P9-EEA-822

The Sun and Its Planets:

Countries Using Torture on an Administrative Basis in the 1970s, With Their Parent-Client Affiliations†

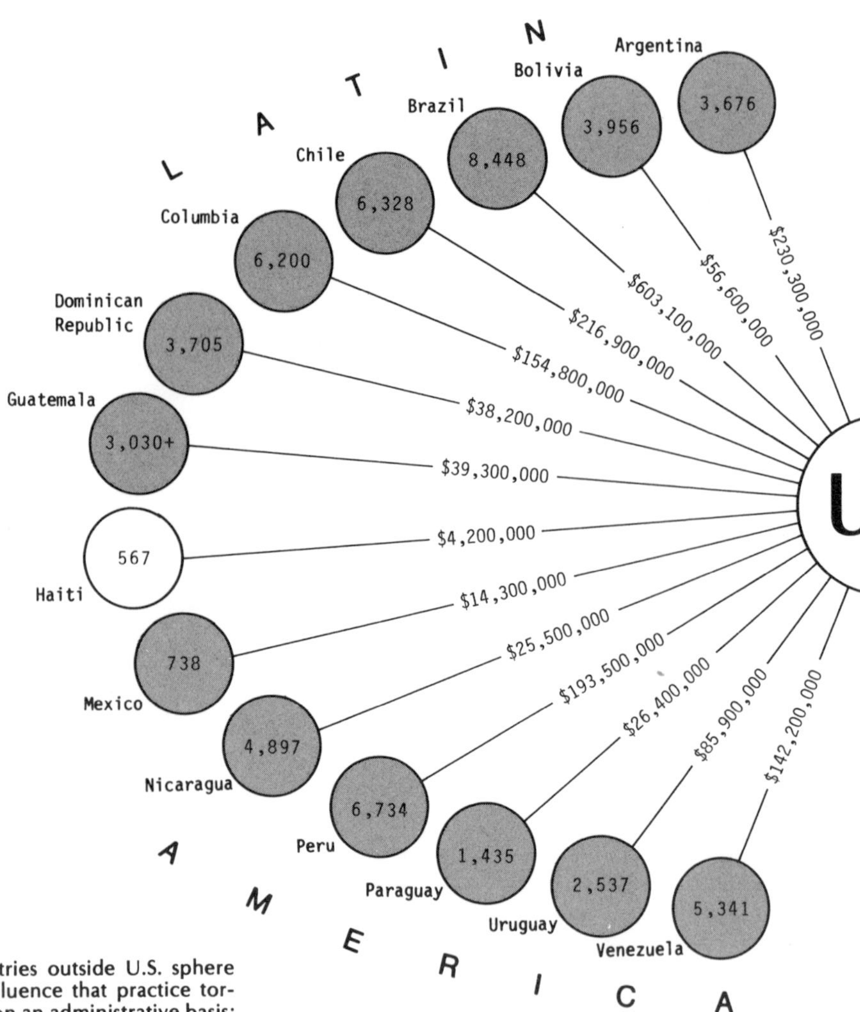

Countries outside U.S. sphere of influence that practice torture on an administrative basis:

Burundi
Guinea
Iraq
Malawi
Rhodesia
South Africa
Soviet Union
Syria
Uganda

No. of U.S.-trained military personnel 1950-1975 (in circles)
Total U.S. military aid 1946-1975 (on lines)
Gray tone indicates U.S. aid or training to police.
(For sources, see Frontispiece Footnotes, p. 361, note 2.)

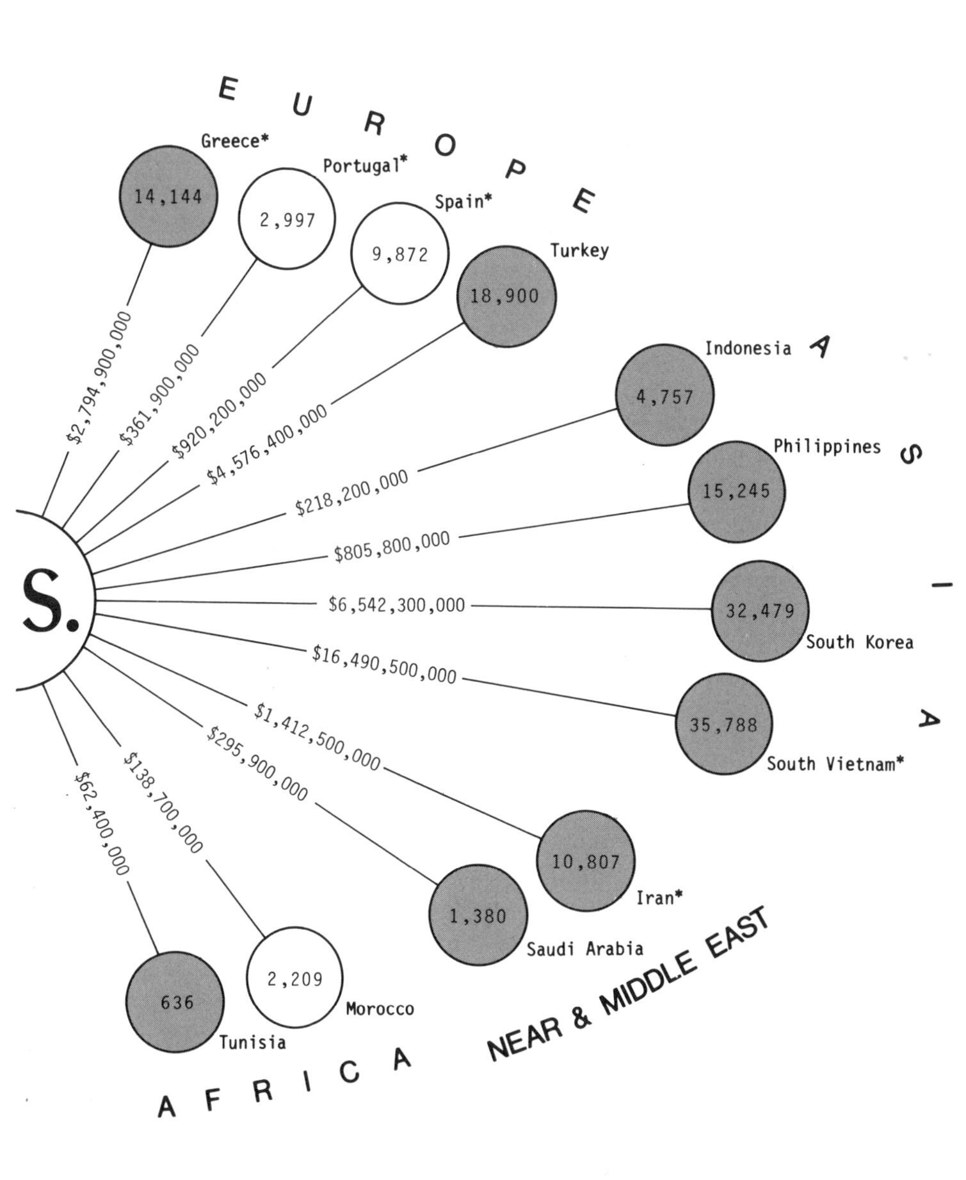

† For a discussion of this classification system, including both the basis for inclusion of countries and the criteria of parent-client relationship, see Frontispiece Footnotes, p. 361, note 1.

* These countries underwent a significant political change during the 1970s, and are included here because they fit the classification—used torture on an administrative basis—for some part of the period.

\+ Figure applies from 1950-1963.

THE POLITICAL ECONOMY
OF HUMAN RIGHTS - VOLUME I

The Washington Connection and Third World Fascism

Noam Chomsky
and
Edward S. Herman

SOUTH END PRESS
BOSTON

First Edition

Library of Congress Card Number: 79-64085
ISBN 0-89608-090-0 paper
ISBN 0-89608-091-9 cloth
Cover design by Ann L. Raszmann/
Boston Community School
Frontispiece design by Clark University Cartography Dept.
Printed at Maple Vail, U.S.A.
Design, typesetting, and paste
up were done by the collective at

South End Press
Box 68, Astor Station
Boston, MA 02123

Table of Contents

The nationalist not only does not disapprove of atrocities committed by his own side, but he has a remarkable capacity for not even hearing about them.

George Orwell, "Notes on Nationalism," 1945

Preface

This study, consisting of two related volumes, deals with relations between the United States and the Third World. It has a dual focus: on facts and on beliefs. The basic *fact* is that the United States has organized under its sponsorship and protection a neocolonial system of client states ruled mainly by terror and serving the interests of a small local and foreign business and military elite. The fundamental *belief*, or ideological pretense, is that the United States is dedicated to furthering the cause of democracy and human rights throughout the world, though it may occasionally err in the pursuit of this objective.

Since 1960 over 18 Latin American regimes have been subjected to military takeovers—a "domino effect" neglected in the West. U.S. influence has been crucial in this process, in some cases by means of deliberate subversion or even direct aggression, but invariably important given the substantial economic and military penetration and presence of the superpower. The phenomenon itself is neither new nor confined to Latin America. The fate of Guatemalan democracy, subverted by the CIA in 1954 in favor of a regime of torture and oppression, can be matched with that of Iran a year earlier; and the Philippines, brutally subjugated at the turn of the century has now been stripped of its short-lived democratic facade without a word of protest by the United States. This, and the subsequent sharp increases in economic and military aid to the martial law government of Marcos, not only reflect a familiar and traditional pattern, they are also compelling evidence of approval and support.

The ugly proclivities of the U.S. clients, including the systematic use of torture, are functionally related to the needs of U.S. (and other) business interests, helping to stifle unions and contain reformist threats that might interfere with business freedom of action. The proof of the pudding is that U.S. bankers and industrialists have consistently welcomed the "stability" of the new client fascist order, whose governments, while savage in their treatment of dissidents, priests, labor leaders, peasant organizers or others who threaten "order," and at best indifferent to the mass of the population, have been most accommodating to large external interests. In an important sense, therefore, the torturers in the client states are functionaries of IBM, Citibank, Allis Chalmers and the U.S. government, playing their assigned roles in a system that has worked according to choice and plan.

With the spread and huge dimensions of the empire of Third World fascism, complete with death squads, torture and repression, the gap between fact and belief has become a yawning chasm. The ideological institutions—the press, schools and universities—thus face a growing challenge. It is, one might have thought, a formidable task to transmute increasing numbers of fascist thugs into respectable "leaders" worthy of our subsidies and active support. Equally serious is the problem of depicting the United States itself as fit to judge and assess the human rights record of other states, in this context of sponsorship of an international mafia, and immediately after its prolonged and brutal assault on the peasant societies of Indochina. Nevertheless, these formidable tasks have been accomplished without notable difficulty, and the credibility gap has been successfully bridged by a very effective system of rewriting recent history and selecting, processing and creating current "information". As we describe in detail throughout this work, on fundamental issues the mass media in the United States—what we will refer to as the "Free Press"—function very much in the manner of a system of state-controlled propaganda, and their achievements are, in fact, quite awesome.

The first volume is devoted to analyzing the forces that have shaped the U.S.-sponsored neo-colonial world, the nature of the client states, and the processes and rationales that the ideological institutions have employed to defend and justify the proliferating terror. The coverage is far from exhaustive; we have selected only a few instances to explore in varying degrees of detail. Our primary concern is the United States: its global policies, their institutional basis in the domestic society and its mechanisms of propaganda. We do not discuss at all the important matter of relations among the powers within the First World of industrial capitalism, or relations between these powers and the Soviet Bloc or China. We also will not consider the background and nature of the movements called "socialist" or "Communist" in the Third World. Nor do we discuss the Soviet empire and the characteristics and effects of that lesser system of Sun and Planets.

Volume II, entitled *After the Cataclysm*, is devoted to "postwar Indochina and the reconstruction of imperial ideology" (the subtitle). It deals with the postwar condition of Indochina, the sources of its problems, Western responses to the travail of its populations emerging from the wreckage. In addition to considering each of the three Indochinese states, we look at the question of refugees and postwar retribution in historical context and give considerable attention to the Western media's use and misuse of the Indochinese experience to rehabilitate the bruised doctrinal system of the imperial powers.

The picture that emerges from this inquiry seems to us a very grim one, both at the level of fact and with regard to the capacity of Western ideological institutions to falsify, obscure and reinterpret the facts in the interest of those who dominate the economy and political system. But this system is not all-powerful, as millions of people learned from their own experience during the U.S. war in Indochina. Until 1965, it was virtually impossible to gain a hearing for any principled opposition to the U.S. military intervention in Indochina, already well-advanced by that time. By "principled opposition" we mean opposition based not on an estimate of national costs and benefits but on the view that the United States has no unique right to exercise force and violence to gain its objectives. Later, a hearing of sorts did become possible, partly through organizations and publications associated with the peace movement itself, and partly as a result of the news value of peace activism as it assumed mass proportions. The Free Press remained largely closed to direct access by the movement throughout the war. The peace movement also had to overcome the obstacle of active state hostility to its efforts. It is now well known that the U.S. government deployed its national political police in a major effort to undermine and destroy the mass movements of the 1960s. Nevertheless, they continued to grow and undoubtedly had an impact on the decisions ultimately taken at the center, without, however, modifying the structure of domestic power in any meaningful way.

This experience shows that even the effective system of ideological controls of the United States has its limitations. It is not impossible for substantial groups to gain some real understanding of social and political reality and to organize and act to modify state policy. The large interests of the country dominate foreign policy, which cannot be altered in its essentials without a change in the internal structure of power or the external environment. But while far-reaching internal changes are not likely in the short-run, organized opposition at home can sometimes make enough of a difference to allow struggling peoples a little breathing space. U.S. failures in Indochina and the 1978 upheavals in Iran are two examples out of many showing the very real possibilities of loss of control in the outer reaches of the empire.

While the U.S. and its allies have armed the neo-fascist elites of the Third World to the teeth, and saturated them with counterinsurgency weaponry and training, long-term elite control of the underlying populations is by no means assured. The abuse of Third World majorities in the empire is so flagrant, and their leaderships are so corrupt, inept and visionless, that explosions and loss of control are highly likely in many states over the next several decades. The voiceless majorities can be helped by outsiders in many ways: among them, maximum world-wide exposure of the actual impact of the West on these peoples; strenuous efforts to stem the huge flow of aid and support to official terrorists; and helping to create an ideological and political environment that will make open intervention difficult when explosions do occur.

It is possible that developments in the United States and other industrialized states might alter the present pattern of sponsorship and support for Third World tyrannies. The arms race and the struggle to control Third World countries are contrary to the interests of the majorities of the *developed* countries, and while the system of indoctrination makes it difficult for them to break out of the machine's ideological control, the growing irrationalities and problems of the West, including the extravagant use of energy, the difficulty of controlling externalities, inflation, inadequate work opportunities for increasing numbers, and the enormous waste on arms may create pressures that will increase awareness or cause systemic shocks that may bring real issues to the fore. It is most probable, unfortunately, that a real crisis would result in a shift toward rightist totalitarianism, a "Brazilianization" of the home country. But prediction in this dynamic era has not been notable for its successes. Educational efforts on the true workings of the machine, and organizational actions that build toward altering its basic mechanisms, may yet yield their benefits, even without the major structural changes required to establish democratic control over the basic social and economic institutions, a prerequisite to a truly democratic politics.

The post-Vietnam war collapse of the movement has relieved U.S. imperial authorities of much of the earlier constraining pressure, and they have been able to continue the enlargement and protection of the neo-fascist empire without significant internal impediment. This can only be changed by a renewal of active involvement of large numbers. It is hoped that this book will show that serious concern is urgently demanded by the facts of the situation.

This book is a major revision of a small monograph written in 1972-73 and then suppressed by the corporation that owned the publisher, as described in the Prefatory Note that follows. Many friends and associates have read parts of earlier drafts of the manuscript and have provided information and critical comment that have helped us immeasurably. We will refer to some of them, quite inadequately, in separate sections that follow. Special mention should be made of Josh Markel for his research assistance and Bonnie Wilker for both research and general help in preparation of the manuscript. Finally we would like to express our thanks to the South End Press collective for their assistance throughout, and in particular, for their care, efficiency, and dedication in producing these books under unusually difficult conditions.

A Prefatory Note by the Authors on the History of the Suppression of the First Edition of This Book

An earlier version of this volume was originally contracted for and produced as a monograph by Warner Modular Publications, Inc., a subsidiary member of the Warner communications and entertainment conglomerate. The publishing house had run a relatively independent operation up to the time of the controversy over this document. The editors and publisher were enthusiastic about the monograph and committed themselves to put it out quickly and to promote it with vigor. But just prior to publication, in the fall of 1973, officials of the parent company got wind of it, looked at it, and were horrified at its "unpatriotic" contents.[1] Mr. William Sarnoff, a high officer of the parent company, for example, was deeply pained by our statement on page 7 of the original that "the leadership in the United States, as a result of its dominant position and wide-ranging counterrevolutionary efforts, has been the most important single instigator, administrator, and moral and material sustainer of serious bloodbaths in the years that followed World War II." So pained were Sarnoff and his business associates, in fact, that they were quite prepared to violate a contractual obligation in order to assure that no such material would see the light of day.

Although 20,000 copies of the monograph were printed, and one (and the last) ad was placed in the *New York Review of Books*, Warner Publishing refused to allow distribution of the monograph at its scheduled publication date. Media advertising for the volume was cancelled and printed flyers that listed the monograph as one of the titles were destroyed. The officers of Warner Modular were warned that distribution of the document would result in their immediate dismissal.

The publisher struggled to keep open the possibility of distributing the monograph. Since one ostensible reason for suppression was the "one-sidedness" of the document, a compromise was worked out for its release upon roughly concurrent publication of a work that supports the counterrevolutionary violence of the United States; in this case a reprinting of a series of articles by Ithiel de Sola Pool. The concept of a publishing house not being permitted to publish something without either the work itself, or the publisher's list, meeting somebody's notion of "balance," is an extraordinary one. Needless to say it is never applied in the case of pro-establishment productions or potential big money-makers, and the application of the "balance" approach in this case was hardly designed to encourage the free flow of ideas. It was, on the contrary, a means of cutting off one side that has great difficulty in gaining a hearing in the United States.

The officers of the parent corporation had regarded the "absence of balance" argument as a reason for refusal to permit distribution of our monograph, rather than as calling urgently for publication of material offering a version of the facts more compatible with their needs and perceptions. The idea of a "balancing publication" was reluctantly accepted by the officers of Warner Modular, the publisher, only as a last resort, a means to salvage a monograph to which they were committed and to meet their moral and legal obligations to the authors. The officers of the parent corporation initially went along with this proposal, presumably because the outright suppression of the monograph would have been a little too blatant, and, of course, in violation of the legally binding contract. But they accepted the compromise without enthusiasm, and before it could be implemented, they decided to close down the publishing house and sell its stocks of publications and contracts to a small and quite unknown company loosely affiliated with the parent conglomerate, MSS Information Corporation. This company is not a commercial publisher and lacked distribution facilities. It did not promote its list and at first did not even list the monograph, adding it only after a considerable period on an additions sheet. The monograph could be purchased by someone with prior knowledge of its existence and of the fact that MSS had taken over the rights to it, or by readers of *Radical America,* a small left-wing publication that distributed some copies that they had obtained.

The monograph had a remarkably different history abroad. While unadvertised, unsold, unreviewed, and unnoticed in the U.S., it was translated into French and several other European languages. The French edition appeared with an introduction by Jean-Pierre Faye which discussed the issue of suppression and put the material discussed in the monograph in the context of a Western "Gulag Archipelago" of extensive proportions. In France it went into a second printing and the suppression in the U.S. became a minor cause celebre. The establishment media in France claimed that the monograph was not sold simply because Warner Modular went into bankruptcy, a complete fabrication. To our knowledge, the only notice of the monograph in the English language can be found in the English translation of Jean-Francois Revel's book *The Totalitarian Temptation* (Penguin, 1977). Here, in the course of a denunciation of the French left for its alleged carelessness with regard to fact, Revel presents an entirely fanciful account of the publishing history, based on his own telephone call to an unidentified friend in the United States.

Despite the substantial interest abroad, it has so far been impossible to provoke any discussion in the country where it was written and to whose population it was addressed either on the merits of the case presented in the monograph or the matter of its effective suppression by the parent corporation. Well-known advocates of freedom of expression who were apprised of the matter have regarded it as insignificant, presumably on the grounds that there is no issue of state censorship but only of corporate censorship. This reflects, we believe, a characteristic underestimation of the importance of the selective policing of the flow of ideas by means of private structures and constrained access, while all the legal forms of freedom are in place. At a given level of quality, the more critical the message the smaller the proportion of the population that will have an opportunity to consider it at all, and there will be no exposure to such messages day after day (as there is, say, to the merits of a new automobile or low tar cigarette, or to the inflationary effects of government regulation, or to the allegations that North Vietnam committed "aggression" in Vietnam or that a bloodbath would follow the "loss" of Vietnam).[2]

The history of the suppressed monograph is an authentic instance of private censorship of ideas per se. The uniqueness of the episode lies only in the manner of suppression. Usually, private intervention in the book market is anticipatory, with regrets that the manuscript is unacceptable, perhaps "unmarketable".[3] Sometimes the latter contention is only an excuse for unwillingness to market, although it may sometimes reflect an accurate assessment of how the media and journals will receive books that are strongly critical of the established order. With rare exceptions (e.g., C. Wright Mills' *Power Elite* or Seymour Hersh's books on the My Lai massacre and cover up), such works are ignored and allowed to fall still-born from the press, or if reviewed, are dismissed with contempt. In the case of the first edition of this work, events showed that there was an international market, even if the parent corporation was able to prevent a test of the domestic market. But the details of the publication history show that the suppression was strictly a function of the contents of the monograph, not of potential profitability.

By coincidence, the parent corporation that was the agency of the suppression is the publisher (through an affiliate) of the paperback edition of Richard M. Nixon's memoirs. Both Warner and the hardback publisher of the memoirs, Grosset & Dunlap, have been criticized for their payment of $2 million for rights to publish and market aggressively the work of a self-confessed prevaricator. The president of Grosset & Dunlap denounced such criticisms in vigorous terms:

> I find it difficult to understand such sentiments. It is incredible that anyone should suggest that a book not be published. If we abridge the freedom of any one writer or publisher, we effectively abridge the freedom of all.

The *New York Times* reported that "also in the audience, but not commenting, was William Sarnoff, chairman of Warner books..."[4]

CHAPTER 1

Introduction: Summary of Major Findings and Conclusions

1.1 Freedom, Aggression and Human Rights

The common view that internal freedom makes for humane and moral international behavior is supported neither by historical evidence nor by reason.[1] The United States itself has a long history of imposing oppressive and terrorist regimes in regions of the world within the reach of its power, such as the Caribbean and Central American sugar and banana republics (Trujillo in the Dominican Republic and the Somozas in Nicaragua were long-lived progeny of U.S. intervention and selection). Since World War II, with the great extension of U.S. power, it has borne a heavy responsibility for the spread of a plague of neofascism, state terrorism, torture and repression throughout large parts of the underdeveloped world. The United States has globalized the "banana republic." This has occurred despite some modest ideological strain because these developments serve the needs of powerful and dominant interests, state and private, within the United States itself.

The Vietnam War experience is often cited to prove the importance of freedom and dissent in constraining state violence. This assessment seriously misreads the facts of the case. Peace movement activism, growing from and contributing to the popular movements for equality, freedom and social change within the United States, did succeed in raising the domestic costs of the U.S. assault, thus helping to limit in some degree its scope and severity and contributing to the eventual decision that the game was not worth the candle. It did so, of course, mainly by employing modalities that were outside the framework of existing institutions: demonstrations, nonviolent resistance, grass roots organizing, and wide ranging educational efforts needed to counter the deep commitment of existing institutions to the protection and furthering of the interests of state and private power. The established "free" institutions supported the war, for the most part enthusiastically and uncritically, occasionally with minor and qualified reservations. The principled opposition, based on grounds other than cost-ineffectiveness, functioned outside the major institutional structures. It is, of course, an important fact that a movement was allowed to organize with relatively modest state harassment and violence, and that this movement could make some impact on the course of events. Such developments and the costs of overcoming these and other forms of resistance that impede the actions of national elites are also problems in totalitarian societies, though the toll imposed on protestors in Iran, Argentina, and the Soviet Union is often far more severe. The value of being allowed to protest relatively unmolested is certainly real, but it should not lead to a disregard of the fact that established institutions, with overwhelmingly dominant power, tend to line up in goose-step fashion in support of any state foreign venture, no matter how immoral (until the cost becomes too high).

The peace movement frightened Western elites. The response of the U.S. (indeed Free World) leadership to the politicization of large parts of the population during the 1960s provides a revealing indication of their concept of "democracy" and of the role of the public in the "democratic process." In 1975, the Trilateral Commission, representing the more liberal elements of ruling groups in the industrial democracies, published a study entitled *The Crisis of Democracy* which interprets public participation in decision-making as a *threat* to democracy, one that must be contained if elite domination is to persist unhindered by popular demands. The population must be reduced to apathy and conformism if "democracy," as interpreted by this liberal contingent, is to be kept workable and allowed to survive.[2]

The most crucial fact relating freedom to the Vietnam War experience is that, despite its free institutions, for over two decades

(1949-1975) the United States attempted to subjugate Vietnam by force and subversion, in the process violating the UN Charter, the Geneva Accords of 1954, the Nuremberg Code, the Hague Convention, the Geneva Protocol of 1925, and finally the Paris agreements of 1973.[3] For almost a decade the peasants of Indochina served as experimental animals for an evolving military technology—cluster bombs, rockets designed to enter caves where people hid to escape saturation bombing, a fiendish array of anti-personnel weapons; new versions of the long-outlawed "dum-dum" bullet were among the more modest weapons employed.[4] The population was driven into urban slums by bombing, artillery, and ground attacks that often degenerated into mass murder, in an expanding effort to destroy the social structures in which resistance was rooted. Defenseless peasant societies in Laos and Cambodia were savagely bombed in "secret"—the "secrecy" resulting from the refusal of the mass media to make public facts for which they had ample evidence. Freedom was consistent not only with this expanding savagery, but also with interventions explicitly designed to preserve non-freedom from the threat of freedom (e.g., the invasion of the Dominican Republic in 1965)[5] and to displace democratic with totalitarian regimes (e.g., the open subversion of Guatemala in 1954; the slightly more *sub rosa* subversion of democracy in Brazil in 1964 and Chile in 1973).[6] Free institutions were able to accept, indeed quietly approve of huge massacres in the name of "freedom," as in Indonesia in 1965-1966—interpreted by U.S. liberals as evidence for the far-sightedness of U.S. intervention in Vietnam. Massive atrocities committed by U.S. client regimes against their own populations or against foreign populations they hope to subdue (e.g., the Indonesian massacres in East Timor) have also proven compatible with freedom and are regularly disguised or ignored by the Free Press.

Whatever the attitudes of the U.S. leadership toward freedom at home—and as noted, this is highly ambiguous—systematic policies towards Third World countries, described in detail below, make it evident that the alleged commitment to democracy and human rights is mere rhetoric, directly contrary to actual policy. The operative principle has been and remains *economic* freedom—meaning freedom for U.S. business to invest, sell, and repatriate profits—and its two basic requisites, a favorable investment climate and a specific form of stability.[7] Since these primary values are disturbed by unruly students, democratic processes, peasant organizations, a free press, and free labor unions, "economic freedom" has often required political servitude. Respect for the rights of the individual, also alleged to be one of the cardinal values of the West, has had little place in the operating procedures applied to the Third World. Since a favorable investment climate and stability quite often require repression, the United States has supplied the tools and training for interrogation and torture and is thoroughly implicated in the vast expansion of torture during the past decade.[8] When Dan Mitrione came to Uruguay in a police advisory function, the police were torturing with an obsolete electric needle:

> Mitrione arranged for the police to get newer electric needles of varying thickness. Some needles were so thin they could be slipped between the teeth. Benitez [a Uruguayan police official] understood that this equipment came to Montevideo inside the U.S. embassy's diplomatic pouch.[9]

Within the United States itself, the intelligence services were "running torture camps," as were their Brazilian associates, who "set up a camp modeled after that of the *boinas verdes,* the Green Berets."[10] And there is evidence that U.S. advisors took an active part in torture, not contenting themselves with supplying training and material means.[11] During the Vietnam War, the United States employed on a massive scale improved napalm, phosphorus and fragmentation bombs, and a wide range of other "anti-personnel" weapons that had a devastating effect on civilians. The steady development of weaponry and methods of "interrogation" that inflict enormous pain on the human body and spirit, and the expansion of use of this technology in U.S.-sponsored counter-insurgency warfare and "stabilization" throughout the U.S. sphere of influence, is further evidence that the "sacredness of the individual" is hardly a primary value in the West, at least in its application beyond an elite in-group.[12]

The rationale given for the U.S. buildup of Third World police and military establishments and regular "tilt" toward repressive regimes, is the demands of "security". This is a wonderfully elastic concept with a virtuous ring that can validate open-ended arms expenditures as well as support for neo-fascism. When it is said that we must oppose Goulart in Brazil or the NLF in South Vietnam for reasons of security, this obviously does not mean that they threaten our survival; it means that their success would be disadvantageous to U.S. interests, and not primarily military interests. It is possible that "security" for a great power and its client government corresponds to heightened insecurity for large numbers within the dominated "secure" state.[13] This seems to be very much the case for the majorities in Brazil, Chile, and Paraguay, for example.

As Jan Black points out:

> The delimitation of what must be secured expands to accommodate what a nation, class, institution, or other social entity has, or thinks it should have. It follows, then, that it is often the nations, groups, or individuals whose wealth and power would appear to make them the most secure who are, in fact, most paranoid,...[14]

—a comment that applies with striking accuracy to the United States after World War II. In the specific case of the United States, she notes that the concept of security is "all-encompassing, involving economic and political hegemony as well as strictly military considerations...."[15] This flows from the fact of inordinate power and is the propaganda counterpart of the imperial leader's assumption of the natural right to intervene to keep its subordinates in line. It has the great public relations advantage, also, of built-in self-justification. Who could object to the pitiful giant's efforts to protect its own security?

1.2 The Semantics of "Terror"

Among the many symbols used to frighten and manipulate the populace of the democratic states, few have been more important than "terror" and "terrorism". These terms have generally been confined to the use of violence by individuals and marginal groups. Official violence, which is far more extensive in both scale and destructiveness, is placed in a different category altogether. This usage has nothing to do with justice, causal sequence, or numbers abused. Whatever the actual sequence of cause and effect, official violence is described as responsive or provoked ("retaliation," "protective reaction," etc.), not as the active and initiating source of abuse. Similarly, the massive long-term violence inherent in the oppressive social structures that U.S. power has supported or imposed is typically disregarded. The numbers tormented and killed by official violence—wholesale as opposed to retail terror—during recent decades have exceeded those of unofficial terrorists by a factor running into the thousands. But this is not "terror," although one terminological exception may be noted: while Argentinian "security forces" only retaliate and engage in "police action," violence carried out by unfriendly states (Cuba, Cambodia) may be designated "terroristic". The question of proper usage is settled not merely by the official or unofficial status of the perpetrators of violence but also by their political affiliations.

These terminological devices serve important functions. They help to justify the far more extensive violence of (friendly) state authorities by interpreting them as "reactive," and they implicitly sanction the suppression of information on the methods and scale of official violence by removing it from the category of "terrorism". Thus in Latin America, "left-wing terrorism is quiescent after a decade and a half of turmoil," the *New York Times* explains in a summary article on the state of terrorism;[16] it does not discuss any other kind of violence in Latin America—CIA, Argentinian and Brazilian death squads, DINA, etc. Their actions are excluded by definition, and nothing is said about the nature and causes of the "turmoil". Thus the language is well-designed for apologetics for wholesale terror.

This language is also useful in its connotation of irrational evil, which can be exterminated with no questions asked. The criminally insane have no just grievance that we need trouble to comprehend. On the current scene, for example, the *New York Times* refers to the "cold-blooded and mysterious" Carlos; the South African government, on the other hand, whose single raid on the Namibian refugee camp of Kassinga on May 4, 1978[17] wiped out a far larger total (more than 600) than the combined victims of Carlos, the Baader-Meinhof gang, and the Italian Red Brigades, is not referred to in such invidious terms. Retail terror is "the crime of our times"[18] in the current picture of reality conveyed by the media; and friendly governments are portrayed as the reassuring protectors of the public, striving courageously to cope with "terror".[19]

The limited concept of "terror" also serves as a lightning rod to distract attention from substantive issues, and helps to create a sensibility and frame of mind that allows greater freedom of action by the state. During the Vietnam War, students were the terrorists, and the government and mass media devoted great attention (and much outrage) to their frightful depredations (one person killed, many windows broken).[20] The device was used effectively to discredit the antiwar movement as violence-prone and destructive—the motive, of course, for the infiltration of the movement by government provocateurs[21]—and it helped to divert attention from the official violence that was far more extensive even on the home front, not to speak of Vietnam, the Dominican Republic, and elsewhere. The ploy was amazingly successful in light of the facts, now documented beyond serious question, even though it did not succeed in destroying the antiwar movement. The terrorism of the Vietnamese enemy was also used effectively in mobilizing public opinion, again a tremendous testimonial to the power of brainwashing under freedom, given the real facts of the matter (discussed in chapter 5 below).

1.3 The Shift in the Balance of Terror to the Free World

Over the past 25 years at least, not only has official terror been responsible for torture and killing on a vastly greater scale than its retail counterpart, but, furthermore, the balance of terror appears to have shifted to the West and its clients, with the United States setting the pace as sponsor and supplier. The old colonial world was shattered during World War II, and the resultant nationalist-radical upsurge threatened traditional Western hegemony and the economic interests of Western business. To contain this threat the United States has aligned itself with elite and military elements in the Third World whose function has been to contain the tides of change. This role was played by Diem and Thieu in South Vietnam and is currently served by allies such as Mobutu in Zaire, Pinochet in Chile, and Suharto in Indonesia. Under frequent U.S. sponsorship the neo-fascist National Security State and other forms of authoritarian rule have become the dominant mode of government in the Third World. Heavily armed by the West (mainly the United States) and selected for amenability to foreign domination and zealous anti-Communism, counterrevolutionary regimes have been highly torture- and bloodshed-prone.

In the Soviet sphere of influence, torture appears to have been on the decline since the death of Stalin. In its 1974 *Report on Torture*, Amnesty International (AI) notes:

> Though prison conditions and the rights of the prisoners detained on political charges in Eastern Europe and the Soviet Union may still be in many cases unsatisfactory, torture as a government-sanctioned, Stalinist practice has ceased. With a few exceptions (see below) no reports on the use of torture in Eastern Europe have been reaching the outside world in the past decade.[22]

In sharp contrast, torture, which "for the last two or three hundred years has been no more than a historical curiosity has suddenly developed a life of its own and become a social cancer."[23] Since it has declined in the Soviet sphere since the death of Stalin, it would appear that this cancerous growth is largely a Free World phenomenon. The frontispiece describes its distribution within the

U.S. sphere of influence. It has shown phenomenal growth in Latin America, where, as AI points out:

> There is a marked difference between traditional brutality, stemming from historical conditions, and the systematic torture which has spread to many Latin American countries within the past decade.[24]

Amnesty International also notes that in some of the Latin American countries "the institutional violence and high incidence of political assassinations has tended to overshadow the problem of torture."[25] The numbers involved in these official (wholesale) murders have been large: for example, AI estimates 15,000 death squad victims in the small country of Guatemala between 1970 and 1975, a thousand in Argentina in 1975 before the military coup and the unleashing of a true reign of terror.[26]

The AI Annual Report for 1975-1976 also notes that "more than 80%" of the urgent appeals and actions for victims of human torture have been coming from Latin America.[27] One reason for the urgency of these appeals is the nature of this expanding empire of violence, which bears comparison with some of the worst excrescences of European fascism. Hideous torture has become standard practice in the U.S. client fascist states. In the new Chile, to savor the results of the narrow escape of that country from Communist tyranny:

> Many people were tortured to death [after the military coup of 1973] by means of endless whipping as well as beating with fists, feet and rifle butts. Prisoners were beaten on all parts of the body, including the head and sexual organs. The bodies of prisoners were found in the Rio Mapocho, sometimes disfigured beyond recognition. Two well-known cases in Santiago are those of Litre Quiroga, the ex-director of prisons under the Allende government, and Victor Jara, Chile's most popular folksinger. Both were detained in the Estadio Chile and died as a result of the torture received there. According to a recurrent report, the body of Victor Jara was found outside the Estadio Chile, his hands broken and his body badly mutilated. Litre Quiroga had been kicked and

> beaten in front of other prisoners for approximately 40 hours before he was removed to a special interrogation room where he met his death under unknown circumstances.[28]

Such horrendous details could be repeated for many thousands of human beings in Argentina, Brazil, Chile, Uruguay, Paraguay, Guatemala, Nicaragua, Indonesia, U.S.-occupied South Vietnam up to 1975, Iran, and in quite a few other U.S. client states. They clearly reflect state policy over a wide segment of the U.S. sphere of influence. As already noted, much of the electronic and other torture gear is U.S. supplied, and great numbers of client state police and military interrogators are U.S.-trained.[29]

Latin America has also become the locus of a major diaspora, with hundreds of thousands of academics, journalists, scientists, and other professionals, as well as liberals and radicals of all social classes, driven into exile. This has been a deliberate policy of the military juntas, which one distinguished Latin America journalist calls a "lobotomization" of intellect and the "cultural genocide of our time,"[30] with the purpose of removing any source of social criticism or intellectual or leadership base for the general population. Another aspect of the same strategy is, of course, the widespread use of torture and political assassinations to create "a climate of fear and uncertainty to discourage any form of opposition to the ruling elite."[31] To find comparable flights into exile on a continental scale, one would have to go back to the experience of fascist Europe, 1933-1940, which provides numerous parallels.[32]

1.4 The Churches Versus the Totalitarian Free Enterprise "Development Model"

The client fascist states have behaved with such inhumanity toward the majority of their populations that the conservative churches throughout the U.S. sphere of influence have been driven into an unprecedented opposition, again reminiscent of fascist Europe.[33] The military juntas and assorted dictators have allied

themselves with a small local elite and foreign busin
governments in a joint venture to exploit both the local
and the 80% or more of the population whose welfare is of no
interest to these joint venture partners. An important function of the military juntas has been to destroy all forms of institutional protection for the masses, such as unions, peasant leagues and cooperatives, and political groupings, making them incapable of defending themselves against the larger interests served by the state. As in Europe in the 1930s, only the church has survived as a potential protector of the majority.

The development model applied by the partners is so blatantly exploitative that it has required terror and the threat of terror to assure the requisite passivity. Church documents point out with pungency how the chosen model of development "provokes a revolution that did not exist" and necessitates a National Security State because its brutalities would elicit such indignation "that the only solution has been to impose absolute silence."[34]

This and numerous other church cries of protest have received minimal attention in the United States. The "development model" in question is serviceable to U.S. economic interests, one of the joint venture partners, so that the imposition of "absolute silence" by terror is given a respectful, parallel and almost complete silence in the heartland of freedom. The imposition of the development model will be interpreted there, as in a *New York Times* editorial on Brazil, as a bold showing of "more intent on applying corrective medicine than on courting political favor," with "an early tackling of social reforms" likely to follow a recovery already in sight.[35] In short, the churches and people of Latin America and the rest of the client fascist empire stand alone.

1.5 How the Media Cope with Client Fascist Terror (I): Suppression Plus an Emphasis on the Positive

Since the installation and support of military juntas, with their sadistic tortures and bloodbaths, are hardly compatible with human rights, democracy and other alleged Western values, the media and intellectuals in the United States and Western Europe have been hard-pressed to rationalize state policy. The primary solution has been massive suppression, averting the eyes from the unpleasant facts concerning the extensive torture and killing, the diaspora, the major shift to authoritarian government and its systematic character, and the U.S. role in introducing and protecting the leadership of this client fascist empire. When the Latin American system of torture and exile is mentioned at all, it is done with brevity and "balance". The latter consists of two elements: one is the regular pretense that the terror is a response to "left-wing guerilla" terror and that the killings on each side are in some kind of rough equivalence. The second is the generous and preponderant attention given to the rationales, explanations and claims of regret and imminent reform on the part of the official terrorists. When elements of the mass media go a little beyond this pattern, as they do on occasion, their efforts are not well-received by other members of the establishment. Thus, an unusually frank ABC documentary on "The Politics of Torture" was greeted by the *New York Times* with petulance and hostility for failing to see the problems posed by "security and economic interests" and/or neglecting the abuses of the Communists.[36]

Although, as noted, the torture and killing of political prisoners appears to be more extensive in the Free World than in the Soviet Union and its satellites, the mass media do not dramatize the abuse of individuals in our client states as they do in the case of Soviet intellectuals. Russians dissidents are international heroes, and their trials, personal and legal, and proclamations on all sorts of political and cultural issues, receive front page attention. Who has even heard the names of their vastly more numerous counterparts in the U.S. client states?

The mass media also feature heavily the positives of our military juntas, especially any alleged "improvements"—a release of political prisoners, an increase in GNP, an announced election to be held in 1984, or a slowing up in the rate of inflation—typically offered without reference to a base from which the alleged improvement started. The parlous state of affairs that made the military takeover a regrettable necessity is also frequently emphasized, in preference to any discussion of the needs and interests of international capital. The military juntas and dictators in the U.S. sphere of influence have become quite adept at making the appropriate gestures, timed to coincide with visits of U.S. dignitaries or congressional consideration of budget appropriations. By these tokenistic and public relations devices the dictators demonstrate improvement, our leaders show that we are a force for liberty, and possibly a small number of prisoners may be freed, all this without seriously disturbing the status quo. Client fascist tokenism is often a collaborative effort of dictator and U.S. sponsor, both concerned with improving an image without changing anything fundamental. The Free Press can be counted on to accept these tokens at face value and without analysis or protest.

A striking example of these procedures is the case of Iran, where a brief experiment with democracy and independence was terminated by a CIA-sponsored coup in 1953, leading to the imposition of a regime that became one of the terror centers of the world. According to a report of the International Commission of Jurists:

> The tremendous power wielded by the SAVAK [secret police] is reflected in the fact that the chief is given the title of Deputy Prime Minister. The SAVAK permeates Iranian society and is reported to have agents in the political parties, labor unions, industry, tribal societies, as well as abroad—especially where there are concentrated numbers of Iranian students.[37]

The number of officially acknowledged executions of political prisoners in the three years prior to 1977 was some 300; and estimates of the total number of political prisoners run from 25,000 to 100,000. They are not well-treated. Martin Ennals, Secretary-General of Amnesty International, noted that Iran has the

> ...highest rate of death penalties in the world, no valid system of civilian courts and a history of torture which is beyond belief. No country in the world has a worse record in human rights than Iran.[38]

The Iranian secret police has received generous training and support from the United States, which has deluged its Iranian client with arms, "priming" it, as a Senate report noted, to serve as the gendarme for U.S. interests throughout the crucial oil-producing regions of the Middle East. When the Iranian people rose in an astonishing and completely unexpected demonstration of mass popular opposition to the terror and corruption of the Shah, the Free Press obediently described this bloody tyrant as a great "liberalizer" who was attempting to bring to his backward country the benefits of modernization, opposed by religious fanatics and left-wing students. *Newsweek* described the demonstrators as "an unlikely coalition of Muslim fundamentalists and leftist activists" (22 May 1978) while *Time* added that "the Shah also has a broad base of popular support" (5 June 1978). Citing these and many other examples in a review of press coverage, William A. Dorman and Ehsan Omad write that "We have been unable to find a single example of a news or feature story in the mainstream American press that uses the label 'dictator' to describe the Shah."[39] There is barely a mention in the media of the facts on the magnitude of corruption, the scale of police terror and torture,[40] the significance of the fantastic expenditures for arms[41]—the police and military establishments are probably the only elements of Iranian society that could be described as fully "modernized"—and the devastating effects on the majority of the population of the agricultural reforms and urban priorities.[42]

As the Shah's U.S.-armed troops murdered hundreds of demonstrators in the streets, President Carter sent his support, reaffirming the message he had delivered in Teheran several months earlier, when he stated at a banquet:

> Iran under the great leadership of the Shah is an island of stability in one of the more troubled areas of the world. This is a great tribute to you, Your Majesty, and to your leadership, and to the respect, admiration and love which your people give to you.[43]

Meanwhile, the Pentagon dispatched arms and counterinsurgency technology,[44] while the press deplored the failure of the Iranian people to comprehend the Shah's beneficence or described him as "not repressive enough"—the "saddest aspect of developments in Iran," according to the liberal *New Republic*.[45] Much emphasis was placed, as usual, on his promises of reform. The servility of the media could hardly have been more dramatically displayed.

The annual survey of human rights put out by the U.S. State Department has this primary characteristic: it strives consistently and without intellectual scruple to put a good face on totalitarian states within our sphere of influence. The bias is so great, the willingness to accept factual claims and verbal promises of military juntas is so blatant, the down-playing of the claims and pain of the victims of official terror is so obvious, that *these reports are themselves solid evidence of the primary official commitment to the dispensers of terror rather than its victims*.[46] They constitute a defense of client fascism, not of human rights. The highly touted "human rights program" must be understood in this context.

The technique of "emphasizing the positive" is also used in other ways to whitewash the behavior of the prime sponsor of Third World fascism. A familiar device is the self-congratulation that regularly attends any decrement in barbarism or aggression. For example, the regular Washington correspondent of the *New Yorker*, regarded as a leading liberal commentator, wrote in 1974 that "we have brought ourselves satisfaction and at least a modicum of self-respect by withdrawing our combat troops from Indo-China."[47] The *Washington Post* also assures us, in an editorial retrospective on the "good impulses" that led to such tragic error in Vietnam, that the United States "in the last days, made what seems to us an entirely genuine and selfless attempt to facilitate a political solution that would spare the Vietnamese further suffering"[48]—very touching, after a quarter-century of brutality and terror, and also untrue.[49]

Perhaps a search through the records of Murder Inc. would also reveal documents praising the thugs in charge for their display of humanitarian benevolence in offering a temporary respite to its victims.

1.6 How the Media Cope with Client Terror (II): The Pretense that the U.S. Is an Innocent Bystander, Rather Than Sponsor and Supporter of Client Fascism

The military juntas of Latin America and Asia are *our* juntas. Many of them were directly installed by us or are the beneficiaries of our direct intervention, and most of the others came into existence with our tacit support, using military equipment and training supplied by the United States. Our massive intervention and subversion over the past 25 years has been confined almost exclusively to overthrowing reformers, democrats, and radicals—we have rarely "destabilized" right-wing military regimes no matter how corrupt or terroristic.[50] This systematic bias in intervention is only part of the larger system of connections—military, economic, and political—that have allowed the dominant power to shape the primary characteristics of the other states in its domains in accordance with its interests.

The Brazilian counterrevolution, as we have noted (cf. note 6), took place with the connivance of the United States and was followed by immediate recognition and consistent support, just as in Guatemala ten years earlier and elsewhere, repeatedly. The military junta model has been found to be a good one, and the United States has helped it flourish and spread. Torture, death squads and freedom of investment are related parts of the approved model sponsored and supported by the leader of the Free World. Terror in these states is functional, improving the "investment climate," at least in the short-run, and U.S. aid to terror-prone states, as we show below, is *positively related to terror and improvement of investment climate and negatively related to human rights* (Chapter 2, section 1.1, Table 1). It turns out, therefore, that if we cut through the propaganda barrage, *Washington has become the torture and political murder capital of the world.* Torture and political murder in the United States itself are absolutely and relatively low, and obviously provide no basis for such a harsh judgment. But the United States is the power center whose quite calculated and deliberate policy and strategy choices have brought about a system of clients who consistently practice torture and murder on a terrifying scale.

Some of the regimes in our sphere of influence have a fair

amount of autonomy and may do things on occasion that our leadership does not like, much as Rumania or Poland in Eastern Europe may press the limits of Russian tolerance. When Guatemala or the Dominican Republic go too far in seeking independence or major socio-economic change incompatible with the approved model, however, the mailed fist will strike, as in Hungary or Czechoslovakia.[51] Brazil, a substantial power in its own right, can go its own way in part, though how far is not clear; it was only as far back as 1964 that the United States intervened to help mold Brazil into a state more to the taste of the U.S.-business community. The U.S. sphere of client states is as homogeneous—and as agreeable to the interest of the dominant power—as the states of Eastern Europe in relation to the USSR.

It is convenient to pretend that Guatemala, South Korea and the Philippines are "independent" in contrast to Rumania, Poland, and Hungary which are puppets of the Soviet Union. In this manner U.S. responsibility for terror in its sphere can be dismissed, while the Soviet Union's imposition of tyranny and crushing of freedom in its sphere can be sanctimoniously deplored. Given our role in creating and sustaining our terror-prone clients, our training and supply programs, our continued support for them on all fundamentals, their relative homogeneity and role in the U.S.-dominated global economy, their alleged independence and our posture of innocent and concerned bystander must be taken simply as principles of state propaganda.

1.7 How the Media Cope with Client Terror (III): "Atrocities Management" and the Demand for Communist Abuses

Another established technique for diverting attention from the ongoing torture and bloodbaths and deteriorating social-political environment in Argentina, Brazil, Chile, the Dominican Republic, and Indonesia (to cite a few examples) is to concentrate attention on Communist abuses, real and mythical. Although Communist terrorism in Vietnam was always relatively modest compared to that of the Saigon government, and paled into virtual insignificance when compared to our own,[52] the U.S. government and mass media created the opposite impression by selective emphasis of fact, outright lies, and a very effective program of "atrocities management." The contention by right wing critics of the press that the media overplayed our bad behavior and understated that of the Vietnamese enemy can be properly interpreted in this way: if the disproportion of violence was 100 (U.S.) to 1 (NLF),[53] and the media attention ratio was 1:1, then while the media would have been underplaying our violence by 100:1, the right-wingers had a point that we were still allowed to see *something* of what we were doing to our victims.[54] Nevertheless, as we show in the text below, the media's massive suppressions and institutionalization of lies and myths in the face of one of the most savage attacks on a helpless population in history, does it credit as an effective instrument of state propaganda.

As we have pointed out (see section 5, this chapter), the media occasionally present a glimpse of the real world of subfascist terror, a departure from orthodoxy that evokes predictable outrage on the part of guardians of the faith. Tom Buckley's *New York Times* review of the ABC documentary on torture in the U.S. sphere (see note 36) nicely illustrates the techniques that are used to overcome such occasional deviations. According to Buckley, ABC "can't get it through its head that the United States cannot easily transform repressive and unstable governments into humane ones..." and that "the United States, despite its best intentions, must balance what are perceived as its security and economic interests with the effort to improve human rights." Typically, it is presupposed, not argued, that the United States has "good intentions" but is limited in its ability to bring about reforms. Buckley evidently "can't get it through his head" that the United States has in fact imposed and supported these repressive governments and provided them with the means to remain "stable" in the face of popular reaction to their torture and repression. Buckley complains further that the ABC documentary "fails to establish a historical or social context," by which he means: fails to provide appropriate apologetics for the U.S. role. His comment is particularly interesting in the light of the fact that ABC, in a rare departure from the standards of the Free Press, did in fact make some mention of the role of U.S. economic interests in the subfascist empire; that is, did touch on the actual historical and social context, a serious lapse from the point of view of the *New York Times*. Buckley further laments the failure of the documentary to point out that "we haven't done badly on behalf of the Jews of the Soviet Union"—which is false, but even if true would be about as relevant as a defense of Soviet human rights practices by a Russian Buckley who objects that "we haven't done badly on behalf of the Wilmington 10." Finally, in this review of a documentary focusing on Chile, Iran and the Philippines, Buckley writes: "More to the point is the fact that Communist dictatorships" do not permit free inquiry into their repressive practices. Why this has any point bearing on the facts of torture in the U.S. client states or proper U.S. policy towards that problem, Buckley fails to explain.

In the post-Vietnam War era the need for Communist abuses has been no less pressing than before. More facts have come to light on the scope of U.S. violence in Vietnam, Cambodia and Laos, the extent to which U.S. officials lied to the public with regard to their programs and methods, and the brazenness with which these officials defied treaty obligations and international law. Much as the government and the media tried to isolate the scoundrelism of Watergate from the much more profound immorality of the "secret" devastation of Cambodia, the linkage between the two could not be entirely concealed and therefore tended to discredit still further the campaign to bring "freedom" to South Vietnam. Counterrevolution, torture and official murder in Argentina, Guatemala, Chile, and other U.S. satellites was also reaching new peaks. Thus, if Cambodian terror did not exist, the Western propaganda systems would have had to invent it, and in certain respects they did, a matter which we will discuss at length in Volume II, chapter 6.[55]

Three features of the propaganda campaign with regard to Cambodia deserve special notice. The first is its vast and unprecedented scope. Editorial condemnation of Cambodian "genocide" in the mainstream media dates from mid-1975, immediately following the victory of the so-called "Khmer Rouge."[56] After that time the Western media were deluged with condemnations of Cambodia, including not only regular reporting in the press and news weeklies but also articles in such mass circulation journals as the *Readers Digest* (with tens of millions of readers in the United States and abroad), *TV Guide*, and for the intellectual elite, the *New York*

Review, the *New Republic*, etc. In contrast, interpretations of developments in Cambodia that departed from the theme of systematic genocide received virtually no attention. The volume of the chorus proclaiming "genocide" and the careful exclusion of conflicting facts (and the context or history) made the occasional expression of scepticism appear pathological, much as if someone were to proclaim that the earth is flat.

A second major feature of the propaganda campaign was that it involved a systematic distortion or suppression of the highly relevant historical context as well as substantial fabrication—the grim reality evidently did not suffice for the needs of propaganda—and fabrication persisted even after exposure, which was regarded as irrelevant in the face of a "higher truth" that is independent of mere fact. Furthermore, the more inflated the claims and the more completely the evidence was presented in a historical vacuum, attributed strictly to Communist villainy, the greater the audience likely to be reached.

A third striking feature of the campaign was the constant pretense that the horrors of Cambodia are being ignored except for the few courageous voices that seek to pierce the silence, or that some great conflict was raging about the question of whether or not there have been atrocities in Cambodia. In France and the United States, in particular, such pretense reached comic proportions. This particular feature of Western propaganda was apparently internalized by the intelligentsia, who came to believe it in dramatic defiance of the obvious facts. To cite one example, in the *New York Times* (22 September 1977) the well-known philosopher Walter Kaufmann, often a thoughtful commentator on moral and political issues, had an article entitled "Selective Compassion" in which he contrasts "the lack of international outrage, protests, and pressure in the face of what has been going on in Cambodia" with the compassion that is felt for the Arabs under Israeli military occupation. His comparison is doubly remarkable. By September 1977, condemnation of Cambodian atrocities, covering the full political spectrum with the exception of some Maoist groups, had reached a level and scale that has rarely been matched, whereas the situation of the Arabs under Israeli military occupation (or indeed, in Israel itself) is virtually a taboo topic in the United States. For example, the U.S. media are outraged over the fact that children work in Cambodia (rarely inquiring into conditions or circumstances or comparing the situation in other peasant societies), but accept with equanimity what is called in Israel "the Children's market," where children as young as six or seven years old are brought at 4 a.m. to pick fruit at subsistence wages or less for Israeli collective settlements.[57] Similarly the odes to Israeli democracy that are a constant refrain in the U.S. media are careful to exclude any mention of the fact that a system of quasi-national institutions has been established (to which U.S. citizens make tax-deductible gifts) to ensure that land use and development funds are reserved to those Israeli citizens who are Jews—comparable anti-Semitic regulations in the Soviet Union would be a major scandal, and would certainly not be subsidized by the U.S. government. Even the human rights organizations in the United States have been scrupulous in suppressing information about the treatment of Arabs. (See chapter 3, note 67.)

In the light of the indisputable facts, how can we explain the fact that a literate and serious person can believe that "selective compassion" in the United States is devoted to Arabs under Israeli rule while "strikingly" avoiding what has been going on in Cambodia, and can express this astonishing view without challenge—indeed, it is received with sage nods of approval. Only on the assumption that Arabs intrinsically lack human rights, so that even the slightest attention to their fate is excessive, whereas the principles of Western ideology are so sacrosanct that even a vast chorus of condemnation of an enemy still does not reach some approved standard—that is, only by a combination of chauvinist and racist assumptions that are quite remarkable when spelled out clearly, though standard among the Western intelligentsia.

1.8 Cambodia: Why the Media Find It More Newsworthy Than Indonesia and East Timor

The way in which the media have latched on to Cambodian violence, as a drowning man seizes a lifebuoy, is an object lesson as to how the U.S. media serve first and foremost to mobilize opinion in the service of state ideology. When somewhere between 500,000 and a million people were butchered in the anti-Communist counterrevolution of 1965-1966 in Indonesia, almost total silence prevailed in Congress and in editorials in the U.S. press—a few tut-tuts, many more "objective" statements of how this is beneficially affecting the structure of power in Southeast Asia, how it shows the effectiveness of our Vietnam strategy, which is providing a "shield" for "democracy in Asia," and some suggestions that the "Communists" got what they deserved in a spontaneous uprising of "the people."[58] This bloodbath involved *approved victims* and a political change consistent with U.S. business and strategic interests—what we refer to as a "constructive bloodbath" in the text below. Even today, as regards East Timor, where our corrupt and brutal Indonesian satellite (authors of the 1965-1966 butcheries) has very possibly killed as many people as did the Khmer Rouge, there is a virtually complete blackout of information in the Free Press.[59] This is a bloodbath carried out by a friendly power and is thus of little interest to our leaders. It is a "benign bloodbath" in our terminology.

An effective propaganda apparatus disregards such cases of violence. It also downplays lesser but significant terror and bloodshed such as has prevailed in Argentina in the years 1975-78 since, in the words of David Rockefeller, "I have the impression that finally Argentina has a regime which understands the private enterprise system."[60] Important lessons are not to be drawn from official terror in states that understand the private enterprise system, but Cambodian terror, although in crucial respects a derivative of U.S. terror, could usefully be served up to the U.S. public on an almost daily regimen.

1.9 Media Self-Censorship: Or Why Two Soviet Dissidents are Worth More Than 20,000 Tormented Latins

The system of self-censorship, which pursues Communist abuses avidly while studiously ignoring the terror-ridden states of Latin America, is not a product of any explicit conspiracy. There *are* powerful governmental and media interests that do try deliberately to dredge up Communist abuse stories as part of a systematic effort at brainwashing. Many examples will appear below. But many media agencies engage in the same kind of selectivity out of their own ideological conditioning and the pressures of larger interests that encourage attention to Communist terror and discourage undue attention to abuses in client states. There are no powerful interests embarrassed by tales of Khmer Rouge terror, a Moscow dissident's trial, or the suffering of postwar Vietnam; in fact, interests opposed to a larger role for government in social welfare and supportive of the arms race favor such emphases on grounds of ideological serviceability. In the summer of 1978, the *New York Times* featured attacks on Secretary of State Vance for not calling off strategic arms talks with the Soviet Union because of the trial of two dissidents. The prime source of pressure was alleged to be the Coalition for a Democratic Majority, a super-cold war group whose concern for dissidents *west* of the Elbe has been negligible.[61] Nothing is more obvious than that Soviet human rights victims were being used by this group for larger political purposes, and that the alleged concern for human rights was strictly a strategic ploy.

There would be strong objections to a constant stream of stories on U.S.-created orphans, prostitutes, starving children, destruction of fields and forests, and the continuing hundreds of deaths in Indochina from unexploded ordnance, or on the depredations of U.S. client states using U.S. arms, as in East Timor. No less hostility would be engendered by a daily focus on the prisons, tortures, disappearances, and accounts of refugees from Argentina, Brazil, and Chile—these are *our* clients and our banks and major multinationals are pleased with the "stability" brought by the torturers.[62] "Security" seems a more acceptable basis for supporting gangsters and torturers than mere money-making, so the former is always adduced disingenuously as our sole source of interest.

The mass media everywhere tend to serve the important interests that dominate the state and select and suppress facts so as to convey the impression that national policy is well-intentioned and justified. Much the same is true, quite commonly, of those areas of academic scholarship that deal with contemporary affairs or social issues. The difference between a society with official censorship (e.g., the Soviet Union) and one without (the United States) is real and significant,[63] but the extent and especially the policy consequences of such differences are often overrated. There is a corresponding tendency to underestimate the significance of self-censorship and the strength of the underlying factors that make for unified mass media support for foreign policy—notably, the force of nationalism, government pressure and resources, and the overlap and community of interest among government, media, and business leaders, who jointly dominate state policy-making. Thus, if the dominant interests of a free society call for a policy of foreign aggression, the mass media will voluntarily mobilize the population as effectively as under a fully censored system.[64] Mild indications of doubt and reservations on grounds of cost-ineffectiveness have little influence on policy, but do serve to convey the erroneous impression that the imperial effort is based on democratic decision-making. Fundamental criticism that openly rejects the basic premises of the propaganda system, especially the assumption of the essential justice and decency of any major foreign venture, may be granted token appearance as an oddity in the mass media, but is generally confined to journals and pamphlets that are guaranteed to reach no more than a tiny fraction of the population. Exceptions to these generalizations are rare and unusual.

In the summer of 1978, the trials of Aleksandr Ginzburg and Anatoly Shcharansky in the Soviet Union received far more news coverage in the mass media of the United States than was accorded the last 20,000 cases of severe torture and murder by U.S. satellite governments in Latin America. Since official torture and murder in Latin America now appear to surpass the level of such abuses in the Soviet bloc and are carried out by governments nurtured, trained, and financed by the United States, and the international financial institutions it dominates, this is not a matter of the pot calling the kettle black; it is the *stove* calling the kettle black! Yet the self-censorship and ideological conditioning of the media is such that even the few remaining liberal columnists seem hardly aware of the ludicrous and hypocritical imbalance. They write as if the United States were struggling valiantly, devotedly, and with clean hands for a better world in which human rights will be respected, and just happened to locate two victims in the Soviet Union, and miss, by chance, the 20,000 brutalized in its own backyard. (See also Chapter 3, note 78)

1.10 Corruption as a Primary Characteristic of U.S. Client States

In Vietnam the legendary corruption of "our" Vietnamese—and their unwillingness to fight—always presented to U.S. imperial officialdom a puzzling contrast to the apparent honesty and superb fighting qualities of the Vietnamese enemy. The explanation was always simple—the Vietnamese willing to serve the United States were "denationalized," that is, they had lost touch with their own culture, and were essentially rootless mercenaries. The Vietnamese elite had a deep contempt for their own people and were quite prepared to cooperate with a "superior" culture and power in destroying their own society. The world-view of this elite was formed out of its own institutional interests, increasingly tied to the largesse of the external power and to the anti-Communist and counterrevolutionary ideology of the Godfather.

There is a close similarity of ideology among the predominantly military leaders of the U.S. client states, based on a incredibly simple Manichean view of the forces of evil (Communism) versus the forces of good (the United States, military officers, and free enterprise), all of it about on a John Birch Society level of sophistication. There is a regular pattern of identifying reform and any criticism of the status quo with Communism, and seeing in any such outcroppings external and subversive evils that must be extirpated.[65] There is solid evidence that this fascistic ideology has flowed in good part from the training and viewpoints of the U.S. military and civil establishment.[66]

The denationalized client fascist elites of such countries as pre-1975 South Vietnam and post-1964 Brazil have had a usually weak internal minority base of comprador and conservative business interests and a dominant external support base in a foreign economic and military establishment. Devoid of any economic ideas of their own, these elites resort to a dogmatic adherence to free enterprise (good enough for the emulated superpower) and an open door to foreign investment as the road to prosperity.[67] Economically illiterate, pretending to be "nonpartisan" technocrats who are going to clean up civilian corruption, these elites are perfect instruments of corruption. In state after client state, from Argentina to Zaire, the installation of military juntas has brought with it a new power and role for foreign business and *corruption as a system*. U.S. businessmen and their spokesmen contend that the spread of bribery as a means of doing business is not their doing—they claim that it is usually extortion, and that competition forces it upon them. What is neglected in this kind of rationalization (which understates the frequent reciprocity involved in payoffs) is that the regimes that are so corruption-prone are products of U.S. initiative. They are part of a package that includes rule by a denationalized minority, repression of the majority, and corruption flowing out of the dependent status of rulers and the interests of their external sponsors.

1.11 Corruption and Terror as a Feedback Process: How the U.S. Undermines Its Own Democratic Order as It Sustains Counterrevolution Abroad

In the early 1960s Robert McNamara, with his characteristic insight and prescience, argued for expanded support and training of the Latin American military on the grounds of the beneficial effect of their contact with democratic values. Between 1960 and 1969, 11 constitutionally elected governments were displaced by military dictatorships. This further enhanced the power of the U.S. military, given their closer relationships with the new dictators and the need to aid them further in consolidating their minority positions and improving "security".[68]

Since World War II, as the CIA and U.S. military have expanded their operations abroad to counter popular threats, their power within the United States itself has increased. They have been able to evade congressional mandates and define and enlarge their own missions; and, concomitantly, it is plausibly argued that despite the immense growth in armaments and frequent intervention abroad our "security" has declined. It probably *has* declined not only in the sense of a greater *feeling* of insecurity (based on symbolic manipulations by the military and its cold war allies), but because the nuclear arms race has steadily increased the capacity for mutual destruction. Counterrevolutionary violence and the growth of U.S. intelligence and military forces have created a huge vested interest in weapons, fear, insecurity, and ideologies conducive to further enlargement of the military-industrial-intelligence complex.

Counterrevolutionary violence abroad has also fed back to the home front in other ways. The spinoff of U.S.-sponsored terror groups has become positively embarrassing, with former CIA operatives like Orlando Bosch and other fascistic Cuban exiles trained to invade and subvert Cuba, now "old boys in the Latin American terrorist network,"[69] bombing and killing in Miami and elsewhere,[70] but often virtually "prosecution proof" because of CIA connections. Even more important has been the cross-country murder network of Argentina, Brazil, Chile, Paraguay, and Uruguay, whose secret police and death squads range freely over one another's territory in the hunt for dissidents. This is an achievement of the U.S. military—a matter of pride, as one of its objectives has been to foster "the coordinated employment of internal security forces within and among Latin American countries...."[71] These official terrorists have become more bold, engaging in kidnappings and political murder outside the co-fascist sphere. The murder of Orlando Letelier and Ronnie Moffitt on the streets of Washington, D.C., arranged by the Chilean secret police, was a mistake, however; the imperial power cannot allow its own capital to be the scene of the kind of unseemly operations that are daily occurrences within the territories of its clients.[72]

The feedback of corruption from South Korea to the U.S. Congress has also provided impressive evidence of the convergent tendencies of client fascism and its parent.[73] The most interesting aspect of the case is the fact that the Nixon administration knew that a foreign power was illegally bribing U.S. legislators and did nothing about it. The South Koreans were bribing the right people for a sound purpose, so that the flow of money could be considered analogous to the financing of CREEP from illicit sources. The CIA would forge documents to discredit foreign politicians in Brazil or Chile, and the Nixon administration would forge documents to discredit Kennedy or some other enemy politicians. In Brazil, a CIA front organization would use extorted and laundered U.S. money to subsidize amenable politicians, and a scholar on Brazil finds it an "overwhelming temptation to compare the modus operandi of this organization (a Brazilian front of the CIA) to that of Richard Nixon's Committee for the Re-election of the President (CREEP)."[74] Brazil, was in fact, a model for Nixon.[75] John Connally, a spokesman for a wide spectrum of U.S. business interests, asserted that "the United States could well look to the Brazilian example to put its own economy in order."[76] With our huge military and intelligence establishment, and a business community impressed with the technocratic "efficiency" of Brazilian fascism in keeping the lower orders passive as living standards decline under the "economic miracle," and in general in providing a superb industrial climate, is it possible that "convergence" will consist not in their becoming more like us so much as in our becoming more like them?

1.12 The New Vietnam: Or How To Abuse and Boycott a Savaged Victim That Is Behaving In a Way Contrary To Official Forecasts

While Cambodia has received maximum attention in the media, the treatment of Vietnam has been equally illuminating on the possibilities of brainwashing under freedom. The allegedly murderous and vengeful instincts of the Communists and the inevitability of a postwar bloodbath were a war propaganda staple from 1965-1975, endlessly and uncritically repeated.[77] Given the brutal character of the Vietnam War, the killing of collaborators and torturers and just plain vengeance killing were plausibly to be expected. In a phenomenon that has few parallels in Western experience, there appear to have been close to zero retribution deaths in postwar Vietnam. This miracle of reconciliation and restraint, instead of receiving respectful attention in the West and generating some soul-searching over another exposed layer of official fabrications, has been almost totally ignored.[78] The search has been exclusively for flaws. Instead of killing collaborators and torturers, the victors sent them to reeducation camps, so the media focus on that atrocity.[79] There is poverty and hardship in this ravaged land, and many people who were habituated to the affluence of war and a corruption-based totalitarian free enterprise economy have fled, along with many others unhappy with the harsh economic conditions or the authoritarian discipline of the new regime, or fearing retribution for collaboration and war crimes.

The media have focused on these refugees, whose flight is interpreted as a mark of failure of post-Thieu Vietnam, rather than on the huge majority who are attempting to rebuild their country, or the hundreds of thousands of orphans, drug addicts, prostitutes, or seriously wounded, whom the Vietnamese leadership is trying to rehabilitate in an effort to overcome the legacy of a shattered economy and social order left by their U.S. benefactors.

The concern for refugees, much like other aspects of the new "human rights" commitment, is highly selective. Thus refugees from postwar Indochina arouse memories of the holocaust and their suffering is portrayed with great indignation, while there is near total silence when 200,000 Burmese Muslims flee to Bangladesh in a two-month period in the spring of 1978 or when 140,000 Filipino refugees escape their oppressors, not to speak of the vast flow of exiles from the torture chambers constructed under U.S. auspices in Latin America. Furthermore, the compassion for refugees from Communism is not coupled with any thought of helping the countries ravaged by the United States to overcome the conditions that are surely a major cause for their flight. Mennonite social workers inform us that many thousands of children face death from starvation in Laos, while in Vietnam too there is hunger, even starvation, as a consequence of the war and natural catastrophes. Even the most saintly of regimes would be forced to resort to Draconian measures under such circumstances. But we read nothing of this in the mass media, which have no time for such trivialities. It is much more convenient to depict the conditions of Indochina as though they result solely from the depravity of the Communists, and to reserve sympathy for those who flee.

The portrayal of a drab Vietnam, with a harsh life, flight of refugees, and political prisoners, has several functions. First, it is offered as "justification" for our earlier efforts and helps us maintain our self-esteem by showing that life did turn out to be pretty bad under the Communists. This requires disciplined avoidance of any focus on the fact that the Indochinese are compelled to struggle upward from stone-age conditions largely of our making. Second, the grim prospects, and the suppression of the U.S. responsibility for them, helps to justify our continued hostility and refusal to aid the victims.[80]

1.13 The U.S. Record in Vietnam—and What Our Obligations and Policies Would Be on the Basis of Minimal Justice

As we discuss in the text below, the historical record, including an accumulating body of official documents, shows that the U.S. leadership knew from its earliest involvement that the Communists in Vietnam were the only political movement with mass popular support and that the faction it supported was a foreign implant (Diem, in fact, was imported from the United States). Joseph Buttinger, an early advisor to Diem and one of his most outspoken advocates in the 1950s, contends that the designation "fascist" is inappropriate for Diem because, although his regime had most of the vicious characteristics of fascism, he lacked the mass base that a Hitler or Mussolini could muster.[81] This is true of other U.S. junta-satellite regimes, which should perhaps be designated "subfascist," lacking the degree of legitimacy of a genuine fascist regime. (Henceforth in this book we will use the term "subfascist" as an appropriate designation for the members of the system of U.S. sponsored client fascist states.)

The U.S. assault on the Indochinese was quite consciously undertaken to smash them into submission to minority, subfascist agents chosen by the U.S. government. By a reasonable use of familiar terms this was plain aggression. If the facts were faced, and international law and elemental morality were operative, thousands of U.S. politicians and military planners would be regarded as candidates for Nuremberg-type trials. And the United States would be paying reparations proportionate to the vast destruction it caused. Although as one Laotian farmer, whose wife and three children were killed by the U.S. Air Force, said to an AFSC representative, when asked what the United States could do to redeem itself: "We want back those lives that were lost."[82]

But given the arrogance of self-righteous power, and the willingness of the media to conceal the central U.S. role as a destroyer without the slightest legal or moral basis for its actions, there will be no reparations and standard U.S. histories will write of a valiant but unsuccessful U.S. effort to protect freedom against Communist terror and subversion.

1.14 The Touch of Racism in U.S. Policy Toward Indochina

There was an important racist underpinning to the assault on Vietnam that was not fundamental to it but greatly facilitated the manipulation and destruction. From MacArthur to Westmoreland, the refrain that Orientals are essentially lower animals who don't feel pain as sensitive Westerners do and who only respect force, had its effect on policy. The Vietnamese have the mentality of six-year olds, and mumble to each other in a vocabulary of a few hundred words, so we learn from the head of the U.S. Information Agency in Saigon, John Mecklin—a critical supporter of U.S. involvement.[83] "Ours has been a reasonable strategy," another liberal analyst of the U.S. war explained, but it was "the strategy of those who are rich, who love life and fear 'costs'." For us, "death and suffering are irrational choices when alternatives exist," but we failed to comprehend that such a strategy will not be effective when applied against those who do not love life or try to avoid suffering. Thus the weak invite us to carry our "strategic logic to its conclusion, which is genocide," but we balk, because we recognize that "genocide is a terrible burden to bear" and would contradict "our own value system."[84]

Penalties against illegal attacks on "our" Vietnamese were so light that military lawyers in Vietnam coined the phrase, "mere Gook rule," to describe military-judicial treatment of offenders.[85] The corruptibility of our own puppets furthered this contempt, as did the very poverty and helplessness of the peasant victims (who thus "invite us" to destroy them) in a frustrating war where the superior race could kill and destroy but not conquer. It is easier to ignore the destruction of "mere gooks" than non-gooks, and to become enraged over the killing of whites in Rhodesia as compared with mere Africans in Mozambique or Namibia.

1.15 The New Human Rights Movement— Only Victims East of the Elbe Need Apply

In the post-World War II era the "Washington connection" has been strongly correlated with the proliferation of regimes of terror and oppression. As we have noted, the linkage arises out of the significant positive relationship between subfascism and "a favorable investment climate" and the long-standing predominance of investment criteria over human rights considerations. Under "conservative" administrations the United States supports subfascism aggressively and with little bother for the public relations aspects of human rights issues. Under "liberal" auspices, the United States supports subfascism no less aggressively—sometimes even more so—but sometimes urges its leaders to give it a more human face.

Despite this linkage, the people who brought us Tiger Cages, Provincial Interrogation Centers, saturation bombings as a device to "urbanize" South Vietnam, death squads, and military juntas, and their spokesmen and apologists in the mass media and academia, are now deeply concerned with human rights—but almost exclusively in the Communist world. Anthony Lewis explains this apparent bias as a consequence of the fact that within the Soviet sphere "the afflicted individuals are enough like us so that we identify with them—and because their stories are often such nightmares of cruelty."[86] The likeness hypothesis may have an element of truth; the endless suffering of peasants and slum dwellers rarely elicits from the privileged more than an occasional clucking of tongues or a remark on the cruelty of fate. But the hypothesis is still difficult to sustain. Chiang Kai-shek was not very much "like us," but we had little trouble "identifying with him," or so the actions of our democratic government would indicate. The numerous murdered and tortured intellectuals of Uruguay, Argentina, and Chile include many who are much more "like" U.S. writers than Solzhenitsyn and Sakharov, but their brutalized bodies rarely make it to the *Times* or the *Post*. As for "nightmares of cruelty," there is an endless supply that could be culled from just Indonesia and East Timor if anyone with dependable access to the media were interested. People are dying today throughout Indochina from starvation, disease, and unexploded ordnance that are one small part of the legacy of the U.S. war, but the new advocates of human rights seem to have little concern. There is not a whisper of protest in the press when the president states that we owe the people of Vietnam no debt and have no responsibility to rebuild what we have destroyed because "the destruction was mutual," no less.[87]

The linkage between U.S. interests and power, on the one hand, and severe human rights violations, on the other, is systematic, not accidental. A potent complex of business and financial interests, military-intelligence-State Department bureaucrats, and politicians are concerned exclusively with investment climate and the dependability of military clients, and this structure of interests has long determined the broad sweep of policy. Liberals and humanitarians in public office have found "business confidence" sagging and hostile forces quickly mobilized when they push too far, even verbally, in the direction of taking human rights values seriously. The system has its own dynamic, which has spawned the human rights arrangements that we now find in Chile, Paraguay, and the Philippines. The U.S. defeat in Indochina led to no institutional changes within this country. Even the doctrinal system, bruised by the revelations of the war, has been quickly restored. It is sheer romanticism, under these circumstances, to expect that a sudden concern for human rights might significantly influence the foreign policy of the United States.

Thus far, in fact, the Carter human rights campaign—mainly one of words rather than deeds, in any case—has been relatively strong on Soviet and Cambodian violations of civil rights and weak or nonexistent on human rights in U.S. client states. Arms sales, credits, gifts and training programs continue virtually unchanged in 1977-1978 to the Philippines, South Korea, Thailand, and Indonesia, countries with established records of serious human rights violations; and the cuts to other gross violators on the U.S. taxpayers' dole have not only involved small amounts, they have also been compromised by continuing deliveries based on unexpended credits from the past and the sanctioning of private sales. Huge arms sales have been approved for Iran, and some small arms and training for the Iranian secret police are included in the fiscal 1979 Carter budget, despite flagrant human rights violations. The upheavals in Iran in the fall of 1978, as we have already noted, led to no slackening of support. On the contrary, President Carter even went out of his way to communicate personally, and repeatedly, his warm backing for the Shah who was offered new supplies to help him quell any opposition or objections to his subfascist priorities.[88] Morocco, engaged in a counterinsurgency war in the Western Sahara of doubtful legality and gross incompatibility with human rights, has also received substantial military credits and training grants, and U.S. corporations linked to the Pentagon are reportedly helping to install a modern electronic sensing system that will improve Moroccan efficiency in violating human rights.[89] The Human Rights Administration has followed its predecessor in providing Indonesia with the military supplies it desperately needs to pursue its war of annihilation in East Timor. The vast flow of armaments to Saudi Arabia and Israel proceeds with utter lack of concern for the human rights policies of the tiny Saudi Arabian elite or of the Israeli military occupation. The Carter Administration is also hoping to realize the long-term aim of U.S. policy to remove Egypt from the Middle East, where it has posed a threat to U.S. interests in the oil-producing states, and turn it towards Africa, one of the major aims of Camp David. Correspondingly, Egypt too is being armed, not out of a devotion to human rights, but for the "new mission" which "is well known to almost everybody: an army of African intervention."[90]

Argentina, rated by Amnesty International as one of the world's premier violators of human rights, with death squads and torture teams still on a rampage,[91] has been an important test of administration human rights policy. Military assistance and sales to Argentina were terminated on September 30, 1978 by congressional action, and even before that the administration had refused to clear some requests for sales of arms and spare parts. Export-Import Bank financing of a major commercial loan to Argentina was denied, and the administration voted against (or abstained from voting on) quite a few loans up for action at the World Bank and Inter-American Development Bank. All military and training programs were not cut off, however,[92] even after September 30, 1978. The flow of funds from both international and private U.S. institutions has increased without interference under the regime of terror. And there has been no interference with normal trade; such drastic action is reserved for serious crimes, such as Cuba's expropriation of U.S. property. All of this suggests a less than maximim adminstration effort and/or structural obstacles to taking human rights seriously.

The Ex-Im Bank loan had been denied in the summer of 1978, over strong objections from the business community. The Bank chairman noted that he was obliged under law "to take into account the observance and respect for human rights in countries receiving exports we support with loans or financial guarantees." By September, business pressure had reached such a level that the law was forgotten, and the State Department reversed its denial of the loan. "While no one pointed to human rights improvements as a reason for the reversal, a State Department spokesman said the administration had 'expectations' of improvement," the *Washington Post* reports.[93] The same report cites regular military sales to Argentina and approval of training slots for Argentine officers at U.S. military installations. These were described by U.S. ambassador to Argentina Raul Castro "as evidence of the new incentives policy," which is replacing the Carter "policy of imposing largely ineffective and often counterproductive sanctions against the junta in favor of incentives to encourage human rights improvements." As if to highlight the effectiveness of these "incentives," the *Post* on the same day reports an account of torture by a political prisoner in Argentina who was never charged with any crime through his 12 months of captivity and 11 days of torture, adding that the transcript of his conversation with Western diplomats recounting the details of his torture "is known to be in the possession of the U.S. government."[94] The same report points out that his "experience is not atypical. Although somewhat improved over the last year, Argentina still ranks among the world's leading human rights offenders." That will all change, no doubt, now that the Human Rights Administration is shifting from ineffective and counterproductive sanctions to a new incentives policy.

In brief, the clients that we nurtured and supported through past years of human rights deterioration find that human rights will continue to be at best a side issue in U.S. policy. Even the verbal spankings will be light, and in the case of clients with money and power, such as Iran, our leaders will join hands with theirs in expressions of common devotion to human rights.

There is no reason to be so restrained with Communism, however, where both our responsibility for human rights violations and our power to alleviate abuses are small; and our bold leaders can (and will be pressed to) speak out more forcefully. The result is that the Carter human rights campaign has had an impact on Soviet attitudes, but not those pertaining to human rights; rather, it has added to Soviet suspicions of U.S. interest in controlling the arms race. Carter's mobilization of power in Congress has not been sufficient to prevent the conservative House from voting against aid to Cuba, Vietnam, Mozambique, and several other exclusively left-oriented states, while preserving it intact for subfascism. Thus, whatever Carter's real intentions, his human rights movement thus far has worked out in practice to exacerbate cold war tensions and affect minimally human rights in areas under United States influence.

But while the new moralism is not likely to have a large impact on human rights, it may well be effective as an instrument of propaganda. After the horrors of Indochina, some dramatic initiatives were needed to reconstruct the image of U.S. benevolence that has proven so useful a cover for external intervention. With our concern for "human rights" reestablished, the United States will be able to return to the "activist" foreign policy that is essential for preserving the global interests of U.S. capitalism. If human rights are violated in the process, ideologists will speak of unexplained "inconsistencies" and "deviations".

Still, in spite of these basic considerations, there may be some marginal gains to human rights from the new propaganda offensive. The expressed concern for human rights may offer opportunities for people who are genuinely interested in the issue. They can exploit the new rhetoric, and should, to try to alleviate the suffering and oppression of the victims of terroristic states, and may even be able to enlist some support from political forces in the United States, when this is not unduly expensive. But it is hardly reasonable to expect that the recent discovery of human rights violations will offset the systematic factors that impel the United States to impose and support client fascism, factors based on powerful and compelling economic interests that have in no way been diminished by recent developments, domestic or international.

1.16 Individual Morality and Human Rights Policy

Several moral issues arise in protests concerning atrocities and violations of human rights. If the purpose of such protests is self-aggrandizement, service to one's state, establishing credentials with one's compatriots or deity, or other self-serving motives, then it is clear how to proceed; join the chorus of protests organized by the government or the media with regard to the iniquity of the current enemies of the state. Such protest may be directed towards genuine abuses of human rights, but it is at the moral level of protest for pay. We understand this very well in the case of official enemies. Suppose that some Russian intellectual condemns U.S. behavior in Chile or Vietnam. What he says may be quite true, but we do not admire his courage or moral integrity. Similar remarks apply here, and for the very same reasons.

Suppose that the purpose of protest is to relieve human suffering or defend human rights. Then more complex considerations arise. One must consider the plausible consequences for the victims of oppression. It is for this reason, for example, that an organization such as Amnesty International urges polite letters to the most miserable tyrant. In some cases, public protest may be positively harmful, a fact familiar to people seriously concerned with human rights. Recently Jiri Hajeok, formerly foreign minister in the Dubcek government and now a leading Czech dissident, "criticized President Carter for an 'over-tough' approach which, he said, will hinder the struggle for greater political latitude in the East bloc."[95] If the purpose of the "human rights crusade" is to restore U.S. prestige after the battering it has taken in the past decades, then such considerations are irrelevant. In fact, Washington had already made its position clear on the matter: "The Carter Administration issued a pointed warning yesterday that it will not be dissuaded from its public campaign for human rights around the world [sic] by the harassment of individual dissidents in foreign countries."[96] But people with a genuine concern for human rights would react quite differently, and give serious consideration to the likely effects on the victims. Such calculations are not always easy ones but the issue will not be lightly dismissed by people who engage in protest for other than self-serving or strategic motives.

Such persons will also consider how their finite energies can be distributed most efficaciously. It is a cheap and cynical evasion to plead that "we must raise our voices" whenever human rights are violated. Even a saint could not meet this demand. A serious person will try to concentrate protest efforts where they are most likely to ameliorate conditions for the victims of oppression. The emphasis should, in general, be close to home: on violations of human rights that have their roots in the policies of one's own state, or its client regimes, or domestic economic institutions (as, e.g., in the case of U.S. investment in South Africa), and in general, on policies that protest may be able to influence. This consideration is particularly relevant in a democracy, where public opinion can sometimes be aroused if circumstances allow a sufficient breach in the conformism of the ideological institutions (the media and academic scholarship), but it applies as well in totalitarian states that rely in part on popular consent, as most do. It is for this reason that we honor a Medvedev or Grigorenko who denounce the crimes of the Russian state and its satellites, at great personal risk. If, as in these cases, they also condemn the criminal acts of the United States, that is well and good, but far less significant. In the case of Solzhenitsyn, who comes to the United States to call for a holy war against Communism and criticizes us for not resorting to still greater violence against our enemies, the most generous reaction must be pity—and distress at the fact that the Soviet state has reduced so many of its most courageous dissidents to such blindly destructive hostility.

For privileged Western intellectuals, the proper focus for their protest is at home. The primary responsibility of U.S. citizens concerned with human rights today is on the continuing crimes of the United States: the support for terror and oppression in large parts of the world, the refusal to offer reparations or aid to the recent victims of U.S. violence. Similar considerations apply elsewhere. French intellectuals may, if they choose, devote their energies to joining the chorus of protest against Cambodian atrocities that has been conducted by the international press (including the *New York Times*, the Soviet Press, indeed virtually every articulate segment of opinion in the industrial societies). As long as such protest is honest and accurate—often it is not, as we shall see—it is legitimate, though further questions may be raised about its impact. This small increment to the international barrage on Cambodia had little if any effect in mitigating harsh practices there, though it had a powerful effect on ideological renewal in the West and helped prepare the ground for the Vietnamese invasion of Cambodia in January 1979. These effects were predictable, and predicted. French intellectuals interested in doing something to alleviate suffering in Southeast Asia where their impact might be positive would have been better advised to expend their efforts in protesting the announcement by their government that it proposes to join in the glorious massacre in East Timor by supplying arms, setting up an arms industry and providing diplomatic cover for Indonesia.[97] If victims of oppression in Russia, Uganda, or Cambodia can be helped by public protest, then it is justified; otherwise, it is empty rhetoric, or worse. The ultimate vulgarity, perhaps, is the spectacle to which we are now being treated in the U.S. (indeed, Western) media, where many people who supported U.S. savagery in Indochina or perhaps finally turned against the war on "pragmatic grounds"—the United States could not reach its goals at reasonable cost—now feign outrage and indignation over oppressive or murderous acts that are in large part a consequence of the U.S. violence that they tolerated or supported. What they say may in fact be true—although it often is not—but it reeks of hypocrisy and opportunism. We would react no differently if some German intellectual who tolerated or supported Hitler expressed his indignation over the atrocities committed by the French resistance after liberation.

Even those who took part in protest or resistance against the U.S. war in Vietnam cannot escape these questions. Should they, for example, protest atrocities in Indochina in the pages of the *New York Times*, in a context of continuing distortions on atrocities (and on all facets of the war) and a very effective, ongoing official and media propaganda campaign, which has direct and very harmful consequences for the victims of U.S. barbarism in Indochina? Again, individuals seriously concerned with human rights and human dignity will carefully consider the potential human consequences of their acts. Will particular forms of protest help to alleviate the condition of those who suffer, including victims of earlier violence? Or will they contribute to rebuilding the ideological foundations for new violence and depredations? The future victims of counterrevolutionary violence will not thank even honest protestors who thoughtlessly contribute to these ends. These questions are not easy to answer and honest people may reach differing conclusions concerning them, but they deserve serious thought, far more than has been publicly expressed during the postwar period of ideological reconstruction.

CHAPTER 2

The Pentagon-CIA Archipelago

The Vietnam War has been digested by the U.S. political system with hardly a trace. Essentially the same people manage national affairs, and possess virtually exclusive access to the mass media; the critics of the war have lapsed, or been forced, into silence; and the media have not allowed the vast accumulation of sordid details about our Vietnam involvement to disturb the myth of U.S. benevolence and concerned pursuit of democracy abroad. This myth has remained unruffled even in the face of the accelerating "Brazilianization"[1] of the Third World over the past several decades, very often under active U.S. sponsorship, with frequent displacement of democratic governments and extensive and growing resort to repression, including physical torture, imprisonment, death squads, and mysterious "disappearances," all within the U.S. sphere of influence.

At the end of World War II, if some prescient commentator had described the terror regimes that now dominate Latin America, liberals would have derided this visionary for spelling out the likely consequences of a Nazi victory. Such liberal critics would have been right, although liberalism has accommodated well (and has contributed much[2]) to the institutionalization of sub-fascism under U.S. tutelage. In this context, the state which has sponsored and supported the Somoza family, the Shah, Marcos, Park, Pinochet, Suharto, Mobutu, the Brazilian generals, and their many confederates in repression and violence, can announce a campaign for human rights throughout the world and be taken with the utmost seriousness.

2.1 Neo-Colonialism and the Washington Connection

Since World War II there has been a steady deterioration of political and social conditions in Latin America and generally throughout Third World areas that are within the Free World. Liberal ideologists treat this as fortuitous and independent of U.S. choice and power, claiming that as a democracy we support democratic institutions abroad, while any contrary trends are based on exogenous forces over which the United States has no control. In the process it is necessary to suppress and belittle the long-standing relations between the U.S. political-military elite and the military juntas and comprador elements in such states as Argentina, Chile, and Brazil, the economic advantages of Third World fascism to U.S. economic interests, and the evidence of positive U.S. political and economic support for brutal dictatorships and frequent hostility to reform as well as radical change in the Third World.

2.1.1 The Systematic Positive Relationship Between U.S. Aid and Human Rights Violations

The *real* relationships, as opposed to the standard ideological expressions of devotion to democracy and humanism, are indicated on the accompanying table, which relates U.S. economic and military aid (and that of U.S. dominated international lending agencies) to various political and human rights and economic factors. The table focuses on a series of strategic changes, whose dates are shown in column 1, for 10 U.S. client countries. Columns 2-4 describe the effect of these events on the political environment and human rights, with minus signs (-) indicating an adverse effect on human rights, i.e., a decline in democratic institutions and an increased use of torture and larger numbers of political prisoners—and positive signs (+), the reverse. Column 5

Table 1

U.S. Aid, Investment Climate, and Human Rights in Ten Countries

Country	Strategic Political Dates[1] (1)	Positive (+) or Negative (−) Effects on Democracy (2)	(−) means an increased use of torture or death squads (3)	(−) means an increase in No. of political prisoners (4)	Improvement in Investment Climate: tax laws eased (+) (5a)	Improvement in Investment Climate: labor repressed (+) (5b)	Economic Aid (% change) (6)	Military Aid (% change) (7)	(6) + (7) (% change) (8)	U.S. and Multi-national Credits (% change) (9)	Total Aid (8) + (9) (% change) (10)
Brazil	1964	−	−	−	+	+	+ 14	−40	− 7	+ 180	+ 112
Chile	1973	−	−	−	+	+	+558	− 8	+259	+1,079	+ 770
Dominican Republic	1965	−	−	NA	+	+	+ 57	+10	+ 52	+ 305	+ 133
Guatemala	1954	−	−	NA	+	+	NA	NA	NA	NA	+5,300
Indonesia	1965	−	−	−	+	NA	− 81	−79	− 81	+ 653	+ 62
Iran	1953	−	−	−	+	+	NA	NA	NA	NA	+ 900
Philippines	1972	−	−	−	+	+	+204	+67	+143	+ 171	+ 161
South Korea	1972	−	−	−	+	+	− 52	−56	− 55	+ 183	− 9
Thailand	1973	+	+	NA	−	−	− 63	−64	− 64	+ 218	+ 5
Uruguay	1973	−	−	−	+	+	− 11	+ 9	− 2	+ 32	+ 21

Sources: 1. Information on torture and political prisoners mostly from the *Amnesty International Report on Torture*, 1975 and *The Amnesty International Report, 1975-76*, 1976. Supplemented with data from newspaper articles, journals, and books on the specific countries. Data on investment climate largely from articles, journals, and books on the specific countries.

2. Data on aid taken from *U.S. Overseas Loans and Grants and Assistance from International Organizations*, A.I.D., 1972 and 1976 editions, for years 1962-1975. Data previous to 1962 taken from *Historical Statistics of the United States*, Bicentennial Edition, Dept. of Commerce, 1975.

shows the effect of these events on the "climate of investment": 5a shows + if tax and profit repatriation laws were eased; 5b is + if government controls were put on wages or independent labor organizations were weakened or destroyed. Columns 6-10 show percentage changes in aid and credits from the United States and international organizations for the two or three years after the political change as compared with the comparable period prior to the events.[3] For example, under Brazil, 1964 is a strategic date as noted in column 1. We can see that human rights deteriorated, investment climate improved, and overall aid and credits by the U.S. and multinational lending organizations went up 112% (column 10) in the three years following the coup as compared to the three years preceding the coup.

There are a number of problems associated with this table.[4] Trends in torture and numbers of political prisoners are not easy to establish, and in a few instances the evidence is tentative. Aid figures can also be misleading, as other factors may temporarily distort a real relationship; e.g., the decline in aid to South Korea after the Park coup of 1972 was greatly influenced by the withdrawal of South Korean mercenaries from South Vietnam and the resultant decline in U.S. payments for these hired soldiers.[5] The reduction in military aid to Chile after the fascist coup of 1973 is also misleading, since the high rate of military aid under Allende reflected U.S. support for the right-wing military in the interests of counter-revolution—economic aid to the civil society declined precipitously under Allende. The collapse of international organization aid to Chile during the Allende period, and its rapid recovery under subfascism, reflects the dominance of U.S. economic and political interests in the decision-making processes of the international agencies.[6]

For all its limitations this table bears out in graphic form a set of relationships that should be obvious to any student of recent Third World history. For most of the sample countries, *U.S.-controlled aid has been positively related to investment climate and inversely related to the maintenance of a democratic order and human rights.* Only in the case of South Korea and Thailand is the pattern reversed. The South Korean exception we have explained above. The row for Thailand shows a sharp reduction of U.S. economic and military aid following the moves toward democratic

Table 2

U.S. Military and Economic Aid to Selected Human Rights Violators, Fiscal Years 1973-78
(Current dollars, in millions)

Fiscal Years 1973-77

Country:	Military aid grant[1,3]	Military sales credits[1]	Total arms sales[1,4]	Total economic aid[2,5]	Number of military trainees[1]	F.Y. 1978 Proposed military aid (grants & credits)[1,6]
ARGENTINA	2.2	134.0	98.6	—	689	15.7
BRAZIL	3.4	230.7	258.3	93.3	1,062	50.1
CHILE	2.5	27.4	146.6	226.7	1,391	—
ETHIOPIA	53.2	46.0	200.6	111.0	736	12.1
INDONESIA	107.9	54.7	91.8	634.2	1,272	58.4
IRAN	0.3	—	15,677.3	5.4	—	—
PHILIPPINES	124.4	60.0	194.7	383.5	1,460	41.4
SOUTH KOREA	601.1	552.4	1,333.1	487.0	2,741	280.4
THAILAND	229.4	74.7	220.3	91.4	2,655	40.5
URUGUAY	9.0	12.0	16.9	22.8	717	—
Totals:	1,133.4	1,191.9	18,238.2	2,055.3	12,723	498.6

[1]Source: 1973-76 data: U.S. Department of Defense, *Foreign Military Sales and Military Assistance Facts* (Washington, 1976); 1977-78 data: U.S. Department of Defense, *Security Assistance Program, Presentation to Congress,* F.Y. 1978 (Washington, 1977).

[2]Source: U.S. Agency for Development, *U.S. Overseas Loans and Grants, July 1 1945-June 30 1975* (Washington, 1976), and additional tables supplied by USAID.

[3]Includes deliveries of excess defense articles and training costs under the International Military and Education Training Program.

[4]Includes the Foreign Military Sales and Commercial Sales programs.

[5]Includes economic assistance (loans and grants), Food for Peace aid, Security Supporting Assistance, and smaller provisions.

[6]Includes MAP grants, training costs, excess defense articles, and FMS credits.

This table is reproduced with permission, from Michael T. Klare, *Supplying Repression*, Field Foundation, 1977, p. 9.

government in October 1973, slightly more than offset by U.S. international organization credits. But the bulk of the credits consisted of a large World Bank loan made in 1974 while control by the Thai elite was still intact. In 1975 World Bank loans fell to zero for the first time in a decade. It should also be noted that there was a large influx of U.S. military aid into Thailand in 1976 (not shown on the table), which no doubt facilitated thc counter-revolutionary coup of October, 1976. (See chapter 4, section 2.)

Each of the 10 countries shown on Table 1 was a major violator of human rights during the past decade, but each received military and economic aid and police training assistance from the United States in the 1970s. For a slightly different group of 10 Free World violators of human rights,[7] Table 2 shows for the 5 year period 1973-1978 that the 10 received total economic aid from the United States of over $2 billion along with military aid and credit of $2.3 billion, they were sold arms in excess of $18 billion, and they had 12,723 officer trainees at schools in the United States or in U.S. bases abroad. The table also shows that 7 of the 10 violators were proposed recipients of military grants and credits in the Carter "human rights" budget for fiscal 1978. The author of Table 2, Michael Klare, concludes that

> rather than standing in detached judgment over the spread of repression abroad, the United States stands at *the supply end of a pipeline of repressive technology* extending to many of the world's authoritarian governments. And despite everything this administration has said about human rights, there is no evidence that this pipeline is being dismantled. In fact, its relative durability suggests that the delivery of repressive technology to authoritarian regimes abroad is a consistent and *intentional* product of our foreign policy, rather than a peripheral or accidental one.[8]

2.1.2 U.S. Military and Police Aid and Training and the Spread of Fascism

Military training and supply, the build-up and cultivation of the military and intelligence establishments, as well as CIA surveillance and destabilization, have been key elements of the "Washington connection," employed to protect U.S. interests in its client states in the post-World War II era. The United States trains client military personnel in some 150 bases and training schools, and sends mobile units and advisors to serve on an in-country basis. This training has placed great weight on ideological conditioning and has "steeped young Latin officers in the early 1950s anti-Communist dogma that subversive infiltrators could be anywhere."[9] In addition to the ideological cement of this world view, U.S. military training has purposefully helped build a network of personal relationships between United States and Latin American military cadres.[10] This tie has been further consolidated by military aid from the wealthier power as well as cooperative maneuvers and logistical planning. Over 200,000 Latin American military personnel have been trained in the U.S., and since 1949 over 35,000 Latin American officers have trained in the School for the Americas alone; a school identified in Latin America by its historic function as the "school of coups."[11]

In testimony before Congress, there has been a pretense by spokesmen for the military and foreign policy establishment that our training and contacts will have a "pro-democratic" impact and will serve to bring more "humane" methods to the Latin American police and military. Precisely the opposite effects have occurred. Our training and aid have enhanced the power of the military, and our ideological and moral support and training have encouraged them to assert themselves politically. They have become more "pro-American," but any spinoff of democratic values is as yet undetectable.[12] In the Brazilian coup, the U.S.-trained faction took the lead in overturning constitutional government, and throughout Latin America graduates of U.S. military training—including Pinochet and Leigh of Chile, Geisel of Brazil, Massera of Argentina, and scores of others—have led the march to sub-fascism. Furthermore, *inhumane* methods of interrogation and general treatment of prisoners have grown steadily, in parallel with the increase in U.S. training and supply of modern tools of repression. The Amnesty International *Report on Torture* pointed out that today "much of state torture is carried out by the military forces, usually elite or special units, who displace the civil police in matters of political security. Their military training and their post-World War II theories about 'unconventional war' make them particularly apt for the practice and enable them to apply the concept of 'war' to any situation of civil political conflict no matter how mild."[13]

From Brazil, and with continuing U.S. assistance, torture spread throughout much of Latin America in the 1960s and early 1970s, with Brazil serving as a torture-aid subcontractor. Jean-Pierre Clavel states that

> secret steps were taken in Brazil in the early 1960s by a group of senior military and police officials to create a coordinated autonomous torture and "death squad" network to crush political opposition. To train personnel, illustrated lectures and live demonstrations of torture were conducted, using political prisoners as guinea pigs, by *Operacao Bandeirantes*, once described as "a type of advanced school of torture." Subsequently, trained Brazilian torturers traveled to military academies in neighboring nations to conduct courses in what is euphemistically called "interrogation".[14]

Clavel notes that "refinements" have continued, based on programs of technical and medical research designed to develop techniques for intensifying pain without causing death. He quotes Dr. Timothy Shallice of London National Hospital: "Torture which was once a craft has become a technology."

Brazil is apparently not the only subcontractor for torture-aid. In a series of reports from Iran, Richard Sale commented that "innumerable Iranians, including many in a position to know, told me that the Israelis oversee SAVAK's techniques," which have been reported by Amnesty International and others in gruesome detail.[15]

The creativity of U.S. specialists in this area has been impressive. A Vietnamese prisoner in South Vietnam remembered a visit by U.S. prison experts: "Usually we were chained in a kind of ordinary shackle in the form of a number 8, where the legs and hands go through the two holes of the number 8. Then, one day, three Americans came and inspected the shackles and chains...A couple of days later, the number 8 cuffs were replaced...[With the new ones] whenever the prisoners tried to move their legs, the fetters would lock further and further one step and yet another step through them."[16] During the Vietnam War the United States supplied funds and technology for Tiger Cages, interrogation centers, and electronic and other equipment used for torture, and at a very minimum the United States gave its moral sanction for the huge expansion of torture as a standard practice. SAVAK, the Iranian secret police noted for its sadism and frequent use of torture, was set up by the CIA in 1957, and the military officers who ran it from its inception "received special training at the Marine base in Quantico, Va., and attended orientation programs at C.I.A. headquarters at Langley, Va. More SAVAK agents received U.S. training under police programs financed by the Agency for International Development, which spent more than $2 million on 'public safety'."[17] Jan Black notes that in Brazil "the marked expansion of the [police] training program also coincided with an increase in documented reports of the systematic torture of political prisoners and of the murders of petty criminals, as well as alleged subversives, carried out by the 'Death Squads,' reportedly composed of off-duty policemen."[18]

There is considerable evidence that U.S. military and intelligence services have provided training in torture to Third World police and military,[19] but this is of small consequence given the established fact of moral support, massive supply of torture technology, and the widespread adoption of torture as an administrative practice by client fascist states so supplied and protected by the United States. The Amnesty International *Report on Torture* provides an excellent case study of the history of torture under the Colonel's regime in Greece, 1967-73, noting that "American policy on the torture question as expressed in official statements and official testimony has been to deny it where possible and minimise it, where denial was not possible. This policy flowed naturally from general support for the military regime."[20] This generalization could be applied to the *system* of torture regimes, as we will show in many cases below, and it tells us a great deal about the ultimate source of this "cancerous growth."

2.1.3 The Scope and Variety of CIA Subversive Activities

CIA destabilization operations have assumed many forms, of which only a few will be mentioned briefly here. First is the outright murder of political leaders like Lumumba (to be replaced by the more amenable Mobutu), or General Schneider in Chile,[21] and the numerous attempts on the life of Castro.[22] Second, and also familiar, are the direct conspiracies with terrorists, mercenaries or (usually) military factions within a country to disrupt or overthrow a government in disfavor. Among the more conspicuous and acknowledged successes with heavy CIA involvement have been the Belgian Congo, Chile, Greece, Guatemala, Indonesia, and Iran; among the failures, the abortive 1958 rebellion in Indonesia and the Bay of Pigs fiasco of 1961. In the case of Laos, the CIA actually organized and directed a mercenary army of hill tribesmen in an effort to destroy the indigenous social revolution, cynically abandoning its proteges when they were largely decimated and no longer needed.[23] In this general category, we may also note such activities as terrorist attacks, crop-poisoning, etc., as practiced extensively by the CIA under Kennedy and subsequent administrations in an effort to undermine the Cuban regime and disrupt Cuban economic development.[24] The total number of cases of CIA involvement in active subversion of established governments (and attempts at political murder) runs into the hundreds or even thousands. Third is political bribery and the funding of foreign politicians. In the case of Brazil, the inflow of CIA money in the pre-1964 period was so huge, involving so many hundreds of politicians, that it provoked a scandal and a government investigation, which was conveniently terminated by the 1964 coup.

Fourth is propaganda, which can take a wide variety of forms, but is invariably undercover (and thus dishonest as to its source) and is often carried out by subsidies to researchers, research institutes, publishers, and journalists. It can be massive in scale and scope, as in pre-coup Brazil, where in 1962 the CIA mounted a "saturation campaign," with 80 weekly radio programs, 300 additional hours of radio-TV advertising, a flooding of the press with canned editorials and "information," large quantities of billboard ads and pamphlets, etc. It kept "dozens" of journalists on its payroll and edited a monthly magazine, using top quality paper and free distribution. It even rented the editorial page of Rio's evening paper, *A Noite*. And it subsidized the publication of numerous conservative books, "distributed free and without attribution."[25]

In its propaganda campaigns the CIA has long engaged in forgeries designed to discredit its enemies. In Brazil, for example, in order to undercut the position of a peasant leader threatening reform, the CIA printed leaflets announcing his presence at non-existent meetings, and printed Marxist literature to be distributed after the coup to prove the existence of a Communist threat.[26] In Chile, the CIA forged and disseminated documents in 1973 to prove that the Communists intended a bloody coup, featuring the beheading of the top echelons of the military, in part to frighten and provoke the military into pushing ahead with their own takeover and massacre.[27]

A fifth type of CIA destabilization operation is the organization and funding of demonstrations, important in the subversion process in both Brazil and Chile. Philip Agee noted in his *Diary* that "the Rio station and its larger bases were financing the mass urban demonstrations against the Goulart government, proving the old themes of God, country, family, and liberty to be as effective as ever."[28] The same tactic was employed in Chile as part of the CIA subversion program. A sixth CIA tactic is the infiltration of unfavored organizations and political parties. This has informational value and it allows confusion to be sown and agent provocateurs to function. In Brazil, the most important effort of this sort was implemented in collaboration with the AFL-CIO through the American Institute for Free Labor Development (AIFLD), which carried out an anti-Communist propaganda campaign, worked diligently to split and discredit any independent Brazilian unions, and in the end proudly supported the coup that definitively ended free unionism in Brazil.[29]

Finally, the CIA collects information, which is used in various ways. Most interesting is the extent to which it regularly provides information to rightist thugs and conspirators against constitutional government. The Chilean military were given lists of "enemies" and the Brazilian right was constantly fed information prior to the coup.[30] The political orientation and role of the CIA are such that no clandestine agents were stationed in South Africa before 1974, while both before and after 1974 the CIA has had a close and "cordial" relationship with the South African secret police.[31] CIA destabilization of inconvenient democracies has been commonplace, but it takes a vivid imagination to conceive of them subverting South Africa in the interests of ending apartheid.

Attention is focused above on Brazil precisely because it is such a large and relatively powerful country.[32] In spite of this the CIA was able to bribe its journalists, subsidize its politicians, conspire with military factions, infiltrate and subvert the labor movement, and engage in extensive propaganda campaigns—in short, it could virtually disregard the sovereignty of this large and theoretically independent country. The catch, of course, is that Brazil was *not* an independent country—U.S. penetration was already enormous by the 1960s and U.S. leaders acted as if they had a veto over Brazilian economic and foreign policy.[33] The Brazilian military and much of its economy were already "denationalized," with strong ties and dependency relations to the United States; and U.S. business had a substantial presence in Brazil, controlling, among other things, about half of the advertising industry and a rapidly expanding and significant fraction of the mass media.[34] It was hard to separate U.S. business and CIA activities in Brazil before 1964. Levinson and de Onis claim that U.S. business, in close touch with the CIA, helped organize and finance anti-Goulart demonstrations in the early 1960s,[35] and Richard Helms himself reported that business served regularly as a CIA cover.[36] Hanna Mining not only funded anti-Communist conferences, but made a more direct defense of freedom by providing trucks for the Minas Gerais troops that launched the "revolution."[37]

A curious aspect of this massive subversion operation in a country such as Brazil is that it is not regarded as subversion. If the Cubans are found to provide weapons to insurgents in Venezuela such a discovery is given great publicity as evidence of Cuban perfidy[38]—*this* piddling and one dimensional effort is subversion.

The subversion of Brazil by the United Statess in the years leading up to the coup of 1964—weapons on a huge scale, bribery, black propaganda, practically open conspiracy with military officers, massive institutional subversion—this multi-dimensional effort is the natural right of power—where domination is so taken for granted that the hegemonic power intervenes by inevitable and unquestioned authority. We are benevolently protecting our children in their own interest—can parents be considered alien to their children or conspire against them? Can the cat looking after its 20 mice have any interest antagonistic to theirs?

2.1.4 The Pre-Eminence of Favorable Investment Climate

The pattern in the exercise of power by the cat among the mice is clear, persistent, rational, and ugly. Human rights have tended to stand in the way of the satisfactory pursuit of U.S. economic interests—and they have, accordingly, been brushed aside, systematically. U.S. economic interests in the Third World have dictated a policy of containing revolution, preserving an open door for U.S. investment, and assuring favorable conditions of investment. Reformist efforts to improve the lot of the poor and oppressed, including the encouragement of independent trade unions, are not conducive to a favorable climate of investment. Democracy is clearly not conducive to a favorable business climate. As noted by Edward A. Jesser, Jr., chairman of the United Jersey Banks, in a speech to the American Bankers Association: "Quick and tough decisions can be made in a relatively short time in a country such as Brazil compared to the difficulty there is in reaching agreement on what actions to take in a democracy.'[39] So much for democracy. Democratic threats to the interests of foreign investors, such as a Philippines Supreme Court ruling prior to the 1972 coup prohibiting foreigners from owning land, or a Brazilian dispute over a mineral concession to Hanna Mining Company, or agrarian reform in Guatemala, or nationalization of oil in Iran, are expeditiously resolved in favor of the foreigner by dictators and military juntas. Marcos, for example, quickly reversed the land ownership decision and, "According to one oilman, 'Marcos says "We'll pass the laws you need—just tell us what you want'."[40] (This is a nice illustration of how, under client fascism, the constituency of the leadership shifts to foreign interests.) This case exemplifies what has been a consistent pattern.

2.1.5 The Economic Role of Terror: Preserving and Enlarging Military, Comprador, and Foreign Income Shares

We have seen that there is a positive relationship between U.S. aid, investment climate, and terror. A grim further fact is that the terror is not a fortuitous spinoff but *has a functional relationship to investment climate.* Special tax privileges to foreign business and dependence on foreign investment for economic growth are not easy to achieve under a democratic order in this era of Third World nationalism. Neither are wage controls and other actions conducive to a favorable investment climate. These actions have involved the deliberate "marginalization" of over 80% of the population by their total exclusion from political processes, from legal and broader "human rights,' and from the policy calculations of the elite leadership.[41] The necessary linkage between terror and economic policy has been expressed time and again by spokesmen for the Catholic Church in Latin America, for whom the the connection is a part of daily experience:

> The situation provoked by the chosen model of development is such that it in effect provokes a revolution that did not exist. In order to impose the model of development which gives privilege to small minorities, it was necessary to create or maintain a repressive State which in turn provokes a situation of civil war. The very theoreticians of the system insist on the necessary link between development and security; they recognize that the development they wish to impose on the country can only provoke indignation among the people...If there were any type of freedom left, the cries of protest would be so great that the only solution has been to impose absolute silence.[42]

In short, the "new order" in the U.S. colonial sphere is blatant and violent class warfare, with the combined interests of the denationalized military leadership, some local business, and multinational enterprise (with its foreign state adjuncts) literally seizing the state to accomplish their objectives, shattering the organizational defenses of the majority of the population, and striving to reduce it to passivity, clearing the decks for subfascist economic policy and "development".

The economics of subfascism involves a rapid shift to a wide open door to foreign trade and investment, tight money, and social welfare budget cuts—that is, the economic policies called for by the interests of the dominant power and its institutional affiliates, the IMF and World Bank. Priority is given to servicing the foreign debt via increased exports and decreased imports, with the burden falling largely on the underlying population in the form of reduced wages and serious unemployment. There is a return to the "free market," in theory, but it is selectively applied, with no serious control over monopoly power, employer organizations and collective action, but with control over wages, both directly and by means of a banning of strikes and the destruction or state control of unions.

Deflationary policies and an open door tend to weaken domestic business and enhance the power of foreign companies that can borrow abroad at relatively low interest rates. Thus, foreign investment often takes the form of buying out "non-competitive" local businesses in an accelerated process of denationalization.[43] Takeovers are financed commonly with resources raised in the poorer country, either in local capital markets or through reinvested local earnings. A 1968 Brazilian Commission of Inquiry study—suppressed in Brazil—showed that over an extended time period 11 major multinationals had brought into Brazil only $298.8 million in capital from the outside. They had reinvested $693 million and remitted abroad $744.5 million. The ratio of the surplus generated by these companies in Brazil to the capital they had brought in was 5 to 1.[44] Although the Brazilian state has become more active in economic affairs in the 1970s, the coup increased the dependence of that country on foreign capital, which controls some 50% of Brazilian manufacturing sales and 59 of the 100 largest manufacturing companies, dominating the motor vehicle, pharmaceutical, machinery, rubber, plastic, and other industries of strategic importance.[45] In Argentina, Brazil, and Chile, the early client fascist years have been characterized by a massive displacement of smaller domestic firms by larger local, and, more importantly, foreign multinationals.

A persistent and crucial characteristic of neo-colonialism is the preservation of labor as a cheap commodity. In the Philippines, for example, real wages have declined sharply for both rural and urban workers, and in "an era of rising commodity prices, labor remains the cheap component...Manila remains one of the few capitals of the world where a taxi ride from the airport to the center of the city costs less than a dollar with tip."[46] Plantation labor in the Philippines in the mid-1970s was 10¢ an hour and in the industrial park of Bataan averaged 85¢ a day;[47] not enough for minimal nutrition, apart from other human necessities, but superb for keeping labor costs at attractive levels. The 1972 agricultural census of Brazil showed that 78% of the rural workers of Brazil earned less that 150 cruzeiros (about $38) per month. This enormous and impoverished reserve army is kept unorganized by force, uneducated by neglect, and constantly replenished by state encouragement and subsidizing of rural agribusiness mechanization.[48] Still lower wages have been obtainable by the use of prison labor. In Colombia, for example, where the minimum wage in 1975 was $1.33 per day, Container Corporation of America, B.F. Goodrich, and dozens of other companies have employed thousands of prisoners at still lower rates under programs put forward as "rehabilitation," although 75% or more of the prisoners have never been tried, but are "caught up in the Colombian system of justice."[49]

Cheap labor is, of course, good for keeping down business expenses, but doesn't it limit the scope of the market for goods to be sold? The answer is that neo-colonial economies are increasingly export-oriented, with a heavy emphasis on the export of raw materials, so that the mass of the population can be regarded by its leaders as merely a cost factor. In a famous 1973 statement signed by six Brazilian bishops, and widely discussed—outside of the United States—the role of exports is described as follows:

> "We must export!" Many industrial and agricultural companies are formed for the purpose of export. They have credit, tax incentives and other advantages so that they can export.
>
> Why? To earn money, to stabilize our balance of payments, etc. But could not the same objective be reached with an increase in the internal market? In Brazil, only five

> percent can buy what is produced. With credit, about 15% of the working class can purchase a little above their basic needs. The other 80% practically buy nothing other than what they need to keep them from dying. Why? Because the economy is not based on the people, but rather on a moneyed minority. Thus, the thing is to export.
>
> They try to export everything they cannot sell here at home, that which the people cannot afford to buy. It is not only a matter of luxury goods. For example, we are exporting shoes; in 1974 and 1975 exports will account for one-third of our production of footwear. And here our people go barefoot, and will go barefoot! And meat exports? Is there too much meat on our tables? Exports guarantee financing and the profits of corporations pure and simple.[50]

The perspective of the U.S. business community on marginalization, repression, and related matters, was illuminated in a 1976 Special Report by *Business Week* on "Reversal of Policy: Latin America Opens The Door To Foreign Investment Again."[51] The editors are positively ecstatic about these new developments. The report is studded with such terms as "pragmatic," "realistic," "stability," "tough," and "confidence". The words "democracy" and "torture" do not appear in the Special Report, nor is there any discussion of trends in income distribution or the allocation of budgetary resources to arms, business subsidies, and education and medical research. The word "repression" appears once, in the following context:

> A unifying theme of Latin military governments is that they stand—or claim to stand—for social and economic progress, not just law and order. Faced with a choice, however, they are likely to postpone social improvement as a goal secondary to economic consolidation [sic: whatever this means] and political stability, imposed with varying degrees of repression.

A unifying theme is that the juntas "claim to stand" for social progress, but they may not get around to it in our time.

These muddled apologetics exhaust *Business Week's* analysis of welfare, income distribution, and political trends in Latin America. *Business Week* is even quite pleased with Chile, "whose economy had been reduced to a shambles" by Allende—no mention of the CIA-ITT contribution. Fascist achievements "have been obscured by a deep recession and by the harsh austerity measures"—industrial output fell marginally under Allende, whereas the index went from 113 to 78 under the junta. Apologetics can hardly be more crass and incompetent. The important point, though, is that a magazine that represents "enlightened" U.S. business interests displays such unqualified enthusiasm for Third World fascism, based clearly on its favorable impact on U.S business. Any adverse effects on the majority of the population are completely irrelevant.

There is also a convergence of economic and military-strategic interests in support of Third World fascism, as the military juntas in charge usually have a client relationship to the U.S. military establishment, are cooperative on U.S. bases, and specialize in the cleaning up of any subversives and protestors who challenge the satellite relationship. The military-strategic interest may have some small degree of autonomy of its own, but the size, role, and global spread of the U.S. military establishment cannot be explained with any degree of plausibility except as derivative from a global economic interest that is well understood by the strategists of "containment".

In the light of the role of client fascism as a system of institutionalized class repression and warfare, it is little wonder that the income share of the top 5% of income receiving units in Brazil rose from 44% in 1960 to 50% in 1970, that the share of the poorest 80% fell from 35% to 27.5%, and that only the top 10% of the population increased its relative income share. The Gini coefficient, a widely used measure of income inequality, reached its highest national level ever recorded in Latin America in Brazil in 1970.[52] According to *Business Week,* the *real* wages of the lowest 80% of the Brazilian population "have been steadily dropping since 1964—the year the generals took over—despite a tripling of the gross national product to $80 billion."[53] In 1971, 65% of Brazil's economically active population subsisted on a monthly income of $60 or less; only 1% earned $350 per month and over, but many of these earned $5,000 a month or more. In entire provinces of Brazil the average income is under 10% of that of other provinces.[54] "Hunger in the Northeast has taken on the characteristics of an epidemic," and undernourishment not only kills large numbers of infants and small children (half the children born in Northeast Brazil die before 5) but has contributed to an alarming rate of feeblemindedness among those who remain.[55]

Just as in Thieu's South Vietnam, so in Brazil very high quality medical service is available in the larger cities for the upper 5% of income-receiving units, but negligible medical resources are available in the countryside. Vastly more resources are applied to the police than to medical research and facilities, although "Northeast Brazil, whose 35 million residents form the greatest concentration of poverty in Latin America, is a virtual human laboratory of third world ailments."[56] The serious disease schistosomiasis is very widespread in Brazil, the fatal disorder chagas affects 500,000 people, 30,000 new cases of tuberculosis appear each year, and contagious diseases account for 22% of all deaths. Nonetheless the Ministry of Health's share of the national budget fell from 4.29% in 1966 to 0.99% in 1974. On the other hand, the allocation for defense *tripled* in real terms between 1963 and 1973.[57]

Clearly the new Brazil, so pleasing to *Business Week* and the U.S. business community, is not exactly a welfare state. The large majority of the population is a means, not an end—in the same class as pack animals, only more dangerous, needing regular doses of terror to "maintain stability." Terror keeps the neo-colonial elites in power and the investment skies sunny. The victims are numerous, but can be disregarded because of their remoteness and passivity. If necessary we can blame them for their own laziness and excessive production of offspring.

In their study *Economic Growth and Social Equity in Developing Countries*, Irma Adelman and Cynthia Taft Morris state that "the results of our analyses came as a shock to us...we had shared the prevailing view among economists that economic growth was economically beneficial to most nations. We had also not greatly questioned the relevance today of the historical association of successful economic growth with the spread of parliamentary democracy. Our results proved to be at variance with our preconceptions."[58] On the basis of an elaborate analysis of data for 43 less developed countries, they found that

> the position of the poorest 60 percent typically worsens. both relatively and absolutely, when an initial spurt of narrowly based dualistic growth is imposed on an agrarian subsistence economy...The gains of the top 5 percent are particularly great in very low income countries where a sharply dualistic structure is associated with political and economic domination by traditional or expatriate elites.[59]

These elites "need" any growth dividend to meet a rising international consumption standard and the needs of the external constituency, so that with sufficient force at their command they and their allies may capture all surpluses and depress even further the real incomes of the masses (frequently via inflation in a context of police state control over money wages).

Adelman and Morris found sociopolitical factors to be of great importance in explaining cross-country differences in income distribution; in case after case, "the more firmly entrenched the expatriate financial, commercial and technical elites, the greater the concentration of income in the hands of the top 5 percent...;" and "broad-based economic growth provides a way to achieve redistribution only where accompanied by social and educational development as well as substantial broadening of political participation."[60]

In brief, then, income distribution has tended to worsen in the poor countries of the Free World because growth has generated wealth that has been used not to improve the condition of the masses but to serve the growing consumption needs of a neocolonial elite and the demands of foreign business and finance. The preservation of their position has required a costly diversion of resources into the military (the "insurance policy") and a subordination of development and welfare needs to the consumption-oriented demands of U.S. open-door entrants and affluent domestic consumers. Suharto, Marcos, etc., all have in common institutionalized venality, terrorization of the masses, and service to the needs of "the expatriate financial, commercial, and technical elites" specified by Adelman and Morris as tied in closely with a worsening income distribution.

2.1.6 Counterrevolution and the "Shakedown" States

The military juntas and dictators sponsored and/or supported by the United States usually proclaim as one of their objectives the cleaning up of civilian and democratic "corruption". But corruption is "built-in" to these regimes and is normally carried to new heights when they achieve power. The graft and amassing of huge fortunes by the leadership of the collaborating elites have been so widespread that we may refer to them as "shakedown states." This is not new. In the case of Chiang Kai-shek's "old China," General Stilwell's lengthy experience with the Kuomintang led him to the oft-expressed conclusion that they were simply "gangsters," who believed (accurately it turned out) that they could "go on milking the United States for money and munitions by using the old gag about quitting if...not supported."[61] As Kolko remarks, "No serious account of China during the period 1942-1945 differs on the proposition that the corruption and venality of the ruling elite was its sole consistent characteristic."[62] A study of $43 million in U.S. savings certificates and bonds put up for sale in October 1943 showed that the bulk was in the hands of Kuomintang leaders: T.V. Soong held $4.4 million; K.P. Chen, $4.1 million; H.H. Kung $1.4 million; and so forth.[63]

In the case of South Vietnam, huge fortunes were being made by comprador elements even before the escalation of 1965 brought in really large resources capable of being stolen. General Khanh, leader of the South Vietnamese state by U.S. choice for a brief period in 1964-1965,[64] and an expatriate shortly thereafter, prided himself on his restraint in having built up an estate of only $10 million prior to his exit.[65] A 1968 report of the Senate Subcommittee on refugees stated that

> corruption pervades all aspects of Vietnamese life, and it is brazenly practiced...Government jobs are bought and paid for by people seeking a return on their investments. Police accept bribes. Officials and their wives run operations in the black market. AID funds and hospital supplies are diverted into private pockets...In the field of refugee care and in many other fields the [Thieu] Government of South Vietnam has been engaged in the systematic looting of its own people.[66]

Strongly reminiscent of the Kuomintang were the daily reports in 1974-1975 of the pocketing by Cambodian and South Vietnamese officers of the pay of "phantom troops" or the rice rations of live refugees, and the stealing and smuggling of medicine, scrap metals, and military supplies. Even new jet fighter planes were converted into ready money by the Saigon corruption machine, a 1976 police raid uncovering in an illegal scrap metal depot the wings of at least 15 A-37 aircraft (large numbers of which were rushed to Saigon just prior to the cease-fire, at a cost to the U.S. taxpayer of $500,000 per airplane). In 1974 there was also a sensational scandal involving the siphoning off into speculative hoards of 150,000 tons of fertilizer, another gift of the U.S. taxpayer, by a group of importers and officials, including Thieu's brother-in-law, who sold it off later at high black-market prices.[67]

The Philippines exhibit the same pattern. An early post-coup analysis in *Business Week*, in expressing skepticism on the likelihood that Marcos would stamp out corruption, noted that

> the President and his close associates are hardly free from suspicion. Since taking office seven years ago as a man of relatively moderate wealth, Marcos has become one of the Philippines' top ten taxpayers. In a country with its share of multimillionaires, that is not bad on his official salary of $4,500 a year. It is also well known that Marcos has demanded that he and his associates in the government be cut in on the profits of local businesses.[68]

Recent evidence indicates that the Marcos revolution against corruption has involved: (1) a transfer of wealth, by expropriation, from some old wealthy families, out of favor with Marcos, to Marcos's family and friends; (2) the concentration of the flow of graft, undiminished in size, into the hands of a new elite; and (3) the more aggressive use of state power to reward favored individuals, to destroy others, and to protect favored looters.[69] Similar processes on a somewhat larger scale are discussed below in the case studies of Indonesia and Thailand. (See chapter 4.)

In the U.S. view, all of this is treated as a rule of "Asian nature." As pointed out by Donald Kirk, Far Eastern correspondent of the *Chicago Tribune* "Kim [a South Korean poet] blames the suffering of his people in large part on the kind of bribery and chicanery that American officials smilingly dismiss as 'routine' in 'all Asian countries'— notably those allied with the United States."[70] Paul R. Strauss, a long-time U.S. financial correspondent in Asia, assures us that "what we fail to realize is that corruption is a way of life in Asia," and that what is bad is not graft but *unsystematic* graft (such as one finds in the Philippines, as compared with the *efficient* graft of South Korea).[71] Actually, Strauss and U.S. officialdom are correct, insofar as the "Asian nature" familiar and relevant to Americans is of those willing to cooperate with the imperial powers in suppressing revolutionary nationalism and maintaining Free World control—what the Vietnamese called "country-selling" Asians. Peter Dale Scott quotes a Council on Foreign Relations document that refers to a certain Indonesian group as possessing "rare qualities of leadership," which, Scott observes, includes this special characteristic: "their recently-demonstrated willingness to plot with the CIA against a popularly elected and supported government."[72] "Asian nature" and "rare qualities of leadership" are clearly often interchangeable expressions.

We therefore expect to find the same characteristics in "African nature" and "Middle Eastern nature." The Zaire regime of Mobutu has replicated the Asian scene with the human nature and "rare qualities of leadership" of Western choice. Michael Kaufman reports in the *New York Times* that

> [Mobutu's] system of patronage and payoffs has created an extortionate culture evident at all levels of society that is becoming increasingly oppressive...The President is also said to have a huge fortune in Swiss banks and in residences abroad...What angers the Zairians more is the spread of this rapaciousness through every rank of the bureaucracy, particularly in the army.[73]

This is the regime which the West put into power initially, and rushed frantically to preserve in power in 1978, with the aid of some traditional cold war demagoguery and fabrications.[74] Much of the loot carried away by the leaders of the Zaire shakedown state, as is so frequent throughout the U.S. empire, is a straight donation by imperial agents of funds provided by the U.S. taxpayer. One recently publicized episode was the $1.4 million given to Mobutu by the CIA for distribution to U.S.-supplied counterrevolutionary groups in Angola—Mobutu simply pocketed the money.[75]

"Middle-Eastern human nature," as manifested in the CIA-produced regime of the Shah of Iran, repeats the familiar pattern, although oil wealth has made possible greater high-mindedness at the top and a partial sloughing off of some of the cruder forms of graft. As in the Marcos case, the line between the interests of the state and the ruler is fuzzy. Expenditures of the imperial court of the Shah are provided for in the Iranian state budget, which in 1976 gave the Shah, among other incidentals, a discretionary fund of $1 billion.[76] The Shah's personal assets are not published, but the Pahlavi Foundation controlled by the Shah owns property estimated as worth about $3 billion and direct family holdings of land, banks, insurance companies, hotels and industrial companies runs the family asset totals to unknown further large sums.[77] Graft has long been endemic to the Shah's Iran, and in the 1950s there was a major scandal involving allegations of massive looting of U.S. aid money by the Shah himself.[78] The bribery revelations of recent years have pointed to the regular use of position by family and military insiders to "expedite" contracts, at a fee. There have been periodic anti-corruption campaigns in Iran, the renewal of which indicates the nature of their success. The effect of the vigorous anti-corruption campaign starting in 1974,[79] according to one foreign company official, "is that we now must pay to the people holding still higher positions in the country's hierarchy."[80] In 1978 the Shah announced that members of the Royal family would no longer be allowed to accept commissions and serve as intermediaries in contracting, suggesting that the family members, large numbers of them millionaires, are so conditioned as to find it difficult to keep their hands out of the till.[81] The popular uprising of late 1978 led to new promises that now there would be reform.

There are several compelling reasons for the pervasiveness of graft under client fascism. One of the most crucial is the power and nature of the interests of the support base: a privileged local elite and a usually even more powerful foreign establishment. These interests expect rewards for their support (or that of their government), and they have the power to exact their toll. Hanna Mining, in dispute with the democratic governments of Brazil from 1956-1964 over mineral rights claims, was able to settle immediately after the coup on its own terms, gaining in addition exclusive harbor rights and other special privileges.[82] In fact, every subversive overthrow of reformist and democratic governments in the U.S. sphere has been quickly followed by tax, profit-repatriation, and mineral claims "adjustments" that reflect a reestablishment of hegemonic authority and special privileges for U.S. corporate interests.[83]

A second and related factor in graft is the quality and ideology of the leadership of the various military juntas and dictatorships. Under U.S. auspices, the native leadership consists of elite military and comprador elements who, in meeting U.S. criteria, will hardly possess any independent social vision relevant to their own country or any basis or capacity to mobilize large numbers of their compatriots.

As Malcolm Browne wrote about "our" Vietnamese in the early 1960s:

> Some military officials, especially those who served in the Viet Minh in the war against the French and later switched to Diem, are excellent officials by any standards. But they are exceptions. Unfortunately, most of the really intelligent, dedicated and patriotic men and women who form the stuff of sound leadership stayed with the Viet Minh.[84]

In the 1970s the same situation holds for the general run of Free World junta leaders, drawn from the same elite groups as Diem and Thieu, standing in the same relation to their own population and an external power, and performing the same functions. Nonmilitary dictators like Marcos tend to be crass and self-serving opportunists. The military leaders of the Third World who have allowed themselves to be mobilized for the crusade against "communism" (i.e., change threatening any reduction in privilege),[85] have tended to be fanatical and naive, as well as opportunistic, not a healthy or inspiring combination. In brief, the support base of privilege and the entire network of arrangements, including the selection of leaders *qualified to do the work to be done*, makes corruption integral to the system.

A general cynicism soon pervades the privileged in a shakedown state, as it is observed that the leadership is feathering its own nest, that the foreigner has special rights not available to the ordinary member of the club,[86] and that privilege is arbitrarily structured within the local elite. Thus graft tends to spread horizontally and vertically among the military and other bureaucratic and elite members; and in the shakedown state, "the government man [when questioned about his right to demand a bribe in a "Latin American customer nation"] points to his own pocket and says *that* is the true resting place of the court of inquiry."[87] This flows naturally from control by denationalized elites in a system of suspended law and arbitrary privilege. Those members of the elite who, awakening to their role, develop qualms about graft, denationalization, and forcible repression, may find themselves cast in the role of subversives themselves and treated accordingly.[88] The system of corruption has its own internal protections since democrats and reformers who oppose corruption and sympathize with the poor are a "security threat" and can be appropriately terminated as part of a system of preventive countersubversion, with the assistance of the CIA, U.S. police advisory groups, and the appropriate communications and torture technology.

2.2 Brainwashing Under Freedom

Despite the clear link between U.S. sponsorship and support, on the one hand, and the use of terror and serious human rights violations, on the other, the nature and importance of the "Washington connection" are generally ignored in the West and the United States is regarded as in the vanguard of the defense of human rights. To some extent this faith rests on the facile—and still widely prevalent—assumption that external misbehavior is closely related to internal repression and limitations on freedom of dissent. As should be obvious from the most cursory examination of history, however, internal freedom is quite compatible with exploitative and inhumane external conduct extending over many decades.[89] Even in the fountainhead of Western democracy, ancient Athens, the development of a military establishment (a naval fleet) "made Athens securely democratic and incurably aggressive...Moreover, the aggressiveness of the Athenian polis was enhanced when rowers' pay and plunder became, for a surprisingly large proportion of the Athenian citizenry, a necessary or at least highly desirable addition to the family resources. Against this background, Athens' ruthless and incessant naval enterprise, which kept the entire Greek world in turmoil from 480 to 404 B.C., becomes intelligible."[90] The cruel plundering of India, China, the East Indies, and Africa by the relatively liberal and open societies of Western Europe from the 17th well into the 20th centuries also shows that internal freedom and long-term external viciousness are entirely compatible.

More important, however, the neglect of the scope and significance of the "Washington connection" is a testimonial to the greatly underrated capacities of what we may call "brainwashing under freedom." The ability of the system—that is to say, the important power factions in the system and their intellectual and media spokesmen—to reconstruct and shape the perspectives of history and the interpretation of current events in accordance with its own interest is truly impressive.

Just as slavery and institutionalized racism could be rationalized and reconciled with the idea of the United States as the land of liberty and equality of opportunity (mainly by *not looking*), so the "Washington connection" with spreading Third World terror can be reconciled with a United States keen on "human rights" by a suitable combination of diversion, prevarication, and refusal to contemplate. To achieve this result without explicit government censorship is the genius of the Western way.

The background against which human rights issues have arisen in the period since 1945 includes an unparalleled, worldwide economic expansion by the United States, its establishment of a global military presence with a peak of over 3,000 foreign military bases "virtually surrounding both the Soviet Union and Communist China,"[91] and interventions in the affairs of other states that are unmatched in number, scale, violence, and global reach. In the face of these developments, the myth has been successfully established in the public mind, and in liberal circles in Western Europe, that the United States is just "containing"other "expansionist" powers! During the early phases of the Vietnam

War, by a blatant misrepresentation of Lin Piao's call for "peoples' war"—suppressing his reiterated statement of the need "to adhere to a policy of self-reliance...on the strength of the masses in one's own country"—and by a general propaganda barrage, the *Chinese* were established by the mass media as "expansionist," while the United States, engaged in the wholesale destruction of a distant small country on the border of China, with bases around China, and supporting Chiang and Taiwan, was *responding* to China's aggressiveness,[92] preventing dominoes from falling, protecting freedom, etc. Rarely was the United States portrayed in the mass media or mainstream academic scholarship as engaged in the positive pursuit of its own economic-imperial interests at the expense of any people standing in its way; nor are its exploits described as subversion or outright aggression.

The hypocrisy and sheer silliness of much political commentary in this regard is truly remarkable. At the outer limits of absurdity, we find the *Wall Street Journal* deriding the "simple-minded myths" that "the problems in Indochina stem from things like American imperialism and its military-industrial complex" (editorial, 31 August 1978). Such phrases as "American imperialism," ordinarily under a strict taboo, are occasionally permitted in such contexts as these. Readers are carefully protected from exposure to any serious discussion of the concept that arouses such horror. We were in Indochina not because of any U.S. material interests motivating a "forward" foreign policy, but as a matter of higher principle, exactly as when we aid and support Stroessner in Paraguay or the Shah in Iran. And it goes without saying that U.S. military exploits or "social engineering" programs in Indochina could hardly be responsible for any current problems.

To cite another example, William V. Shannon, liberal commentator for the *New York Times* and later President Carter's ambassador to the Republic of Ireland, laments the failure of U.S. policy in these terms (28 September 1974):

> For a quarter century, the United States has been trying to do good, encourage political liberty, and promote social justice in the Third World. But in Latin America where we have traditionally been a friend and protector and in Asia

> where we have made the most painful sacrifices of our young men and our wealth, our relationships have mostly proved to be a recurring source of sorrow, waste and tragedy.

Even in Chile, he explains, our "benevolence, intelligence, and hard work have proved not to be enough," as we intervened "with the best of motives." We will be trapped in "ironic paradoxes" if we persist in our noble crusade to "advance our moral ideals" throughout the world.

As these examples illustrate, self-deception can reach quite extraordinary heights. Suppose that Fidel Castro had organized or participated in at least eight assassination attempts against the various presidents of the United States since 1959. It is safe to conclude that the *New York Times,* CBS News, and the mass media in general would have portrayed him as an international gangster and assassin, who must be excluded from the community of civilized nations. But when it is revealed that the United States has made or participated in that many attempts on Castro's life,[93] it's just "one of those things that governments do." The press will hardly suggest on the basis of such information that the world's "nations have to evaluate the U.S. potentiality as a responsible world citizen," to paraphrase a *Christian Science Monitor* editorial that had the gall to assert that the United States after the record of the past 30 years, is entitled to stand in judgment over Vietnam for its alleged violations of human rights!

Suppose further that Fidel Castro had arranged for his agents in the United States to disperse various disease carriers in agricultural regions in an attempt to poison and destroy livestock and crops. Can one imagine the hysteria of the *Wall Street Journal* and the *Times* on the depths to which barbarian evil can sink under Communism? The United States actually did carry out such acts against Cuba, reported in the press in early 1977 as minor news items—500,000 pigs had to be destroyed in Cuba as a result of a deliberately spread viral disease. And according to a recent statement of a Canadian adviser to the Cuban government, as early as 1962 he was paid $5,000 by a Defense Intelligence Agency representative to infect Cuban poultry with a viral disease.[94] Editorial outrage has been modest, to say the least.

President Carter has kindly offered to move toward normalizing relations with Cuba, but under conditions that are worth presenting in his own words:

> If I can be convinced that Cuba wants to remove their aggravating influence from other countries in this hemisphere, will not participate in violence in nations across the oceans, will recommit [sic] the former relationship that existed in Cuba toward human rights—then I would be willing to move toward normalizing relations with Cuba, as well.[95]

It is *Cuba* that must cease its "aggravating influence" in this hemisphere and refrain from the use of force in international affairs if normal relations are to be established, not the superpower that has instituted subfascist regimes throughout the hemisphere and pounded the countries of Indochina to dust, among other recent exploits. But even put that aside. Eight admitted attempts on Castro's life, a sponsored invasion, innumerable acts of sabotage—and still Carter can talk about Cuban external violence *and not be challenged or ridiculed by anyone whose voice can be heard.* Carter's reference to the state of civil rights in Cuba under the Batista dictatorship, to which he urges that Cuba should "recommit" itself, also elicited neither criticism not satire. Where such hypocrisy and distortion can pass without comment, it is evident that the mass media are maintaining a system of thought control which can establish and nourish the Big Lie as effectively as any system of state censorship.

All of this may be regarded as commonplace.[96] In any society apologists will seek to portray external ventures in a favorable light, and the force of nationalism assures that their view prevails. Nevertheless, despite massive evidence to the contrary, liberal and social democratic opinion in the United States and Western Europe continues to regard the United States as an "exception," a country in which ideas flow freely and without discrimination and where the truth wins out over falsehood (*vide* Vietnam and Watergate). The myth is reinforced by material success and power, which have helped generate a high degree of self-righteousness and respect. And it is promulgated by an enormous propaganda apparatus that tends to dominate the domestic and international flow of "information". Power has also meant innumerable links and dependency relations with elites throughout the world, and thus strong psychological and interest pressures influencing them to perceive issues from the viewpoint of the U.S. leadership. The British Labor government's consistent support for the U.S. assault on Vietnam, with only the mildest admonitions and occasional foot-dragging, represents the typical governmental and leadership response outside the Communist world. (The Swedish government's open and sharp criticism was virtually unique in the "Free World," despite an unprovoked aggression of extraordinary savagery.) U.S. beneficence and good intentions are presumptions abroad that sustain self-righteousness and self-deception at home.

2.2.1 Brainwashing Under Freedom: Sources and Processes

One of our main concerns in this work is the process of brainwashing under freedom as manifested in the selection and analysis of issues by the media and the relationship of such practice to human rights, to U.S. economic and political interests and to truthfulness. We will not attempt to unravel the detailed mechanisms of thought control—e.g., the mechanisms by which editors decide what to publish and how to present it—but rather the general principles to which their practice conforms. We focus on the fact, for example, that the mass media bewail the fate of Cambodian victims of Communist terror on an almost daily basis,[97] while entirely ignoring or rationalizing Indonesian massacres in East Timor which are, on the available evidence, no less fearsome, and are being perpetrated in the course of unprovoked aggression—considered to be a rather serious matter since Nuremberg—and are carried out with U.S. weapons and *de facto* support.[98] The most extreme claims regarding Cambodian violence are immediately given credence and extensive publicity, and even if proven false are, with insignificant exceptions, not correctible in the mass media. We note, in contrast, that as regards East Timor, when the mass media on rare occasions touch gingerly on this subject, the "facts" offered are not only often false, but are also regularly skewed in the direction of apologetics for Indonesian terror, exactly in accord with the U.S. government propaganda line. We will also review in detail how the mass media systematically ignore, deny, or construct apologetics for subfascist terror, in striking contrast to their technique with regard to the Communist enemy.[99]

An interesting methodological counterpart to this dichotomous treatment is that in regard to the states to be treated negatively (e.g., postwar Indochina), refugees or other victims are taken as the primary or exclusive source of information, even when other sources are available, and neither the selection of refugee testimony, the circumstances under which it is obtained, or the credibility or bias of those transmitting their version of this testimony is subjected to critical analysis; whereas in the case of subfascist clients (Indonesia in East Timor, Guatemala, Brazil, etc.), the victims of terror are almost entirely disregarded as sources of information and the officials administering the terror or their public relations services are relied upon for "the facts."

The pattern is, to be sure, a very familiar one, and one of the most striking illustrations of the effectiveness of the process of brainwashing under freedom is that the obvious truth is so rarely perceived. The pattern just described, which we will illustrate in considerable detail below, is just what we find in the totalitarian states, where conformity is ensured by application or threat of force. We are not surprised to discover, for example, that the Soviet press is indignant over the actions of the CIA and U.S. corporations in Chile or over U.S atrocities in Vietnam, while it finds that Russian intervention in Hungary or Czechoslovakia is an expression of the solidarity of the Russian people and their worker's state with the toiling masses who are defending themselves against CIA-fascist plots. And if Ethiopia attempts to suppress Eritrean liberation forces with violence and terror during the period when it is a Soviet client, one would hardly expect to find an indignant factual account in *Pravda.* While all of this is obvious in the case of a totalitarian state, replication of a similar pattern in the Free Press passes without notice in the West, an indication of a form of "convergence" between the major socioeconomic systems that is a bit different from those sometimes discussed.

As regards both Indochina and the subfascist states, a clear "line" is discernible in the U.S. media (and to a significant extent, throughout the Free World). Indochina is subject to regular, almost daily attention, focusing with laser-like intensity on terror and oppression.[100] In keeping with this preoccupation, we find a gravitation to the most inflated estimates of repression and violence, a stripping away of the crucial historical context, a high moral tone, and non-correctibility of falsification and error. The line with regard to the U.S. client fascist states is just the reverse: only episodic attention, deemphasis of terror and avoidance of the human effects of subfascist processes, understatement of facts concerning state violence, stress on GNP (abstracted from the human consequences of a rise in GNP under subfascist conditions) and on alleged or promised "improvements," and the correctibility of error if it is hostile to the subfascist state. Thus for each class of cases the volume of "information," the tone, the emphasis and the interpretation are loaded with bias in favor of the doctrinal system preferred by those with power, and they function to implant in the public mind selected truths with all the effectiveness of a system of government censorship.

The "line" dispensed in this fashion by the Fress Press conforms well to the economic interests of the U.S. multinational corporations and other large interests of dominant social groups. Cambodia, for example, is a Communist state. A focus on Cambodian terrorism, carefully extricated from the relevant historical context, serves important U.S. interests by allowing strong ideological points to be scored against radicalism, socialism, egalitarian ideals, and the dangers of Third World nationalism. Socialist terror, real or fabricated for the occasion, is useful, a fact that may help explain why distortion and fact-creation are permissible and uncorrectible. Cambodian terror also diverts attention away from the terror and violence that have been growing by leaps and bounds throughout the entire subfascist empire. Thus, Communist terror is positively and urgently needed as a diversion and to show that while we may be awful they are worse. Pained outcries about human rights violations in East Timor, Indonesia, Brazil, or Uruguay, while incomparably more significant in actually helping to relieve human suffering than the focus on Communist iniquity, would upset U.S. businessmen, bankers, and military-intelligence and other government officials, who are not only pleased with subfascism but whose interests explain active U.S. sponsorship and support for it. Mass media selectivity, suppressions, exaggerations, and sometimes plain lying are thus subject to an entirely rational explanation in terms of primary systemic interests, whatever may be the precise mechanics whereby the system's "line" is implemented.

Alternative views and analyses are available in the United States, in fringe media that reach a minuscule sector of the population, probably less than 1%. Thus the "line" that Vietnam is now solely a land of "woes," refugees, and would-be refugees victimized by cruel oppressors—not a country suffering from the legacy of U.S. violence—is the virtually uncontested portrayal in the *New York Times* (daily circulation over 800,000 and enormous influence beyond) as well as in less reputable but even more widely circulated publications such as the *Reader's Digest* (circulation over 18 million in the U.S. alone) and *TV Guide* (circulation over 19 million). In contrast, a visiting Quaker delegation, including Vietnamese-speaking relief workers with long experience in Indochina, gains no access to the mass media, though its members are free to report their perception of a nation attempting to rebuild from the wreckage of the U.S. war in *New England Peacework* (monthly circulation 2,500). On Cambodia and East Timor, while the mass media adhere to an almost undeviating line, the balance is righted by some excellent coverage in the *International Bulletin* (circulation 6,000), and dissidents who expose press fabrications are, on rare occasions, permitted a letter to the editor. Typically, reports that emphasize the destruction caused by the United States in Indochina or the efforts and commitment of the victims reach a tiny circle of peace activists. Reports that ignore the U.S. role and find only woes and distress—attributed exclusively to Communist villainy—reach a mass audience and become part of the established truth.

Facts contrary to the line are available in the mass media in small, isolated doses lacking context, and may be culled out by the assiduous reader aware of the overwhelming built-in bias. Where powerful domestic interests are at odds over an issue (Nixon and Watergate, or to a lesser extent, Vietnam) there may be no uniform line, or the line may be subject to a fair amount of undercutting in the mass media. These deviations, mostly small but occasionally substantial, are important and valuable, and they help make a so-called "Free Press" in a wealthy society considerably better than a state-censored press, as does the sheer volume of news. But the adulation (including self-adulation) of the Free Press has long neglected the extent to which it also follows a "party line," especially on foreign affairs where the interests that shape policy are powerful and without any substantial internal opposition. Because it is not censored by the state, the Free Press enjoys an aura of even-handedness and dedicated pursuit of truth—an illusion and a dangerous one—as we shall document throughout this work. Especially where the issues involve substantial U.S. economic and political interests and relationships with friendly or hostile states, the mass media usually function much in the manner of state propaganda agencies. And their pronouncements should be treated accordingly.

The impact of economic and political interests and power on the mechanics of mass media processing of the news is complicated and can only be summarized briefly here. One factor is ownership interests. Mass media enterprises are big business. Many of them are now divisions of conglomerates with a wide variety of activities, including the production and sale of weapons (e.g., Westinghouse, RCA, GE, and General Tire and Rubber); and their owners and managers share the interests and values of their business peers.[101] They are an important part of an elite group that benefits from the status quo and plays a crucial role in the selection of editors and other key personnel, in policy decision criteria, and in fixing the "practical possibilities" of news selection. Advertisers are also important to the mass media, and the need to attract and maintain good relations with them helps define the limits of tolerable controversy. Sponsors and media together want to produce an output that will help sell goods, will not seriously disturb any substantial consuming group, and will be ideologically and politically compatible with the business system and the multinationals that increasingly dominate mass media advertising.

On television, the news itself is easily overrated in importance for ideology and attitude formation in comparison with the commercial and "entertainment" messages that combine dramatic intensity and uniformity of ideological substance. The action-drama-spy series of the immediate pre-Vietnam War era, continuing throughout the war, gave an ideological underpinning to the U.S. intervention. Especially the FBI espionage-type series, featuring the omnipresent Communist threat, "all quickly acquired sponsors" and "set the tone: excitement, patriotism, freedom, crusade":[102]

> Exciting "entertainment" provided the escape route—seemingly unrelated yet subtly supportive of what was being done...the drama could have meaning only if viewers accepted, consciously or unconsciously, its underlying premise: that "we" faced enemies so evil and so clever that "the intricate means used to defeat them are necessary."

News reporting proper only rarely upsets the supportive tone fixed by the more important commercial-entertainment avenues, but it hardly could, given the dominance of the government and business in news supply and the underlying business involvement in U.S. global efforts. The relationship between newsmen and business leaders was described by Walter Cronkite himself, considered one of the more critical members of the fraternity, as "symbiotic". He observed that "newspapers, broadcasting networks and outlets survive on the advertising revenues that come from business... Journalism can thrive only as long as the business community remains healthy enough to provide the funds. Business on the other hand, depends on journalism to foster its own growth—through the dissemination of information through news and advertising."[103] Because of this symbiotic relationship, media efforts that focus on matters which business does not want discussed are rare (e.g., wage rates and labor conditions in the Dominican Republic, or the use of police torture in states offering excellent opportunities to U.S. business, such as the Philippines and Brazil, or regular and in-depth treatment of occupational diseases). Such efforts would involve serious potential costs in conflict and lost goodwill. Documentaries on such subjects would not sell well.[104] Since all of this is understood in advance, self-censorship causes them not to be prepared in the first place.

The government is another potent factor that mass media businesses must treat with care. It is an important source of news, has power in many spheres, and even directly regulates TV and radio mass media firms. The mass media find it in their self-interest to portray government actions in a favorable light.[105] On foreign affairs the government and business interests are major sources of news; and if their policies and interests are such that the daily murder of dissidents in Argentina, Uruguay, Brazil, and Guatemala is not only irrelevant but tends to discredit "friendly" regimes, they will not supply such information to the media and will even regard any featuring of such facts as offensive and contrary to the "national interest."

The highly concentrated wire services are also closely linked to the U.S. government, business, and the mass media, and they are sensitive to the "national interest" as seen by dominant power groups. They are also tied in important ways to foreign governments in the U.S. sphere of influence, depending on them for news and as buyers of wire service copy in local media (including government operated stations and papers). Thus the wire services will tend not to seek out abuses of individual rights in Brazil or the Dominican Republic, even if quite severe, but will concentrate instead on Palestinian terror and Soviet and Cambodian violations of human rights. When Richard Arens and Survival International tried to interest the U.S. wire services and media in the destruction of the Paraguayan Indians, they found no response.[106] The stories had plenty of "punch" and would be highly salable, we believe, if the atrocities had occurred in an enemy state. But Paraguay is "friendly" and a responsive client state which grants ready access and privileges to U.S. corporate interests. Hence, the State Department consistently downplays its abuses. No significant interest groups in the United States are troubled by a "final solution" for the Indians of Paraguay.

The "lines" followed by the Free Press thus seem to be readily explained as a function of the structure of U.S. interests and power that feed in to the media selection process at many levels. No central authority tells the mass media to "lay off" the Indonesian assault on East Timor or the daily abductions and murders in subfascist Latin American states. It is sufficient that occasional editorial boldness in dealing with these off-the-agenda matters could well result in significant flak from government officials, interested businessmen, or representatives of the terror states. Normally, self-censorship does the job. The self-censorship is conducted within the journal (or station) by news selectors who have developed a feel for the "line," and who can identify and excise hot items likely to generate too much negative reaction upstairs or from important people outside.

News reporters and columnists also develop a feel for what is acceptable, and self-censorship thus occurs at their level on the basis of learned and understood limits of subject matter, tone, balance, and the like. A failure to self-censor on the part of reporters will result in the production of unused copy, as well as the loss of goodwill at the top in the face of such irresponsibility. Several people concerned with U.S.-backed massacres in East Timor, for example, have informed us that reporters did write stories that were "highly newsworthy" by the standards of professional journalism, but when these reporters found that such material was not going to be published, they simply stopped writing on this taboo topic. We have discovered in our own experience a different device that the media use to ensure that the unspeakable is not spoken. Thus journals refuse to publish material on East Timor, or on the media suppression of the ongoing massacres, on the grounds that this is not a story that will interest people, since no one has heard of it! Cambodian atrocities, in contrast, are an interesting story because they are in the spotlight of world attention. Thus a feedback process operates to ensure that the public remains properly indoctrinated. The process is set off in the right direction at the initiative of one or several of the perhaps dozen giant mass media enterprises (e.g., *Readers Digest, Time, NBC, New York Times,* etc.), or the U.S. government, which by themselves are easily able to focus the spotlight of attention on some worthy subject.

Even liberal commentators rarely focus on the *systematic character* of the U.S. support for right wing terror regimes and the simple economic logic of this "Washington connection." This evasion may even be said to define the limits of permissible liberalism in the mass media—one may occasionally denounce torture in Chile and "death squads" in Brazil, but (1) it is unacceptable to explain them as a result of official U.S. policy and preference and as plausibly linked to U.S. economic interests; and (2) it would be highly advisable even when merely denouncing subfascist terror to show "balance" by denouncing Soviet and left terror in equally vigorous terms. Otherwise, your days are numbered in those parts of the media that reach 99% of the U.S. population. Liberals are under such ideological pressure that when a Shcharansky or Ginzburg trial comes along, or an alleged Communist massacre, they hop onto the bandwagon with relief in their eagerness to rejoin their fellow citizens in the mainstream.[107] Needless to say, a similar balance is not required of establishment and extreme right wing commentators. One rarely finds any criticism of *Gulag Archipelago* for balance as a picture of Soviet society and its evolution, let alone for its neglect of unpleasant aspects of the Free World.

An amusing feature of the current U.S. media scene is that Soviet dissidents can publish almost at will in the New York Times Op Ed columns and receive publicity via press conferences, while U.S. dissidents have lost the limited access available to them at the height of the Vietnam War and are frozen out, unless they wish to petition for the rights of victims of Communism. The 99% of the population unreachable by U.S. dissidents are subject to the selective processes of the mass media that do not allow serious criticism of patriotic myths and untruths, with a brainwashing effect comparable to that of systems with explicit government censorship.

2.2.2 The Case of the Lost Bloodbath: the Supply of and Demand for Communist Atrocities

If we ask, for example, what the U.S. public has been allowed to learn about the "bloodbath" that Nixon, Rockefeller, Douglas Pike, Patrick Honey, and the mass media in general protrayed as a virtually certain result of a Communist victory in South Vietnam, the answer must be that the post-1975 media suppressions and distortions neatly complement the deception on violence *during* the war that made these predictions plausible. Since the bloodbath threat was an important rationale for intervention, and was reiterated time and again by our leaders, it might be expected that in the interests of the alleged victims that we were "saving" the media would have followed closely and reported on this matter.[108] Also, public education might be thought to require follow-ups on the solemn predictions on this subject by political leaders, experts, and editorialists. That is not the case, however. There has been no bloodbath, so far as is known; nothing like what happened in France in 1944 after the Germans were expelled, for example, despite the long and horrendous provocations (see Volume II, chapters 2, 4). But this remarkable fact and the reconciliatory behavior of the Vietnamese Communists, which is unusual by historical standards as we shall see in Volume II, has been acknowledged grudgingly if at all in the small print of news reports. There have been few if any editorials pointing out the striking contrast with the behavior of the U.S. clients in Indonesia and Chile, for example, though the motives for revenge in Vietnam were incomparably greater. And there have been no analyses of the contrast between the official forecasts and the long portrayal of the enemy as barbarians bent on mass murder, on the one hand, and the currently available facts on the lost bloodbath, on the other. On the contrary, it is not unusual to describe the postwar situation in Vietnam as if there had indeed been unprecedented retribution and atrocities.[109]

As we have pointed out and will examine at length in the next volume, the promised Vietnam bloodbath not having materialized, the mass media have found a new haven and basis for humanistic concern in Communist Cambodia. An important virtue of Cambodia from the standpoint of mass media serviceability is that information is not only sparse but is also dominated by reports of refugees—which are often selected and transmitted by sources of limited credibility and extreme ideological bias. The limited and controlled information also facilitates the standard technique of attributing to Communist iniquity all suffering, troubles, and deaths arising from a complex of causes, one of them being the quickly-forgotten U.S. devastation and killing from 1969, particularly in the 1973 saturation bombing. Many people have been murdered and oppressed by the Communist regime and its cadres since its triumph in 1975, but the distortions and exaggerations on the part of the Western media in the search for a nefarious bloodbath have reached staggering proportions, and—as we shall show in detail demonstrate as clearly as any topic considered in this study the workings of the Free Press as a system of propaganda.

The mass media take Communist atrocities where they can find them and invent them where they cannot. Since such atrocities serve a useful "educational" purpose—bringing the community together in support of a vast and growing military budget and whatever new imperial ventures the political leadership wishes to pursue—the veracity of the allegations is irrelevant. Even if ultimately proven to be fabrications, these proofs can be disregarded and a useful lie can be institutionalized by reiteration and suppression (see chapter 5 below and Volume II, for many examples). The same is true of false predictions. To cite only one of innumerable examples, the *Wall Street Journal* published a forecast by former CIA analyst, Samuel Adams, that 100,000 people would be murdered in the event of a Communist victory in Vietnam, which relied heavily on a hysterical propaganda tract by Craig Hosmer put out by the Rand Corporation.[110] The *Journal* refused at the time to publish any criticism of the Adams piece and has subsequently never gotten around to discussing where the Adams forecast went wrong. For readers of the *Journal,* the Vietnamese Communists might be said to have killed 100,000 people in a postwar bloodbath, an "Asian Auschwitz" (see note 109, chapter 2).

It is one of the public functions of both right-wing and official think tanks like the Rand Corporation, the Hoover Institution, the Hudson Institute, and academic social science scholarship more broadly, to show that *they* are evil and *we* are good—though we occasionally err. A liberal acknowledges that we also have flaws; a conservative tends to neglect ours entirely. But for both, Communist flaws (and bloodshed) are front and center, a matter of the "Communist essence," while such Western defects as may be noted and deplored are "aberrations." A Max Lerner, for example, treats the human rights issue as a potential plus for the United States; his premise is an explicit Cold War chauvinism that defines the United States as the force for good in the world, which "can strengthen its world position" by this vehicle.[111] Lerner will not discuss the U.S. role in violations of civil rights in the Third World or even address the question of our disproportionate focus on civil rights East of the Elbe—Lerner would no doubt like the United States to pursue freedom instead of propping up little tyrants and torturers all over the world, but if our leaders choose otherwise a "responsible" liberal will not explore the systematic factors involved and will pretend that people who do apply normal canons of rationality to

U.S policies and their origins must be either "apologists for Communism" or otherwise outside the spectrum of tolerable discussion.

The media are only one component of the general system of indoctrination and thought control. A fuller discussion of the processes of brainwashing under freedom would explore the schools and universities as well. When the media want an "expert opinion" on some topic of current interest, they naturally turn to academic specialists in that area. And the state propaganda system is generally well-served by this device. The academic professions rarely stray from orthodoxy in interpreting matters of sensitive concern or private power. Like the media, academic scholarship in general cautiously refrains from analytic investigation of U.S. foreign policy and its roots in domestic power. Crucial documentation that illuminates these issues is simply placed under a ban, for example, the high-level planning studies of the Council on Foreign Relations and the State Department during World War II. Dangerous topics, such as the role of corporate interests in foreign policy, are studiously avoided, as if under a taboo. Young scholars who might wish to undertake a systematic and rational analysis of the nature and exercise of U.S. power and its domestic determinants are steered in other directions, made to understand that there is little future in this direction. A network of pressures, including grants, promotions, access to external (state and private) power, class interest, the comforts, prestige and privilege that are natural concomitants of what Hans Morgenthau once called "our conformist subservience to those in power"—all of these factors and others combine to provide an intellectual milieu in which few serious questions will be raised about sensitive issues. Those who may, nevertheless, choose to raise and pursue them can either be weeded out (if they are young and unprotected) or simply ignored or dismissed as "unreasonable," much as organized religion in the period of its dominance could insulate itself from unworthy thoughts.[112]

In such ways, a doctrinal system is constructed that is responsive to the demands of the establishment. Questions that will be serviceable to its interests are intensively explored while potentially embarrassing topics are put aside, and state and private power are protected from critical scrutiny. The doctrinal system that evolves in this way is available to be sampled by journalists and commentators who have their own reasons to keep close to the "party line."

We have not discussed other crucial elements of the system of brainwashing under freedom, for example, the organized and quite extensive efforts of business to control the contents of school curricula on sensitive topics, or to manage the flow of news directly through the mechanisms of what specialists in public relations call "the engineering of consent."[113] Nor have we attempted to elaborate the network of shared associations—class solidarity, common educational background, social contact, and status, etc.—that link elite groups in the private economy, the state, publishing, the news corporations, the universities, and the professions. These too are major factors in helping to create a world view that is protective of established power and that insulates it from unwelcome inquiry. A fuller investigation of these questions would also consider the occasional exercise of brute force when needed as a technique for undermining and disrupting radical tendencies or popular movements, even those with aims that are within the theoretical framework of shared belief such as the civil rights movement. A fuller study would also explore the historical roots of the U.S. system of indoctrination in an immigrant society that by a unique combination of natural advantages was, for a long period, able to offer a share in expanding wealth and power to those who were willing to toe the line. These topics, barely noted here, are also rarely investigated within the framework of orthodox opinion that dominates the academic world, the schools, the mass media, and the outlook of the great mass of the population, which has little opportunity to inquire into its character and limits.

CHAPTER 3

Benign Terror

3.1 The Semantic of Terror and Violence: Retail Violence as "Terror"—Wholesale Violence as Maintaining "Order" and "Security"

The words "terror" and "terrorism" have become semantic tools of the powerful in the Western world. In their dictionary meaning, these words refer to "intimidation" by the "systematic use of violence" as a means of both governing and opposing existing governments. But current Western usage has restricted the sense, on purely ideological grounds, to the retail violence of those who oppose the established order. Throughout the Vietnam War these words were restricted to the use of violence in resistance to regimes so lacking in indigenous support that Joseph Buttinger rejects General Lansdale's own designation "fascistic" as too complimentary.[1] The essence of U.S. policy in South Vietnam, and elsewhere in Indochina, was intimidation by virtually unrestrained violence against the peasant populations. Nevertheless, this was not terror or terrorism, invidious words reserved for the relatively small and much more selective use of force by the NLF, from the time when the former Viet Minh were authorized to use violence in self-defense against official U.S.-backed terrorism in the late 1950s.[2]

In the Third World, the United States set itself firmly against revolutionary change after World War II, and has struggled to maintain the disintegrating post-colonial societies within the "Free

World", often in conflict with the main drift of social and political forces within those countries. This conservative and counterrevolutionary political objective has defined the spectrum of acceptable and unacceptable violence and bloodshed. From this perspective, killings associated with revolution represent a resort to violence which is both reprehensible, and improper as a means for bringing about social change. Such atrocities are carried out by "terrorists". The word "violence" itself, like "terrorism," is generally confined to the use of force by elements and movements which we oppose. An AID report of 1970, for example, refers to the improving capability of the South Vietnamese police, then very possibly the most extensive employers of torture in the world, as "preventing the spread of violence."[3] And the 1967 "moderate scholars" statement on Asian policy, sponsored by Freedom House, defended the U.S. assault on Vietnam and passed in silence over the mass slaughters in Indonesia, referring delicately only to the "dramatic changes" there as encouraging, while at the same time explicitly condemning those who are "committed to the thesis that violence is the best means of effecting change" (presumably the NLF, DRV and the Indonesian Communists).[4]

Bloodbaths carried out by counterrevolutionary forces are regarded in a more favorable light, as they are in the interest of a return of Third World populations to the desirable "measure of passivity and defeatism" that prevailed before World War II,[5] also commonly referred to as "stability",[6] or "political equilibrium." Killings undertaken to return these populations to passivity are rarely described as bloodbaths or as involving "terror" or the use of violence—they are "readjustments" or "dramatic changes" tolerated or applauded as necessary and desirable. This is true whether the bloodbath destroys both the organizational apparatus and the population base of radical movements (as in Indonesia), or kills more modestly, merely disorganizing and terrorizing a population sufficiently to permit rightist totalitarian rule (as in the Dominican Republic, Guatemala or Brazil).[7]

The same Orwellian usage was standard on the home front during the Vietnam War. Students, war protestors, Black Panthers, and assorted other dissidents were effectively branded as violent and terroristic by a government that dropped more than five million tons of bombs over a dozen year period on a small peasant country with no means of self-defense. Beating of demonstrators, infiltration of dissident organizations, extensive use of agent provocateur tactics, even FBI complicity in political assassination were not designated by any such terms.

In the 1970s this usage has been institutionalized as a device to facilitate an exclusive preoccupation with the lesser terror of the alienated and the dispossessed, serving virtually as a disguised form of apologetics for state terror and client fascism. Many analysts simply *define* "terror" as retail and unofficial terror, and will talk of nothing else. Thus Walter Laqueur, in his general study of terrorism, writes: "My concern in the present study is with movements that have used systematic terrorism as their main weapon; others will be mentioned only in passing."[8] The state is not a "movement," although with an interest in quantitatively significant violence, the terminology could easily have been adjusted to include governments captured by terror-prone "movements," such as the Nazis or the fascist military cliques in Latin America. This would be incompatible with Laqueur's purposes; and, ruling out state terror, all that remains is "terrorism from below," for which he reserves the term "terrorism" by definition, much as one might use the title *Terrorism* for a study of Jewish violence against the Germans, 1933-1945.

The victims of "terrorism" in this restricted sense have been far fewer throughout the world than those killed by any number of individual states; Laqueur gives an aggregate figure of 6-8,000, more than half in Ulster and Argentina, between 1966-1976 (p. 213). Nevertheless, his study of "terrorism" is limited to retail terror. This terminological decision affords endless possibilities for dredging up incidents of anti-establishment violence and for demonstrating its frequent senselessness and lack of specific connection with any injustice, while enhancing the general disregard for the wholesale terror of the established states. It is consoling to the privileged in the West to learn that the troublemakers of the world are evil and irrational outsiders, not responding to just grievances. It is also helpful to self-esteem, patriotism and business-as-usual to have ruled off the agenda any details on ripping out fingernails or attaching electrodes to genitals and nipples of the trouble-makers, now standard practice among Free World forces engaged in combating "terrorism".

It is interesting to observe Laqueur's fine discrimination as he exploits the possibilities. He manages to get in a great many gratuitous digs at the "enemy" while ignoring or playing down more significant state terror. For example, he twice mentions the alleged killing of several thousand administrative cadres in South Vietnam in the 1950s and 1960s by Communists, although he concedes that this example does not conform to his concept of terrorism since such violence was not the primary political means of the NLF—but nowhere does he mention U.S.-Diem terror in South Vietnam, which occurred earlier, was far greater in scope, was a primary cause of Communist terror, and was the *principal* political means employed by Free World forces.

Laqueur's treatment of Latin American terror is particularly illuminating. He says that

> most of the terrorist operations [in Brazil] took place in Rio de Janeiro and Sao Paulo and the number of victims, excluding terrorists, was relatively small—about one hundred killed over a period of five years. But the terrorists had an excellent flair for publicity and good connections with the media and their exploits were extensively reported all over the globe. There is no reason to disbelieve the reports about systematic torture used against captured terrorists; but it is also true that the terrorists had few, if any, scruples; their victims included farm workers who had stumbled on terrorist hideouts, motorists killed by terrorists who needed their cars, and boatmen cut down after a getaway at gunpoint.[9]

In context, these remarks amount to barely disguised apologetics for neo-fascism and torture. Consider that:

(1) Laqueur can only grudgingly admit that terrorists in Brazil may be tortured ("no reason to disbelieve").
(2) He gives no details on the nature and extent of official torture, but does give specifics on selected examples of retail terror.

(3) He fails to point out that large numbers have been tortured in Brazil who were *not* terrorists and that torture began, proceeded, and continues quite apart from the existence of any perceived terrorist threat.

(4) In discussing the "scruples" of the Brazilian terrorists, he ignores the question of whether these exclude torture, perhaps because they *did* seem to have scruples on that score or perhaps because the issue does not seem to him of much importance.

(5) He fails to mention that the terrorists in Brazil along with many non-terrorist dissidents are hunted down like animals and threatened with torture and death upon capture, whereas the official torturers do their work at their leisure and with impunity.

(6) He denigrates the terrorists by snide remarks about their flair for publicity and access to the media, not mentioning that non-violent dissidents had no access to the media in Brazil and no machinery for bringing about peaceful social change after the U.S. backed military coup. Nowhere is there a single paragraph of discussion of the nature and quality of neo-fascism, its impact on the population, its origins, or its role in eliciting the terror to which he devotes his exclusive concern.

Where there is an obvious connection between terrorism and injustice, as Laqueur grudgingly concedes in the case of Latin America, he simply raises the question whether the terrorists' solutions would be preferable to those of the military junta, without discussing the nature of the grievances, their sources, or the nature and availability of other modes or terms of resolution. By this evasive ploy and his own limited concept of "terrorism" Laqueur leaves no viable option to fascism-as-usual.

As soon as we investigate real instances of retail terror, we begin to see the importance of avoiding such detail in maintaining the preferred message in studies such as Laqueur's. Consider, for example, the sensational kidnapping of the American Ambassador to Brazil, Burke Elbrick, in 1969.[10] His kidnappers certainly wanted to reach the media, long closed by military censorship; they insisted that a manifesto be read over radio and television as a condition for the Ambassador's release. Their second condition was that the military junta "free those men and women who were being tortured most savagely," including one sick 70-year old Bolshevik who had spent 20 years in prison under various regimes and was one of the first political prisoners abused after the 1964 military coup when "a Brazilian army major had tied him to the back of a jeep and dragged him bleeding through the streets of Recife." After these demands were met, Elbrick was released. He was sufficiently impressed by his treatment and the political discussions he had with his terrorist captors so that "he could not bring himself to denounce" them but could only say "that they were misguided, that their tactics were wrong," though there was no denying "their bravery or their dedication or the consideration they had shown him." At that point, though Elbrick did not know it, "his diplomatic career was over." The released prisoners, meanwhile, had a good deal to say about the horrendous torture they had suffered at the hands of the army, navy, and police in torture rooms decorated with the familiar red, white, and blue symbol of U.S. AID.

A look at the other torture chambers of the Free World, to which we return, quickly reveals the significance of what escapes Laqueur's tunnel vision. In *Le Monde* (7 September 1978), Jean-Pierre Clerc reports an interview with Wilson Ferreira Aldunate, the Uruguayan conservative who received the largest number of votes in the last presidential election and is now in exile, one of the half-million inhabitants of this country of 2.7 million people who have fled since the military coup of 1973 with little notice in the U.S., and who succeeded in fleeing his refuge in Argentina after the military coup there in 1976. He recounts the destruction of Uruguayan democracy, offering as the sole explanation "foreign intervention," i.e., the application of the Kissinger doctrine of establishing "stable regimes" in Latin America; the systematic torture of 25,000 people, counting only the most severe cases; and the decline of real wages to a 1977 level that is at 60% of the 1962 level. A response to "terrorism" in Laqueur's sense? Wilson Ferreira points out that the military coup that turned Uruguay into a chamber of horrors took place after the Tupamaros had been "completely destroyed"; "from June 1973 until today, there has not been a single subversive action. But the government kills, kidnaps, imprisons, tortures." They began by torturing the Tupamaro urban guerrillas, then union activists, then political militants and intellectuals, and finally they have victimized "the entire population, without consideration of ideology, out of habit." But none of this falls under the concept of "terrorism," in the sense of contemporary ideology.

It is a conventional cliché that the media are playing into the hands of the terrorists by offering them publicity. Laqueur is indignant over the access that terrorists in Brazil have to the world's media, which encourages them in their nefarious anti-state activities, while J. Bowyer Bell is upset over the fact that "as skilled producers of irresistible news, terrorists can control the media." [11] This conception of media control by terrorists contains a germ of truth; occasionally the retail terrorists do succeed in publicizing a message that they wish to convey, as in the Brazilian case just mentioned. But this characterization neglects a more salient feature of the situation, namely, that the media almost always suppress or distort the issues pressed by the terrorists and discredit them by an almost exclusive focus on their violence or threats of violence. Thus the media allow the terrorists to "use" them only for media purposes; to inflate the importance of retail terror, obfuscate its nature and sources, and distract attention from more significant issues such as official terror and institutionalized injustice. Laqueur and Bell represent the somewhat more sophisticated establishment commentary on terror. A cruder version is offered by Arnold Beichman in one of a featured pair of articles in the *Boston Globe* (2 April 1978) on "the historical use of terrorism and the punishment for those who practice it." In the introductory article, James Joll warns of "the romantic appeal that terrorism still has for some people, who, while deploring terrorist actions, have too bad a conscience about the evils of contemporary society to condemn such acts when carried out by others"; the noted historian failed to identify those who refuse to condemn terrorist acts, and indeed they would be hard to find, though it is a common and convenient illusion that they represent some significant force in the West. But Beichman far excels his British colleague as a demonologist. He too warns of the danger of the alleged support for terrorism among the intellectuals, asking whether the

Red Army Faction appeals "to some dark side of the German intelligentsia as did the Weather Underground to a surprisingly large sector of the American intelligentsia" (which he does not identify, naturally, since this "surprisingly large sector" is a figment of the imagination). He then warns of the "desire to spread the guilt of the terrorists among friends, relatives, class, society." As evidence, he offers the following gem: "Thus, Anthony Lukas's 1971 book on the student terrorists was titled *Don't Shoot, We Are Your Children*."[12] But, Beichman thunders, "the terrorist who has unilaterally declared war on innocent people cannot be regarded as a misguided utopian or benevolent revolutionary: terrorists are not our children." We should deal with them as follows: "The terrorist who attacks the innocent must know in advance that a drumhead court-martial will follow his apprehension; and execution, his conviction. There can be no forgiving the literal killer of the literal innocent."

It need hardly be noted explicitly that for Beichman, like Laqueur, the term "terrorism" never includes a bombardier on a B-52 mission over Indochina wiping out entire villages of "literal innocents," nor the higher authorities ultimately responsible for such attacks—at a certain level of apologetics, state terror, no matter how gross, occupies a sacred place exempt from invidious language. But Beichman's hysteria over dissidence is so great that for him, civil rights workers become indistinguishable from bomb throwers in the frightening array of opponents of the holy state. Lukas's book, whose "terrorist" children so enrage Beichman, is a study of 10 selected young "1960s people," of whom only one participated in a true act of violence—a drug addict, she was bludgeoned to death. The ten include tenant organizers, civil rights workers, pacifist war resisters, ghetto organizers, etc., whose acts of violence extended to burning draft cards or, on occasion, occupying university buildings. Most of those in the group did not even reach these heights of terrorist atrocity. In the group are young men and women who represent the finest moments of high principle and courage in modern U.S. history, as they braved the real terror of racist violence at the cutting edge of the civil rights movement, or steadfastly bore witness against the barbarism of a state for which Beichman was an outspoken apologist. These are the "terrorists" who have "unilaterally declared war on innocent people."

It is quite possible that this leading academic specialist on terrorism did not look beyond the title of Lukas's book and is merely guilty of egregious incompetence in jumping from the "terrorism" of Lukas's children to his own drum-head court-martials. But in the current state of fright among establishment intellectuals, who were indeed shaken by the youthful challenges of the 1960s, such subtle distinctions as may exist between civil rights workers and bomb-throwers are blurred. In the eyes of the Lord they are all one or another form of "terrorist", challenging the established order.

On the theory that there is no form of apologetics for state violence that will not be found in the current productions of the intelligentsia, we might next ask whether it is possible even to find justification for torture to complement Beichman's proposals for drumhead court-martials for retail terrorists.[13] Anyone familiar with U.S. intellectual life will turn to the *New Republic*, long a primary organ of the U.S. liberal intelligentsia, to see whether even this stage of moral degradation has been achieved. Indeed it has, and it will also cause no surprise to find it emerging in relation to Israeli policy. Since its smashing victory in 1967, Israel has played a role among the U.S. intelligentsia that is reminiscent of the Soviet Union in the Stalinist period (though the reasons are different the style is similar). Reviewing the detailed *London Sunday Times* study of torture in Israel and the Israeli government response (but not mentioning the devastating reply of the *Sunday Times* to the Israeli rebuttal), Seth Kaplan explains in the *New Republic* that "the question of how a government should treat people who regularly detonate bombs in public places is not susceptible to simple absolutism, such as the outright condemnation of 'torture'.[14] One may have to use extreme measures—call them 'torture'—to deal with a terrorist movement whose steady tactic is the taking of human life."[15]

To our knowledge, nothing comparable has appeared in the West in recent years apart from ultra-right circles in France during the Algerian War. But it is not very surprising that an explicit defense of torture should appear in a leading journal of U.S. liberalism—eliciting no comment or protest—when the victims are

Arabs and the agents are Israelis. The selective Western view of Mideast terrorism over the years deserves a study in itself, particularly, since Palestinians have been made the very symbol of "terrorism" in the course of the recent efforts to identify "terrorism" (in the Laqueur-Beichman sense) as the primary scourge of modern life with little attention to its origins.[16]

In mass media jargon today, Argentine guerillas attacking a police station are terrorists, while the police, military and officially protected "death squads" and thugs are "maintaining order"—even when the guerillas are exterminated and the abduction and murder of union leaders, scientists, political activists, priests, and the wives and children of people objectionable to the regime continues unabated. The widely respected Permanent Assembly for Human Rights in Argentina estimates that the number of persons detained by the armed forces or security organizations who have "disappeared" since the 1976 coup is "not less than 15,000."[17] Martin Ennals, Secretary General of Amnesty International reported recently that altogether "about 30,000 people have disappeared in Latin America in the last 10 years after being seized by official security forces or their sympathizers"; this in a 50-word news item in the *Boston Globe* (26 Nov. 1978), exceeding by 50 words the coverage in the national press. By contrast, the State Department's Office for Combatting Terrorism estimates a worldwide total of 292 deaths caused by "retail terrorism" from 1973 through 1976.[18] The daily Argentine official and semi-official abductions and murders, largely ignored in the United States, are sometimes reported as simply three-liners on the back pages in the language of the handouts of the government implementing the terror, or written up by Juan de Onis in the *New York Times* very even-handedly—the extremists of the left and right are engaged in disturbing mutual violence, in which the right seems to have the edge in the killing competition, with General Videla in the "middle," sincerely trying to contain the deterioration but frustrated by unexplained forces.[19]

Similarly, "normal" police intimidation, killing, and torture in such countries as Guatemala or Brazil are barely newsworthy in the United States. The Brazilian death squads, also recruited from among the police, came into existence in 1964 and have thrived ever since. They even own property and operate a newspaper, *O Gringo*. And they are responsible for murders running into the thousands. The *Jornal do Brasil* of April 20, 1970, reports:

> In Guanabara and in the state of Rio alone, the number of deaths attributed to the Death Squad is more than 1,000, that is, almost 400 a year. The victims show signs of unnecessary cruelty. For example, between January 11 and July 1, 1969, 40 bodies were found in the waters of the Macacu River, buried in the mud near the bridge between Maje and Itaborai. All of the bodies, in an advanced state of decomposition, still showed the marks of handcuffs and burns caused by cigarettes and multiple bruising; some of them were still handcuffed. According to the findings of the autopsy, it was noted that many had been tortured, shot, and then drowned.

In the review *Veja* of March 3, 1971, the director of the periodical states that out of 123 homicides attributed to the death squad in Sao Paulo between November, 1968 and June, 1970, only five had been investigated by the magistrate. It is evident that these killings are carried out under the authority and protection of the state. They are numerous, sadistic, and reveal a Nazi-like social pathology that should be highly newsworthy and deserving of editorial attention. A Brazilian Bishop can refer to these official terrorists as "thugs" (see below, p. 258), but such language will not be found in the Free Press. The Brazilian junta is U.S.-sponsored, very friendly to U.S. business—if not to its own dissenters and poor—and is regarded with positive enthusiasm by our bankers and businessmen. Wholesale violence by fascist client states is not "terror".

3.2 Benign and Constructive Terror

In the official version of pre-1975 Vietnamese history only we and our spunky Saigon ally stood between the 17 million people of South Vietnam and a bloodbath by the barbarian hordes of North Vietnam (DRV) and their southern arm, the Vietcong. The impression conveyed in the standard media fare was one of humanitarian concern for the victims of "violence" on the part of U.S. leaders, and the public was even led to believe that our presence in Vietnam and the regrettable (perhaps even excessive) use of force that accompanied it was a result of the resort to violence and threat of a bloodbath on the part of others.

Even a cursory examination of recent history, however, suggests that concern over violence and bloodbaths in Washington (in Moscow and Peking as well) is highly selective. Some bloodbaths seem to be looked upon as benign or even positive and constructive; only particular ones have been given publicity and regarded as heinous and deserving of indignation. For example, after the CIA-sponsored right-wing coup in Cambodia in March, 1970, Lon Nol quickly organized a pogrom-bloodbath against local Vietnamese in an effort to gain peasant support. Estimates of the numbers of victims of this slaughter range upward from 5,000, and grisly reports and photographs of bodies floating down the rivers were filed by Western correspondents. Some 330,000 out of a total of 450,000 Vietnamese in Cambodia are estimated to have been expelled or to have fled the country in the course of this campaign.[20] The United States and its client government in Saigon invaded Cambodia shortly thereafter, but not to stop the bloodbath or protect its victims; on the contrary, these forces moved in to support the organizers of the slaughter, who were on the verge of being overthrown. The small-scale Lon Nol bloodbath was, of course, followed by a major bloodbath with the bombing and invasion of Cambodia by the United States and its Saigon affiliate. In the words of one observer with an intimate knowledge of Cambodia:

> Cambodia has been subjected in its turn to destruction by American air power. The methodical sacking of economic resources, of rubber plantations and factories, of rice fields and forests, of peaceful and delightful villages which disappeared one after another beneath the bombs and napalm, has no military justification and serves essentially to starve the population.[21]

Those who paid close attention to the U.S. slaughter of Cambodians in 1969-1971 would have had no reason to be surprised by the intensive bombing of heavily populated areas in a last-ditch effort to delay the collapse of the U.S. backed regime three years later.[22] This was simply a minor variant of a policy, consistently pursued in Cambodia, which President Nixon called "the Nixon doctrine in its purest form."[23] Nor should the slight concern of the U.S. media with the disappearance of "peaceful and delightful villages [and human beings]...beneath the bombs and napalm" from 1969 (and even earlier[24]), in contrast with the intense preoccupation over the plight of Cambodians *after* the fall of Phnom Penh to the Khmer Rouge,[25] surprise anyone who follows the principles of mass media selection of worthy victims.

The regularly publicized and condemned bloodbaths, whose victims are deserving of serious concern, often turn out, upon close examination, to be largely fictional. These mythical or semi-mythical bloodbaths have served an extremely important public relations function in mobilizing support for U.S. military intervention. This was particularly true in the case of Vietnam. Public opinion tended to be negative and the war-makers had to labor mightily to keep people in line. The repeated resort to fabrication points up the propagandistic role that the "bloodbath" has played in Washington's devoted attention to this subject.

The great public relations lesson of Vietnam, nevertheless, is that the "big lie" can work, despite occasional slippages of a free press. Not only can it survive and provide service regardless of entirely reasonable or even definitive refutations,[26] but certain patriotic truths also can be established firmly for the majority by constant repetition. With the requisite degree of cooperation by the mass media, the government can engage in "atrocities management" with almost assured success, by means of sheer weight of information releases, the selective use of reports of alleged enemy acts of atrocity, and the creation and embroidery of bloodbath stories and myths. These myths never die; they are pulled from the ashes and put forward again and again whenever the government needs some renewed public fervor for bloodshed, although repudiating evidence is readily available and is occasionally permitted to reach the printed page as a presentation of the "other side" of the question.[27]

At the same time, our own atrocities can be dismissed as the "unintended consequences of military action,"[28] or as an historical inevitability for which we bear no responsibility,[29] or as "isolated incidents" for which the guilty are punished under our system of justice. Thus that distinguished spokesman for the sacredness of each individual, William Buckley, Jr., concluded from the Vietnam experience that

> ...there are nations more civilized than others, for reasons of history and providence however freakish. We would not, in America, in this day and age, treat prisoners of war the way the Vietnamese did. And we are, however humbly, reminded that we fought in Indochina to repel the atavistic forces that gave historical and moral justification to the torture and humiliation of the individual.[30]

While awaiting Buckley's reflections on the atavistic forces that seem to have turned U.S. client states into charnel houses, we note that his moralizing was provoked by the reports of returning U.S POWs. Even if we were to grant the precise accuracy of their reports, they hardly begin to compare in horror with the explicit and detailed reports by U.S. veterans of the treatment of Vietnamese prisoners (not to speak of the civilian population) by the U.S. armed forces.[31] Foreign observers, less circumspect than Buckley, commented that "the Nixon administration has had nothing to say about the atrocities which have been going on for many years in [Saigon] prisons and which still go on, often under the direct supervision of former American police officers" and noted that the U.S. POWs "who talked of Oriental tortures were all able to stand up and speak into microphones, showing scars here and there," whereas the handful of prisoners released from the U.S.-run Saigon jails "were all incurably crippled while prolonged malnutrition had turned them into grotesque parodies of humanity."[32]

More balanced minds than Hook or Buckley perceive that "unfortunately, the record is not unflawed" and that "the highest United States authorities cannot escape responsibility" for certain "violations of the spirit if not the letter of international law...even if the violations were not expressions of official policy"—while insisting, to be sure, that the "damning indictment of the Vietnamese communists...cannot be erased by the pious denials of the North Vietnamese or their apologists in this country" and that "a compelling case can and should be made against the North

Vietnamese for their clear violations of the Geneva Convention of 1949..."[33]

In chapter five below and in Volume II, we will touch upon the amply-documented record of the "spirit" of the U.S. assault on Indochina and its relation to both law, morality, and enemy violence.

3.3 Post-Colonial Rot and Permanent Counterrevolution

That revolutions are costly in human life and that those undertaking them should weigh these heavy costs against any potential gains is obvious enough. Less attention has been paid to the enormous human costs that have resulted from counter-revolutionary attempts to forestall revolution and successful "stabilization". On the evidence of recent decades of U.S. sponsored counterrevolution, a good case can be made that these are far more bloody, on the average, than revolutions. This is conspicuously so where modern technology is put to work in direct counterrevolutionary intervention. Here the indiscriminate violence puts into operation a feedback process of "Communist creation" that affords the intervention legitimacy in the eyes of the imperial power while at the same time giving it a genocidal potential.

Since the role of counterrevolution is to allow local and foreign elites to preserve and enlarge privileged positions, terror may be required on an institutionalized and durable basis. Sometimes an initial wave of savage repression that destroys mass organizations and their leadership may weaken resistance, reduce the population to apathy, and permit elite rule with only modest doses of follow-up violence. The prospects for pacification without continuing terror are questionable in an age of improving communications and revolutionary ferment, when the subfascist states so often combine minimal domestic support, increasing exploitation and great ineptitude. Under these circumstances, durable and periodically intensified repression may be necessary and even occasional foreign intervention against "internal aggression" by the populace.[34] Ideally, the proper role of the military junta in post-Vietnam U.S. thinking is to *prevent* Cubas and Vietnams by anticipatory counter-subversion, which nips any radical or seriously reformist tendencies in their earliest stages before they become "problems". In the words of General Maxwell Taylor:

> The outstanding lesson [of the Vietnam War] is that we should never let another Vietnam-type situation arise again. We were too late in recognizing the extent of the subversive threat. We appreciate now that every young [sic] emerging country must be constantly on the alert, watching for those symptoms which, if allowed to develop unrestrained, may eventually grow into a disastrous situation such as that in South Vietnam. We have learned the need for a strong police force and a strong police intelligence organization to assist in identifying early the symptoms of an incipient subversive situation.[35]

This is a call for counterrevolutionary police states, one that has been widely heeded in the U.S. sphere of influence.

Consistent U.S. support for counterrevolutionary violence in the Third World flows from structure and interests. Since this real and fundamental drift of policy flies in the face of proclaimed democratic and egalitarian ideals, the United States periodically announces that it is turning over a new leaf and will henceforth support "reform" and "structural change" (more recently, also, "human rights"). The leaf has always turned out to be of the fig variety. The Alliance for Progress was proclaimed with great fanfare as a program designed to help bring about critically needed reforms in Latin America, but like "land reform" in South Vietnam the program was quickly thrust aside in favor of plain repression. The basic conflict between changes that would benefit the Third World's masses and the interests of the United States and its chosen instruments has always been decisive. The organizational power necessary for change and campaigns for reform and for the redistribution of income and rights are quickly seen as a subversive threat incompatible with "security" (that is, U.S. domination and assured economic and military access). This was painfully evident in the U.S. reaction to what were essentially reformist efforts by Brazilian leaders in the 1950s and early 1960s, a crucial episode in recent history that we have already briefly mentioned.

Prior to the Brazilian military coup of 1964, U.S. policy makers felt threatened by the efforts of Kubitschek, Quadros and then Goulart to strengthen internal labor and peasant organizations as a counter-weight to the United States and to U.S.-related comprador and military interests. Such developments would have allowed the Brazilian leadership some freedom of action to carry out an independent economic policy and a program of social reform by freeing it from the tremendous constraints of U.S. economic power. This was intolerable to the United States and led it to take steps and encourage forces that steadily sapped Brazilian democracy and, finally, to collaborate in the 1964 coup. The successor regime of generals has allowed no independent labor or peasant organizations that might contribute to change internally or disturb external dependency and semi-colonial status. The military junta has identified all criticism of the United States and any reformist (let alone radical) tendencies as Communist-subversive and deserving of torture or death. According to one authority, "subject to United States military influence on anti-Communism the professional army officer becomes hostile to any sort of populism."[36] Forcible repression of reform or of any effort to organize or speak in the interest of the exploited majority has been a key function of the military in Brazil, and despite some tut-tuts over torture and political murder, the new Brazil has been warmly approved and rewarded by the U.S. elite. Accordingly, its methods for maintaining "stability" have been extended widely in the U.S. sphere of influence. The numbers tortured and murdered by these U.S. agents of permanent counterrevolution run into the scores of thousands.

Beyond the costs of repression *per se* are the human costs of "success" in keeping Third World populations in the desired state of "passivity and defeatism," such as has been achieved in Brazil, the Dominican Republic, or Guatemala. In these countries, there has been a restoration of a corrupting dependency on a foreign power, rule by a reactionary exploiting elite, social polarization, degradation and insecurity for large numbers, and a low level of morale and cultural esprit. As has been pointed out in a series of eloquent Brazilian church statements, the majority of the population constitutes a "whole universe of atomized workers, powerless and obliged to humiliate themselves before the power of the landlords."[37] Large numbers of Brazilian *posseiros* (squatters) colonized and cleared unoccupied land, but

> now, without land or legal protection, they are being expelled from the places they cleared, where they worked and had their children. Any resistance to this expulsion is overcome by hunger, beatings, house burnings or death.
>
> The life of the Indians, the first and real owners of the land, is a little like that of the posseiros. Our Indians are also moved off their land. The scandals and injustices that are done to these people are now widely known. Every day a new fraud takes away another piece of land from the Indians.
>
> The peons who live without any labor guarantees, make up a totally unprotected social class. They are separated from their families, live like animals, and are easy prey to alcoholism and vice. Beyond that, in the intensive system of cattle raising, with cutting down the forest and planting grass, there is little left over for the small farmer. Mechanization on the large haciendas makes it more and more difficult to find work.[38]

While the U.S. establishment has succeeded in reconciling all this with its Christian-libertarian conscience, the churches of Latin America have been driven into the struggle by their recognition of the enormity of the injustices built into the U.S. system of client fascism:

> The socio-economic, political and cultural situation of our people is a challenge to our Christian conscience. Undernourishment, infant mortality, prostitution, illiteracy, unemployment, cultural and political discrimination, exploitation, growing discrepancies between rich and poor, and many other consequences point to a situation of institutionalized violence in our country.[39]

In the Brazilian church document just quoted there follows a call for a dismantling of this system of violence with its extreme and unjust privilege. But there is a recognition of how difficult this will be with forcible repression and with a media and educational system dedicated to "lulling asleep vast strata of the population, aiming at the formation of a type of man resigned to his alienation." The smug apologetics and cultivated ignorance of the U.S media help to disguise our own self-interested complicity.

The generals placed in charge of these systems of institutionalized violence are encouraged by their foreign sponsors to look down on their own peoples and cultures, and they come to think of their emulation of foreign ways as a mark of their own sophistication and superiority. The Brazilian generals describe themselves as non-partisan technocrats preserving old-time values from foreign subversion, when, in fact, they are visionless creatures of U.S. imperial policy aping their masters, subordinating the Brazilian economy and culture to precisely those external interests and disciplining mechanisms that U.S. elites prefer. The Greek colonels in the junta interlude of 1967-1973 also pretended to a technocratic and moral superiority. But while talking of "cultural purity" like their Brazilian counterparts, the Colonels placed primary emphasis on encouraging tourism, diversification via "eye-popping incentives" to foreign capital, and a huge influx of U.S. commodity-culture mix. In Brazil, "Atop a high hill dominating the quiet waters of Botafogo Bay in Rio de Janeiro stands a giant Coca Cola sign...[which] flashes its silent mockery through the long Brazilian night."[40] These strutting bantam cocks chosen by the U.S., convinced of their own autonomy and superiority while doing their master's bidding with brutality and ineptitude, call to mind Rostand's Chanticleer, proud of the responsiveness of the sun each morning to his crowing command.

In contrast with this Free World scene of military elites repressing populist or mild reformist tendencies and using systematic and institutionalized terror to allow a redistribution of income upward and outward, consider North Vietnam, lost to the Free World in 1954 and thereafter under the iron grip of Communism. The failure of North Vietnamese society to show the smallest signs of disintegration under one of the most ferocious assaults in history was a puzzle to Western analysts. In seeking the "sources of strength" of the DRV in 1971, Rand specialist Konrad Kellen noted the absence of any "signs of instability," the lack of "resort to the kind of pressure against their population in the North that might have alienated the people"; and he concluded that

> the Hanoi regime is perhaps one of the most genuinely popular in the world today. The 20 million North Vietnamese, most of whom live in their agricultural cooperatives, like it there and find the system just and the labor they do rewarding.[41]

The contrast with Free World controlled areas of South Vietnam throughout the period of Western hegemony is startling.[42] The difference between "our Vietnamese" and their opponents in South Vietnam was also a great puzzle to such U.S. analysts as Kennedy adviser Maxwell Taylor, later ambassador to Vietnam, who bemoaned the "national attribute" ("Asian nature" once again) which "limits the development of a truly national spirit" among the South Vietnamese, perhaps "innate" or perhaps a residue of the colonial experience, though for unexplained reasons the Vietcong showed an amazing ability "to rebuild their units and to make good their losses"—"one of the many mysteries of this guerrilla war," for which "we still find no plausible explanation."[43] Bernard Fall, writing in the early 1960s, raised the same question and provided a partial answer:

> Why is it that we must use top-notch elite forces, the cream of the crop of American, British, French, or Australian commando and special warfare schools; armed with the very best that advanced technology can provide; to defeat Viet-Minh, Algerians, or Malay 'CT's' (Chinese terrorists), almost none of whom can lay claim to similar expert training and only in the rarest of cases to equality in fire power?
>
> The answer is very simple: It takes all the technical proficiency our system can provide to make up for the woeful lack of popular support and political savvy of most of the regimes that the West has thus far sought to prop up. The Americans who are now fighting in South Vietnam have come to appreciate this fact out of first-hand experience.[44]

3.4 Benign Terror

In surveying the selective concern with terror, bloodbaths, and human rights, we will focus initially on instances where attitudes in the United States have been characterized mainly by sheer indifference. The terror and violence in these cases we designate as "benign". The reasons for the indifference, typically shared by our allies and the Communist powers as well, lie in the lack of significant community or interest group identification with the victims, or the fact that the terror is being carried out by a power whose goodwill and prosperity weigh more heavily in policy-making than mere human suffering, however large its scale. If the terror is carried out by an unfriendly state, "humanitarian concern" tends to play a larger role in expressed policy and action. Where the terror actually makes a direct contribution to *our* ends and interests, as in the case of counterrevolutionary bloodbaths that destroy radical and reformist political movements and clear the way for an "open door," we designate the terror as "constructive" (and we shall see below that it is so treated by U.S. officials and media).

In several cases that we discuss below as "benign," there is some kind of U.S. political-economic interest that contributes to acquiescence in terror. Real world cases rarely fall into one category exclusively, and those discussed are ones in which the indifference factor is large, although "constructive" elements sometimes affect official attitudes. The Burundi case is perhaps closest to purely benign. The East Pakistan butchery was acceptable in part because of the political "tilt" towards Pakistan by Nixon and Kissinger. The destruction of the Latin American Indians and the people of Timor has both political and economic "positive" components: the governments of the genocidal states are our friends and clients. In Latin America, the destruction of the natives (as in the United States in past centuries) is, furthermore, an aspect of economic development in which U.S. corporations are often involved, while Indonesia is one of the great prizes of the Free World in Asia.

3.4.1 East Pakistan: Tilting Towards Massacre

A revolt of the Bengals of East Pakistan against the rule of the dominant Moslems of West Pakistan in the early 1970s led to a large-scale military effort at suppression by the West Pakistanis that quickly degenerated into a huge rape and slaughter. This terrible carnage was given considerable publicity in the West and a small segment of the U.S. public became aroused and active in opposition to U.S. policy in this area. This resulted in part from the sheer magnitude of the onslaught, which one authority described as "the most massive calculated savagery that has been visited on a civil population in recent times."[45] For the Nixon administration, nevertheless, this was a "benign" bloodbath, and its scope and brutality failed to deter Washington from continuing military and economic aid to the government engaging in the slaughter. This was a bloodbath imposed by a friendly military elite with which U.S. authorities had a traditional affinity—"notorious in Mr. Nixon's case" as Max Frankel pointed out[46]—and U.S. policy "tilted" toward Pakistan just enough to maintain the friendly relationship with the ruling junta required by U.S. strategic planning for the Persian Gulf and South Asia.[47] Consequently the matter was regarded as "purely internal"[48] to Pakistan, the bloodbath was benign, and Washington was "not nearly so exercised about Pakistani suppression of the East Bengalis as about what they saw as Indian aggression against Pakistan."[49]

3.4.2 Burundi: "The Limitations of U.S. Power"

During the spring and summer of 1972 perhaps 250,000 people were systematically murdered in Burundi by a tribal minority government that attempted "to kill every possible Hutu male of distinction over the age of fourteen."[50] According to an American Universities Field Staff report on Burundi, which U.S. officials judged accurate, the extermination toll included

> ...the four Hutu members of the cabinet, all the Hutu officers and virtually all the Hutu soldiers in the armed forces; half of Burundi's primary school teachers; and thousands of civil servants, bank clerks, small businessmen, and domestic servants. At present (August) there is only one Hutu nurse left in the entire country, and only a thousand secondary school students survive.[51]

The Prime Minister of Belgium advised his cabinet as early as May, 1972 that Burundi was the scene of "veritable genocide," and in June the term "genocide" began to appear in State Department internal memos and cables. Yet after a small news flurry in June, and speeches on the subject by Senators Kennedy and Tunney, the U.S. press and Congress lapsed into virtual silence.[52] In confirming a new ambassador to Burundi in June, 1972, the Senate Foreign Relations Committee showed itself to be not only uninformed on the history and recent events in that country, but also quite unconcerned with the massacre.[53]

The Carnegie Endowment study of the U.S. policy toward the Burundi massacres states that "the United States has still not uttered a single public word to describe the immensity of the crime against humanity in Burundi—or to condemn it."[54] Although the United States buys 80 percent of the main export crop (coffee) of Burundi, at no point in the unfolding of the massacre was a threatened or actual withdrawal of this fundamental support to the massacre leadership ever considered.[55] In fact, no serious or potentially effective action was taken by the United States government, despite its detailed knowledge of events in Burundi (kept out of the public domain insofar as possible), and despite an internal memorandum prepared within the African Bureau that suggested a U.S. legal obligation to act in the face of massive abuses of human rights.[56] The Carnegie study observes that this was

> ...one of those rare episodes in recent American foreign policy in which the ostensible humanitarian concern of the United States had not collided with competing interests. In Bangledesh, the human disaster had been subordinated to Washington's relationship with Pakistan and the tangled secret diplomacy with Peking. In Biafra, relief seemed choked not only by the politics of a civil war, but also by a State Department policy which placed more value on good relations with the regime in Federal Nigeria. Yet there appeared to be no comparable interests in Burundi to weigh against the human factor.[57]

In the end, however, the relevant considerations were the absence of significant U.S. political or economic interests, along with "the conviction in the African Bureau that avoiding the disapproval of African States was more important than the human lives or the international legal issues in Burundi."[58] This was an unremarkable, or benign bloodbath.

A final word of justification for the U.S. handling of the Burundi massacres was provided in an article in the *New York Times* (27 October 1974) by Thomas P. Melady, the U.S. Ambassador to Burundi. "There is no doubt about how horrible the situation was," he observes, adding his eyewitness testimony of "trucks weighted down with bodies of Hutus, leaving the city for burial." He praises the United States for having delivered relief supplies "in the critical first two weeks of the tragedy," and expresses his understanding for those who thought that more might have been done: "Deep concern about stopping such a tragedy is understandable and praiseworthy," but the critics who have accused the U.S. government of having ignored the Burundi tragedy are mistaken. The role of the U.S. as world policeman "has faded," and it would now be improper for the U.S. "to interfere in the affairs of small states," for example, by "boycotting trade." Rather, "we should focus on long-term solutions and through education seek ways that will assist all people in developing nations and that will diminish the possibilities of genocide...The Burundi tragedy is a good example of the limitations of United States power." He mentions specifically the crucial importance for human rights of developing and supporting institutions "that will defend the rights of all men and women," perhaps referring to our contributions to such institutional developments in Chile during the preceding year.

While U.S. actions were praiseworthy in Burundi, Melady continues, others failed in their duty, notably the United Nations and Organization of African Unity, which, by their inaction, "left themselves open to the serious charge of being selective about their concern for human rights." But "the United States, in my opinion, followed the role of a responsible major power in the Burundi affair," with its relief aid and "efforts to stop the killings" (which unfortunately were not successful, given the failure of others to act with comparable concern, humanity, and forthrightness); "there is no other road for a major power like the United States to follow in a world where many governments carry on repressive activities."

These guidelines for non-intervention are, to be sure, not precisely the ones that the United States follows elsewhere in the world. One "direct action" that this humanitarian regards as inappropriate, the boycott, is employed by the United States on a vast scale (although generally for crimes against property rights); and the United States has not hesitated to offer quite vociferous words of protest when real or alleged violations of human rights take place in enemy territory. The United States has also been known to intervene occasionally to install or protect in power governments that have not thus far shown a readiness "to take the lead in the struggle against man's inhumanity to man."

The ambassador's effort to "reappraise...how in today's world of great concern for human rights such a large number of people [he offers estimates of 90,000 to 250,000] could have been liquidated without any country or organization attempting to stop the mass murder," thus manages to evade every important point. Taken in the abstract, Ambassador Melady's recommendations on non-intervention might merit consideration. Placed in their historical context, they reveal a startling degree of cynicism or capacity for self-deception.

3.4.3 The Indians of Latin America: The Non-Civilized in the Way of "Progress"

Commenting on the systematic massacre of the Aché Indians of Paraguay, the distinguished U.S. anthropologist Eric R. Wolf writes:

> In Latin America, this battle of the civilized against the non-civilized is fought by men who classify themselves as 'men of reason' (*gente de razon*) against those who, bereft of that particular reason, can be classified with the animals...The progress of civilization across the face of the earth is also a process of primary accumulation, of robbery in the name of reason. Nor is this process confined to Latin America. What goes on there now is but what went on in North America when the land was "discovered" and taken from its first occupants. It is only that in North Ameria the process has been dignified by the passage of centuries: "dead men tell no tales."[59]

Wolf points out that "the Roman Catholic Church of Paraguay has spoken out against the genocide of the Aché and informed the Holy See" and that Paraguayan anthropologists have protested at great risk.[60] But, he goes on:

> What about the Great Protestant Conscience, represented on the Guayakí reservation by the New Tribes Mission, which has seen fit to be handmaiden, gunbearer, and prison warden for the killers? What about the government of these United States, always so quick to employ the rhetoric of human rights when its interests are threatened? It gives aid to the government of Paraguay under whose aegis the campaign of extermination is being waged. Americans have good cause to listen to the Aché weeping songs. We can no longer listen to moans of the dying at Wounded Knee or of those who did not survive the Long March. But maybe there is still time to save a few Aché. [61]

The chances are slight. The massacre of the Aché is a case of a benign bloodbath. As Wolf notes, "Paraguay has never offered any product of interest to the growing world market, and the country has been too peripheral to be of strategic concern to any of the great powers which direct the game of international power politics." Still, the U.S. economic and political stake in Paraguay, while not large, is growing, and easily tilts the balance in favor of indifference and apologetics where human rights violations are concerned.

Mark Münzel, a German anthropologist, was the first to call attention to the massacre of the Paraguayan Indians, with whom he lived for a year. He points out that "the Aché are inconveient"—particularly, for the few enterprises with a majority of foreign (Brazilian, United States, and Western European) shares that dominate the Paraguayan economy, and for the Stroessner dictatorship that has imposed its terrorist rule with substantial U.S. support, as did its murderous predecessors. As the forests are cleared for domestic and foreign mining and cattle-raising interests, Indian removal, using some combination of outright killing and forcible resettlement, is a normal facet of "development" policy. In the case of a "poor-man's Nazi" regime such as Stroessner's Paraguay, the nature of the resettlement ("comparable to those in Nazi concentration camps"[62]) is such as to make the charge of genocide an appropriate one.

Münzel records the campaign against the Indians by manhunts, slavery, and deculturation. In manhunts with the cooperation of the military, the Indians are "pursued like animals," the parents killed and the children sold (citing Professor Sardi). Machetes are commonly used to murder Indians to save the expense of bullets. Men not slaughtered are sold for field-workers, women as prostitutes, children as domestic servants. According to Sardi, "there is not one family in which a child has not been murdered." The process of deculturation aims at the intentional destruction of Indian culture among those herded into the reservation. Little effort is made to maintain secrecy about any of this, except by agencies of the U.S. government and by the U.S. media. For example, Münzel was offered teenage Indian girls by the Director of Indian Affairs of the Ministry of Defense, who "sought my good will," and he comments that "slavery is widespread and officially tolerated." Slaves can be found in Asunción, the capital city.[63]

Indians who survive the manhunts are herded into reservations where, according to Münzel, they are "subjected to stress and psychological degradation calculated to break the body as well as the spirit." Torture and humiliation of Indian chiefs is a "standard procedure designed to produce the disintegration of group identity." Medication and nourishment are purposely withheld. When spirits are broken, the reservation is used "as a manhunt center where tamed Indians are trained in fratricide." In a recent visit, Arens was impressed with the "striking absence of young adult males," the horrendous condition of the children, with festering sores, distended abdomens and widespread symptoms of the protein-deficiency disease kwashiorkor, and the refusal of medication and medical care as a general and deliberate practice.[64] Arens, even on a guided tour, was aghast at the systematic maltreatment and felt himself "engulfed by the collective gloom of a people who had given up on life."[65]

The systematic humiliation and ethnocide, Münzel writes, "produces docile Indians who are sometimes taken to Asunción and exhibited to the public. Thus, the 'good image' of the reservation (as illustrated by the well-fed and smiling Aché photographed by a *New York Times* reporter in 1974) is preserved." Not all reporters are so easily fooled, however. As Arens notes, contrasting the contemptible behavior of the U.S. media with the more serious treatment abroad, "where a reporter for the *New York Times* had discovered a clean reservation, peopled by smiling and happy Indians, Norman Lewis [of the *London Sunday Times*] had found a death camp." This is also what Wolf reports in his survey and Arens found in his 1977 guided tour of the Paraguayan camps.

The reservation in question is run by U.S. fundamentalist missionaries, one of whom "has himself been observed participating in Indian hunts within the forest areas and, beyond that, in the lucrative sale of captives in his charge" (Münzel). The takeover of the extermination camp by missionaries "has meant the end of overt brutality" and the beginning of reforms which appear to be "window dressing," Münzel reports. "Fundamentalist missionaries have followed the official line of the Paraguayan Indian Affairs Department with greater cruelty than their predecessors; they have attempted and continue to attempt to secure the rapid cultural 'integration' of the Aché at almost any cost." Their technique is "civilizing with a sledgehammer," in the words of the Director of the South American section of the Hamburg Ethnographic Museum, who discusses their "racist feeling of superiority" and suggests that their disdain for Indian culture may be the reason why they were selected by the government to run the reservation. Indians are forced to give up their names, customs and traditions, and taught to think "that anything connected with their own culture is shameful." For example, when a child died of hunger in a camp after capture, Münzel reports, his parents were forbidden to bury him in the forest in the traditional manner but were required to bury him close to the house in a Christian rite:

> Denial of the Aché rites was seen by the Aché as compelling the spirit of the child to remain close to the house of the parents and to bring retribution to the mother should she engage in sexual intercourse with her husband. The couple, therefore, abstained from sexual relations, waiting for the chance to perform the necessary rites which had been forbidden. While attempting to maintain this abstinence, the grieving mother was repeatedly raped by the administrator and other men.

Christian values are taught in other ways as well. A Paraguayan rancher writes that he "was struck by the fear that this man inspires in these Indians," referring to Jack Stolz of the New Tribes Mission ("the most influential of the North Amcrican Protestant missions in Paraguay"), administrator of the "Guayaki Colony" (Norman Lewis). When Stolz arrived to return a group of Indians to the reservation, "they started to run away into the forest"; women wept that they did not want to return to the camp "because there they were given no food." Stolz proceeded to claim payment from the rancher for work done by the Indians. Other missionaries commented to Lewis that they are making good profits by the sale of Indian handicrafts produced by "the tame Makas under missionary control." Stolz, who seemed to be "virtually a functionary of the Paraguayan government," and who had himself participated in manhunts according to one of his colleagues, "attempted to hide the fact that the Indians were still hunted and their children enslaved," Lewis reports after an October, 1974 trip. Stolz reported that all evidence of Indian culture had been suppressed and admitted that he had made no converts and had not learned the language: "The missionary believed that all those Indians who remained, without hope of conversion, were doomed to spend eternity in Hell"—perhaps the reason why the missionaries are preparing them with a hell on earth.

There are, however, other possible reasons for the fact that observers who do not report for the *New York Times* are reminded of "Nazi extermination centers" when they visit the missionary-run reservations. Paraguay has been a haven for escaped Nazis, including "Josef Mengele, the exterminating angel of Birkenau" (Elie Wiesel). In Argentina and Paraguay, according to Frances Grant, "The Nazis became mentors of the dictators' prison guards, with the local police establishments sharing an expertise won in the concentration camps of Europe."

With a combination of Nazi advisors and racist missionaries along with the complicity of international corporations, the U.S. government and the press, the future looks bleak for the Aché. Perhaps they are the lucky ones, however. Paraguayan liberals, according to Lewis, fear that the same "or even more ruthless methods" are being extended to other regions where corporations are exploiting natural resources and "the role of North American fundamentalist missionaries in that area suggests a fate for those Indians comparable to that of the Guayakí-Achés..."

Frances Grant, who has had a long experience in human rights affairs in Latin America, points out that "the story of the Aché Indians is the clinical microscopic study" of the "most malignant cell" in the "general examination of a diseased body":

> Even as these pages are being written, the obbligato of imprisonments and tortures goes on—priests, students, anthropologists, educators are all drawn into the maw of hidden dooming centers of interrogation or confinement...few are the families whose members have not been ravished, imprisoned, or humiliated during the course of the years that Alfredo Stroessner and his civilian and military satraps have ruled, like incubi of terror and vampirism, over their people.

The archives of human rights organizations, she notes, "overflow with contributory evidence, past and present: declarations of the tortured; futile protests to the presumed protectors of the human person, the regional and international organizations; numberless lists of the summarily imprisoned, with details of their arbitrary confinements and tortures (many since 1956 without trial); names of prisons and concentration camps, covering the country like a spider web." Most of the stories are known through the efforts of "a few courageous protestors within Paraguay and the more than half a million refugees who keep their vigil on the borders of the neighboring countries."

Grant finds U.S. support for the bloodier dictators "puzzling", though she notes that "North American, British, and Dutch Oil Companies, vying for prerogatives in Latin America, found dictatorships highly amenable to their courtships." There is nothing "puzzling" in the support of Nazi-style dictatorships by the country that has taken upon itself the international role of maintaining a favorable climate for oil companies and other corporations. The business climate of Paraguay has not been ideal, with corruption and terror of almost suffocating levels, but on such details the United States is tolerant—especially since, as Arens was informed by his hosts in Paraguay, Stroessner's is a *very* anti-Communist regime which "tolerated no iron-curtain embassies or missions and was a haven for U.S. investment, which was not subject to the fluctuations of less carefully regulated markets like North America."[66] Well-taken points. Accordingly, U.S. support for Paraguayan subfascism has been dependable, with an actual spurt in aid in the liberal years of Kennedy and Johnson. Total aid from 1962-1975 aggregated $146 million, and both military and economic aid have been alloted to this regime in the Carter "human rights" budgets. The direct aid given Paraguay by the United States has not been large, but it has had an economic and political significance not measured by the dollar totals—it constitutes a seal of approval by the U.S. government, and the granting of such an imprimatur opens up lending and grants from public and private lending institutions. It also symbolizes a supportive relationship by the United States, quite important in the case of a weak tyranny like Stroessner's that might not last without U.S. props. This support is manifested in the extreme protectiveness of the U.S. embassy in Paraguay, the State Department and the U.S. mass media in apologizing for, and denying and suppressing information on human rights abuses in that client state.[67] Amnesty International even notes ironically that "although Stroessner has said that he considers the American Ambassador to be an ex-officio member of his Cabinet, the U.S. has never officially acknowledged or taken steps to prevent the use of torture by a government which appears to be very much within its sphere of influence."[68]

In an afterword to the book he edited (see note 59), Arens notes correctly that

> our ability to bend the Paraguayan government to our will by measures well short of war or threats of war is unquestioned. The silence which has enveloped the Paraguayan extermination of the Aché Indians is therefore infinitely more shameful than our failure to condemn an act of genocide in Asia and Africa.

He also notes that it is "ironic" that there has been no call to evacuate the pitiful survivors who "perish at the hands of their persecutors," though "there are no known assassins, torturers, or other criminals among that wretched refuse of humanity" as there were, alongside of many innocent victims, among those evacuated from Vietnam. Furthermore, "United States policy in Paraguay mirrors United States policy for all of Latin America and beyond it for our other 'spheres of influence'," a crucial and accurate observation.

Given that U.S. influence might bring this benign bloodbath to an end, how have the government and the media reacted to the information that has been made public? Arens gives a detailed rundown. As for the government, when apprised of the arrest and torture of courageous anthropologists and others who attempted to defend the Indians, or the arrest and expulsion of priests and Protestant missionaries engaged in relief work, "it has remained silent at every official level, notwithstanding protests by private citizens and Congressmen" (as of May 1976, when the book *Genocide in Paraguay* went to press; see note 60). Efforts by Senator James Abourezk, who noted denunciations of "Paraguay's genocidal policies" by "European governments and their press," while the United States is silent and continues "dumping massive amounts of foreign aid into Paraguay," were equally unavailing. Abourezk has often been a solitary voice of conscience in the U.S. Senate, defending the rights of American Indians and others. It is small wonder that he decided not to seek office again to continue his lonely efforts.

In April, 1976, the State Department continued to refer to torture as an internal Paraguayan matter. The subsequent State Department Human Rights reports are barely more than a derisory whitewash, as is standard for U.S. domains.[69] Arens flatly asserts that the 1978 Report involves "overt fraud." It states that a study by anthropologist Robert Smith "appears to support" its denial of the charge of genocide when Smith, in fact, claims explicitly that "genocide has occurred and is occurring," with the Paraguayan government primarily responsible, the U.S. government serving as an accomplice.[70] It states that Arens was invited "to examine firsthand the situation of the Aché Indians" but makes no mention of his findings on this guided tour (see "Death Camps in Paraguay" and the report on his visit in *Survival International*, both published a month before the Report was submitted).

After *The Nation* had published a rare—indeed unique—article on genocide in Paraguay (24 September 1973), the State

Department received an inquiry concerning the allegations in the article from the Chairman of the Subcommittee on Inter-American Affairs of the House Committee on Foreign Affairs. The Department replied that there had been isolated incidents and "until recently the administration of the reservation left much to be desired and the administrator was a poor choice," but the "situation has now changed with the appointment of a new, and more suitable administration"—namely, Jack Stolz of the New Tribes Mission, whose ministrations to his charges are noted above and described in more detail in the Arens collection. The State Department further reiterated Paraguayan government denials and stated that the U.S. government does not believe "that there has been a planned or conscious effort on the part of the government of Paraguay to exterminate, molest, or harm the Aché Indians in any way." It did not go so far as lauding Stroessner,[71] who has yet to be treated like his predecessor Morínigo who was in power from 1940 to 1948 and was responsible for introducing a "nazified Paraguayan police force" among other notable contributions, and whose "final years in office were enhanced by gratifying visits to the other Americas, ending in his hearty reception in the United States and with the laurels of an honorary degree from Fordham University" (Frances Grant).

The self-censorship of the U.S. mass media neatly complements the official support of Paraguayan fascism. Arens documents the striking contrast between Western Europe, where press, radio, and TV have featured reports of Paraguayan abuses of the Indians, and the United States, where the media have imposed an almost complete blackout. Occasional reports in the *Miami Herald*, the *Missourian*, or the *Oakland Tribune* merely highlight the complicity of the national media in the massacre of the Indians; we note again Arens' crucial observation that the silence has enveloped the extermination of a people in a country very much subject to U.S influence.

In general, apart from finding tame happy Indians in death camps, on the rare occasions when the national press has deigned to discuss the matter, it has tended to follow the State Department line: "The horror was past for all practical purposes, a new administration had taken benevolent charge of the Indian reservation, and, in effect, the good life for the Aché Indian was just beyond the next banana tree" (Arens). The national media and government maintain this pose by the simple expedience of ignoring the contrary evidence presented to them. Thus, letters to the *New York Times* by Dr. Münzel and other specialists protesting misleading coverage, including distortion of Münzel's own remarks, were not published and documentary material presented to the media or studies in the foreign press are regularly consigned to the waste basket. The press has contented itself, by and large, with silence or at most mild rebuke to the Paraguayan authorities for their past deficiencies. Religious organizations in the United States have also refused to take any action, pleading that the issue is "one of extreme delicacy" (Arens). Even condemnations of genocide in Paraguay by the Roman Catholic Church (April, May, 1974) never made it to the national media in the United States.

The Arens book, as noted, was an effort to pierce the veil of silence imposed by the media and government. The same was true of a January 3, 1978 *Survival International* document embodying Arens' report on his 1977 trip, and also a June, 1978 *Survival International* supplement on the Paraguay Indians, an early June press conference on the subject in England, and the January, 1978 article by Arens in *Inquiry* on "Death Camps in Paraguay" (see note 62). The press conference in England was covered by the British and Western European media and led to a Parliamentary debate and Resolution. The Reuters dispatch describing these events was picked up in Latin America—even in Paraguay—but it was almost totally ignored in the U.S.

One might imagine that it is the U.S. tradition of brutal maltreatment of "inconvenient natives" (merely a chapter in the sordid history of European colonial expansion), or standard racist unconcern, that keeps the media from taking allegations of genocide seriously in U.S. domains. While there is no doubt some truth in that explanation, it is only a partial one. Thus, the *New York Times* offers front-page coverage to threats posed to native hill tribesmen in postwar Indochina, fabricating the required evidence, as we shall see below (Volume II, chapter 4). And the *Times* promptly reviews each book condemning Cambodia—though not ones that depart from the official line, as we shall see—but has yet to get around to a review of *Genocide in Paraguay,* which is ignored by the media and unknown to the reading public; total sales amount to under 2,000 copies.

The story of the Paraguayan "Guayakí" is hardly unique within U.S. domains, and, needless to say, has its analogues elsewhere, e.g., in the extermination of the aboriginal population of Tasmania. It is an important fact, however, that one is more likely to find direct reporting on benign terror in the U.S. sphere in the foreign rather than in the U.S. press. As a further example, the London *Observer* (5 March 1978) contains an extensive discussion of the fate of the Indians of Bolivia. The cover shows a photograph of a young Indian woman holding an infant with the caption: "The price of civilisation: To stay alive this Bolivian Indian sells herself at the roadside for 13p." Other pictures show Indian slaves, "fiestas" organized by the Church "to encourage the peasants to spend their money and so keep them in a state of manageable subjection," dying Indians in a mission compound who had their water supply cut off as a punishment, Indians at a mission camp who "appeared dazed with apathy and did not move for hours" and others who walked 250 miles in search of food and "now, in the alien urban world of the whites,...are a prey to every exploiter."

Still other photos indicate the deeper problem: for example, a picture of a burial ground in a tin-mining town where, according to a report by a delegation of the British National Union of Mineworkers in 1977: "It is estimated that an underground tin worker contracts first degree silicosis within five years. At the age of 30 he will have second degree silicosis and by the age of 35 he will have progressed to the stage where he cannot be saved." Or another, showing migrant cane-cutters who work a 15-hour day (13 hours on Sunday, so that they have time for purchases at the estate owner's shop in a nearby village) with wages so low that "90 percent of workers are victims of the debt-bondage system: debts not worked off during their lifetime are passed on to their children."

Such facts, easily documented throughout domains of the Free World, do not fall under the concept of "human rights violations" in the sense of the recent human rights campaign; to achieve this status, deaths from overwork or otherwise must be in the "right place at the right time" (see the discussion of Cambodia, volume II, chapter 6, in particular the dismay expressed by reporters over the fact that Cambodians are alleged to work a nine-hour day in cooperatives).

The text of the *Observer* article, by Norman Lewis, explains how "the Indians of Bolivia, already exploited by a military dictatorship, will have to take up more of the white man's burden if South African and Rhodesians accept an invitation to colonise the country" as Western civilization is driven from some of its historic conquests. Dr. Guido Strauss, Bolivian Under Secretary for Immigration, announced a plan to settle 150,000 whites from the racist regimes of Africa "financed by a 150-million-dollar credit to Bolivia offered by the Federal German Republic," appropriately enough. He also alleged that "Britain, the U.S., and France between them were ready to put up 2,000 million dollars to indemnify white Rhodesians, 'who would be unable to resist the process of Africanisation'."

This "rescue effort" will no doubt be highly lauded in the West as an example of traditional Christian humanitarianism if it is conducted as Dr. Strauss outlines it. But the Catholic Church in Bolivia has a different view. A conference of religious leaders warns that the South African whites, "with their violent racial mentality," can be expected to "import the principles of apartheid" to Bolivia, "the richest of the Latin American countries, requiring only an advanced technology for the exploitation of its raw materials" and now populated largely by those referred to disparagingly by the South Africans as "illiterate natives." The conference cites "the contemptuous remarks of some of our own authorities who say, 'The Indians cost more to keep than animals. They have to be fed, and work less'."

But, Lewis continues, the Church authorities, though well-meaning, are naive, "since in some ways apartheid already exists in a purer and more extreme form in Bolivia than the version professed by the racists of South Africa," as "a visitor to the country quickly discovers." The Indians, he writes, "have been forcibly Christianised, and enslaved over four centuries, and they are still fantastically exploited," though now, "with the Church turned benign, they are no longer compelled to carry priests in chairs on their backs, or scourged for persisting in their ancient worship..."

Penny Lernoux reports that 30,000 white Africans are being invited to settle in Eastern Bolivia in lands that had been earmarked for impoverished Indians, while "one-third of the Bolivian work force lives in exile because it lacks land and infrastructure—the very things the government is offering the white Africans." Some 700,000 Bolivians have left the country because of poverty and repression, she estimates, most of them to Argentina where they work as plantation labor. But, as Dr. Strauss explained to a U.N. Commission, his government's objective is to construct "a white Bolivia." A South African delegation meanwhile reported in the *Sunday Times* of South Africa after a visit to Bolivia that white South Africans, with their "inbred intelligence" and "racial purity," could easily take over the Bolivian economy, "run by a small minority of white immigrants from Europe who keep the Spaniards and local Indians well and truly in their place."[72]

Dr. Strauss explained how the South African settlers will be absorbed in this "promised land" after the government develops the infrastructure in areas where they are to be settled, some of which are now occupied by Bolivian Indians. To pursue the question further, Lewis, following Strauss's suggestion, talked to the director of the Summer Institute of Linguistics (SIL), "the largest group of North American evangelical missionaries working in Bolivia," a group regarded by every Bolivian he met "as the base for operations of the CIA in Bolivia; possibly in South America itself."[73] The SIL is perhaps the richest and most powerful of the "North American religious bodies devoted to the spiritual advancement of South America," Lewis notes, and is supported by the government under the Ministry of Culture and Education. One of its main activities is Bible translation—with a few modifications for local consumption as when the phrase "Let every soul be subject unto the higher powers" becomes "Obey your legal superiors, because God has given them command."

Lewis then discusses some of the past history of spiritual advancement, for example, the description by a German anthropologist of how missionaries allowed Indians "to die in cold blood, after establishing contact with them," by holding back medicine, with the following argument: "In any case they won't allow themselves to be converted. If I baptise them just before they die, they'll go straight to heaven."

The standard missionary technique when an uncontacted group is found is to leave gifts along forest paths to draw the Indians to the mission compound, where "often at the end of a long journey, far from the Indian's source of food, his fish, his game, [the trail] comes abruptly to an end." The Indians are then taught that they must work for money on local farms and they agree, "when they realise that there's no going back," according to the head of SIL, an official of the Ministry of Culture and Education.

This official, Lewis writes, "is the first human link in the chain of a process that eventually reduces the Indians to the lamentable condition of all those we saw in Bolivia," namely, a state "too often indistinguishable from slavery." He is one of hundreds of missionaries all over South America, "striving with zeal and with devotion to save souls whose bodies are condemned to grinding labour in an alien culture"—virtual slaves on white-owned farms or in the tin mines of the international corporations.

The North American missionaries, he continues, "have become—often officially—the servants of such right-wing military dictatorships as that of Bolivia," which is not above sending in planes or tanks to kill those who show "too spirited a resistance to its authority," but which generally is more "like a digesting crocodile" in a state of "watchful inactivity." The Roman Catholic Church, after centuries of complicity in torture and oppression, is now attempting to defend the native population, as we describe further below.[74]

The role of Christian missionaries in the historical and current practice of Western expansion is interesting and complex, not only in Latin America. The ideological commitments that lie behind it are sometimes remarkable. Evidently, missionary activities will be facilitated, in general, by the success of Western penetration, military and otherwise. This fact is sometimes interpreted in terms of fundamentalist doctrine. Consider, for example, the following comments on Southeast Asia in the journal *Translation* of the Wycliffe Bible Translators (closely linked if not virtually identical to SIL):

> God uses military troops, but He has other methods also. God turned the tables in Indonesia on the eve of a Marxist revolution, and the spiritual response of thousands turning to Christ has been tremendous. Cambodia put all missionaries out of their country in 1965, and it seemed God's work there was finished. Suddenly—a coup d'etat and a new responsiveness to missionary work...
> We are looking to God for the purchase of new headquarters in Saigon and trusting Him for advance into Cambodia and other new tribes as He leads...[75]

God's work in the case of Indonesia in 1965, included the massacre of hundreds of thousands of people; the missionaries' reference to this spiritual achievement recalls the comments of the "moderate scholars" of Freedom House on the "dramatic changes" that had proven so beneficial in Indonesia as the massacre was consummated, sure evidence that the United States was on the right track—perhap's on God's side—in Vietnam. (see p. 86, above). And God's agents in Indochina turn out to be the avenging angels of the U.S. Air Force. Small wonder that whatever their private goals and individual justifications, the fundamentalist missionaries so often find themselves accomplices in ethnocide or even genocide.

Indians who attempt to resist white depredations are captured and tortured by police, Lewis continues. Those "who have only recently been driven or enticed from the jungle...are at the bottom of the pyramid of enslavement," even below those forced to labor as virtual slaves on farms and in mines. After passing through the mission, where they have "been deprived of their skills and been taught the power of money," they are forced into slavery to subsist or must sell their women for food. Lewis visited a mission where the scene "was a depressingly familiar one: the swollen bellies, pulpy, inflated flesh, toothless gums and chronic sores of malnutrition, the slow listless movements, the eyes emptied by apathy," with no edible food visible and with the water supply "cut off by the missionary in punishment for some offence," as shown in the accompanying pictures: "The Indians, several of them ill, and with sick children in the camp, had been without water for two days."

The missionary in charge confirmed the collective punishment, ordered after two or three children had broken into a store. Water would be withheld, he said, until the culprits were found "and brought into his compound, there to be publicly thrashed." He deplored the fact that "the conception of corrective chastisement seemed to be beyond their grasp." The missionary "spoke of this aversion to punishment as of some genetic defect inherited by the whole race." The chief of the captured tribe, "grotesque in his dignity," attempted suicide with an axe.

Elsewhere, Indians give away their children—usually girls—to white families in the hope that at least they may be saved, though a form of slavery is the common lot. These children are the "untouchables of Latin America, whose existence went unnoticed," though this form of slavery is "barely disguised" and causes no particular response among the civilized whites—the "men of reason"—who are now accustomed to the practice.

Many of the leading citizens are Germans, "the most successful and affluent of the foreigners in Bolivia," who are now committed to bringing in South Africans to displace the native population, as discussed above. Many remain loyal Nazis, Lewis reports. Lewis attended a fund-raising dinner for a German school, where "many of the guests were ex, or actual, Nazis." What he found "most extraordinary...was to be assured that German Jews in Bolivia had sunk their differences with their old Aryan persecutors, and now fraternised at such gatherings, joining the chorus of 'Horst Wessel' along with the rest; a case of cultural solidarity in an alien background overcoming even racial prejudice." "Cultural solidarity," in this case, is buttressed by the economic opportunities afforded by the rich resources that await exploitation when the Indians are sufficiently christianized by the missions that are devoted to this task.

Lewis concludes with the following observation:

> Together with the powerful German-Dutch minority already in place, these newcomers [from South Africa] could transform Bolivia into a strong white-dominated, ultra-right, anti-Communist state in the heart of Latin America. This vigorous transformation would discourage the future covetousness of neighbouring states, and it

would delight the United States by laying forever the ghost of Che Guevara—himself once attracted to empty spaces in Bolivia.

There, Guevara was killed by the CIA and local authorities, after an abortive and ill-conceived effort to organize the native population to better their lot.

It is perhaps too much to say that the United States is delighted by the extermination, enslavement, and torture of the native populations and their replacement by Nazis and racists who can serve more effectively the needs of the industrial democracies. Rather, it is a matter of no particular moment, worthy of no protest, no display of the kind of emotion reserved for Russian dissidents, and deserving no comment in the nation's press.

Turning once again to the State Department's Human Rights reports, we discover (March, 1977) that "most Bolivians enjoy a relatively orderly and peaceful society and are normally secure from abuses" although "despite significant progress over the past generation, however, a majority of the people are still not protected from occasional infringement of the right to life on the part of military and security forces" (the "most recent example" was January, 1974). Meanwhile the country is "currently experiencing a period of relatively rapid economic growth." There were cases of inhuman treatment in earlier years, but thankfully things have improved as President Banzer assures us that his government will remain in power "in order to continue its avowed program of nation-building, economic development and internal political stabilization"—who could doubt his word? Needless to say, there is no mention of the situation described by anthropologists, the local Catholic church, or European reporters.

The 1978 Human Rights Report is no less cheery in tone. It tells us of "a series of significant improvements in the status of human rights" along with economic progress that "has also undoubtedly improved the situation of some of the poorest segments of Bolivian society and contributed to the economic and social cohesion of this country." Again, the material just reviewed has somehow escaped the assiduous researchers of the State Department, even though their commitment to human rights is so intense and single-minded as to have come under sharp attack from realistic liberals such as Joseph Kraft, who warns that the United States does not "have the luxury of sniffing at corruption" or "playing liberal missionary on human rights" or "being a supersleuth on weapon sales."[76]

The *London Sunday Times* carried a lengthy illustrated report on the situation of the Indians in Brazil, where a population of 3 million at the time of the white conquest has been reduced to less than 100,000 by "disease, alcohol and demoralisation" (Brian Moynahan, "The Last Frontier," 18 June 1978). Sometimes they are simply murdered, by the traditional method of offering them blankets infected with smallpox or sugar laced with arsenic, or by the more modern technique of dropping dynamite sticks from planes. Or they are treated by missionaries and others to the civilizing process already described. In Brazil, too, the German community has achieved high rank in both numbers and investment. Many immigrants have recently left Europe, which they describe as "a continent submerged in decadence and Socialism." In this group, for example, is a former French Army sergeant from Africa who manages a Brazil nut plantation and says forthrightly: "Je suis raciste...The Brazilians are white niggers. Not a thought for tomorrow, all rhythm and shit. They're kids. You've got to push them...The Amazon is white man's country. Any European winds up boss." Not like France, where "some day some Arab will wind up President."

Settlers explain that it is easy to remove the Indians from their (in theory) inalienable lands: " 'Hell, man, banana his friends off.' Which means a couple of aerial bombardments with dynamite sticks." A rancher adds: "Don't get me wrong. I'm Christian. I don't think the only good Indian is a dead Indian, like the Yanks say. But I do believe that the only good Indian is a landless one." A Canadian missionary predicts "total extinction" for the Indians, with the Army moving in for the kill, for development—though Moynahan comments that Brazil is showing a degree of "restraint and decency not paralleled by any other New World country at the height of its venture into the interior and certainly not by the British in Australia"—small comfort.

Moynahan, quite typically, explains the extermination of the Indians in terms of historical inevitability: "What happens on the frontier is harsh, the cruelty unplanned but present. It would be unrealistic, in the face of history, for it to be anything else." Others disagree. Shelton H. Davis, in a study of development and the Indians of Brazil, concludes that "the massive amount of disease, death, and human suffering unleashed upon Brazilian Indians in the past few years is a direct result of the economic development policies of the military government of Brazil," and more generally, the private, state and multinational corporations that have taken over the Brazilian economy, particularly since the U.S.-backed coup of 1964.[77] He notes as well that this particular version of "economic progress," which is far from inevitable, has also led to the victimization of agricultural workers, rural migrants from the poverty-stricken Northeast, and millions of urban poor. He describes the history of extermination of Brazilian Indians on the North American pattern to permit Western colonization, and the failure of attempts to save them from the worst depredations of the advancing "men of reason." From 1900 to 1957, he estimates, the indigenous population of Brazil dropped from 1 million to less than 200,000, and by the latter date many "were enduring the most precarious conditions of life in the greatest misery" (p. 7, citing a Brazilian anthropologist). Hideous atrocities came to light in 1968 when a government commission released a 5,000 page report documenting "widespread corruption and sadism" and the use of biological as well as conventional weapons to wipe out Indian tribes (deliberate spread of smallpox, tuberculosis, measles, etc.; pp. 10f.) He reviews Norman Lewis' study in the *London Sunday Times* (February 1969), entitled "Genocide—From Fire and Sword to Arsenic and Bullets, Civilization Has Sent Six Million Indians to Extinction." Again it is to the European press that one must turn for serious current discussions.

The main point that Davis is concerned to stress is that the destructive policy toward the Brazilian Indians and the maltreatment of the Brazilian poor in general are elements of a specific program of development keyed to the needs of the domestic and foreign elites who dominate Brazilian policy. He notes that with the coup of 1964 "a new partnership has emerged in Brazil between international lending institutions, multinational corporations, and the Brazilian military regime" (p. 42). This partnership has greatly speeded up an export-oriented development strategy that runs roughshod over any obstructive weak elements in society. Thus the Indian regulatory body "was forced to sacrifice Indian land rights for the larger economic interests of state highway programs, large-scale mining prospects, and agri-business enterprises in the Amazon. Such wanton dispossession of native lands had led to the uprooting and destruction of scores of Indian tribes." This process has greatly disturbed some of those who have tried to defend the Indians, for example Antonio Cotrim Soares, "one of Brazil's most dedicated Indian agents," who resigned from the Brazilian National Indian Foundation in 1972 because, he said, "I am tired of being a grave-digger of the Indians...I do not intend to contribute to enrichment of economic groups at the cost of the extinction of primitive cultures" (p. 68).

The "global pattern of ethnic destruction that since 1970 has encompassed the entire Amazon region of Brazil" (p. 73), Davis argues, is related to a program of extraction of natural resources that will offer little benefit to the mass of the Brazilian population, though it will enrich a few and will serve the needs of the industrial countries. If workers are forced to live in "slave camps," in the phrase of a Catholic Bishop describing immigrants brought in from impoverished areas (p.122), the reason is not historic inevitability any more than the continuing massacre of Indians is an inexorable process of history. Citing the same Bishop, Davis notes that "if the incentives given to the oligarchies and trusts from the south of the country had been invested in the peasantry of the country, a very different set of events would have occurred ...'Such investment could have produced a future of hope and development for all of these people in the interior of Brazil, rather than perpetuate the inequities of the latifundia system which is socially and radically unjust' "(p.126).

The actual policies pursued, while benefiting a traditional and foreign elite, are not only destroying the Indians but are severely damaging the Brazilian peasant small-holders and agricultural workers and have, in fact "worsened the already severe pattern of hunger and malnourishment that characterizes the majority of the population of Brazil" (pp. 126, 132). According to Davis:

> One of the major results of this new settlement pattern has been the uprooting of large numbers of poor Brazilian

> peasants who previously formed the pioneer element in central Brazil. It must be stated categorically that the land-tenure situation of these peasant small-holders is no less precarious than that of Indian groups in the Amazon basin. In addition, all attempts to seek legal protection for the land claims of these peasant populations, on the part of such institutions as the Brazilian Catholic Church, have been met by severe repression on the part of local, state, and national officials in Brazil.[78] As a result, over the past decade, agrarian protest and violence have reached epidemic proportions in several areas of Mato Grosso and central Brazil. (p. 161)

But there is more to say about what Davis calls the "silent war ... being waged against aboriginal peoples, innocent peasants, and the rain forest ecosystem in the Amazon Basin of South America" (p. 167). While it may benefit Western capitalism in the short term, a serious ecological disaster may be in the making. Commercial exploitation of the Amazon is disturbing a fragile ecological system with significant potential effects even on the oxygen content of the earth's atmosphere, given the magnitude of the Amazon Basin forests, which are estimated to contain about one-third of the trees on the earth's surface. The matter is poorly understood and is not a consideration within the framework of capitalist development programs.

The director of Brazil's National Institute for Amazon Research suggested recently that the surviving Indians of the Amazon region may be the only ones who know the answer: "We regard the Indian," he stated, "as an inferior being with an inferior culture. But when you talk about living in the Amazon he is far superior because he harmonizes so perfectly with the whole ecological system... The tragedy is that the Indian is one of the main keys to the successful occupation of the Amazon, and as he disappears his vast knowledge is going with him."[79]

Perhaps the native Americans will yet witness a grim harvest reaped by the "men of reason."

3.4.4 East Timor: Genocide on the Sly

We conclude this survey of selected benign bloodbaths by shifting to a different area of the world, Southeast Asia.

On December 7, 1975 Indonesian armed forces invaded the former Portuguese colony of East Timor, only a few hours after the departure of President Gerald Ford and Henry Kissinger from a visit to Jakarta. Although Indonesia has effectively sealed off East Timor from the outside world, reports have filtered through indicating that there have been massive atrocities, with estimates running to 100,000 killed, about one-sixth of the population. An assessment by the Legislative Research Service of the Australian Parliament concluded that there is "mounting evidence that the Indonesians have been carrying out a brutal operation in East Timor," involving "indiscriminate killing on a scale unprecedented in post-World War 2 history." We will return to the evidence, which compares very well in credibility with what is available concerning other areas of the world closed to direct investigation where atrocities have been alleged; Cambodia, to take an obvious parallel in the same time frame.

It is instructive to compare Western reaction to these two instances of reported bloodbaths. In the case of Cambodia reported atrocities have not only been eagerly seized upon by the Western media but also embellished by substantial fabrications—which, interestingly, persist even long after they are exposed. The case of Timor is radically different. The media have shown no interest in examining the atrocities of the Indonesian invaders, though even in absolute numbers these are on the same scale as those reported by sources of comparable credibility concerning Cambodia, and relative to the population, are many times as great. Nevertheless, apart from Australia, and to a lesser degree, the Netherlands, the Western reaction has been almost total silence. In the United States, lack of concern has been coupled with some show of hostility to the bearers of unwelcome tidings. On the rare occasions when the press deals with Timor it generally presents as fact the latest handout of the Indonesian propaganda agencies, as we shall see, or else reports the iniquity of the resistance, compliments of Indonesian generals. The State Department observes the same conventions.

The difference in international responses is revealing. Specifically, it reveals once again how hypocritical is much of the "human rights" clamor in the West. The difference reflects the concern of ideologues to divert attention to the crimes of enemies of the state they serve, while obscuring atrocities for which they share a measure of responsibilty. The major point we wish to emphasize is that the United States and its allies are participants in the Timor massacres through the agency of the regime they support in Jakarta. The United States could have prevented the invasion and might have used its influence (and still can) to bring the subsequent atrocities to an end, while in Cambodia, where much of the post-1975 suffering has been a direct consequence of U.S. barbarity in the recent past, the vast outpouring of indignation in the West was unlikely to have a positive effect in improving the lot of victims of barbarism or oppression. From this simple observation, as obvious as it is ignored, we learn something about the sudden concern for "human rights" that has moved to stage center just at the moment when the lustre of classical colonialist and interventionist ideologies has dimmed.

In the next chapter we will turn to United States relations with Indonesia, which provide the framework for understanding the attitude that the U.S. government and the Free Press have taken with regard to Indonesian aggression in East Timor. The crucial event was the military coup of October, 1965, which had two major consequences regarded with much admiration in the West: first, Indonesia rejoined the Free World as a fully-accredited member, a paradise for investors, free to be plundered by the industrial societies and its own rulers on a joint venture basis; second, the mass-based Communist party, which had posed a barrier to the kind of freedom offered to the underdeveloped world by the industrial West, was destroyed with the incidental murder of hundreds of thousands of people. Since recording these achievements, the military government of Indonesia has been the beneficiary of the full range of support from the United States: military, economic, diplomatic and ideological. In particular, the U.S. government has not only provided its Indonesian client with the material means to conduct its programs of pillage, oppression and massacre, but has also exerted strenuous efforts to obscure them, with the loyal assistance of the Free Press. We will see many examples as we turn to the Indonesian aggression in East Timor, but it is important to be aware of the more general context.

Before turning to the direct consequences of the Indonesian invasion, a few words of background.[80]

The island of Timor was a region of conflict between Dutch and Portuguese imperialism until 1904 when the Luso-Hollandesa treaty assigned East Timor to the Portuguese empire and West Timor to the Dutch. A rebellion against the Portuguese was quelled with over 3,000 Timorese killed in 1912, after two years of bitter fighting. During World War II, "intervention by Australian and Dutch troops, and finally by Japanese forces plunged East Timor into the war, and inevitable occupation by the Japanese" (*Dunn Report*). Australian commandos resisted for over a year, attributing their success to support from the Timorese in the mountains, where most of the population lives. "During the Second World War the few towns of Timor and many of the villages were either destroyed or badly damaged, largely as a result of Allied bombing" (*Dunn Report*). Portuguese authorities estimated the number of Timorese who died at over 50,000. In contrast, the Australian commando force of 400 suffered 40 deaths (Jolliffe, p. 46).

Indonesian independence did not affect the Portuguese colony of East Timor, which remained a backwater, undeveloped apart from some improvement in the few towns (primarily the capital city of Dili), where the economy was largely in the hands of Chinese. The Church had long cooperated with the imperial power. "Critics of the Church, among them the Jesuits and other missionaries, sometimes observed that the Church in Timor seemed to concentrate more on helping its flock to come to terms with their plight rather than on pressing for social reforms" (*Dunn Report*), a typical colonial manifestation. "In all Portuguese colonies the Catholic Church had been the linchpin of Portugal's 'civilizing mission'," recognized in the Portuguese Constitution as one of the "centres for spreading civilisation" (Jolliffe, p. 93). The same was true throughout the Spanish and French colonial systems.

For the people of Timor, colonialism was a disaster. The slave trade flourished under the Dutch as well as the Portuguese until well into the nineteenth century. In 1947 representatives of the Australian government observed "forced labour under the whip...

from dawn to dusk" as the Portuguese "live with the same mixture of civility and brutality as they had 350 years ago." An Australian journalist visiting in 1963 wrote that "I have never been so sensible of fear-paralysed hostility as I was in Timor" (Jolliffe, pp. 47, 55).

East Timor was never included within the colonial or post-colonial boundaries of Indonesia and "Indo-Javanese and Islamic influences barely can be noted."[81] After World War II, mountain people "have proclaimed repeatedly their right to self-determination" and eagerly welcomed the steps toward independence which followed the 1974 Portuguese revolution.[82]

As soon as the Portuguese announced that independence would be granted to the colonies in April, 1974, the tiny elite of Timor (numbering perhaps 3,000) formed three political parties (and later, a few minor parties): UDT, FRETILIN, and APODETI. "Among the founders of the UDT were mainly Timorese who had benefited from Portuguese rule" (Hill), including several leaders associated with the fascist parties in Portugal. The UDT is described by Forman as "the offshoot of the old colonial administrative class."[83] "The UDT leadership predominantly comprised Catholics who were smallholders or administrative officials." (Jolliffe, p. 62). Initially regarded as the most influential of the three parties, "its lack of positive policies, its associations with the 'ancien régime,' together with its initial reluctance to support the ultimate goal of full independence led many of the party's original followers to swing their support to FRETILIN which by early 1975 was generally considered to have become the largest party in the Territory."[84] The reasons for the swing were not only the failures of the UDT but also the successes of FRETILIN. "The UDT's inability to articulate a programme of social development or build links with the common people in the hinterland could not provide serious opposition to the FRETILIN literacy and agricultural development campaign" (Joliffe, p. 90). One Australian journalist estimated in February, 1975 that the UDT had the support of about 10 percent of the population and FRETILIN about 60 percent, while about 25 percent "are thought to be too remote, illiterate or apolitical to take part in an election."[85] The remaining 5 percent were said to support the pro-Indonesian party APODETI, a common estimate.

FRETILIN was a moderate reformist national front, headed by a Catholic seminarian and initially involving largely urban intellectuals, among them young Lisbon-educated radical Timorese who "were most eager to search for their cultural origins" and who were "to lead the FRETILIN drive into the villages, initiating consumer and agricultural co-operatives, and a literary campaign conducted in [the native language] along the lines used by Paulo Freire in Brazil" (Jolliffe, p. 69). It was "more reformist than revolutionary," calling for gradual steps towards complete independence, agrarian reform, transformation of uncultivated land and large farms to people's cooperatives, educational programs, steps towards producer-consumer cooperatives supplementing existing Chinese economic enterprises "for the purposes of supplying basic goods to the poor at low prices," controlled foreign aid and investment, and a foreign policy of non-alignment.[86]

The third party, APODETI, "apparently attracted little support and has generally been regarded as the smallest of the three political parties to have emerged by May, 1974."[87] It was the only party calling for union with Indonesia. Its "social base tended to be anti-white and anti-Portuguese, drawing support from conservative full-blooded Timorese Catholics (including some priests), a section of conservative tribal leaders and the majority of the small Timorese Moslem community" (Jolliffe, p. 82). Its president, Arnaldo dos Reis Araújo, was a Japanese collaborator jailed after the war,[88] and was selected by the Indonesian invaders to head the Quisling regime that they instituted in East Timor after the December, 1975 invasion.[89]

In January, 1975 the UDT and FRETILIN formed a coalition, which collapsed when the UDT withdrew in May. In August the UDT staged a coup, setting off a bloody conflict that ended a few weeks later in a complete victory for FRETILIN." According to an assessment made by a team of the Australian Council for Overseas Aid (AFCOA) which visited East Timor in October 1975, between 2,000 and 3,000 people lost their lives in the civil war, most of them in the area around the central mountain zone."[90] The figures are worth noting, since the United States, after reports of later Indonesian atrocities began to surface, has tried to claim that many of those killed were victims of the civil war.

One major factor in FRETILIN success, apart from popular support, was that the small Timorese military forces trained by the Portuguese were pro-FRETILIN, and indeed were initially confined to barracks by the Portuguese for this reason. At the time of the coup, the Portuguese appear to have aided the UDT, arresting FRETILIN leaders. An Australian pilot, who seems to be a major source for tales of FRETILIN atrocities circulated by Indonesia and the United States, flew men and guns for the UDT and dropped what he called "improvised bombs" on Dili.[91] What reached the international press was largely the version approved by Indonesia, which "had the monopoly on information from the territory" (Hill, p. 12; see below for many examples). Foreign visitors later "found that there had been considerably less fighting than had been reported and less people killed" (Hill, p. 12). Dunn and Jolliffe report exactly the same thing.

The handling of the reports by the first foreign visitors after the brief civil war gives a revealing insight into the nature of the news management that has since then prevailed in the United States. The *New York Times* published an account written by Gerald Stone, "an Australian television journalist, who is believed to be the first reporter allowed there since the fighting began" (4 September 1975). In fact, the *Times* story is revised and excerpted from a longer report carried by the *London Times* (2 September 1975). The *New York Times* revisions are instructive.

A major topic of Stone's *London Times* story is his effort to verify reports of large-scale destruction and atrocities, attributed primarily to FRETILIN by Indonesian propaganda and news coverage based on it, then and since. These reports, he writes,

> had been filtered through the eyes of frightened and exhausted evacuees or, worse, had come dribbling down from Portuguese, Indonesian, and Australian officials, all of whom had reason to distrust FRETILIN.

Here are his major conclusions:

> Our drive through Dili quickly revealed how much distortion and exaggeration surrounds this war. The city has been taking heavy punishment, with many buildings scarred by bullet holes, but all the main ones are standing.

> A hotel that was reported to have been burnt to the ground was there with its windows shattered, but otherwise intact...
>
> Undoubtedly there have been some large-scale atrocities on both sides. Whether they were calculated atrocities, authorized by Fretilin or UDT commanders, is another question. Time after time, when I tried to trace a story to its source, I found only someone who had heard it from someone else. Strangely, it is in the interest of all three governments—Portuguese, Indonesian and Australian, to make the situation appear as chaotic and hopeless as possible...*In that light, I am convinced that many of the stories fed to the public in the past two weeks were not simply exaggerations; they were the product of a purposeful campaign to plant lies* (our emphasis).

Stone implicates all three governments in this propaganda campaign.

Of the material just quoted, here is what survives editing in the *New York Times*:

> A drive through Dili showed that the city had taken heavy punishment from the fighting. All the main buildings were standing but many were scarred with bullet holes.

Stone's conclusions about the purposeful lies of Indonesian and Western propaganda are totally eliminated, and careful editing has modified his conclusion about the scale of the destruction. What the *New York Times* editors did retain was Stone's description of prisoners on burial detail, the terrible conditions in FRETILIN hospitals (the Portuguese had withdrawn the sole military doctor; there were no other doctors—cf. Hill, p. 13), "evidence of beating" (this is the sole subheading in the article), and other maltreatment of prisoners by FRETILIN.

The process of creating the required history advances yet another step in the *Newsweek* account of Stone's *New York Times* article (International Edition, 15 September 1975). *Newsweek* writes that "the devastation caused by rival groups fighting for control of Timor is clearly a matter of concern," a comment that is interesting in itself, in view of the lack of concern shown by *Newsweek* for the real bloodbath since the Indonesian invasion. *Newsweek* then turns to "an account of the bloodbath written by Gerald Stone" in the *New York Times*. After quoting the two sentences cited above on the "drive through Dili," *Newsweek* continues:

> Stone went on to report seeing bodies lying on the street and many badly injured civilians who had gone without any medical treatment at all.[92] He also revealed that the Marxist Fretilin party had driven the moderate Timorese Democratic Union (UDT) out of the capital and in the process had captured and systematically mistreated many UDT prisoners...Stone's dispatch supported the stories of many of the 4,000 refugees who have already fled Timor.

From this episode we gain some understanding of the machinations of the Free Press. A journalist visits the scene of reported devastation and atrocities by "the Marxist Fretilin party" (cf. note 86) and concludes that the reports are largely false, in fact, in large measure propaganda fabrications. After a skillful re-editing job by the *New York Times* that eliminates his major conclusion and modifies others, *Newsweek* concludes that he found that the reports were true. Thus the required beliefs are reinforced: "Marxist" terrorists are bent on atrocities, and liberation movements are to be viewed with horror. And the stage is set for general acquiescence when U.S.-backed Indonesian military forces invade to "restore order."[93]

The background for the UDT August coup seems to lie primarily in the erosion of support for the UDT during 1975 as FRETILIN extended its social and political activities throughout the territory, efforts not duplicated by the UDT.[94] The chief of the Portuguese political affairs bureau "said he thought that UDT had been told by the Indonesians that the only way they could be independent would be to establish an anticommunist country" (Hill, p. 11). Just prior to the coup, high-level meetings had been held in Jakarta and Kupang (capital of Indonesian West Timor). After the Kupang meeting, UDT President Lopes da Cruz said: "We are realists. If we want to be independent we must follow the

Indonesian political line. Otherwise it is independence for a week or a month."[95] The Indonesians had made it clear that they would tolerate no "radicalism" in East Timor and only Indonesian-style "independence." "In an interview recently a source close to Lieut. Gen. Alo Murtopo, President Suharto's principal troubleshooter, said: 'Integration into Indonesia is the best solution. Independence has no chance. It is too weak and small and will create a problem for us in the future. If it becomes radical we will take care of it.'"[96] In his congressional testimony, Benedict Anderson stated that "my understanding is that the situation which precipitated the civil war in East Timor was a coup by the UDT, which was instigated by Indonesian intelligence," referring to the August coup.[97] This seems to be the general view among qualified observers. Declining in internal strength, UDT leaders appear to have concluded that their only hope for power lay in associating themselves with Indonesia's drive for dominance.

Shortly after the UDT coup, the Portuguese sent a peace-keeping mission to try to prevent civil struggle, but they were unable to reach East Timor because of Indonesian obstruction. It was only after a formal protest by Portugal that a Portuguese peace-maker was permitted to arrive in the area, after full-scale fighting had begun (Jolliffe, pp. 124-5). Again, this would seem to indicate that the Indonesians may have been hoping that civil strife would provide them with an excuse for intervention.

The colonial administration departed just prior to the FRETILIN victory in September, "taking with them the only remaining doctor and a large supply of the colony's food, and leaving behind an administrative vacuum which was filled by FRETILIN" (Hill, p. 13), which received no material assistance from outside. Indonesia refused entry to journalists from their side of the border, but from mid-September to the Indonesian invasion of December there were accredited Australian journalists present and also Australian visitors. The Western press outside of Australia again tended to rely on Indonesian sources, while the U.S. State Departments claims (and reveals) ignorance, as we shall see.

The Australians who were in East Timor have given quite a favorable account of the brief interlude of semi-independence from September to the Indonesian invasion of December 7. Dunn, who led the Australian aid mission in October, wrote on the basis of his visit that:

> The Fretilin administration was surprisingly effective in re-establishing law and order, and in restoring essential services to the main towns. By mid-October, Dili was functioning more or less normally and the Chinese shops were beginning to re-open. The towns and villages visited by the ICRC [International Red Cross] and ACFOA [Australian aid mission] members reflected an overall improvement in the situation... The Fretilin administration had many shortcomings, but it clearly enjoyed widespread support from the population, including many hitherto UDT supporters. In October, Australian relief workers visited most parts of Timor and, without exception, they reported that there was no evidence of any insecurity or any hostility towards Fretilin. Indeed, Fretilin leaders were welcomed warmly and spontaneously in all main centres by crowds of Timorese. In my long association with Portuguese Timor, which goes back some 15 years, I had never before witnessed such demonstrations of spontaneous warmth and support from the indigenous population.[98]

Other visitors gave similar reports. Testifying before the UN Security Council in April, 1976, Ken Fry, Labor member of the Australian Parliament who visited the territory in mid-September, found it at peace apart from some border clashes with forces operating from Indonesian West Timor:

> We found the FRETILIN administration to be responsible and moderate and it obviously enjoyed strong support from the East Timorese people. The prisoners were being well cared for and it is worth noting that the prisoners included some FRETILIN supporters who had been apprehended for breaches of discipline...[99] Although the FRETILIN administration faced serious supply and economic problems, order had been restored and the people were going back to the villages to tend their crops. The civil war had ended....Like all other Australians who

> visited Portuguese Timor during this period, I came away full of admiration for the Central Committee of the FRETILIN party. I was tremendously impressed by their moderation, by their integrity and by their intelligence in dealing with a very difficult situation.[100]

Jill Jolliffe, who was working at the time as a journalist in East Timor, describes the FRETILIN program, as it was evolving during this period, in the following terms:

> Most observers of the FRETILIN administration in the last months of 1975 are generally agreed that there was nothing to suggest that an independent East Timor under FRETILIN would have been other than a moderate government pursuing a foreign policy of non-alignment and regional co-operation. Its programme of social reform is moderate, based principally on establishment of agrarian co-operatives (rather than land expropriation) and mass education. Its hallmarks are fervent nationalism, populism, political pragmatism, and while FRETILIN thinking has been stamped in the mould of Third World nationalism rather than western social democracy, the future of an independent East Timor would lie open to political change (p. 298; cf. pp. 193f.).

"Throughout this period FRETILIN repeatedly requested foreign governments, particularly those of neighbouring countries, to send observers and fact-finding missions to East Timor to ascertain the situation in the Territory" (*Decolonization*, p. 25). They refused on the grounds that Portugal retained sovereignty. Until mid-November FRETILIN leaders requested that Portuguese authorities return to the territory to resume and complete the process of decolonization (*Dunn Report*, p. 70).

It might be noted, at this point, that Indonesia had previously indicated its support for independence of Timor. In a letter of June 17, 1974, to José Ramos-Horta of FRETILIN, Foreign Minister Adam Malik of Indonesia wrote that the Portuguese change of government offers "a good opportunity to the people of Timor to accelerate the process towards independence" and stated that the Government of Indonesia adheres to the following principle:

"The independence of every country is the right of every nation, with no exeption [sic] for the people in Timor." He also stated that Indonesia had no designs on the Territory.[101] Dunn was present in Dili when Ramos-Horta of FRETILIN returned from Jakarta with the Malik letter, believing that the prospects were so good that his party might consider "conceding foreign affairs and defence powers to Indonesia."[102]

The facts proved to be quite different. With the victory of FRETILIN in the civil war, Indonesia at once began its armed intervention on the pretext of assisting anti-FRETILIN Timorese, a pretense which, as we will see, is generally accepted in the West, though it has absolutely no basis in fact, so far as we can determine. Indonesian border raids began on September 14; an Indonesian corporal captured during these raids said that he had crossed the border as part of a task force on September 9 (Jolliffe, p. 146). Indonesian attacks continued, reaching a significant level when a force of about 2,000 Indonesians along with some 80 Timorese in support roles attacked and captured the town of Balibó about 10 km. from the border on October 16. In the course of this attack 5 Australian newsmen died, an event which caused some uproar in Australia as evidence of Indonesian responsibility began to mount. A few days later Dunn observed an Indonesian warship "shelling positions well within Fretilin territory to the East of Balibó, near the Loes River. Throughout October and November heavy hand-to-hand fighting took place between Fretilin and Indonesian troops, and gradually the Indonesian forces were able to establish control over much of the territory to the west of the Loes River."[103]

Like Hill (see above), Dunn points out that during this period the foreign press (at times including *Pravda*) relied heavily on Indonesian reports (p. 80). Jolliffe, one of the few journalists actually working in East Timor during this period, also comments on "the incidence of false reports, many of which were carried uncritically in the Australian and international press," from Indonesian sources, particularly after the fall of Balibó (p. 198). In mid- and late-November Indonesian military activity increased; heavy supporting fire from artillery and naval vessels as well as use of aircraft was observed and reported by Australian journalists Michael Richardson and Jill Jolliffe.[104]

Fighting in the border areas increased after the Indonesian capture of Balibó, though there were no new Indonesian offensives. Indonesian naval bombardment continued in November. On November 14, Indonesian naval forces began bombarding the town of Atabae, which had become the front line after the fall of Balibó to the Indonesian invaders. The Australian journalist Roger East, later killed at the time of the December 7 invasion, observed regular air attacks some 30 km. inland from Atabae at this time. "After fourteen days of intense aerial and sea bombardment Atabae fell to Indonesian occupation at 7 a.m. on 28 November."[105] The air and naval bombardment was also witnessed by Michael Richardson.[106]

These attacks evidently convinced FRETILIN leaders that Indonesia was determined to invade. Appeals for a negotiated settlement by FRETILIN and Portuguese had been rejected by Indonesia, and FRETILIN leaders were coming to believe "that Portugal and Australia, the only third parties showing an interest in the conflict in Timor, could not or would not take steps to deter Indonesia from attaining her objective by military means" (*Dunn Report*, p. 81). In this context, FRETILIN declared the independence of East Timor, which it had been governing for almost three months, on November 28.

A full-scale Indonesian invasion was generally expected at this point. Australia instructed all nationals to leave on December 2. "It was clear that an attack on Dili was imminent and that the Australian government had advance knowledge from Indonesian intelligence sources." Australia relayed to the International Red Cross the information that Indonesian forces had threatened to kill Australians remaining in Dili. "The threats were evidence of a final effort by Indonesia to clear the territory of foreign observers before the invasion began." It was important to ensure that no independent witnesses would be present, including the Red Cross, whose absence "would mean that the important work of enforcing the Geneva Conventions could not be done." To this day, the International Red Cross has been barred by the Indonesians. For the Australians, the fate of the reporters at Balibó "had set a precedent which they could not afford to ignore."[107]

On December 6 President Ford and Henry Kissinger visited Jakarta and the following day the Indonesian army carried out the expected full-scale invasion, setting in motion a process described by Forman as "annihilation of simple mountain people"[108] and by others as simply genocide.

It is important to bear in mind that this is not ancient history. In October 1978, a group of Australians who entered Dili harbor on a disabled yacht saw "frigates, patrol boats, barges crammed with Indonesian soldiers, and many aircraft and helicopters," heard explosions in the distance, and "were left without doubts that Dili was still a war zone" (*Canberra Times*, 20 October 1978). The narrow limits of Indonesian control in East Timor and the necessity for continuing military action to extend these limits and to suppress the population are implicitly conceded even in Indonesian propaganda. In July, 1978, the Indonesian news-weekly *Tempo* published an interview with one of the Timorese collaborators, Guilherme Goncalves, ex-chairman of APODETI and now head of the East Timor Provincial Assembly established in Dili by the Indonesian invaders.[109] Asked whether East Timor would participate in the forthcoming Five Year Plan, Goncalves responded:

> There must first be peace and calm among the people. As of now the people can only get on with their jobs in places where our troops are concentrated, such as Dili, Same or Maliana [which is a few miles from the border with Indonesian West Timor].

The implications of this remark, two and a half years after the full-scale Indonesian invasion and two years after the "integration" of East Timor into Indonesia (to which we return), seem obvious enough.

The Indonesian campaign to suppress the independence movement of East Timor continues. The annihilation of simple mountain people goes on with barely a whisper of protest in the Western industrial democracies that are providing material support and ideological cover.

The United States government professes to know very little about anything that was happening during the pre-invasion period. This is a constant refrain of government witnesses during the *March* and *June-July Hearings*. A few examples will be cited below. The pretense is quite outlandish. As already noted, the press had long been reporting Indonesian intentions to take over East Timor. Furthermore, Australian intelligence was well aware of Indonesian military activities in East Timor in late 1975, though the Australian government also feigned ignorance in public.[110] There can be little doubt that U.S. intelligence was privy to the information available to Australia. It was revealed shortly after the invasion that the Australian Ambassador in Jakarta, Richard Woolcott, had cabled advice to the Australian Department of Foreign Affairs on October 29, 1975 "that Australian knowledge of Indonesian intervention be concealed," to avoid complications with Indonesia. "A Ministerial statement was altered last year to conceal the fact that Australia knew Indonesian troops were active in East Timor, more than a month before the all-out Indonesian invasion of the territory on December 7."[111] Juddery comments that this new material adds to the "mounting body of evidence that Australia had many months foreknowledge of Indonesian intentions but actively collaborated in its plans to 'integrate' East Timor with the republic, and that this collaboration continues behind a cloak of ostensible disapproval." The primary difference between Australia and the United States in this respect is that in the United States the cover-up continues in the media as well (and, of course, direct U.S. complicity by means of military and other support is far greater).

The pretense of ignorance is only one aspect of the U.S. charade with regard to this period. The government also claims to have suspended military assistance to Indonesia from December 1975 until June, 1976.[112] The temporary sanction was "unannounced and unleaked" (Lescaze). It was also a fraud. "We stopped taking new orders. The items that were in the pipeline continued to be delivered to Indonesia," General Howard M. Fish testified before Congress. (*March Hearings*, p. 14). Benedict Anderson testified in the *February 1978 Hearings* that according to a report "confirmed from Department of Defense [Foreign Military Sales] printout" new offers of military equipment were also made during the period of the alleged ban:

> If we are curious as to why the Indonesians never felt the force of the U.S. government's "anguish," the answer is quite simple. In flat contradiction to express statements

> by General Fish, Mr. Oakley and Assistant Secretary of State for East Asian and Pacific Affairs Richard Holbrooke, at least *four* separate offers of military equipment were made to the Indonesian government during the January-June 1976 "administrative suspension." This equipment consisted mainly of supplies and parts for OV-10 Broncos, Vietnam War era planes specially designed for counterinsurgency operations against adversaries without effective anti-aircraft weapons, and wholly useless for defending Indonesia from a foreign enemy. The policy of supplying the Indonesian regime with Broncos, as well as other counterinsurgency-related equipment has continued without substantial change from the Ford through the present Carter administrations.[113]

This violation of their own secret policy was admitted by State Department and Pentagon officials who told the committee, however, that "certainly the Department of State is not deliberately engaged in any deception or violation of the law."[114] They certainly weren't deceiving the Indonesians. In fact, it turns out that the "aid suspension" was so secret that Indonesia was never informed of it. Rep. Fraser commented that the aid suspension reminded him "of the Cheshire cat in 'Alice in Wonderland'; all we have is the grin left."[115]

Of the $44.5 million that had been proposed for the period of July, 1975 to June, 1976, 84% was already "in the pipeline" when the December secret "suspension" allegedly took place. Military aid during this period actually was above what the State Department had originally proposed to Congress, and has been increased since.[116]

The Indonesian invasion in December, 1975 was of course reported in the U.S. press, which kept largely to the Indonesian version of the facts, as usual. David Andelman's story in the *New York Times* is headed "Indonesians Hold Portuguese Timor After Incursion" (8 December 1975; dateline Sydney). The Indonesians actually held only the capital city of Dili. The difference is of some significance, given that the United States has consistently been claiming that the fighting is essentially over, and that whatever we may think about the past, now we must recognize the Indonesian annexation as a fact of life and, with our traditional humanitarianism, urge the Indonesians to turn to aid and reconstruction (as of course they are planning to do). Andelman also reported falsely that the civil war (which had ended in early September) had been proceeding until the "incursion" and implied that Indonesia had offered no material assistance to the anti-Fretilin forces: "while at the beginning Indonesia offered no material assistance to the anti-Fretilin forces, now vast resources of food, ammunition and manpower are arrayed against the remaining Fretilin fighters." These deceptive comments are true in a perverse sense; that is, since Indonesia was itself conducting the military operations while falsely alleging that "anti-Fretilin forces" were doing so, it is true, technically, that Indonesia was not offering "material assistance to the anti-Fretilin forces."

The same deception persisted in the "Week in Review" (*New York Times,* 14 December 1975). Here it was alleged that Indonesian forces had "ousted the leftist Revolutionary Front for an Independent East Timor (Fretilin)"; as noted, FRETILIN had been "ousted" from Dili.[117] The *Times* went on to assert, in utter defiance of the facts but in accordance with Indonesian propaganda, that since August "Fretilin forces...have been trying to overcome several other groups which sought union with Indonesia"; the only such group involved in the fighting in any significant way since September had been the Indonesian Army itself. The *Times* claimed that "the Indonesians, however, provided support for the anti-Fretilin forces," which is about like saying that the Russians provided support for anti-fascist Czech forces in 1968.

The *New York Times* did publish an editorial condemning the Indonesian invasion (13 December 1975), while repeating the standard falsehoods produced by the Indonesian propaganda services. "By any definition," the *Times* editorialized, "Indonesia is guilty of naked aggression in its military seizure of Portuguese Timor." But the *Times* added thoughtfully that "to be fair there was provocation in the unilateral declaration of independence last month by the leftist Revolutionary Front for an Independent East Timor, known as Fretilin, which had seemed to be winning the civil war handily against pro-Indonesian forces until Jakarta began to intervene." Note again the series of false claims: Indonesia had not "seized" East Timor, but rather held only the capital city. FRETILIN did not "seem" to be winning the civil war but had won it by early September. It was in September that Indonesia began to intervene (though there was no outright invasion until December 7), not in support of "pro-Indonesian forces" but on its own, under the cover of assisting pro-Indonesian forces. None of the background just reviewed is mentioned. The *Times* editors also do not explain why FRETILIN ascendancy or the declaration of independence was a "provocation" to Indonesia, which had no claims to East Timor, and they say nothing about *Indonesian* "provocation" noted above. The *Times* editors also believe, on grounds that they do not explain, that "there is an ethnic and economic case to be made for voluntary integration"—on the "ethnic" case, see Forman's testimony, cited above. With its traditional concern for human rights, the *Times* concludes that "the real losers are Portuguese Timor's 620,000 inhabitants, whose interests and desires have been ignored by all parties to this deplorable affair"—including the independence forces. Perhaps similar statements were expressed by thoughtful British commentators in July 1776—though recall that Indonesia had no claim at all to East Timor.

On December 25, 1975, a *New York Times* editorial again reproached the government of Indonesia for its "aggression in seizing Portuguese Timor early this month to back up parties favoring union with Indonesia," again repeating the falsehoods provided by the Indonesian propaganda agencies and dimissing the facts as irrelevant. Neither then nor subsequently did the *Times* make clear the fact that on that very day the Indonesian Army had landed an additional force of 15-20,000 men to try to expand its control beyond the capital city of Dili (see note 117).

It is unclear whether the *Times* reference in the December 13 editorial to "a lightening takeover" of East Timor by Indonesia, and comparable misrepresentations in its "news columns" and editorials, was an example of incompetence or deceit. It is nevertheless characteristic and, we stress again, quite important. Since shortly after the outright Indonesian invasion, the U.S. government, with the Free Press trailing loyally in its wake, has alleged that "East Timor is effectively part of Indonesia,"[118] so that no useful purpose would be served by protesting the Indonesian invasion or withholding arms from Indonesia (much as we regret their possible use in the past in this "internal" matter).[119] The basic government line, throughout, is as expressed by Richard Holbrooke, Assistant Secretary for East Asian and Pacific Affairs, discussing a forthcoming Asian tour in Washington with Australian correspondents. Asked about reported atrocities in East Timor, he said:

> I want to stress I am not remotely interested in getting involved in an argument over the actual number of people killed. People were killed and that is always a tragedy but what is at issue is the actual situation in Timor today...

As for the numbers killed in the past, "we are never going to know anyway." So let us put that aside as unknowable history, and turn to the current problems.[120]

The same stance is adopted by State Department spokesman Robert Oakley in the *February 1978 Hearings.* He introduced a report of the State Department expressing their belief "that we have been on the right track in seeking to concentrate our efforts on encouraging the Indonesian government to do a better job of assisting the people of the territory," reiterating the position expressed in the 1977 hearings. Oakley does not outline the good job that the Indonesian government is already doing, which should be made even better. We will return to the character of this good job. Oakley then adds his personal comment that "we have directed our efforts toward urging Indonesia to institute an administration in East Timor which is as responsive as possible to the needs of the people and to enlist the assistance of international humanitarian organizations" (p. 66).[121] Meanwhile we supply them with military equipment to continue the massacre.

These references to the complete Indonesian victory are regularly interspersed with indications that the fighting continues. A remarkable example occurs in the testimony of State Department legal representative George H. Aldrich in the *June-July Hearings*, pp. 46-47. Discussing the formal incorporation of East Timor into Indonesia on July 17, 1976, recognized by the United States but few other countries, Aldrich observes that this incorporation "followed unanimous approval by the People's Council of East Timor on May 31, 1976, of a petition asking Indonesia to accept integration of East Timor into Indonesia." On this farce, which was acceptable in the United States on the authority of the Indonesian government, the sole source of assurances of its legitimacy, see note 148. Aldrich continues: "We actually know very little about the selection process for these delegates, although the process itself took place at a time of military occupation by Indonesia during which considerable fighting was still going on." Actually, the U.S. government knows all that needs to be known about the "selection process"—the feigned ignorance compares with the pretense concerning the pre-invasion period—but it is striking that on the basis of this pretended ignorance the United States was willing to recognize the takeover while at the same time recognizing that considerable fighting was still going on, "renewing" the arms shipments to Indonesia which, in fact, were never halted. The duplicity of the government is matched only by that of the loyal media.

By its adherence to government claims in news reporting and editorial commentary, the Free Press has played its role in permitting the U.S. government to contribute effectively to the massacres and atrocities in East Timor on the pretext that whatever may have happened (and of course we will never know, etc.), it is now a matter of history. A comprehensive collection of articles from December 8, 1975 to the present reporting that fighting is over and Indonesia is now in control, and dismissing past reports of atrocities as "exaggerated" but in any event now irrelevant, would constitute a revealing record of media subservience to the state, to be placed alongside the refusal to acknowledge the ongoing atrocities—again in conformity with the higher purpose of insuring good relations between the United States and its valuable subfascist client. A number of examples are reviewed below.

We will not undertake to review the scanty coverage by academic specialists. To cite one example, the well-known Southeast Asia scholar Michael Leifer of the London School of Economics described "Indonesia's decisive intervention" as a case "in which the imperatives of force and order have not necessarily been matched by justice"[122]—one wonders what the reaction would have been had his colleagues concerned with Eastern Europe described Russia's "decisive intervention" in Hungary in 1956 in the same cautious and modulated tones.

New York Times coverage of the events leading up to the Indonesian invasion gives further insight into the workings of the Free Press. We have already discussed the remarkable distortion of Gerald Stone's account by skillful editorial revision and deletion. This was followed a few weeks later by a special filed from Dili giving an account of the situation which was surprisingly accurate, noting in particular that FRETILIN "is in de facto control of the territory."[123] The regular *Times* correspondent, David Andelman, turned to the topic on November 26, in a dispatch from Jakarta.[124] He noted that Indonesia badly needed Western aid, and with Ford coming for a visit and congressional approval for new military grants still pending, "Indonesians, in the words of a senior military official, will be 'on our best behavior'." He did not have anything to say about what their "best behavior" had been in the preceding months but wrote instead that the Indonesians "point to their hands-off policy with respect to the civil war that is engulfing Portuguese Timor" (there was no civil war and had not been for two months but rather a limited Indonesian invasion). Continuing, Andelman explained that U.S.-supplied Indonesian destroyers "cruise the waters around Timor to prevent infiltration of arms by sea to the left-wing rebels who seized control of the colony last August" (at that point Atabae had been under naval bombardment for 12 days, and fell to Indonesian occupation two days later). Andelman continues: "American supplied Indonesian troops patrol the Indonesian side of the border on the Island. Last week it was announced here that Indonesian forces would be supplying and training refugee opponents of the rebels in 'self-defense' before they are returned to the eastern part of the island." This is six weeks after the fall of Balibó to an Indonesian military attack. Finally comes this insight: "The Indonesian forces reportedly at the direct orders of President Suharto, who has been urged by military men to intervene, have been showing remarkable restraint, for what is at stake [is military aid]." This "remarkable restraint," as we have seen, existed only in the pages of the country's leading paper; and in the *Times* index, where the phrase identifies the article.

On November 30, two days after the Indonesian forces captured Atabae, the *Times* carried a Reuters report stating that "...pro-Indonesian forces advanced from the border toward [Dili]," which in translations means: Indonesian forces accompanied by some Timorese collaborators from the groups that had lost the civil war months earlier were advancing toward Dili.

The rare and uninformative articles scattered through the *Times* during this crucial period have another striking characteristic. While there are references to allegations by FRETILIN of Indonesian involvement in the fighting (e.g. October 19), the Indonesian version is presented not as claim but as fact. Thus: "Latest reports from Portuguese Timor, *where a civil war is raging between rival political factions,* said that the bodies of five foreigners were found in Balibó, but there was no confirmation that they were the missing Australians."[125] Or: "The pro-Indonesian forces have been engaged in a war with the left-wing Revolutionary Front for an Independent East Timor..." (December 2). Again, the Indonesian version repeated as fact by the *Times* is completely false, according to all independent observers.

A review of the *scope* of *New York Times* coverage of Timor also gives some understanding of how the Free Press functions. For the year 1975, when the Portuguese revolution and the fate of the Portuguese colonies was a matter of great concern in the West, the *New York Times* index has six full columns of citations to Timor. In 1976, when Indonesian troops were carrying out a major massacre, coverage dropped to less than half a column. For 1977, when the massacre advanced to a point that some feel amounts to genocide, there are five lines. These five lines, furthermore, refer to a story about refugees in Portugal. Actual coverage of East Timor is a flat zero.

Since the Indonesian invasion of December 7, 1975, the country has been effectively closed to the outside world by the Indonesian military. Nevertheless, evidence is available as to what has taken place. Much of the information is based on interviews with refugees in Portugal conducted by James Dunn, who testified before Congress during the *March Hearings;* the Western press, always passionately concerned with reports of refugees from Communist tyranny, has carefully avoided these refugees[126]—or to be precise, has, as we will see, described their present plight while carefully avoiding their testimony about the events in East Timor. Other information has been received from Catholic priests in Timor who, as in Latin America, have vainly attempted to arouse the conscience and attention of the Western world, and from other sources, to which we return, which have also been assiduously ignored by the Free Press.

Dunn's congressional testimony was given a largely hostile reception and was generally ignored and quickly forgotten in the nation's press, which has also disregarded other pertinent material on this annoying subject. Congressman J. Herbert Burke, then ranking minority member of the House subcommittee on Asian and Pacific Affairs, wrote:

> I have my own suspicions respecting what might be behind the testimony [of Dunn's], and I agree with you that it is in all our interests to bury the Timor issue quickly and completely.[127]

Burke's suspicions, which are based on no evidence that has been made public, simply reflect the natural outrage over the fact that someone dares to provide information concerning crimes for which the United States bears no small responsibility. Any Russian functionary would react in the same way to charges of atrocities in the Soviet sphere. His concern that the Timor issue be quickly and completely buried is also easy to comprehend. If there were anything resembling a free and honest press in the United States (indeed, most of the West), the issue of Timor would be of major international concern for the reason already noted: the "annihilation of simple mountain people" proceeds as a direct consequence of Western aid and silence, therefore complicity.

Burke's concern that the issue of Timor be "buried" is understandable given that the United States had provided crucial diplomatic and material support for these continuing atrocities. Rep. Helen S. Meyner, who visited East Timor in a congressional delegation that was permitted a 23-hour guided tour, reports that the Commander of the Indonesian forces, asked whether U.S. weapons had been used in the invasion, responded: "Of course, these are the only weapons we have."[128] That is actually a slight exaggeration, it seems. Asked by Congressman

Fraser whether it is true that "We armed [the Indonesian military] so that they were able to carry out the use of force," the Deputy Legal Advisor of the State Department, George H. Aldrich, replied: "That is correct. They were armed roughly 90% with our equipment." He evaded the question of use of U.S. arms, apart from a "guess" that they might have been used, pleading ignorance: "...we really did not know very much. Maybe we did not want to know very much, but I gather that for a time we did not know."[129]

As to this "ignorance," it is a fact that the West generally, the United States specifically, does not want to know, preferring that the issue be quickly buried, forgotten along with the mass graves and demolished villages of East Timor.

Introducing the 1977 congressional hearings, Chairman Donald Fraser observed that they were called to consider "allegations of genocide committed by the Indonesian forces against the population of East Timor," allegations which "are extremely serious both particularly in terms of the human tragedy which is depicted as well as the implications concerning both past and present U.S. policy."[130] He presented his final impressions of the last day of the hearings in the following words:

> That is, that the United States was apprised, at least in general, perhaps specifically because I think Secretary Kissinger was in Djakarta the day before the invasion, we were apprised of the intention of the Indonesian government but we made no serious objection to what they proposed to do; that as soon as the military operations, which were by the testimony of other members of the State Department at least initially quite violent, within a matter of months after the major military operations came to an end and what I would regard as a facade of self-determination was expressed, the United States immediately indicated it was satisfied with what had transpired and resumed shipments of military assistance which it never told Indonesia it was suspending. U.S. arms were used in all that and continue to be used today, there is a degree of complicity here by the United States that I really find to be quite disturbing. Even if one sets

> that aside, to write off the rights of 600,000 people because we are friends with the country that forcibly annexed them does real violence to any profession of adherence to principle or to human rights.
>
> I am deeply disappointed that this administration has continued that posture. It seems to me that on this score they have come out with a very bad rating...[131]

Some witnesses went further. Thomas M. Franck, Professor of Law at New York University Law School, stated that if the new administration, with its highly touted concern for human rights, did not reverse existing policy, "it will be adding blatant hypocrisy to earlier malevolence."[132] The policy has not been reversed, nor so far as is known, even reassessed.

Congressman Fraser's reference to past and present U.S. policy is apt. The United States has been officially involved with the Indonesian military since 1958 (the year of an abortive CIA effort to overthrow the Sukarno government). Military aid flowed generously prior to the 1965 coup. Its purpose was explained by Pentagon official Paul Warnke, a reputed dove, in congressional testimony:

> The purpose for which it was maintained was not to support an existing [i.e. the Sukarno] regime. In fact, we were opposed, eventually and increasingly to the then existing regime. It was to preserve a liaison of sorts with the military of the country which in effect turned out to be one of the conclusive elements in the overthrow of that regime.[133]

—not to speak of the subsequent massacre. The same technique was used to good advantage later in Chile under Allende. In following years the United States expanded its military aid and training of the military and police. The Country Officer for Indonesia in the State Department, David T. Kenney, is capable of saying, with a straight face, that one purpose of U.S. military aid to Indonesia is "to keep that area peaceful" (*March Hearings,* p. 19); this, in testimony on the Indonesian invasion of East Timor.

The United States attitude toward the Indonesian invasion of East Timor is explained as follows by Aldrich, speaking for the

State Department:

> My impression is that we made it clear to [the Indonesian government] that we understood the situation they were in, we understood the pressures they felt and their concern about the fighting that was going on and the potential for instability that would be caused by developments as they saw them.
>
> We certainly did make them aware, if they were not already aware, of the problems that would be posed under our law if they took action with equipment they had received from us, contrary to the agreement. But it is not my impression, and as I say I am probably not fully informed on this, but it is not my impression that we pressed them terribly hard about it. We simply told them what I suspect they already knew, that there might be problems under our military assistance laws.[134]

The evidence available supports the judgment that the United States not only took no significant action but also gave its tacit or explicit approval to the invasion. It was certainly known that an Indonesian invasion was imminent when President Ford and Henry Kissinger arrived in Jakarta; Australia had, in fact, already evacuated its nationals.[135] The invasion took place just as the U.S. visitors departed.

The official U.S. view is "that resolution of the matter would be best reached by the parties directly involved—the Indonesians, the Portuguese, and the Timorese."[136] No attempt is made to reconcile this position with certain simple and evident facts: (1) the legitimacy of the Indonesian "involvement" is precisely what is at issue, not to be assumed in advance by fiat; (2) the Portuguese strenuously opposed the Indonesian involvement and in fact broke relations with Indonesia; (3) the Timorese government that was in de facto control of the territory apart from the border areas already conquered by Indonesia certainly opposed Indonesia's invasion, with overwhelming popular support so far as is known, and continue to do so insofar as they are able to resist. One may argue about this or that detail, but there seems ample reason to accept the judgment of Jill Jolliffe that "the avowed willingness of most of the political associations formed after April 25, 1974 to now fight alongside FRETILIN [which had won handily in the brief civil war and was governing with success and popular support] epitomises the truth that the force now seeking to assert itself is that of Timorese nationalism..." (p. 297). The official U.S. government position therefore reduces to acceptance of Indonesian aggression and its consequences, whatever the attitudes of the other "parties directly involved," and surely irrespective of the attitudes of the primary party, the people of East Timor themselves.

The invasion took place while Ford and Kissinger were on their way from Jakarta to Hawaii:

> When he landed at Hawaii, reporters asked Mr. Ford for comment on the invasion of Timor. He smiled and said: "We'll talk about that later." But press secretary Ron Nessen later gave reporters a statement saying: "The United States is always concerned about the use of violence. The President hopes it can be resolved peacefully."[137]

Henry Kissinger, travelling with Ford, had already given his reactions. He "told newsmen in Jakarta that the United States would not recognize the Fretilin-declared republic and 'the United States understands Indonesia's position on the question'."[138]

As for the failure of the U.S. to take any significant action, that is sufficiently clear from the record. We have already mentioned the fraudulent "suspension" of military aid. A secret cable sent in August, 1975 from the Australian Ambassador to Indonesia, Richard Woolcott, to the head of the Australian Foreign Affairs Department was leaked to the press in May, 1976. In it, Ambassador Woolcott, recommends "a pragmatic rather than a principled stand," because "that is what national interest and foreign policy is all about": "As I stressed in Canberra last month, we are dealing with a settled Indonesian policy to incorporate Timor—as even Malik admitted to me on Friday." Recall that this was July-August, 1975; again, it is hardly credible that the United States did not receive this or comparable information. Woolcott continues:

> The United States might have some influence on Indo-

> nesia at present as Indonesia really wants and needs U.S. assistance in its military reequipment program. The State Department has, we understand, instructed the embassy to cut down its reporting on Timor. But [U.S.] Ambassador Newsom told me last night that he is under instructions from Kissinger personally not to involve himself in discussions of Timor with the Indonesians on the ground that the U.S. is involved in enough problems of greater importance overseas at present. I will be seeing Newsom on Monday, but his present attitude is that the U.S. should keep out of the Portuguese Timor situation and allow events to take their course.[139]

The U.S press, to our knowledge, has never discussed this material or its significance.

A report in the Australian press, noting that "the United States will double its military aid to Indonesia this year even while condemning Indonesia's military presence in East Timor" cites a State Department official who repeats the official view, while expressing its content a bit more clearly than usual:

> In terms of the bilateral relations between the U.S. and Indonesia, we are more or less condoning the incursion into East Timor...We don't want to make a strong stand one way or the other. The problem of East Timor is basically one for the countries involved—Indonesia, Portugal and the near neighbors, such as Australia. The United States wants to keep its relationship with Indonesia close and friendly. We regard Indonesia as a friendly, nonaligned nation—a nation we do a lot of business with.[140]

A review of U.S. behavior at the United Nations supports this assessment.[141] On December 12, 1975 the General Assembly adopted resolution 3485 (72 votes to 10, with 43 abstentions), which "*strongly deplores* the military intervention of the armed forces of Indonesia in Portuguese Timor" and "*calls upon* the Government of Indonesia to desist from further violation of the territorial integrity of Portuguese Timor and to withdraw without delay its armed forces from the Territory in order to enable the people of the Territory freely to exercise their right to self-determination and independence." Coming immediately after the Indonesian invasion, this response of the United Nations was of crucial importance. The United States abstained as did most of its European allies. There is reason to believe that the United States may have blocked support for the resolution. On January 23, 1976 UN Ambassador Daniel P. Moynihan sent a cablegram to Henry Kissinger and all U.S. embassies entitled "The Blocs are Breaking Up" in which he took pride in the "considerable progress" that had been made by U.S. arm-twisting tactics at the UN "toward a basic foreign policy goal, that of breaking up the massive blocs of nations, mostly new nations, which for so long have been arrayed against us in international forums and in diplomatic encounters generally." He specifically cited the General Assembly vote on Timor (and the Sahara—see note 149), when "the non-aligned were similarly divided in the voting."[142] Testifying before Congress, Thomas Franck commented that "the failure of 53 countries, including the United States, to support this resolution, I contend sent a clear signal to Indonesia that the United Nations lacked the political will to oppose Djakarta's action and that the United States would turn a deaf ear to the demands of the East Timorese to be accorded the benefits of the firmly established international normative right to self-determination."[143]

On December 22 the United States joined in the unanimous approval of what Franck called "a rather wishy-washy compromise resolution," Security Council resolution 384, which "*calls upon* the Government of Indonesia to withdraw without delay all its forces from the Territory." On April 22, 1976 the Security Council passed resolution 389 which repeated this demand. As the *New York Times* commented, the "language is considered ineffectual": "Many delegates and some United Nations officials said privately that the rather bland language of today's Security Council document practically meant that Indonesia was given leeway to consolidate its hold on the former Portuguese colony."[144] Nevertheless, the United States abstained, along with Japan; the resolution was passed 12 votes to none with two abstentions. As the *Times* commented, "Indonesia's stand ...was discretely backed by the United States." The United States voted against the General Assembly resolution of December 1, 1976 (passed 68 votes to 20 with 49 abstentions) which "*rejects* the claim that East Timor has been integrated into Indonesia, inasmuch as the people of the Territory have not been able to exercise freely their right to self-determination and independence." A year later the General Assembly passed a resolution (67 votes to 27, with 46 abstentions) calling on the UN Special Committee on Decolonization to send a mission to the territory. Indonesia announced that it would bar any UN mission. The United States voted against the resolution, along with Japan, Malaysia, the Philippines, Singapore and Thailand, "all of which seek close political and economic ties with Indonesia." The vote came as Indonesia was preparing a new military offensive against FRETILIN, scheduled for December 31, 1977.[145]

The UN made an attempt to carry out an on-the-spot investigation in January, 1976, after the condemnation of Indonesia in December. On December 28, Vittorio Winspeare Guicciardi was selected as UN emissary to East Timor. He visited territories controlled by the Indonesians in late January but was prevented from visiting FRETILIN-held areas, that is, almost all of East Timor. He then attempted to contact FRETILIN through a radio transmitter in Darwin, Australia; the FRETILIN representative in Darwin was immediately arrested and the transmitter seized and confiscated. New contacts were established through the radio of a Portuguese corvette in Darwin harbor, and FRETILIN named four possible landing places. Indonesian forces immediately bombed these areas and mounted a large-scale offensive at one of them. At that point the UN representative abandoned his efforts.[146]

As already noted, the U.S. has consistently attempted to shift the time of the reported massacres to the period prior to the full-scale Indonesian invasion, in conformity with the requirements of its Indonesian client, and with the cooperation of the Free Press. The U.S. estimate of "probably under 10,000" total casualties ("civilian, military, everything else"[147]) is far below any estimate offered by informed observers or even the Indonesian authorities as we shall see. The State Department further claims that though there were "some civilian casualties," these were the result of "a couple of occasions when Indonesian military units, according to our intelligence, did commit excesses in the towns against the civilian population" and "were called back to Indonesia and the commanders were punished," which "reveals ...(that)... the Indonesian Government was not deliberately setting out to do violence to the civilian population; but there were military units that got out of control and this sort of thing did take place." This effort to exonerate the Indonesian military should be compared with the detailed accounts by refugees, local priests and others to which we return, which indicate that the massacres were consistent and deliberate policy, that they were most severe outside of the few urban areas and that they continue at a frightful level until this day. As already noted, the State Department further takes the position that "Timor has effectively become a part of Indonesia" (Oakley, *March Hearings*, pp. 7,16). Thus the integration announced by the Indonesians and confirmed by a faked "people's assembly" is simply a fact.[148] "As a political matter, the United States has recognized the annexation of East Timor and the legality of the exercise of sovereignty there by the Indonesian Government" (Aldrich, *June-July Hearings*, p. 64) The United States has taken no stand, Aldrich continues, on the question whether Indonesia has violated "international standards or norms of conduct of international principles" in "the seizure and annexation of East Timor."

In response to repeated questioning by Rep. Donald Fraser, Aldrich stated that he was not "in a position to judge" the question of the adherence to international standards:

> There certainly was at the time considerable international [sic] strife and killing going on in East Timor. The Indonesians were the only country in a position to put an end to it. Whether they did it properly or did not do it properly, whether they did it with improper motives, I really do not want to go into and try to second-guess. I think that is something which scholars are better able to draw conclusions about than lawyers for the Department of State (p. 65).

Aldrich's reference to "considerable international strife" was presumably a slip of the tongue, as obvious truth overwhelmed diplomatic pretense. His statement is true in one respect; Indonesian intervention was causing strife and killing even prior to the full scale Indonesian invasion of December. To state, under these circumstances, that "the Indonesians were the only country in a position to put an end to" the strife and killing for which they alone were responsible reveals an astonishing degree of hypocrisy, even for a State Department lawyer. As for his reference to scholarship, presumably tongue-in-cheek, Aldrich need have little fear. To judge by the scholarly literature, there will be very few scholars to draw the obvious conclusions that a government functionary must repress—apart from unfortunate slips.

While the State Department professes ignorance about the facts, reserving that matter to the judgment of history, it has a clear insight into U.S. "interests." As Aldrich states, the United States did not question the incorporation of East Timor into Indonesia because it was "an accomplished fact" and "such a policy would not serve our best interests in light of the importance of our relations with Indonesia" (p. 48).

The latter qualification is of course crucial. A report by the Congressional Research Service notes that the United States has "a long history of non-recognition of territorial changes brought about by force," citing many examples and two exceptions: namely, the takeover of phosphate-rich Sahara areas by U.S.-armed and trained Moroccan forces in violation of the will of the indigenous people, and the case of East Timor.[149]

The same apparent inconsistency is stressed by Leonard Meeker, former Legal Advisor to the Department of State. He notes, for example, that "the Department of State has never recognized since 1940 the forcible incorporation of the Baltic States into the Soviet Union," an act that was not conducted by U.S.-armed troops and is surely far more irreversible than the Indonesian takeover of East Timor.[150] Asked about this matter, Aldrich replied that with regard to the Baltic states "I think we did what we thought was the right thing and we have maintained it with a steadfastness that is rare and admirable, but I am not sure that if we did the same thing with respect to East Timor it would be something that we could consider would be a useful advance on human rights."[151]

It is perhaps unfair to record the efforts to justify state policy on the part of a beleaguered functionary. What does deserve condemnation, however, is the general silence and deceit of the mass media[152] and the fact that academic scholarship so commonly refuses to see the implications and seeks to disguise them with no less miserable evasions and falsehoods.

The country officer for Indonesia in the Department of State, David T. Kenney, also presented his thoughts on the matter of integration in congressional testimony.[153] He offered the State Department judgment that "at the present time," that is, March, 1977, 9 months after "integration" about 200,000 people out of a population that he estimated at 650,000 in East Timor "would be considered in areas under Indonesian administration." This estimate by the State Department specialist on the subject contrasts sharply with the claims by the U.S. government that the war was effectively over by early 1976. Kenney was then asked by a congressman whether the "people [are] relatively happy with the fact they are now under Indonesia." He replied as follows:

> Sir, my judgment on this is they are, that given the circumstances and alternatives available to them, which were put in terms of continuing the war on the one hand or possibly Indonesian administration on the other that the people of Timor, as far as we can judge from all those we have talked to, is that they are. They have decided their best interest lies at this time, in incorporation with Indonesia.

Their "decision" was expressed in the "popular assembly" to which we have already referred. Commenting on this amazing testimony, Benedict Anderson noted that Kenney's claim "is tantamount to saying that during World War II the Filipinos decided their best interest lay in incorporation into Japan's Greater East Asian Co-Prosperity Sphere, or that the people of the Baltic states have 'decided *their* best interests lie' in incorporation into the Soviet Union"[154]—even putting aside the more than two-thirds of the population who have as yet not been able to express their "decision" because they are not under Indonesian administration. Or to put it in the terms favored by the State Department, because they are not yet "protected" by Indonesia. As State Department representative Robert Oakley explained:

> We are concerned about the situation in East Timor, and as I stated we would like to see the situation there solved, as we would any conflict, by peaceful means. This has not yet happened [N.B., by February, 1978] There has been a certain change in the situation, in that a large number of people have moved from areas that could be described either as no-man's land or under the control of Fretilin to areas where they could be *protected by the Indonesian Government.*[155]

"Protected," that is, from FRETILIN, the guerrillas who still had over two-thirds of the population under their "control" in March, 1977 according to the State Department. In short, after the U.S.-backed Indonesian military succeeds in bombing and starving the population into submission, the remnants can then "decide" to accept Indonesian administration, under the "protection" of the Indonesian Government. Once again, it would be difficult to find comparable examples of cynicism outside of the totalitarian states. As we shall see, the Free Press accepts these concepts, quite generally, when it turns to the flight of refugees from areas where they have been "forced to live" by the guerrillas.

The United States has not been content with recognizing the Indonesian conquest and ignoring the attendant massacres. It has also pressured its allies to do the same—which is not inordinately difficult, since their interests too are served by tolerating or supporting Indonesian atrocities. The Melbourne *Age* (3 August 1976) reports that "the U.S. has warned Australia not to allow further deterioration of relations with Indonesia over Timor," referring to discussions in Washington between high-ranking members of the Ford Administration and Australian Prime Minister Fraser. The front page headline reads: "Fraser given blunt warning at Washington talks: 'Don't anger Jakarta': U.S. protecting Indon channel for its N-subs." An accompanying cartoon shows President Ford admonishing Fraser, saying "With the bodies of the East Timorese ... we can balance Russia's military might." The story explains that the fastest and safest passage for U.S. nuclear submarines from the Pacific to the Indian Oceans is through the deep water straits north of Timor island, and if this passage were denied by Indonesian action, under its "long-proclaimed archipelagic concept," the submarine journey between Guam and the

Indian Ocean Diego Garcia outpost would be lengthened by 8-10 days. Meanwhile Russian submarines must use "the shallow and overcrowded Straits of Malacca and Singapore, where they have to surface in order to pass through safely," which may explain why the USSR has "kept its criticism of the East Timor annexation to a minimum." Russian interest in sharing in Indonesia's wealth is no doubt also a major if not the major reason for Russian silence, as is also true with regard to Iran, Argentina, and other resource-rich subfascist client states in the U.S. global system. The article continues: "Observers believe the strategic location of East Timor is one reason why the US Administration has readily acquiesced to Indonesia's takeover of the disputed Portuguese colony and to its campaign to crush the Left-wing Fretilin independence movement."

Southeast Asian correspondent Michael Richardson took up the same theme (Melbourne *Age*, 4 August, 1976). Noting U.S. warnings to Australia with regard to criticisms of Indonesia issued through diplomatic channels in Canberra, Richardson asserts that "US officials in South-East Asia confirmed the warning followed two high-powered academic assessments of the importance of Indonesian waterways in current US nuclear strategy," one by Robert E. Osgood of the Johns Hopkins School of Advanced International Studies (closely linked to the State Department) and the other by Michael McCgwire, Professor of Maritime and Strategic Studies at Canada's Dalhousie University. "In terms of America's ready acquiescence in Indonesia's takeover of Portuguese Timor," Richardson adds, "it is significant that the Ombai-Wetar narrows [one of two straits that would fall under Indonesian control under proposals being considered at the UN Law of the Sea conference] are in the eastern half of the island between it and the island of Atauro." These two straits are the only ones (apart from Gibraltar) "through which [the U.S.] needs passage to reach Soviet targets and for which [it] cannot count on Allied permission." Richardson asserts that U.S. officials in Southeast Asia have confirmed these assessments concerning the crucial strategic role of the straits "for the projection of military force from the Pacific into the Indian Ocean" (McCgwire). Richardson reported (*Age*, 5 August, 1976) that Western intelligence sources are apprehensive about the possibility that the USSR might offer to resume the military aid terminated with the 1965 coup, assisting Indonesia's reorganization of its armed forces begun in 1971 with U.S. and Australian assistance, with the aim of making them "more mobile and effective for dealing with insurgency, regional uprisings and foreign infiltration." Particularly important are ground transport vehicles and helicopters, since supplied by the United States and employed effectively in Timor. Actually more is at stake. The straits near Timor are important for the passage of supertankers. Furthermore, as FRETILIN has been claiming for years, the area between Timor and Australia is potentially rich in oil. This is confirmed by Michael Richardson in the *Far Eastern Economic Review* (5 January 1979) in a discussion of conflicts between Indonesia and Australia over the seabed boundary. He notes that the disputed zone is believed to be "part of a very promising offshore oil and natural gas province. The petroleum companies have certainly been queueing up to start a multi-million dollar search," including a U.S. oil company that had "planned to start initial reconnaissance and seismic exploration in 1975" but was delayed by the war. The potential oil wealth has bearing on the claim by the *New York Times* (see pp. 146-47) and others that East Timor would not be economically viable, on the relations between Australia and Indonesia, and on Indonesia's efforts to conquer East Timor with the backing of the industrial democracies.

The *Washington Post* also took note of U.S. concern over the dispute between Australia and Indonesia.[156] "The last thing American diplomats in the area want is a split between the two friends, especially one that current Australian emotions could force into a confrontation in which Washington would be asked to choose sides." The reference to [Australian] "emotions" relates to Australia's concern "that the Indonesian invasion of East Timor is part of a pattern of military expansion by their most powerful neighbor" and to the call for an inquiry into the death of the five journalists in October, 1975. The report notes that José Martins, formerly a Timorese collaborator with Indonesia, "last week gave a detailed version of how the Australians were gunned down by Indonesian troops."[157] What was particularly "infuriating for Australians" was a statement by Indonesian Foreign Minister Malik who "proposed a very Asian answer to the problem of the five journalists' deaths"[158]: "'Let us forget them,' he told a press conference in Jakarta attended by Australian correspondents, 'and we will erect a monument to them.'"

In the *March Hearings*, the most informed and extended testimony was that of James Dunn, who was consul to Portuguese Timor from 1962 to 1964, a member of a fact-finding mission sent by the Australian government to assess the situation after the Portuguese coup ("during the period for which the State Department claims not to have much information"; Dunn) and also led an aid mission in October and November, 1975 "between the beginning of the covert Indonesian attacks, as we chose to call it in Australia, and the events of December, 1975."[159]

After a brief review of the bare facts, Dunn turned to his main topic, the atrocities following the December invasion. "According to accounts from Timorese refugees in Portugal, some of whom were in East Timor at the time of the attack, information from Chinese refugees in Taiwan and Australia, and reports from within Indonesia itself, the move to annex this territory has been a brutal operation, marked by the wanton slaughter of possibly between 50,000 and 100,000 Timorese, by extensive looting and by other excesses such as rape and torture." He submitted a detailed memorandum, published in the *March Hearings* (pp. 31-38) on his interviews with Timorese refugees in Portugal in January, 1977 during a visit made at the initiative of non-governmental agencies including the Australian Catholic Relief and Community Aid Abroad, who funded the trip.

These refugees, Dunn points out, are nearly all supporters of the conservative UDT party. Dunn interviewed about 200 of the 1500 Timorese refugees in Portugal, including more than half of the approximately 25 who had spent some time in East Timor after the invasion. "All accounts of the Indonesian military action against East Timor, and conditions under Indonesian occupation until as late as September, 1976, portrayed a grim picture of the situation in the territory. Even in Indonesian Timor, the Timorese refugees virtually became prisoners in the camps set up by the Indonesians" and were deprived of medical facilities and frequently humiliated, suffering many deaths.[160] Dunn says that he urged the refugees "not to exaggerate or distort their stories," but "without exception, however, they related stories of excesses by Indonesian troops," including people who claimed to have witnessed the incidents and "prominent Timorese who had not been involved in the politics of East Timor, and who had not initially been strongly opposed to 'integration'." "According to informants, many of the Indonesian troops killed indiscriminately from the beginning of their attack on Dili [the capital city]. However, several prominent Timorese said that the killing in the mountain areas was far more extensive than it was in Dili. In the mountain areas, they claimed, whole villages were wiped out as Indonesian troops advanced into the interior." There follow detailed and specific accounts of mass murder, rape, looting, starvation. Refugees consistently agreed that a figure of 100,000 killed was "credible, because of the widespread killing in the mountains [where most of the population lives] and because of the extensive bombing," reportedly including napalm.

Dunn summarizes these interviews by stating that the plight of the Timorese "might well constitute, relatively speaking, the most serious case of contravention of human rights facing the world at this time."

Dunn noted in testimony that there are other corroboratory sources (to which we return), including letters from Chinese in Taiwan and Darwin, one of which alleged that 80% of the Chinese (a community that tended to be pro-Indonesian and that monopolized wealth and commerce) may have been killed by the Indonesians.[161] His account of refugee and other reports appears to be careful and judicious to an extent that is unusual for the genre. He insists that people not accept his account but rather use it as motivation for investigating the reports of refugees directly to check the authenticity of what he has discovered. The refugees in Lisbon, Dunn comments, "fully support my presence here and they would like to present witnesses themselves if this committee was prepared to give them an opportunity to do so"—which of course it was not; the only Timorese permitted to appear before Congress were those selected by the Indonesian invaders. Dunn is neither pro-FRETILIN nor anti-Indonesian, and indeed urged that "it is very important that Indonesia should get as much assistance as possible to meet its development problems." It is doubtful that there is another Westerner who is in a comparable position to present an objective and dispassionate assessment.

Representative Fraser asked the State Department Representative Robert Oakley whether the State Department or any of its agencies had attempted to interview the refugees in Portugal. Oakley responded that they had not.[162] The Free Press maintains the same discipline. There are reports on the Timorese refugees in Portugal, but their experiences in Timor are carefully avoided. Marvine Howe interviewed refugees in Portugal in October, 1976.[163] She writes that "about 40,000 Timorese fled the civil war in East Timor last year and took refuge in West Timor..." She repeats the apparently exaggerated State Department figures (see note 160) and, typically, refers only to the "civil war." The sole reference to Indonesia is that life in Indonesian West Timor was hard. To appreciate the significance of this report, and the general avoidance of the crucial issue that it exemplifies, one must place it in context of the massive effort by the Free Press to elicit any information from refugees that might possibly be incriminating or negative with regard to Indochina.[164]

We return directly to Dunn's reception by the congressional committee and the press reaction, which offer an interesting contrast to the response to testimony on human rights violations outside of the U.S. sphere of influence. But first, it is worth noting that even prior to Dunn's testimony there was evidence that something rather disturbing was underway in Timor. The *New York Times* (15 February, 1976) had published a report that 60,000 people had been killed in East Timor, 10% of the population. This report appeared on page 11 at the bottom of a column below a story on another subject, and merited all of 150 words. This single reference to an ongoing massacre should, once again, be compared to the vast outpouring of denunciation and horror with regard to "genocide" or "autogenocide" in Cambodia, beginning immediately after the U.S.-backed government was deposed and continuing with mounting intensity thereafter. The most extreme allegations offered by those who have actually investigated atrocities estimate the numbers killed at about 100,000 out of a population of 7-8 million, though many other figures have been bandied about freely in the Western media. See Volume II, Chapter 6, for detailed analysis. As we shall see, the sources offering these estimates are of extremely low credibility; comparable work critical of Western actions would be dismissed out of hand. Furthermore, the analysts are uniformly hostile to the Cambodian Communists, whereas the estimates on Indonesian atrocities derive from pro-Indonesian sources (e.g. the Indonesian government itself and Indonesian church officials) or independent analysts whose work has received no critical challenge from those who ignore or disparage it. But even if we accept the estimates by these hostile critics of the Cambodian regime at face value, the comparison to Timor gives a revealing indication of the overwhelming bias and ideological commitment of the Western media.

A more careful look at the 150 words that the *Times* devoted to the reported killing of 60,000 people in Timor reveals the duplicity of the Free Press with still greater clarity. The *Times* report of February, 1976 reads as follows:

> About 60,000 people have been killed since the outbreak of civil war in Portuguese Timor last August, according to the deputy chairman of the territory's provisional government... "The war is virtually over because only a few remnants of the Fretilin forces are fighting in the jungles or hills," Francisco Xavier Lopez da Cruz said. He referred to the Revolutionary Front for Independent East Timor, which has been fight [sic] forces favoring union with Indonesia.

Apart from the estimate of numbers killed, this is simply a handout from the Indonesian propaganda agencies. Da Cruz was Deputy Governor of the puppet regime installed by the Indonesians after the invasion.[165] In the civil war of August-September, 1975, perhaps 2,000-3,000 were killed; the remainder of the estimated 60,000 were victims of Indonesian intervention, primarily the murderous attack of December 7, 1975 and subsequently. The statement by the *Times* that FRETILIN has been fighting forces favoring union with Indonesia is on a par with a (hypothetical) statement by the Nazi press that the French resistance in 1944 has been fighting forces favoring occupation by Germany. The forces "favoring union with Indonesia" had been defeated in September and had played no significant part in the subsequent fighting. These forces did not, in fact, favor such union for the most part, certainly not prior to their defeat and probably not thereafter, if we discount the effects of Indonesian coercion. As for da Cruz's statement that the war is virtually over, that bears comparison with the *Times* headline of December 8 already cited: "Indonesians Hold Portuguese Timor After Incursion," when in fact the Indonesians held the capital city of Dili after an invasion. As we write, the war continues, with thousands of new Indonesian troops dispatched.[166]

But let us leave this testimony to the Freedom of the Press and return to Dunn's testimony and the response to it. The testimony was evidently available in advance to reporters, and a fair factual account of its contents appeared in the *Washington Post*[167] when Rep. Fraser announced the hearings. The *New York Times* carried a briefer story by Bernard Gwertzman,[168] referring to Dunn's testimony but giving no details and also noting the State Department belief that "the reports of atrocities have been greatly exaggerated" though "we know very little"—a curious pair of comments—and that Indonesia had taken "significant steps to minimize possible use of American equipment in the East Timor operation," an evident absurdity given the armaments available, not to speak of the direct reports of the invasion. Gwertzman does not question the remark, but merely notes that "under United States law, a country is prohibited from using American equipment secured under the military sales program for operations not based on legitimate self-defense," drawing no conclusions. Keeping close to the State Department line, Gwertzman describes the background as follows:

> When Portugal withdrew from East Timor in 1975, a civil war broke out between leftists seeking independence; pro-Indonesian troops intervened and are believed to have effectively crushed the so-called Fretilin movement. Last July East Timor was incorporated into Indonesia.

Comparing this with the facts, the civil war was not between leftists seeking independence, and Portugal withdrew during, not before, the civil war. Furthermore, and more important, it was not "pro-Indonesian troops" that intervened but rather the Indonesian army. And still more important because of the policy consequences, even the State Department did not believe that the Indonesian army had effectively crushed the resistance, as we see from Kenney's testimony in the hearings already cited. What is more, the report by Dunn, which was evidently available to Gwertzman, maintained that resistance continues and that "Fretilin troops have been joined by UDT and Apodeti supporters and their extensive guerrilla operations seem to have limited effective Indonesian control to no more than 20% of the territory of East Timor" (*March Hearings*, pp. 31-32), a point that Gwertzman does not mention. The point is significant. For as we have noted, the pretense that whatever unfortunate events may have occured, now it is all over, has been used throughout by the U.S. government as justification for its military and diplomatic support for Indonesian aggression with its continuing large-scale atrocities.

In short, Gwertzman's account satisfies all the state's requirements for a "newspaper of record."

As these references indicate, despite the consistent distortion of the facts in the service of U.S. propaganda, enough information was available to alert people concerned with human rights that something quite extraordinary might have taken place with tacit or direct U.S. backing, and that these terrible events might be continuing.

But the story quickly died. The *New York Times* interviewed Dunn, but ran nothing. There were scattered news stories, before and since. AP reported from Canberra that six members of the Australian Parliament (Labor) sent a report to the international relations committee of the House of Representatives alleging that possibly 100,000 had been killed and asking it to investigate the charges.[169] The AP report—typical for the U.S. press—repeated the Indonesian propaganda line concerning the invasion ("Indonesia annexed the eastern half of Timor island, which is in the Indonesian archipelago, last July after a civil war in which Indonesian forces helped a pro-Indonesian faction defeat a faction favoring independence"), but the report did at least mention the charges and also the *Dunn Report* which was submitted at the same time to Congress. The *New York Times* ran a 9-line Reuters dispatch (1 March 1977) on a petition to President Carter by 94 members of the Australian Parliament "charging atrocities by Indonesian troops" and asking Mr. Carter "to comment publicly on the situation in East Timor"—naively no doubt, in view of the role played by Indonesia in the U.S. system.[170] But 9 lines was evidently considered too much for a topic of such meager interest. The story did not make it to the *New York Times* index because it was deleted from the Late City Edition, which is the newspaper of record for microfilm; *Times* editors and correspondents are much too busy seeking evidence of Communist atrocities to bother with the possible massacre of 100,000 Timorese at the hands of a U.S. client using United States arms.

Robert Shaplen, the Asia correspondent of the *New Yorker,* commented briefly on East Timor in his "Letter from Indonesia," December 12, 1977. According to his reconstruction of history, "Indonesian troops intervened, somewhat crudely and clumsily, in December of 1975, in a war for independence which the East Timorese were ostensibly waging against Portugal." The idea that the East Timorese were fighting Portugal is a novel contribution, but the reference to the massacre of perhaps tens of thousands of people as a somewhat crude and clumsy intervention is about par for the course for the Free Press. Shaplen continues: "the so-called Fight for Freedom had turned into a civil war among five factions, one of which, the left-wing Fretilin, objected strenuously to the manner in which Indonesian troops moved in to take over the former colony." Comment seems unnecessary. "According to neutral observers," Shaplen continues, "some ten thousand East Timorese, including many civilians, were killed by the Indonesian forces..." In fact, "neutral observers"—Dunn for example, and others to whom we return, who are in fact not "neutral" but pro-Indonesian or anti-FRETILIN—have consistently given figures in the range of 50-100,000 killed, and only the U.S. State Department has offered estimates of "some ten thousand" killed. Shaplen's reference to "neutral observers" suggests that he is simply passing "information" from some U.S. government contact, not an untypical technique on the part of the more unscrupulous correspondents. Shaplen then explains that the estimated 600 FRETILIN guerrillas "control parts of the forbidding countryside, with the help of thousands of ordinary villagers whom they induced, by force or persuasion, to take to the hills with them"—that FRETILIN might have genuine popular support for its resistance to Indonesian aggression is excluded on doctrinal grounds. He concludes finally that the Indonesians "don't seem particularly perturbed by the criticisms" that they receive from "many Third World nations," which is natural, given the support they receive from the powers that count and from journalists of the calibre of Robert Shaplen; and Suharto has announced that "on December 31st, the Army will start a new campaign against the guerrillas," a matter that is of little concern to this observer or his colleagues in the Free Press. We discuss below the consequences of this "new campaign," as experienced by the people whose fate Shaplen so lightly dismisses.

One final example of the kind of report that occasionally graces the pages of the U.S. press is a Reuters dispatch from Dili, based on a guided tour, in the *Los Angeles Times* (27 September 1978), explaining that "although the scars of the bitter civil war that preceded the merging of East Timor into Indonesia are still visible on its buildings, this little seaside capital seems to have recovered surprisingly well from its ordeal." The discussion of the "civil war" continues as follows: "After the Portuguese colonial rulers departed in December, 1975, pro-Indonesian forces, later aided by regular Indonesian troops, defeated left-wing Fretilin independence guerrillas in an eight-month civil war." But now things are quite happy under the peaceful rule of "Gov. Arnaldo dos Reis Araujo, who spent 29 years in jail as a subversive element under Portuguese rule" (see note 88, above). Again, comment is hardly required.

A rare exception to the general tendency to bury the issue as quickly as possible is a report from Washington by Richard Dudman.[171] Dudman notes correctly that "amid all the talks about human rights, the country with perhaps the worst record has been getting increasing amounts of economic and military aid from the Carter administration." He discusses Indonesia's horrendous record with regard to political prisoners and reports that Indonesia has been placed by Carter's policymakers in a "not-to-be-criticized" category because of the "bonanza enjoyed by American oil companies and multi-national corporations since the present military regime came to power in 1965," citing Kohen's *Nation* article (see note 80). Turning to the Indonesian invasion, he points out that "aggression was thus converted into suppression of an insurgency, and continuing U.S. military aid could have a facade of legality." Dudman's report, unique to our knowledge in its willingness to cite crucial sources that are beyond the pale for establishment journalism—for example, the delegation of the Democratic Republic of East Timor that has participated in UN debate—and to consider the U.S. role, suffices to show that it was not beyond the capacity of correspondents and commentators to investigate the Timor issue, had their ideological and institutional constraints allowed them to do so.

The congressional reaction to Dunn's testimony was even more appalling than the unconcern in the press. Chairman Fraser apart, most of the questioning was hostile and abusive. Rep. Burke attacked Dunn's credibility, asking "under whose auspices are you here in the United States" (unfortunately for Burke, the answer was that his sponsors were relief agencies supported by Catholic Relief and the Australian Council of Churches) and dismissing his testimony as "hearsay" and "allegations you don't know any more about," whereas "our job...is for us to try to get the truth, not just hearsay or not just talk." Dunn's testimony was indeed "hearsay". As he stressed, he was not himself an eyewitness to Indonesian atrocities during a period when Timor was closed to all outsiders, including even the International Red Cross, and he therefore urged vainly that direct witnesses be called to check the accuracy of his reports. Burke's standards, we need hardly add, are never invoked in the case of alleged atrocities committed by enemies of the state for which he serves as a minor propagandist.

Rep. Goodling (see note 128) went still further, beginning his interrogation by saying that "if I would say I am happy that you are here I would not be telling the truth...I wish you had not been invited because of the political implications." He insinuated that Dunn was repeating FRETILIN propaganda and dismissed Indonesian atrocities as "some indiscretion of the part of a certain unit and they were called on the carpet for that. They were removed. That is past history." He also cited Indonesian claims that Dunn "is vindictive because he has been expelled from East Timor," which Dunn denied. These questions exhausted the concerns of the members of the committee, apart from Fraser and a brief intervention by Rep. Meyner. Goodling later referred to "the fairy tales and the fiction by Jim Dunn"[172] (an attempt at "humor," he later claimed), and dismissed "this Jim Dunn bit here" as contrary to his experience in the staged tour noted earlier.[173] Goodling's further remarks consist of apologetics relying on

Indonesian propaganda, combined with pleas that "I am accused of trying to be too consistent and too realistic...I say all the time that if we are going to talk about human rights one place, let us do it all the places."[174] Thc spectacle was generally disgraceful, and, as noted, contrasts remarkably with the eagerness to seize upon any scrap of evidence of abuses committed by those who have freed themselves from U.S. control, a matter to which we will return in Volume II.

There is substantial evidence corroborating Dunn's testimony based on his extensive interviews with anti-FRETILIN refugees in Portugal. In the *Dunn Report* (p. 108), it is noted that an Indonesian church official who visited East Timor in September, 1976 had been skeptical about a massacre reaching a level of 10% of the population (60,000 people) but added that "when I asked the two fathers (priests) in Dili, they replied that according to their estimate the figure of people killed may reach to 100,000." "This figure certainly does seem exaggerated," Dunn comments, "but it nevertheless came from the Church in East Timor which is more likely to make a frank and objective assessment of the overall social situation than the other authorities involved in the territory." Dunn himself regards the most accurate figure of those massacred as between 50,000-60,000 after the first year of war, and cites various estimates to that effect.

Among those who have offered figures in this range is Indonesian Foreign Minister Adam Malik, as briefly noted in the *Far Eastern Economic Review* (15 April 1977). A fuller account appears in the Australian press. The Melbourne *Age* (1 April 1977) quotes Malik as saying that "50,000 people or perhaps 80,000 might have been killed during the war in Timor, but we saved 600,000 of them." Australian state radio commented that "The [U.S.] State Department is clearly embarrassed by Adam Malik's statement that the number killed in East Timor might have been as high as 80,000." The Washington Bureau of Australian radio tried to obtain a reaction from the State Department to the question of how Malik's estimate relates to their own figures of 2-3000 or perhaps 10,000 killed, but received no answer for 24 hours. A State Department official finally said that they had been unable to obtain information on the Malik statement from Jakarta but "if it is true that Malik said this he is wrong."[175] Nothing about any of this seems to have appeared in the United States.

An AAP-Reuter dispatch from Jakarta in the *Canberra Times* (1 April 1977) quotes Malik as follows, referring to killings in the "civil war":

> The total may be 50,000, but what does this mean if compared with 600,000 people who want to join Indonesia? Then what is the big fuss. It is possible that they may have been killed by Australians and not us. Who knows? It was war.[176]

The claim that Australians may have been responsible for the killings in East Timor was apparently too much even for the U.S. State Department, generally a loyal purveyor of Indonesian propaganda; it is not known to have publicized this allegation. Putting it aside, Malik's admission that the total killed may be 50,000 or perhaps 80,000—about 10% of the population, but no big fuss—is of some significance. The silence accorded it in the Western press contrasts interestingly with the massive publicity accorded an alleged admission of atrocities by a high Cambodian official, which appears to be a propaganda fabrication; see Volume II, chapter 6.

The occasional lapses into veracity on the part of its Indonesian client have been a constant embarrassment to the U.S. government, which understands more clearly the need for *consistent* duplicity, particularly in a period of pretended concern for "human rights." While the media can be trusted to stay fairly close to the party line, leakage is always possible in a system that lacks overt totalitarian controls, and it may prove embarrassing if the Indonesian government speaks out too openly about the scale of its massacres. Hence the State Department's concern over Malik's straightforward admission, though the Department need not have been concerned in this case, since the U.S. media respected the need for silence. Similar problems arise regularly because of the legislation requiring the State Department to submit "human rights" reports to Congress. As we observe throughout this volume, this legislation requires constant deception since obvious problems would arise for an administration that preaches about human rights if the truth were to be told about the actual practices of its client states. Sooner or later, some journalists might comment on the fact that the "human rights administration" is indeed "adding blatant hypocrisy to earlier malevolence," as Thomas Franck had warned (see p. 154, above). In the case of Indonesia, the problem was squarely faced in the first of the State Department attempts to conform to the legislation. Just as the State Department had to inform Australian state radio that the Indonesian foreign minister was wrong in his account of what Indonesian forces had accomplished in East Timor, so it brazenly tells Congress that "as many as 100,000 people were killed" in the 1965 coup in Indonesia, only a few months after the Indonesian chief of security, Admiral Sudomo, had estimated the number of people massacred at half a million.[177]

The Melbourne *Age* reported from Canberra that "a highly confidential report handed to the Government claims that at least 60,000 Timorese have been killed since Indonesian forces invaded East Timor."[178] This confidential document, reportedly prepared by independent relief workers who visited East Timor, and smuggled out of Indonesia, "is regarded by government officials as one of the most authentic first-hand accounts of the situation in East Timor since Indonesian troops invaded the Portuguese colony late last year." The same report is cited by Michael Richardson, Southeast Asia correspondent for the *Age*, on the anniversary of the Indonesian invasion.[179] He states that this document "contains probably the most authentic information we are likely to get about the balance of forces and the state of popular feeling in East Timor, where access for outsiders is severely restricted by the Indonesian authorities." He also attributes it to "independent relief workers" who visited Timor in September. "For anyone with an ounce of conscience—and that should include members of the Australian Government—the disclosures made in the report must be profoundly disturbing," he concludes, summarizing its contents.

The significance of this report increases when we discover that the source is not independent relief workers but rather Indonesian church officials who are strongly anti-FRETILIN and pro-"integration," as the document indicates.[180] This fact underscores the significance of the estimate of 100,000 killed reported by the two Fathers in Dili to the visiting Indonesian Catholic officials. In the document, FRETILIN is described as a minority party, dominated by Communists from Lisbon University in Portugal—

the position of official Indonesian propaganda, denied by independent sources (see above, p. 134 and note 86). But the Indonesian church officials warn that the alleged "desire to integrate with Indonesia is beginning to cool off because of bad experience with the occupying forces. (Stealing, robbery, burning houses, violating girls, etc.)." As an example, they cite a town in which 5,000 people allegedly welcomed "the Indonesian troops"[181] whereas now there remain only 1,000 people in the village, the rest having joined FRETILIN in the mountains. "If this is an exceptional case, then it will be not so bad, but if this is a symptom of the real situation, then it is very bad," they comment. They also report that of the 30,000 people in the occupied capital (Dili), 20,000 want to leave for Portugal while others are "with the Fretilin in the mountains so that in fact the real town people of Dili [sic] numbers only a couple of thousands not counting the Indonesian soldiers"—an interesting observation, given that Dili is widely regarded as the major area where there may have been initial support for the Indonesian invaders on the part of some segments of the population. They go on to describe how difficult it is "to start rehabilitation program because the people we intended to help are still in the mountains"—i.e., with FRETILIN. They describe the Indonesian-imposed East Timor Government as "without any authority," "only a puppet government for the military commander," and indicate that FRETILIN is "now" treating the people well (having "changed its tactic") and is said to be so popular that it would win in a real referendum. They also report that "80 percent of the territory is not under direct control of the Indonesian military forces," with 500,000 people "not under their control." They also report rumors that FRETILIN is supplied ("men and material") from Australia and describe how "villagers steal and rob" under FRETILIN control. The document is interesting as evidence of how the situation is viewed by Indonesian and Timorese Catholic circles strongly opposing FRETILIN and committed to "integration."

This report was described as "significant and disturbing" by the Federal Parliament's Legislative Research Service which examined it and prepared an assessment for MPs. According to the assessment (cited above, p. 130), "information from earlier reports adds substantially to the mounting evidence that the

Indonesians have been carrying out a brutal operation in East Timor," involving "indiscriminate killing on a scale unprecedented in post-World War 2 history."[182]

Church sources have continued to plead for some help or at least attention from the West. A Catholic priest in East Timor managed to have a letter smuggled to Portugal by two nuns, former Dominican missionaries.[183] In this letter, dated November, 1977 and translated from Portuguese, the priest writes that from the December 7 invasion until February, 1976, Indonesian warships bombarded the hills around Dili 24 hours a day while helicopters and military aircraft flew over the country and "inland there are countless tanks and armored cars." He estimates the Indonesian troop level at 50,000:

> In December 76 there was an intense movement in the Dili harbor, unloading war materials and troops. From last December the war was intensified. The war planes dont stop all day long. There are hundreds of human beings who die daily. The bodies are food for the vultures. If bullets dont kill us we die from epidemic disease, villages completely destroyed....Fretilin troops who surrender are shot dead: for them there are no jails. The genocide will be soon: it seems it is next December.

Recall the testimony of Robert Oakley, Deputy Assistant Secretary for East Asian and Pacific Affairs, Department of State, on March 23, 1977: The situation in Timor "today is fairly calm," with a "low level of insurgency" and "very few civilian casualties," surely no more of those occasional "excesses" which were "punished" in the early stages; most of the violence "took place during the period between August, 1975 and March, 1976."[184] It is hardly conceivable that the U.S.-supplied Indonesian forces operate without U.S. knowledge. According to the U.S. legal code, "false, fictitious or fraudulent statements or representations" by government officials in the area of their jurisdiction constitute a crime punishable by heavy fines or imprisonment, a fact that might be brought to the attention of the highly selective contemporary advocates of "law and order."[185] In this case, false representations by the State Department contribute directly to the crimes described by the despairing Catholic priest in Timor, sending his message to the void.

Returning to the letter smuggled to Portugal, the priest writes that the Bishop has resigned and church buildings have been destroyed. The economy, such as it is, has become one of "cabarets and brothels"—reminiscent of Saigon afflicted by the U.S. plague. The people oppose integration, but those "controlled by the Indonesians are like mild sheep that you take to the abattoir because of the oppressive character of the Indonesians"—an image that may also arouse memories in a Western conscience now intrigued by another holocaust that aroused little concern or reaction when it might have mattered. Timor was not "liberated from 'communism'. It was given to islamic indonesians."

The latter comment evoked a response in Australia. "Anti-Christian elements supported by the military were openly persecuting Christians and the Church in East Timor, a Federal Liberal MP [Michael Hodgman] said yesterday," the press reported.[186] "It appalls me that we can be so hypocritical and so morally apathetic," he said, referring to the letter from the Catholic priest, which has somehow entirely escaped the keen and inquiring eye of the U.S. press.

The priest's letter ends with an appeal for help:

> Do something positive for the liberation of the Timor people. The world ignores us and it is a pity. We are on the way to a genocide. Till the end of December the war is to exterminate. All the valid youth of Timor is in the bush. The indonesians only control villages in a radius of one to two kilometers. Ask the justice loving people to save Timor and pray to God to forgive the sins of the people of Timor.

The appeal was in vain. The "justice loving people" of the West to whom the priest's appeal was addressed were spared the pain of reading it. Western governments and the Free Press cannot be troubled by the actions of an important business partner and source of needed raw materials; their outrage is confined to offenders who threaten disturbance of the Free World system. Apart from the minuscule left-wing press, we know of no more attention to this letter in the U.S. than to other evidence of genocidal acts of our loyal ally, certainly no expression of indignation.[187]

Australian Labor Parliamentarian Ken Fry published extracts from a letter of a resident in Dili, also apparently from Catholic sources.[188] The letter appeals to the recipient to "tell my son that for nothing on this earth should he return to Timor. I would rather die without seeing him again than to know that he had returned to this hell." He describes an open-air Mass conducted in Dili by the apostolic Nuncio of Jakarta in October: "The ceremony was responsible for a great wave of emotion to evolve, made manifest in the tears, the cries, and in the sobbing of the orphans, the widows, and the forsaken, so much so that the Mass was interrupted for a quarter of an hour....It would certainly have been difficult to find some one from amongst all of these people who had not had a relative killed, or unheard of, or a prisoner in one of the Indonesian dungeons... Timor is no longer Timor; it is nothing but an oppressed worm." In the streets of Dili one sees no one but Indonesian soldiers and Chinese: "there are very few Timorese for the majority is either in the forest, dead or in jail." Most government personnel have been sent to Jakarta, "And in the meantime, their wives, who have been left behind, are systematically raped by the Indonesian soldiers who do as they please, taking no heed of their superior officers." Again the letter ends with a plea:

> Is the free world going to continue to pretend to ignore the drama of Timor? And will we have to go on watching the sad sight of the Government of our country shaking off the shackles of responsibility? Let there at least be a little respect for the suffering of so many innocent people!

It should be noted that much of the cited material on Indonesian atrocities derives from element of the small urban elite that were initially disposed to accept Indonesian "integration," some with resignation. The bulk of the population is rural, non-Christian, voiceless here as elsewhere, and generally disregarded.[189]

Jill Jolliffe, reporting from Lisbon, presents another letter smuggled from East Timor telling of "a continuing 'hot' war in the mountains, and...widespread starvation, disease and death." The letter was not written for publication, but is a personal letter to friends, "and is thus an unselfconscious personal account of life in Timor as the writer sees it" (Jolliffe). The letter, published in the *Nation Review* (4-10 August 1978) describes the situation as of late 1977 and 1978. It tells of family and friends, one who had a baby "born in the confusion of the bombardment, when they were forced to go to the bush...for almost two months," others whose children had died of starvation "in conditions tragic enough." "As they proceeded in front of the bombing and shooting, only those who could survived. The wounded and dead were abandoned and left for the dogs." Still others "were driven from their home by Indonesian forces, supported by bombing," in January, 1978. "Many elements of the population were killed under inhuman conditions of bombardment and starvation....The waters of the river were filled with blood and bodies. Great was the tragedy people endured during their escape. Husbands, fathers, brothers and abandoned wives, sons and brothers, all in the same agony." Other relatives mentioned "are very thin, skeletons, from the bad times they had in the bush. That they did not die is a miracle. The time they spent in the bush has left them sad and emotional, reflecting on the drama that the Timorese people suffer in the bush: hunger, nakedness, sickness, the continual pounding of bombing and shooting." The letter continues:

> Pray much for us. The war will last indefinitely. Twelve search bombers effect a daily bombardment. The war in the south, near the sea, pounds the earth with artillery fire. The war is conducted with armoured cars numbering in the hundreds and the support of the army, of around 70,000 men in operations in all the territory....[190] But these truths are hidden from the outside world. The ICRC is forbidden to enter Timor also, as any foreign delegation must be authorised by the Jakarta government.... We are threatened by illness and disease, as until now we don't have preventative vaccines (after three years of war!) Medicines are rare. Pray for us that God will quickly send away this scourge of war. The mountains shake with the bombardment. The earth talks with the blood of the people, who die miserably...

The writer, presumably a member of the educated elite, is describing the situation long after the war has ended and the population is now being "protected" by the Indonesians from the depredations of the fierce Marxist guerrillas, according to the version approved in the West, where the industrial powers, great and small, are eagerly seeking to sell arms to Indonesia so that they too can participate in these glorious accomplishments,[191] while the Free Press maintains its silence. Though again, not entirely. Recall Robert Shaplen's breezy commentary on the impending invasion of December, 1977 (p. 172-73, above). The letter we have just reviewed describes its consequences.

The *Australian* (8 October 1977) carried a UP dispatch from Singapore reporting that "30,000 Indonesian troops are still roaming East Timor slaying men, women and children in an attempt to end the persistent but hopeless liberation war." The report is based on the account of French photo-journalist Denis Reichle of *Paris Match*, who was deported from Timor after his arrest by Indonesian soldiers when "he was photographing West Timoreans dancing and cheering around a military truck carrying scores of corpses which were paraded through the garrison town of Atambua as slain communists from East Timor." His cameras and film were destroyed, including the results of a six-day visit to a mountain retreat of FRETILIN in East Timor. Reichle gives "a safe estimate" of 70,000-75,000 East Timorese killed by the Indonesians in 18 months of combat. The Indonesians, he reports, do not seek combat with FRETILIN forces but "were 'systematically wiping out' the populations of villages known or suspected to be Fretilin supporters and destroying Fretilin supply lines and sources." "He said Catholic missionaries, led by the Bishop of Atambua [West Timor], were the only voices in Timor trying to stop the 'systematic killing-off of East Timorese'." The Bishop, he said, "had been trying to get an interview with Indonesia's President Suharto for 2½ months, but his requests had so far been ignored." He reported that "a German priest had been driven insane by the constant killings in his area."

Unable to provide food and medical treatment to a population of half a million under the circumstances described, FRETILIN has been encouraging refugees to move to Indonesian-controlled areas, Dunn reports: "It was therefore not surprising to learn that many of the population were encouraged by Fretilin to return to towns and villages under Indonesian control."[192]

It is interesting to see how this population movement is interpreted in the U.S. press in one of its rare references to Timor. (Recall the review of diminishing *New York Times* coverage, p. 151 above). Henry Kamm, the *New York Times* specialist on Communist atrocities in Southeast Asia,[193] reported that "foreign sources give credence to Indonesian reports of a heavy flow of refugees to regions firmly in Government hands." Explaining this refugee flow, Kamm describes the deteriorating situation in the mountain areas where "scattered Fretilin groups" continue their hopeless fight, "seemingly destined to die by attrition":

> The diminishing of supplies of the Fretilin guerrillas appears to have caused them to lose much of their hold over the significant part of the population of about 600,000 whom they have forced to live in regions under their control.

Now they can be "protected by the Indonesian Government," in the words of the State Department spokesman. (See above p. 163). These characterizations recall the standard reporting style from Vietnam about "Viet Cong control" over parts of the population who had to be liberated and protected by the U.S. It is hardly imaginable that the distinguished correspondent of the *New York Times* would report the observation by Denis Reichle after his brief visit to East Timor: FRETILIN forces "are simply East Timorese who would rather die fighting than submit to what they consider to be Indonesian slavery."

The *Times* Pulitzer Prize-winning specialist on refugees in Asia does not provide the source for his insight into the minds of the refugees fleeing from the regions where they have been "forced to live" by the "scattered Fretilin groups." In his reporting on Communist powers, refugee reports—often second or third hand, or transmitted by prisoners locked in cages under guard—are grist for the Kamm mill, as we shall see in Volume II. But for Indonesia and East Timor, Indonesian officials will suffice. Without any qualification or apparent check, Kamm quotes General Ali Murtopo, Indonesia's Information Minister and the person in charge of the early stages of the Indonesian invasion,[194] as "explain[ing]" that the lack of security that requires Indonesia to keep foreigners away is not caused by FRETILIN forces (which are supposed to be virtually nonexistent according to the Indonesia-U.S.-*New York Times* propaganda line) "but from anti-foreign feelings among Timorese, the origin of which he did not explain. 'When they see a foreigner they have a prejudice and would make moves that make trouble,' he said." It is so difficult to comprehend the inscrutable Asian mind.[195] Perhaps General Murtopo is also Kamm's source for the insight that the refugees are fleeing FRETILIN oppression.

The device of relying on the Indonesian military is not a monopoly of the *New York Times*. In fact, it is common throughout the Free Press. To cite another case, Reuters reports from Jakarta on the imminent collapse of FRETILIN in October, 1978.[196] The report is based on statements by Indonesian military commanders, presented—as usual—as unquestioned fact. Citing these sources, the report expresses deep humanitarian concern over "the plight of thousands of villagers still under FRETILIN control or in refugee camps," in particular, those who "are afraid to leave the mountains into which they had been forced from their homes to grow food for FRETILIN."

Reference to FRETILIN "control" over the people who are "forced to live" with them or "forced to grow food for them," as contrasted with Indonesian "protection" of them, is in fact standard in the Free Press and government pronouncements (assuming that these can be distinguished), as was comparable rhetoric in the case of Vietnam. Those who trouble to exercise their democratic right to petition their elected representatives are treated to similar intellectual fare. In response to a letter to Vice President Mondale, Hodding Carter III, Assistant Secretary for Public Affairs and Department Spokesman for the State Department, wrote that "with respect to East Timor, sporadic fighting continues between Indonesian forces and Fretilin remnants, but we have no information to substantiate charges of a pattern of atrocities by Indonesian troops....The latest reports available to us indicate that some 60,000 persons have voluntarily left areas in which they were exposed to some degree of Fretilin control or pressure and moved into territory secured by Government forces."[197] It might have been written by Henry Kamm himself; or by General Ali Murtopo—again, assuming that there is a difference.

Kamm reports that "Jakarta's military forces are still fighting an anti guerrilla war throughout the eastern half of the island," though the guerrillas have no hope of success. "Their [the guerrillas'] international backing appears to be limited to highly vocal groups of Australian leftwing students who have made of eastern Timor an issue similar to Vietnam, with Indonesia playing the American role."[198]

Kamm's comparison between the opposition to Indonesia's exploits in Timor and the Vietnam War is illuminating. In fact, though this has escaped the attention of the *Times* Southeast Asia correspondent, the international protest over Timor also includes the majority of the states in the United Nations—though this may be irrelevant, since they are exercising that "tyranny of the majority" that has been so deplored in U.S. commentary on the UN ever since it became difficult for the United States to pull the strings. Furthermore, the conference of non-aligned nations in Sri Lanka in August, 1976 added East Timor to a list of "colonial territories" in need of self-determination and "speedy independence," over bitter opposition from Indonesia and well after the U.S. had recognized "integration" as an irrevocable fact.[199]

This support from the non-aligned nations was reiterated at the Belgrade meeting of summer, 1978, which once again affirmed the right of the East Timorese to self-determination, over the objections of Indonesia and a number of other countries that entered "reservations".[200] It also has included major segments of the Australian labor movement.[201] As we have noted, even the *New York Times* took note of the petition to President Carter on the part of the majority of members of the Australian Parliament, though this inadvertent error was quickly rectified; see p. 171, above.[202] Apart from the majority of states of the United Nations, the nonaligned nations (which constitute the majority of the world's population) and the majority of the Australian Parliament and trade union movement, the protest over Indonesian actions has included substantial elements of the Australian press and church circles and even a few misguided souls in Europe or the United States who have not been so successfully brainwashed as the *Times* Pulitzer prizewinner.

To be sure, a precise logician might note that Kamm spoke of "international backing" for guerrillas resisting the Indonesian invasion while the protests are over the invasion and its aftermath; there is a difference, though such standards of accuracy, while relevant to serious reporting, hardly bear on this case. The distinction is one that the *Times* and its colleagues elsewhere have never been able to master in the case of opposition to U.S. aggression and atrocities in Vietnam; such opponents were invariably labelled "supporters of Hanoi," at least if their opposition was on principled grounds.[203]

Returning from the *New York Times* to the real world, many Australian political figures have repeatedly condemned the Indonesian atrocities. Labor representative Ken Fry, who has been a consistent opponent of Indonesian aggression, alleged that the government had confidential information that up to 80 Timorese are being killed daily by Indonesian troops and that if the slaughter continued, "another 25,000 casualties would have to be added to the 50,000 dead already conceded by the Indonesian Foreign Minister, Mr. Malik." He cited infant mortality rates of 50% and lack of medical supplies, a situation which, along with the "slaughter," was "placing in jeopardy the future of the Timorese people."[204] Another one of those "highly vocal leftwing students" who are making an issue of Timor is Michael Hodgman of the Liberal Party, who describes himself as "staunchly anti-communist," so much so that he has been described as "the worst Red-baiter" in the House of Representatives. He mentioned this in response to "a massive campaign," of which Kamm's absurd remark is one small part, "to brand any person concerned about East Timor as 'pro-Fretilin' and therefore, 'pro-communist' ";he adds that "one could hardly call the Catholic Commission for Justice and Peace, headed by Bishop Mulkearns..., a 'leftist' organization." Hodgman writes:

> For us, as Australians, to bury our heads in the sand and turn our backs on what is alleged to have occurred, would be a gross act of national moral cowardice. We would be degrading Australia, and future generations would have to bear the same shame and disgrace which fell upon those citizens of nazi Germany who turned a blind eye to

> Auschwitz by the simple process of saying to themselves: "It does not exist—it has not occurred"... The ghosts of the dead will haunt each and every one of us who seeks solace in silent acquiescence.[205]

How much more true is this of U.S. congressmen, journalists and the public, given the direct U.S. role in implementing the aggression and building a wall of silence around it. More recently Hodgman charged in Parliament that between 30-40,000 people have died in East Timor because defoliants destroyed their crops.[206]

In this connection, Rep. Donald Fraser wrote a letter to Secretary of State Cyrus Vance on December 8, 1977, in his capacity as chairman of the Subcommittee on International Organizations, in which he stated: "We recently received a reliable report that Indonesian forces have been using chemical sprays on crops in areas under Fretilin control and that U.S.-manufactured planes, the OV-10s, are being used to spread these chemicals... We have also received reliable reports that Indonesian troops are engaged in indiscriminate killings in areas under Fretilin control." A response from Douglas J. Bennet, Jr., Assistant Secretary for Congressional Relations, states (surprise!) that "we believe the report [of defoliation] is erroneous" and that "in regard to your other queries, we have received no information to indicate that Indonesian troops are engaged in indiscriminate killings in areas under Fretilin control." The information reviewed above, for example, as well as that to which we return, is so esoteric that State Department intelligence and other intelligence agencies are quite unable to discover it, just as it lies beyond the reach of the Free Press and mainstream U.S. scholarship.

Returning to the "highly vocal leftwing students" who are making of East Timor "an issue similar to Vietnam," the Australian Labor Party has repeatedly voiced its opposition to the Indonesian aggression. In July, 1977 it voted to endorse a cutoff of military aid to Indonesia and to recognize the Democratic Republic of East Timor (FRETILIN). To the best of our knowledge this resolution still stands. Six Australian parliamentarians, including Fry and Tom Uren, then Deputy Leader of the Opposition, urged Representative Fraser to invite Dunn to testify, citing his refugee interviews and also a "confidential report from Indonesian Christian aid sources" (see above) which "documented widespread killings and destruction by Indonesian armed forces."[207] Uren was among the Australian troops captured in Timor after strong resistance to the Japanese invasion; others continued the struggle with the aid of the Timorese, who suffered bitterly for their contribution to the allied war effort and are now reaping the further benefits of their sacrifice.

We have already discussed Fry's testimony before the UN Security Council in April, 1976. During the same Security Council sessions, the Secretary-General of the UN received a letter from José Martins, President of the extreme right-wing KOTA party, a participant in the early stages of the Indonesian invasion and one of the three Timorese collaborators selected by Indonesia to report to the Security Council of the UN immediately after the December, 1975 invasion.[208] He informed the Secretary-General that the entire delegation was forced to attend and "to read what the Indonesians had written." Martins wrote that he had since "managed to escape from the evil Indonesian hands." Originally a supporter of the Indonesian invasion, he quickly discovered that "many thousands of people" were machine-gunned as the Indonesian army ran amok and that apart from a few selected collaborators even the right-wing parties were not permitted to function. He referred to the FRETILIN report to the Security Council for details concerning the situation in Timor and appealed to the Secretary-General "to use your good offices to end the Indonesian presence in East Timor."[209]

The media attention given to the defection of this leading collaborator—one of three Timorese handpicked by the Indonesian military—may be usefully compared with the treatment of Nguyen Cong Hoan, a minor political figure who escaped from postwar Vietnam and was accorded substantial coverage by Henry Kamm and others and invited as the sole witness for the July 26, 1977 Hearings of the Fraser Committee on Human Rights in Vietnam. (See Volume II, Chapter 4.) Martins, in contrast, was ignored by the Committee and in the press (virtually—see above p. 165). Not only is his defection far more significant from a political point of view, but, furthermore, nothing alleged to have taken place in Vietnam after the U.S. was expelled begins to compare with what has been reported concerning Timor, where the United States is a party to the slaughter. The comparisons, once again, are enlightening.

The hearings on human rights in Timor did not call as a witness anyone who spoke for FRETILIN, though such individuals (including José Ramos-Horta, former Minister of External Affairs and Information of the FRETILIN government and currently one of its international spokesmen) were available in New York and had been heard by the United Nations, which, under the "tyranny of the majority," has departed from lofty U.S. standards. The congressional ban, however, was not against Timorese, but only against Timorese who were not Indonesian collaborators. Two Timorese selected by the Indonesians did testify at the congressional hearings, reporting, for example, that no Indonesian army units were in East Timor until after the July 1976 "integration," when for the first time there were "units of uniformed people of security forces, the police and other units." Prior to July, 1976, one of these witnesses reported, he "never saw any Indonesian who carried a weapon or wore a uniform."[210] Such testimony is so radically inconsistent with the facts reported by all serious sources and accepted by the UN and even the U.S. State Department, that one can reasonably conclude that these witnesses were subjected to Indonesian coercion, as Martins had indicated. Representatives of the Timorese resistance to Indonesian aggression would obviously be appropriate witnesses for a congressional hearing, as would the refugees who have indicated their desire to testify, if Timorese were regarded as members of the human race alongside victims of Communist oppression who are much more convenient objects of sympathy and concern on the part of human rights enthusiasts.

If, in fact, Timorese were accorded human status, the media too might listen to what FRETILIN representatives have to say. The estimates of casualties given above are from hostile sources primarily: Adam Malik, Indonesian Church officials, supporters of the UDT, priests, members of the elite. FRETILIN representatives have also given their estimates, but these have yet to reach Congress or the U.S. public. Mari Alkatiri of the FRETILIN Central Committee alleged in an interview in Paris that the number of deaths had passed 150,000. He also criticized the decision of the French government to sell sophisticated weapons to Indonesia which "will be put into operation against our civilian population, our women and children."[211] But this allegation and protest has not yet been noticed by the Free Press.

Alkatiri's concern over French arms sales to Indonesia is quite appropriate. Although according to the State Department the war was effectively over in early 1976, one finds an occasional report in the loyal media revealing that this is far from true. A Western diplomat is quoted by George McArthur in the *International Herald Tribune* as saying that the Indonesians "are running out of military inventory. The operations on Timor have pushed them to the wall."[212] The fight against the guerrillas has "virtually exhausted" military supplies, according to this report, even though "the guerrillas now number only about 600 men." McArthur does not explain how a war against 600 men can exhaust the military supplies of Indonesia, but perhaps one can draw some inferences that the Free Press does not allow. He reports that "arms salesmen from France, Britain, the Netherlands, Italy, Spain, Switzerland, Belgium, West Germany and other places discretely woo the government—their way paved by various embassies." He also claims, contrary to the reported facts, that the Carter administration is "slowing down international armament sales," in particular to Indonesia.[213]

The Free Press continues to mask the obvious significance of the flow of arms to Indonesia. The chief White House correspondent of the *New York Times* explained the "meaningful role" that has been achieved "in the making of foreign policy" by the Administration's official liberal, Vice President Walter Mondale, referring to his visit to Jakarta to discuss "Indonesia's requests for additional military and economic assistance":

> As the talks concluded, an Indonesian minister drew aside an American official. "These sessions have been really useful for us," he said. "Now we have someone at the Friday breakfasts who understands Indonesia's problems." The breakfast the Minister was referring to is the foreign policy review that President Carter conducts over coffee and Danish every Friday.

Mondale showed his understanding of Indonesia's problems while in Jakarta when he discovered that A-4 ground-attack bombers that Indonesia had requested "were indeed important to the Indonesians...Some hurried phone calls back to Washington and a few hours later, the Vice President was given the discretionary authority to grant the plane request if he felt adequate progress could be obtained on human rights. More talks with the Indonesians persuaded him that this was the case. Shortly before he left, he announced the plane sale."[214] The people of East Timor will thank him for his devotion to the cause of human rights.

The British are also wasting no time. In April, 1978, British Aerospace signed a 25 million pound contract with Indonesia for Hawk ground-attack / trainer aircraft, well-designed for counterinsurgency. The managing director commented: "The Indonesian contract is superb news so soon after our recent success in Finland. It is an important breakthrough into the South East Asia market, which is one of great potential."[215] Plenty of defenseless people to kill there.

The Southeast Asia correspondent of *Le Monde*, R.-P. Paringaux reported from Jakarta that Foreign Minister de Guiringaud had laid the basis for sales of military aircraft and other military equipment to Indonesia and for the eventual establishment of a plant for manufacture of light automatic weapons:

> Asked about the position of France with regard to the annexation of East Timor by Indonesia, M. de Guiringaud stated that if that question would again be raised at the next session of the United Nations, France would not place Indonesia in an embarrassing position in any manner. "*The government has so far abstained,*" reported the Minister, who judged his visit to Jakarta to have been "*satisfying in all respects.*"[216]

The United States is also continuing, indeed apparently increasing its arms supplies to Indonesia. Imagine the reaction if the major powers had been pouring arms into Cambodia for use in internal repression.

The point deserves further comment. In France, as in the United States, there is great indignation over repression and atrocities in postwar Indochina, coupled with striking lack of concern for France's participation in continuing massacres elsewhere. Thus the representative of the French news bureau AFP, invited to a news conference at the UN on East Timor, November 30, 1978, declined to attend, stating that the French press is not interested in East Timor. Similarly, Parringaux's report from Jakarta just cited led to no significant protest, to our knowledge. In dramatic contrast, a report a few weeks later by the same correspondent about repression in Vietnam became a cause celebre in France (indeed, in the U.S. press as well, though reports in *Le Monde* are rarely accorded such notice here, in particular, when they deal with U.S. crimes).[217] Similarly in France there has been a vast outcry about "autogenocide" in Cambodia.[218] But when the French foreign minister announces plans to sell arms to Indonesia and establish an arms manufacturing industry there while continuing to support Indonesian aggression, the response is far more muted, though there is little doubt about the consequences, and they have indeed been drawn quite explicitly in France—as distinct from the United States, where the media cover-up has been far more effective. Thus in mid-1976 the French press pointed out that the government of the Democratic Republic of East Timor (FRETILIN) believed that "time is on its side" in the struggle against Indonesian aggression, because Indonesia would not be able to sustain its attack, given the severe costs.[219] But FRETILIN had not counted on the willingness of the Western powers, including those that have compiled such a notable record in Southeast Asia, to provide the material and diplomatic support that is required for Indonesian aggression and massacre to continue.

As we have noted several times, the reports of Indonesian atrocities that have reached the West and on occasion barely penetrated the barrier of silence and "ignorance" derive largely from sources that were anti-FRETILIN and in support of "integration" with Indonesia or initially willing to accept it. Information emanating from FRETILIN sources is excluded from the U.S. press or Congress as a matter of principle. There has been substantial information from such sources, much of it sent directly by radio from East Timor, but it has not been considered worthy of mention (in striking contrast, for example, to material smuggled out by Russian dissidents). In November, 1976 the conservative

Fraser Government in Australia "decided to prevent Telecom, Darwin, from passing on telegrams from the Fretilin forces in East Timor. These Telecom messages are the only way in which the Australian people and the world can find out what is happening in East Timor."[220] This decision, which "cuts off Fretilin's last official link with the outside world,...follows the seizure seven months ago of a mobile transmitter broadcasting to the Fretilin movement from near Darwin."[221] For the Western powers, it does not suffice that the servile press (outside of Australia) pays no attention to the sole regular source of information about Timor—can one conceive of a dispatch from the Timorese resistance in the *New York Times*?[222]—or to the pleas from priests and others for some concern over impending genocide? It is necessary to proceed further and to make sure that the voice of those who dare to resist the depredations of a U.S. client state must be entirely stilled, so that even those "highly vocal leftwing students" who provide their sole "international support," according to Henry Kamm, shall know nothing of their fate. Since even the International Red Cross has been barred from Timor,[223] it is even more certain than before that what reaches any substantial audience in the West will be the kind of "information" produced by the Indonesian generals and loyally transmitted by the Henry Kamms of the international press.

Nevertheless, the voice of the resistance has not been completely stilled. Radio contact continues, contrary to allegations in the press.[224]

A UPI report from Sydney, June 19, 1978, cites a charge by Denis Freney, secretary of the Campaign for an Independent East Timor, that "the CIA has sent military advisers to help Indonesian troops battle guerrillas in East Timor."[225] Freney gave as his source a radio message received from FRETILIN in East Timor, reporting an invasion by 15,000 fresh troops who arrived in May, 1978. The report from East Timor was quoted in a press release by José Ramos-Horta in New York, July 12, 1978:

> American military advisers and mercenaries fought alongside Indonesian soldiers against FRETILIN in two battles in Lekidoe area, 10 miles south of Dili, on June 13, and in the Remexio village, eight miles south-east of the

> capital, on June 21 and 22. In the meantime, American pilots are flying OV-10 Bronco aircraft for the Indonesian Air Force in bombing raids against the liberated areas under FRETILIN administration.

The same press release also cites a report from the same source "that military observers of an ASEAN country have been to East Timor during the month of December last year to watch Indonesian military operations against FRETILIN forces in the village of Ainaro." On the same day, Ramos-Horta addressed a letter to UN Ambassador Andrew Young citing the same reports, and appealing to him, "with faith in your sense of justice and your record as a freedom-fighter for civil liberties in this country...[and] ...your profound convictions in human dignity and liberty [which] are an interpretation of the feelings of the American people at large...to help stop the unjust American intervention in East Timor."

This appeal was unnoticed by the Free Press, and had no discernible effect on or through Ambassador Young.

There have been occasional reports by journalists permitted highly controlled tours by the Indonesian government, but very few. The first appears to have been Richard Carleton, who spent six days in East Timor in July 1977.[226] He reports that wherever he went on his "conducted tour" he was "surrounded by two concentric circles of men from the civil defense forces." He did, however, manage "to give the slip to the dozen escorts, guards, interpreters and hangers-on that the Indonesian government had provided" and "in a darkened room of a building on the outskirts of Dili" met someone whose "integrity is beyond reproach" and whose eyewitness account of Indonesian atrocities, which Carleton reports, was supported by another witness. "The voices of my informers quavered as they spoke, their hands trembled and they perspired freely." Apart from describing to him a massacre that took place in December, 1975, his informants also told him "that here people are still dying of disease and malnutrition every day." They estimated the total number killed to be in the neighborhood of 50,000. Carleton reports that in the streets of Dili, "about one person in five still wears a black armband of mourning." He could see that "for those who survived the fighting the Indonesians have begun a full-scale Orwellian re-education program," complete with indoctrination in the schools and signs reading "go to hell James Dunn" and similar slogans, most of them, however, written "in Indonesian, a language none of the local people speak, let alone write." Meanwhile children sent to welcome him "kept up a continuous chant: 'We are one nation, we are Indonesian'." Carleton was less impressed than his colleagues reporting from Jakarta. He reports what he was told by Indonesian military commanders but also the current assessment of Western intelligence sources in Jakarta which estimated that one-third of East Timor is controlled by the Indonesians, one-third by FRETILIN, and one-third is no-man's-land. He noted, for example, that the town of Remexio, 15 kilometers from Dili, was still under FRETILIN control, and even in Dili he found signs in the native language clandestinely painted by FRETILIN supporters who had heard of his arrival over radio Australia. To determine what was happening in Dili, Carleton reports, "the best one can do is to gather the odd eye-witness account from those not too terrified to talk"; or to translate into the style preferred in the West, from those who are now being "protected" by the Indonesians after having escaped from areas where they were "forced to live" by FRETILIN.

The Indonesian government apparently was not too happy with the results of this "conducted tour." Journalists were barred for a year afterwards. In July, 1978, journalists were permitted to accompany General Suharto on a 24-hour visit to Dili, and in September, 1978, when the Indonesian government brought several foreign diplomats, including the U.S. Ambassador, for a three day visit to sections of East Timor under their control, several journalists were in the party. A report by David Jenkins appears in the *Far Eastern Economic Review,* datelined Remexio; by September, 1978 the Indonesian army had captured this town less than 10 miles from the capital city of Dili, which had been occupied in December, 1975.[227] "In Remexio, as in most other towns," Jenkins writes, "the people are stunned, sullen and dispirited. Emaciated as a result of deprivation and hardship, they are struggling to make sense of the nightmarish interlude in which as much as half the population was uprooted." The diplomats visiting Remexio "found bewildered residents drawn up in two rows, jiggling Indonesian flags and mouthing the words *merdeka* (freedom) to the prompting of local cheerleaders." An East Timorese collaborator said:

> These people are totally stunned by what has happened. Thousands died in this *kabupaten* (district). The people are shocked both by the severity of the killing and by the recent political changes. Four-fifths of them wouldn't know what they are doing. I could give them a Portuguese flag and they would wave it.

The town, Jenkins reports, was almost completely on the side of FRETILIN. Keeping to the standard Western version of events, Jenkins reports that for Remexio "the trauma began in 1975 when rival Timorese factions turned on one another in what was to become an especially horrifying civil war" (the standard misrepresentation, as we have seen). Attacked first by the UDT at the time of the brief civil war of August-September, 1975, according to Jenkins, Remexio "was to suffer even more severely at the end of the year and in early 1976 as Indonesian 'volunteers' let loose their full fury on Fretilin units dug in around the town." Now the inhabitants "are undernourished and desperately in need of medical attention." Many have come in from the surrounding hills where they barely survived on tapioca, leaves and poisonous berries. The children reminded one ambassador of "victims of an African famine."

According to Timorese officials, Remexio is not unique and is, in fact, better off than other "transit camps" in the province. The Indonesian foreign minister, typically, blamed the poverty (worse than "any other part of Indonesia," he said) on the legacy of the Portuguese—not entirely false, despite the cynicism. Church officials estimate that 500 refugees die each month of starvation in one district.

Indonesia has still not granted permission to the International Red Cross or other relief agencies to enter East Timor, though it is willing to accept aid for the dispirited people who remind visitors of "victims of an African famine." But only on certain conditions: "Indonesia is looking for foreign aid for East Timor but the Foreign Minister, Professor Kusumaatmadja, who accompanied the party [of visitors], indicated the donor countries must acknowledge Indonesia's sovereignty."[228] Aid will be accepted, in short, as a device to obtain international recognition for Indonesia's aggression, so far withheld by most countries, though not by the United States, the chief accomplice.

In the UN debate of November, 1978 over East Timor, the representative of Sao Tome-Principe spoke of the East Timorese people "as hostages in their own territory."[229] The cynicism of the Indonesian government on foreign aid confirms this judgment, as do other actions. Jill Jolliffe comments that the reference to the East Timorese is "indeed accurate":

> This is borne out by the attempts of several thousand East Timorese in Dili to emigrate to Australia. Despite an agreement by Australian immigration authorities to accept around 600 of these applicants—a small concession wrung out of Indonesia by the Australian government in reward for de facto recognition of Indonesian control in East Timor—the Indonesian government continues to obstruct the departure of these people.[230]

These facts too are considered unworthy of notice in Western countries that reserve their display of deep humanitarian concern for those who suffer from starvation, disease and oppression in the countries of Indochina

The description of the stunned, dispirited, starving residents of Remexio brings to mind other pictures: for example, the Aché Indians who had "given up on life" in the government death camp so admired by a visiting *New York Times* reporter (cf. p. 111-112, above) or those in the Protestant mission visited by Norman Lewis, where the chief attempted suicide when the missionary in charge withheld water from sick and starving children to teach them "the conception of corrective chastisement" that seemed "beyond their grasp" because of "some genetic defect" (cf. p. 123-124, above).

Jenkins writes of "this enormous humanitarian and development problem" with which Indonesia is "saddled...as a result of its takeover of East Timor in December, 1975," referring in the now-familiar way to the Indonesian capture of Dili in the December invasion, later extended to a near-genocidal attack that apparently still continues, though Jenkins, on the authority of his Indonesian hosts, assures us that only 2-300 scattered FRETILIN guerrillas fight on. Perhaps some troubled German also wrote of the "enormous humanitarian and development problem" that the Nazis were "saddled with" in Poland. Even this level of concern appears to be beyond the U.S. press.

As a grim experiment, we have taken, in recent months, to asking audiences at political talks in the United States if they know in which continent Timor is to be found. Few have even heard the name. U.S. Indonesian clients can persist in their humanitarian endeavors with little fear that they will be impeded or called to account by their Western backers. Perhaps, when enough years have passed and a new Human Rights campaign is launched, thoughtful commentators will evoke some distorted memory of this holocaust as a testimonial to the new day that is dawning as the West turns over still another "new leaf" in its never-ending efforts to bring the message of humanism, freedom, and justice to benighted peoples.

But for the present, silence is deemed more appropriate. A letter to the liberal journal *Newsweek*, inquiring as to its failure to devote a word to the slaughter in East Timor, elicited a response (5 December 1978) explaining that for the past 20 months the situation there has been "stable": "with the responsibility of covering important developments from every corner of the globe each week...we cannot report on a stable situation," the letter explained. The week the letter was sent, *Newsweek* had met this awesome responsibility with a cover story on electronic toys. The letter continues: "We have to wait until some event...brings the area into the spotlight of world attention," for example, a "military offensive"—evidently the major offensive of December 1977 was below the threshold for media attention, as distinct from electronic toys. As for the constant bombardment and terror, the regular new offensives that would have exhausted Indonesian military supplies were it not for Western assistance, the scenes reminiscent of an African famine glimpsed by Western ambassadors, the atmosphere of a war zone in Dili, the anguished pleas of victims and refugees—none of this is newsworthy, since the situation is "stable." Recall *Newsweek*'s profound concern over the "devastation" caused during the civil war, minuscule by comparison even if we were to accept the presentation in the skillfully edited *New York Times* report that *Newsweek* used as a source (see p. 135-137). Note also the emphasis on the obscurity of the events in East Timor, which is not in "the spotlight of world attention." In contrast, atrocities, hunger and repression in postwar Indochina are continually newsworthy, because they remain "in the spotlight of world attention." In short, Catch-22: first suppress the facts, then refuse to report them because they are not "in the spotlight of world attention," while the glare of publicity ensures that material that can be used to teach the proper lessons remains "newsworthy." *Newsweek* also adds that it is "even rumored" that "some guerrillas" remain, but again, the rumors cannot find space in a journal with such serious responsibilities.

With its resort to the concept of "stability," *Newsweek* shows that it has learned the party line very well. By providing diplomatic and propaganda cover and a continuing flow of arms, the U.S. government has enabled its Indonesian client to slaughter at will, to annihilate the simple mountain people who continue to resist, to destroy their crops and drive them to "transit camps" where they sit in stunned silence like the remnants of another holocaust. But the situation is "stable," in the sense of "stability" that has been devised by the U.S. government and the Free Press (see note 6). In the standard sense of U.S. propaganda, "stability" is just the right term to apply to East Timor for the 20-month period preceding this letter.

We conclude this survey by turning to the Human Rights Reports of the State Department.[231] In the March, 1977 report, covering the period when Indonesia launched its murderous attack, *there is no mention whatsoever of Timor*. The omission is rectified in the 1978 Report, which deals with allegations of genocide in Timor as follows, *in toto*:

> Questions have been raised concerning atrocities by Indonesian troops in East Timor in 1975 and 1976 prior to the incorporation of East Timor into Indonesia. The Indonesian Government withdrew and disciplined offending units guilty of individual excesses, but most of the human losses in East Timor appear to have occurred prior to Indonesia's intervention.[232]

The last statement is a blatant lie. Note also the refusal to consider the substantial evidence, some of which we have reviewed, of massacres after the incorporation into Indonesia continuing to this day, and the qualified reference to the earlier period. For the period after mid-1976, State Department Human Rights specialists will not even grant that "questions have been raised."

A study prepared by the Congressional Research Service at the request of Donald Fraser notes that the State Department estimate of fatalities is far below that of Dunn (or others, including Malik!) and reports that William Goodling—an outright apologist for Indonesia—"testified that Timorese and Indonesian sources estimated to him that 40,000-60,000 were killed in the period of civil conflict and the December, 1975-March, 1976 period of Indonesian intervention."[233] Recalling that perhaps a few thousand were killed prior to the Indonesian invasion, we can draw a simple inference as to the estimated casualties resulting from the invasion itself up to March, 1976.

We do not want to suggest that the State Department is unique in its profound show of concern over possible genocide in Timor. As we have seen, journalism and responsible scholarship do not lag behind. To cite still another case, two commentators associated with the *Asian Wall Street Journal* write in *Foreign Affairs* that Indonesia is a "ripe target" for those who might be concerned with human rights violations. There is no mention of Timor.[234]

Press commentary on the 1978 State Department Human Rights Report is interesting. Bernard Gwertzman noted in the *New York Times* (February 10, 1978) that "the report was gentle on alleged atrocities in East Timor, asserting that most lives were lost before Indonesia's intervention in the former Portuguese colony." Neither the *Times* reporter nor its editors felt any need to take note of the glaring falsity of this claim or to comment on the significance of the State Department whitewash, nor did they mention that the Carter Administration had been stepping up aid, including military aid, to Indonesia.[235] Gwertzman is no less "gentle" than the State Department, as we see in his comparison of Indonesia and Cambodia:

> In Indonesia, where thousands have been detained without trial after the Communists were crushed in 1965, there

> has been a decision to release them gradually. In Cambodia, the radical forces that took power in 1975 have allowed no real contact with the outside world. But millions are alleged to have been killed, forced into exile or into bondage.

We return to Cambodia in Volume II, chapter 6. But note how the numbers "detained without trial" in Indonesia have been diminished, while the hundreds of thousands slaughtered have simply disappeared from the record.[236]

East Timor is not the only territory subjected to U.S.-backed Indonesian terror. The Melbourne *Age* reports that "almost 9,000 people have died in two years of bitter guerrilla fighting in Irian Jaya—the forgotten 'Timor' on Australia's northern doorstep." The estimate is given by the "peasant army which has since the mid-1960s been waging a stone-age war against Indonesian control of the land that borders Papua New Guinea," and which claims that 3,515 Indonesian soldiers and 5,269 Irianese villagers and guerrillas have been killed since January, 1976. "The figures are consistent with [Papua New Guinea] intelligence, according to reliable sources." The *Age* reports that it has "been shown detailed documents covering more than 50 separate battles and six village bombing raids by Indonesia over the two-year period," with "dates, places and precise figures for deaths and injury" which constitute "persuasive evidence of a sizeable and strong liberation movement..." The report is based on two weeks spent with the guerrillas by *Age* correspondent Mark Baker.[237]

In a follow-up report on April 27, Baker gives a detailed account of a "movement of people in the sisterland of Papua New Guinea who live in the bold hope of winning an end to 15 years of Indonesian rule...a movement that has survived nearly a generation of poverty, hunger and bombardment" and has, on his account, given pride and hope in ways that "will never be fully comprehended by...Western standards" both to stone age tribes and to "young men who are now leaving the comfort of urban colleges and jobs to fight." Their leader has so far refused Communist military aid in "the vain hope that the West will bring him guns."

It would be unfair to say that the U.S. press has failed entirely to cover this struggle. In September, 1978 the foreign minister of West Papua, New Guinea's Revolutionary Provisional Government was in New York, claiming that "we are fighting against Indonesia's genocide against our people." A report is carried in the Marxist-Leninist *Guardian* (New York, 20 September 1978), along with background discussion. The Free Press lives! Perhaps some day a reference to this liberation movement, which is giving pride and hope to the people, will make its appearance in an academic study of terrorism, that scourge of our age and one of the major problems facing civilized society.

A study of West Irian under Indonesian occupation by an Australian sociologist is reviewed by Richard Franke in the *Bulletin of Concerned Asian Scholars*,[238] giving a rare account of the liberation movement that has developed in "opposition to the brutality and exploitation of the Indonesian generals and their partners at PT Pacific Nickel," 43 percent owned by the U.S. Steel Corporation, and other international corporations intent on exploiting the rich mineral potential of the territory, where Indonesia has imposed an "ethnic caste barrier...to promote use of the region as a place to which the most impoverished peoples of other Indonesian islands might emigrate," among other humanitarian exercises.

A report from Melbourne in the *London Times* (27 July 1978) states that "Australia's tangled relations with Indonesia have been exacerbated by the razing of a border village in Papua, New Guinea, allegedly by Indonesian forces." Australia believes that "Indonesia has gone too far in its efforts to crack down on Irianese rebels" but is "even more concerned with keeping the diplomatic relationship healthy." In the case of East Timor, "Australia was the only Western country to take any real interest in the takeover" and produced a "muted complaint" that was entirely ignored. But the current situation is more serious, in part because of suspicions "that Indonesia has territorial designs on Papua, New Guinea." The *London Times* report continues: "The United States is now much more interested in Indonesia, not only because of the Administration's preoccupation with human rights, but also because it is a big arms supplier to Indonesia." The logic of the last comment is not obvious, given the way in which the "human rights preoccupation" has been spelled out in practice in the case of

Indonesia, Timor, Iran, the Philippines, etc., but it is a testimony to the effectiveness of the U.S. propaganda system, at the very least. One does not wait with bated breath for stern U.S. action to influence Indonesia to terminate the bloodbaths on its borders, or the interminable repression within.

CHAPTER 4

Constructive Terror

The U.S. global effort to maintain and enlarge the areas with a favorable investment climate has necessitated regular resort to terror, directly (as in the case of Indochina) and more often indirectly through subsidy and support for repressive clients. Bloodbaths and terror that contribute substantially to a favorable investment climate are "constructive" in the sense that they advance the end that clearly ranks highest in the priorities of Free World leaders. In such instances, therefore, human rights issues are set aside by right thinking people in the light of the contribution that such terror makes to "freedom" and "security".[1]

4.1 Indonesia: Mass Extermination, Investors' Paradise

The huge massacres in Indonesia, 1965-1969, have a threefold importance. In the first place, they constitute a new phase in counterrevolutionary violence marked by resort to "mass extermination in an attempt to consolidate authoritarian power."[2] Second, they provide the most revealing demonstration of the U.S. establishment's response to a major bloodbath where the political results of the slaughter are regarded as "positive".[3] Third, since the reaction of responsible journalists and political leaders was enthusiastic,[4] and the world protest at the mass killings was minimal, the Indonesian bloodbath set the stage as a viable model for lesser but still large-scale anti-communist pogroms in later years, as in Chile.[5]

The massacre in Indonesia followed an alleged Communist effort at a takeover in October, 1965, in which a small group of left wing army officers assassinated a half-dozen Indonesian generals. This "coup" was extremely convenient, providing the "long awaited legitimation" for the *real* coup and bloodbath that came as its aftermath. The term "mutiny" has been suggested as perhaps more appropriate than "coup" for the precipitating events of October, 1965, and its link to the Communist party is by no means established.[6] The abortive coup or mutiny did, however, provide the military establishment with the excuse to destroy its only serious institutional rival: the Indonesian Communist Party (PKI).[7] The PKI was large and well organized, had a mass base, and its policies and interests were antithetical to those of the generals. The PKI opposed dependence on the U.S., to which the Indonesian military was already closely tied by ideology and growing technological dependency (arms supplies and training). And the PKI was sharply critical of the corruption and mismanagement of the military-dominated bureaucratic capitalism of the early 1960s, which was breaking new ground in looting and shakedowns even before the post-1965 consolidation of military power. In any event, the army quickly established itself in power and proceeded to organize within a four month period one of the most extensive and brutal slaughters in human history.[8]

The Indonesian coup and terror sequel had certain similarities with that of Brazil, which it followed by a year. The CIA had long been involved in Indonesian affairs, had participated in an unsuccessful regional rebellion in 1958 (an abortive Brazilian coup had occured in 1955), and, along with the Pentagon, had supplied cash and political intelligence to the officer corps. Army-inspired anti-Chinese pogroms that took place in West Java in 1959 were financed by U.S. contributions to the local army commander. By the late 1950s the CIA and Pentagon both had built an extensive network of connections with the Indonesian military. As noted, the Indonesian coup was immediately preceded by a legitimizing "Communist coup" to which it was allegedly a response; the Brazilian junta and the sponsoring U.S. leadership could only claim Communist infiltration and bloodthirsty plans—which more than sufficed for the molders of U.S. public opinion, although perhaps more would have been needed to justify mass extermination. As in the case of Brazil, the Indonesian military officer corps had been built and trained by the U.S.; "one-third of the Indonesian general staff had some sort of training from Americans and almost half of the officer corps...[and] the American and Indonesian military had come to know each other rather well. Bonds of personal respect and even affection existed..."[9] One of those closest to the U.S. military and most respected by them. General Nasution, achieved some notoriety by openly demanding the total extermination of all three million Communist party members, plus all their followers and sympathizers.[10] One of the army leaders in the very forefront of the killing, Colonel Sarwo Eddie, had been a CIA contact man while serving in the Indonesian embassy in Australia.[11]

In mid-November of 1965 Suharto formally authorized a "cleaning out" of the Indonesian Communist Party and set up special military teams to supervise this final solution. The army played a key role in this holocaust, doing a large part of the killing directly, supplying trucks, weapons and encouragement to paramilitary and vigilante death squads, and actively stimulating anti-Communist hysteria that contributed greatly to wholesale mass murder. A key part in stirring up a mood of butchery was played by media fabrications, which were concocted with a sophistication suggestive of outside assistance. Photos of the bodies of the dead generals—badly decomposed after three days in a well—were featured in all newspapers and T.V. broadcasts, with accompanying texts claiming that the generals had been castrated and their eyes gouged out by Communist women. (The army later made the mistake of allowing official medical autopsies to be included as evidence in some of the trials; and the extremely detailed reports of the injuries suffered only mention bullet wounds and some bruises, no eye gougings or castration.) The cynically fabricated campaign was well designed to arouse panic about Communist sadism and thus to set the stage for the second largest holocaust of the twentieth century.

The mass killings began in late October 1965 in Central Java with the arrival there of the paratroopers, moved to East Java at the end of November as the paratroopers moved east, and on to Bali about mid-December, again correlated with a move of the paratroopers. Lists compiled by the military were given to right-wing Muslim groups, who were armed with *parangs* and transported in army trucks to villages, where they killed with bloody mutilation. Schoolchildren were asked to identify "Communists," and many so identified were shot on the spot by army personnel, along with their whole families. Many people were denounced as "Communists" in personal disputes, and "on the basis of one word or the pointing of a finger, people were taken away to be killed."[12] The killing was on such a huge scale as to raise a sanitation problem in East Java and Northern Sumatra, where the smell of decaying flesh was pervasive and rivers were impassable because of the clogging by human bodies.[13]

This slaughter was described by the anti-Communist Indonesia expert Justus M. van der Kroef as "a frightful anti-Communist pogrom" where, "it is to be feared, innocent victims of mere hearsay were killed" (as opposed, presumably, to the guilty Communist men, women and children who fully deserved their fate).[14] In 1968 there was a renewal of mass executions, and in one single case in early 1969 army and local civic guards in Central Java "were said to have killed some 3,500 alleged followers of the PKI by means of blows of iron staves in the neck."[15] According to van der Kroef, it was a period of "endless and often arbitrary arrests, brutalization of prisoners, and an atmosphere of distrust in which exhibitions of violent anti-communism are believed to be the best way to convince suspicious local military of one's *bona fides."*[16]

The number killed in the Indonesian bloodbath has always been uncertain, but an authoritative minimum was established in October 1976 when Admiral Sudomo, the head of the Indonesian state security system, in an interview over a Dutch television station, estimated that more than 500,000 had been slaughtered.[17] He "explained" to Henry Kamm of the *New York Times* that these deaths had been a result of an "unhealthy competition between the parties" who were causing "chaos".[18] Other authorities have given estimates running from 700,000[19] to "many more than one million."[20]

For the period of the massacres, the *official* figures for people arrested, exclusive of the 500,000 or more "Communists" killed, is 750,000.[21] AI estimated in 1977 that there were still between 55,000 and 100,000 political prisoners. Of the 750,000 arrested only about

800 have been brought to trial, usually by military tribunals, and usually receiving death sentences. Uncounted thousands died in prison of malnutrition and untreated illness. AI has "not found a single case of a prisoner not being found guilty."[22] Thus, tens of thousands of prisoners today

> are held capitive without trial, or used as servants by local military commanders, or exploited as forced labor, or subjected to an archaic policy of transportation to penal colonies. They are ill-treated by the authorities. The majority have now been held prisoner for more than 11 years without trial. Men, women, and children are held prisoner, arbitrarily and at the discretion of local military commanders.[23]

Conditions in the Indonesian prisons have been and remain appalling and torture has been employed "systematically" in interrogation. According to AI:

> Young girls below the age of 13, old men, people who were frail and ill, were not exempt from torture. It was used not only for interrogation, but also as punishment and with sadistic intent. Cases of sexual assault on women and extreme cruelty were reported to Amnesty International. Deaths from torture were frequently reported up till the end of the 1960s. At the present time, Amnesty International receives reports of cases of torture under interrogation. The worst cases are those of military officers and men suspected of left-wing tendencies, who are tortured by their fellow officers. The Air Force interrogation center in Jakarta is particularly notorious for its use of brutal and prolonged torture.[24]

Meanwhile, this land of mass murder and huge concentration camps quickly became "a paradise for investors."[25] The generals have followed the typical subfascist strategy of alliance with powerful foreign interests for the joint exploitation of the local markets, resources and people. The blind-growth development model was adopted, emphasizing rapid increases in investment and technology through foreign investment and expertise. The Foreign Investment Law of February 1967 provided the requisite tax and other incentives, and a major influx of foreign capital ensued, with the United States leading the way in mining, and the Japanese especially important in textiles. By 1973 foreign interests controlled 59% of the capital invested in forestry, 96% in mining, 35% in industry, 47% in hotels and tourism, and 33% in agriculture and fisheries.[26] The lifting of restrictions on imports and encouragement of foreign investment also led to substantial denationalization in sectors traditionally dominated by local enterprise—batik, textiles, beverages, foodstuffs, and cigarettes—a process hastened by the lack of capital access of local entrepreneurs in a system of priveleged credit and restrictive credit policies.[27]

New agricultural technologies, the monopolization of rural credit by large individual and corporate farmers, and the rise in price of agricultural land also resulted in massive dispossession of peasants and a greater redundancy of agricultural laborers, a fall in agricultural wage rates, widespread hunger, and a widening gap between village rich and poor. Anderson notes that

> ...in the wake of the destruction of the PKI, the modest land-reform and crop-sharing legislation of the Sukarno years had become a dead letter. Much of the land redistributed in the early 1960s had reverted to its earlier owners by the early 1970s. Although the law provided for 50-50 shares in the crop between tenant and landlord, in many areas the actual ratio ran as high as 70-30 or even 80-20 in the landlords' favor. It was only too easy to brand any attempts to enforce the land-reform and share-cropping statutes as "communist". With the memory of the massacres of 1965-66—which took place largely in the villages—still only too vivid, few poor farmers dared to try to organize to defend their legal rights.[28]

Foreign capital has had to pay a steep price for the privilege of entry and in "protection money" demanded by the generals. The pervasiveness and scale of looting in the post-1965 New Order have been unique even for the world of subfascism. In 1977, *Business Week* reported that the foreign business community was "dismayed by the blatant growth of corruption," citing the case of the general manager of Inco's nickel project, brought to court on a libel charge for dismissing an Indonesian company manager, and having the state judge offer to dismiss the case—for $10,000. "Even Jakarta-based businessmen, who are accustomed to wholesale bribery, are disturbed that it took the World Bank's threat to hold back loan funds to squelch the payoff demand."[29]

More widely publicized was General Telephone and Electronics' claim in 1977 that it had lost a telecommunications contract to Hughes Aircraft for refusing to pay a $40 million bribe, Hughes allegedly having paid bribes of 20% or more to Indonesian officials.[30] Even more publicity was given an SEC complaint in 1977 against Pertamina, the state oil company of Indonesia, alleging a shakedown of 54 U.S., European and Japanese companies with Indonesian interests for money to finance the Rayamana Indonesian restaurant in New York City.[31] An internal Exxon memo of February, 1970 says: "I doubt that we can avoid this shakedown...Do you have any suggestions as to amount?"[32]

Licenses to do business, to import, to export, to exploit timber or mineral resources, government contracts, and state bank credit are all up for sale by the military elite, or else they are reserved for groups centered in a military officer or faction. The military clique dominates by controlling access to markets and credit, serving in a manner closely analogous to ordinary gangsters who control a line of business by force and demand payoffs for entry and "protection". In the Indonesian case, the gangsters run an entire country and insist on payment either via "commissions" or in joint ventures where the generals or their agents get 10-25% of the profits for a nominal investment.[33] Besides selling licenses and other privileges, the generals and their families or clients may form their own sole agency companies, frequently using Chinese (*cukong*) managers. Thus a Suharto-associated company owns the Volkswagen agency, General Sutowo owns the Mitsubishi agency and so on down the line. The Suharto interests begin with the Cendana group, containing 15 companies in banking, real estate, cement, flour milling, rubber, logging, trading, and other activities. Suharto, his wife, brother, two brothers-in-law, and other relatives and clients have shareholdings in a wide variety of foreign companies, which regularly receive monopoly rights and subsidized bank credits.[34] The business empires of the generals are "nets of minority shareholdings in joint ventures in which their role is strictly political..."[35]

The diversion of tax monies and foreign aid into privileged pockets has also attained spectacular levels under the New Order. A scandal of 1968 involved the misuse and looting of about 30% of several hundred million dollars of aid made available by foreign governments in that year.[36] Ingrid Palmer, in fact, estimates a 30% corruption drain in Indonesian aid programs in general.[37] An interesting feature of the constantly recurring scandals, and their sequel of promised cleanup, is that while the major looters are at the top, the top is immune from prosecution. "Explaining why all those brought to court were 'small fish', Sugih Arto [Attorney General, in charge of the anti-corruption drive] said, 'for the time being the cases of the 'big fish' cannot be finalized because of technical difficulties.' During 1968, 172 cases were investigated, but none involved members of the armed forces."[38]

Indonesian corruption is so vast that a new language has been required to cope with the "sticky handshake" in its many variants:

> The faint crackle of money changing hands is as pervasive here as the scent of clove in the cigarette smoke. The lucre goes by many names: "smooth money," "lubricating money," "rule 2,000" (which means it will cost you 2,000 rupiahs—about $5). Lately the government has been referring to extortion by low-level civil servants as "illegal levies." "Illegal levies are everywhere, and almost everybody is involved," declares Adm. Sudomo, head of a body known as the National Command for the Restoration of Security and Order.[39]

In 1977 the generals began another campaign to totally exterminate corruption at every level—over a ten year period. A proclamation to this effect was "greeted with great hilarity. There have been many like it, and they all have turned out to be so much hot air. This time, however, the government may have reasons for being serious. The level of public rapacity has grown here in recent years. The higher-ups are taking much more, it's said, and they aren't spreading it around."[40]

Perhaps more important than the "shakedown" forms of corruption just described have been the processes of strictly internal looting of Indonesia by its military elite. In 1957 when large Dutch holdings were taken over by the Indonesian state, the successor companies, although nominally nationalized, were given over to the control and management of the generals. These important enterprises were mismanaged and plundered on a grand scale, part of the looting being for the private profit of individual officers, some of it a conversion of resources to use by the army.[41] Only Pertamina, the state oil company, escaped serious decline or ruin, for a time. Following the introduction of the New Order in 1965, these national enterprises went into relative decline, but they remained absolutely important in several areas such as oil, mining and trading. Internal corruption assumed the form of plain stealing on a new and larger scale, and the discriminatory manipulation of bank credit and the privileged exploitation of state monopolies.[42] As noted by Anderson:

> Most banks operated under military supervision and were compelled to offer huge credits and unrealistically low interest rates to senior officers (or *cukong* working with them). Very often these cheap credits were not used for productive investment, but for real-estate speculation, land grabbing, luxury housing, and so forth. Second was the survival of a number of important state monopolies, which in effect legally excluded indigenous entrepreneurs from certain economic fields. Particularly notorious instances of these were, and are, the state oil company Pertamina, and Bulog, the National Supply Board, which controls the import, marketing, and domestic purchase of basic staples. Not surprisingly, these lucrative monopolies were and are the fiefdoms of important military supporters of Suharto.[43]

The reign of the denationalized and thieving generals has led to a great emphasis on infrastructure investments convenient to the export sector and "exotic" projects, frequently capital intensive and very expensive. The satellite-domestic communications network program, in connection with which the GTE-Hughes dispute arose, is one of the "exotics," to which the state had already allocated $840 million in 1978 "without noticeable effect" on communications even in Jakarta, and the *Times* notes that "many bankers and economists question whether the government and this impoverished nation where nearly half the people earn less than $50 a year can really afford" such projects.[44] But the generals like good roads and modern communications, which demonstrate their modernity, serve the convenience of the small upper class who may wish to see Mohammad Ali on television, and facilitate the monitoring and military control of the population. Given their sensitivities to the needs of the masses, the choices are understandable.

The Indonesian generals, even more than the military in Brazil, the Dominican Republic, South Vietnam, and Thailand, have used power to catapault themselves to the top level of elite economic status. They live in "lavish American-style haciendas renting for $1800 and more a month," while hundreds sleep under the new bridges and overpasses of the expanding road networks, in this country with a per capita income still under $200 per year.[45]

Some of them have become fabulously wealthy. The Jakarta press reports Ibnu Sutomo's personal gifts of mosques and athletic stadiums and Robison claims it is common knowledge that "officials and their families are the owners of a large proportion of the luxury Jakarta housing leased to foreign executives...[and are] moving right into riceland ownership on a considerable scale, significantly changing the power structure in rural Indonesia."[46]

With this institutionalized looting of huge proportions, plus a set of policies whereby the generals "guarantee the interests of their corporate [mainly foreign] partners,"[47] it is little wonder that the immense surge of oil revenues contributed little or nothing to rational economic development or succor for the underlying population. In fact, the state oil company, Pertamina, succeeded in running itself into bankruptcy by excessive borrowing, wild misinvestment, and what one Indonesian source referred to as "undoubtedly the worst plundering of the 20th century, maybe in the world."[48] Its excesses left Indonesia with an added debt burden of over $6 billion and a sharply reduced international credit standing, which will be paid for by the general populace. According to the *Wall Street Journal*, Pertamina investments "catered to foreign oil companies by building roads, bridges, houses and schools...[and on the side it was] channeling money primarily to the army for pet projects of various generals." According to the same source,

> ...government investigators have shied away from the most sensitive area of all: the whisper of a connection between Pertamina's dubious adventures and the family of President Suharto. There are countless rumors to be heard in Jakarta that Lt. Gen. Ibnu Sutowo, Pertamina's deposed president, poured Pertamina money into the private business operations of President Suharto's wife and brother.[49]

All things considered, then, the developments of the past dozen years in Indonesia have been favorable to the predominant interests and priorities of the Free World in general, the United States and Japan in particular. Appropriately, therefore, Vice President Mondale stops in Indonesia for a friendly conference with that fellow devotee of freedom and human rights, Suharto, and is much encouraged by an announced release of political prisoners.[50] It almost goes without saying that the State Department will whitewash the continuing massive violation of human rights within Indonesia, and will continue its annual apologetics for the ongoing Indonesian aggression in East Timor. In each instance the State Department relies on statements by the Indonesian government which it accepts (or pretends to accept) at face value without verification. Once again, since our businessmen and military-intelligence establishment are reasonably happy,[51] massive violations of human rights are entirely irrelevant.

It is also entirely understandable that the U.S. response to the 1965-66 holocaust proper was restrained. No congressman denounced it on the floor of Congress, and no major U.S. relief organization offered aid.[52] The World Bank, unaffected by either terror or the systematic looting of bank money,[53] subsequently made Indonesia its third largest borrower, with about $2 billion in loans over the past decade.

Media treatment of the massacres was sparse, with the victims usually described merely as "Communists and sympathizers." Little mention was made of the large numbers of women and children massacred or the modes and details of the slaughter. A characteristic rationalization was that "the people rose up in anger against the Communists" in a "political upheaval [that] had an air of irrationality about it, a touch of madness even...tinged not only with fanaticism but with blood-lust and something like witchcraft"; "nowhere but on these weird and lovely islands" could such an affair have "erupted."[54] The rationalization is useful in suggesting (falsely) that this was a purely spontaneous popular upheaval, a peculiarly Asian form of "madness," not a mass murder coordinated and stimulated from the top with direct participation by the military forces of the state, which acted with Nazi-like "ruthlessness," demonstrating qualities that U.S. specialists had feared they might lack (see note 8). The U.S. liberals who sometimes offer such rationalizations would find them less appealing as an account of Czarist or Nazi pogroms against the Jews, which had a similar blend of popular hostility and top-level encouragement, planning and organization. We have cited media statements about the "positive" and "hopeful" nature of the changes in Indonesia (no details given). With a little time lapse George McArthur, well-known Far Eastern correspondent of the *Los Angeles Times*, has now produced a complete role reversal between assailants and victims. In discussing relations between Indonesia and China he states that

> the Indonesians broke relations in 1965, when the Mao-inspired Communist Party, now outlawed, attempted to seize power and subjected the country to a bloodbath.[55]

This bland statement that it was the victims of the massacre who "subjected the country to a bloodbath" is no slip of the pen, but rather a characteristic formulation. Elsewhere, the same noted correspondent refers to the "attempted Communist coup in 1965" as follows: "That attempt failed in a national bloodbath that ended the career of President Sukarno, who had tried to ride the Communist tiger."[56] These examples exemplify the outer limits of subservience to the government propaganda system. The more typical pattern is to downplay the bloodbath and repression, which continues to this day.

For the leaders of the United States this bloodbath was a plus. In a Freedom House advertisement in the *New York Times* (30 November 1966), signed by "145 distinguished Americans" including Jacob Javits, Dean Acheson, Thomas D. Cabot, Harry Gideonese, Lewis E. Powell, Whitelaw Reid, Lincoln Bloomfield, and Samuel Huntington, the events in Indonesia were treated as follows: "It [the Vietnam intervention by the United States] provided a shield for the sharp reversal of Indonesia's shift toward Communism, which has removed the threats to Singapore and Malaysia." And as we have already noted, in the statement on Asian policy sponsored by Freedom House and signed initially by 14 leading "moderate" political scientists and historians, later by many others, the series of events that included the huge Indonesian bloodbath were described merely as "dramatic changes" implicitly constructive in character, although these scholars, as noted earlier, condemn "violence" as a mode of achieving social change.[57] This humanistic treatment was paralleled by that of the late Prime Minister of Australia, Harold Holt, who told the River Club of New York City in July, 1966 that "with 500,000 to 1,000,000 Communist sympathizers knocked off, I think it is safe to assume a reorientation has taken place."[58]

Late in 1972 General Maxwell Taylor explained to *U.S. News and World Report* that "Indonesia's independence today and its relative freedom from an internal Communist threat is attributable, to a large degree, to what we've accomplished in South Vietnam." With large U.S. forces moving into Vietnam the Indonesian anti-Communists "were willing to run the risk of eliminating President Sukarno and destroying the Indonesian Communists."[59] That's all. It apparently does not even occur to this "military adviser to four presidents" that any moral issue might arise in "destroying the Indonesian Communists." This was a constructive bloodbath. The victims, once identified as Communists, have lost all claim to humanity and merit whatever treatment they received. What is more, the victims may have been largely ethnic Chinese and landless peasants, and the "countercoup" in effect reestablished traditional authority more firmly.[60] Since the result was the preservation of a neo-colonial economic and social structure and an "open door" to U.S. investment, only sentimentalists will moralize over the bloodbath. The academic, business, political, and intellectual leaders of the United States must turn their attention to more serious matters.

4.2 Thailand: A Corrupt "Firm Base"

An important illustration of U.S. sponsorship and support for subfascist terror regimes of better than average viciousness and venality—and an equally consistent lack of sympathy with any democratic political tendencies—is provided by recent Thai history. Thailand emerged from World War II as the only state in Southeast Asia whose military leadership had collaborated with the Japanese to the extent of declaring war on the United States and Great Britain. Immediately after the war U.S. officials refused to go along with the British desire to dismantle the apparatus of military power in Thailand. Thereafter the United States gradually increased its support of the military faction. As a result, after a few years of constitutional rule characterized by "temporizing" support of the democratic forces by the United States, the military was able to reestablish full control, and Phibun Songkhram became "the first pro-Axis dictator to regain power after the war..."[61] Phibun quickly mastered the art of extracting both moral and material support from the U.S. cold warriors ("milking," to use Joe Stilwell's earthy reference to Chiang), constantly creating alarms of external and internal Red threats, and encouraging local newspapers "to denounce the United States so that his government could appeal for more U.S. aid on the grounds that it would help to pacify this 'anti-American' segment of public opinion":[62] and, of course, serving as a loyal agent of his North American supporters in SEATO and elsewhere.

In the apt language of the NLF's description of the Diem regime and its successors, this was a "country-selling government." In the Orwellian perceptions of Washington officialdom, however, this all reflected the free choice of the Thai people ("Thailand [sic] decided to adopt collective security as the basis for its foreign policy").[63] Phibun used the diplomatic support, money, and arms provided by the U.S. leadership as his primary source of political power in Thailand, frequently timing his violence against his opponents to "coincide with an important meeting of the SEATO alliance, thereby minimizing local and foreign criticism."[64] As the Thai police state consolidated itself and became both more bloody and more corrupt, U.S. support was in no way diminished and criticism by U.S. leaders, public and private, was minimal. In fact, "a notable trend throughout this period was the growing intimacy between the Thai military leaders and the top-level military officials from the United States."[65] Legion of Merit awards were given to three Thai generals in 1954, and in 1955 Phibun himself was given a Doctorate of Laws at Columbia University and the Legion of Merit award by Eisenhower for his services in "the cause of freedom." Vice President Nixon referred to Thailand's "dedication to freedom," while New York Governor Dewey was most impressed with the "settled, orderly situation...a steady improvement toward stability."[66]

When attention is called to the fact that Thailand under U.S. auspices has been a military dictatorship, the official response has been to point to "encouraging" political trends. If none could be dredged up at a particular moment, "Asian nature" and customs have been cited, along with the need to preserve Thailand's "independence."[67] At the time of Ambassador Leonard Unger's appearance before the Senate Foreign Relations Committee in 1969, a constitutional facade was in fleeting existence, and he was greatly encouraged by this development, which "rounds out a system in which the people of the country feel that they do have representation in Bangkok..."[68] But if their democracy is not quite like ours, the Thai people "have their own conviction about the better system of government, about how representation should be carried out...and I personally believe it would be a mistake for us to try to lecture them on the operation of democracy."[69] Our lectures in fact have been accolades to the military dictators; and to fend off criticism at home, philosophical observations on Asian nature have been coupled with the plea that it would be arrogant of us to intrude into the internal affairs of "independent" states. In fact, however, U.S. impact and influence were continuous and decisive in helping the military faction to extinguish the constitutional regime of 1946-1947 and to consolidate military rule thereafter.

The large inflow of U.S. aid and arms, which totalled in excess of $2 billion between 1949 and 1969, in the official (Unger) view, helped Thailand "to improve its internal security forces so that it will be better able to meet the guerrilla and terrorist threats which have been mounted by the Communists."[70] In reality, throughout this period, until the U.S. invasion of Vietnam in 1965, the

Communist "threat" in Thailand was slight, and the obvious and predictable use and effect of this aid was to establish a police state and suppress the substantial non-Communist opposition.

Another facet of the official mythology and propaganda regarding arms aid is that it "contributed to Thailand's economic growth by enabling Thailand to devote a greater share of its resources to economic development."[71] Awkwardly, however, between 1954, the year of the SEATO treaty, and 1959, the value of Thai military expenditures rose by 250%. This was explained by Unger as a result of growth stimulated by military aid, which provided "an expanding income some of which could be devoted to security expenditures."[72] But Thai income per capita in 1959 was well below the levels of 1950-1952.[73] Control by an internally unconstrained military junta, dependent on the largesse of an external sponsor engaged in an anti-Communist crusade, is the key to this huge expansion of military outlays in a country with pressing development needs.

Rising security expenditures were part of the total package of aid-armaments-repression that was immensely advantageous to the Thai military elite and at the same time met the requirements of the selectively benevolent tutelage of the U.S. cold warriors. In this package the military leaders of this "land of the free" (Dulles) not only were able to rely on U.S. support to establish and control a police state, but also were able to convert their political power into graft and monopoly income, including significant contributions by the U.S. taxpayer. From 1948 onward they "took over the directorships of banks, private companies, and government corporations, and they diverted large amounts of public funds to themselves."[74] Each military leader developed a huge private income to finance his own political organization. Police Chief Phao (U.S. Legion of Merit, 1954) "derived most of his funds from the opium trade," while army chief Sarit (U.S. Legion of Merit, 1954) got the proceeds of the national lottery.[75] At his death in 1963 Sarit left a fortune of approximately $140 million, a matter disclosed only when relatives began squabbling over the booty.[76]

As in Indonesia, much income of the military elite has been derived from dozens of state enterprises run by and for military officers. Also reminiscent of Indonesia is the sizable income flow produced by a generalized shakedown—i.e., "it was virtually impossible to run a major business or build a small one into a large one without enlisting the support of military men, which meant money and directorships."[77] The Bangkok Bank during its period of boom growth had on its board four senior army generals and an army Field Marshal, and board members received substantial fees. A banker with close ties to the military said that the late General Kris Sivara, while on only a handful of boards, was paid handsomely by over 200 companies as "he was their protector."[78]

A substantial fraction of U.S. aid has almost certainly gone into the pockets of members of the military juntas, a fact sometimes revealed "in the extensive travel and luxuries they enjoyed after fleeing the country."[79] Former CIA analyst Darling suggested that the military leadership of Thailand was able to siphon off for their personal use a staggering 12% of the national income.[80] The acceptability of this huge plundering to the U.S. leadership can be interpreted as recognition of the "Asian nature" of the elements who could best serve cold war ends (the same people, in this case, who could best serve the aims of the Japanese co-prosperity sphere during World War II), and the necessary costs to the U.S. taxpayer of purchasing the services of these "patriots".

Bloodshed by the Thai military juntas in consolidating this police state has been substantial, but it has not noticeably disturbed their sponsors. Truman's Ambassador Stanton was particularly energetic in urging even more vigorous repression, and "frequently encouraged Phibun to be alert to the allegedly increasing signs of Communist subversion among intellectuals, students, priests, and writers."[81] After the 1957 coup, according to Darling:

> It was also discovered that the police chief [Phao, opium trader and recipient of the U.S. Legion of Merit] had been much more ruthless in suppressing his political opponents than formerly assumed. Some of his atrocities rivaled those of the Nazis and the Communists. The graves of Nai Tiang Sirikhand and four unidentified persons were uncovered in Kanburi province, and further investigation revealed that these victims had been strangled to death while being interrogated by the police. Tiang had been a courageous leader in the Free Thai movement during World War II

> and later served in the National Assembly. Phao claimed that the former Free Thai leader had escaped from Thailand and joined the Communists.[82] The deaths of other victims of the police were also investigated, but the extent of the torture and murder committed by the former police chief will probably never be fully known.[83]

One of the "major assets" of the police chief was

> the extensive assistance he received from the American-owned Sea Supply Corporation which enabled him to build the police force into a powerful military organization which was better led, better paid, and more efficient than the army...By 1954 American assistance enabled Phao to increase the police force to 42,835 men or one policeman for every 407 people. This was one of the highest ratios between policemen and citizens of any country in the world.[84]

The Sea Supply Corporation was a CIA front and Phao was a CIA tool. The 1957 coup that ousted him from power was carried out by the army, which had been built up as a separate military force jostling for control by the Pentagon. U.S. penetration of Thailand was so extensive by the mid-1950s that the dominant factions—all military, and all extremely right-wing—were proxies for competing U.S. military and intelligence factions.[85] U.S. domination was so complete, and the denigration of civilian rule so thorough, that the U.S. construction of bases in Thailand was begun in the early 1960s without the knowledge of the Thai foreign minister or any other civilian leaders of that puppet state.[86] Militarization of Thailand went steadily forward after the 1957 coup, with heavy U.S. involvement in counterinsurgency and police programs. As noted by Thadeus Flood:

> Not only did massive, purely military assistance intensify the militarization of Thailand during the Sarit regime, but the so-called "economic aid programs," which to most Americans mean bettering peoples' health and welfare, did the same. From FY 1967 through FY 1972, "almost $100 million in 'economic aid' went to civil police administration, an aspect of the counterinsurgency pro-

> gram, and the Accelerated Development Program, another counterinsurgency program.[87]

All of this was *before* the U.S. counterinsurgency experts themselves claimed the existence of any armed insurgency in the Thailand countryside, which was in 1965.[88] This was a form of bribery, a *quid pro quo* to the Thai military police elite for turning over their country to the U.S. military. Lobe notes that

> a number of U.S. officials saw no other explanation for the dramatic increase in aid levels when no objective emergency existed. No significant battles between the police and guerrillas occurred until mid-1965, and the training and new equipment that OPS had already so generously granted the Thai police had not been demonstrated deficient.[89]

The Vietnam War made Thailand even more thoroughly an occupied satellite of the United States, with 50,000 U.S. military personnel using Thailand as a "landlocked aircraft carrier" in 1968 for bombing raids against the Indochinese peasant societies. Thai mercenaries were also used extensively in Laos and Vietnam. The period of war boom and U.S. occupation brought with it inflation, an influx of foreign capital, a huge bar and prostitution industry—the corruption of Bangkok in this regard was notorious—and an artificial prosperity that temporarily covered over intensifying economic and social problems. The ending of the U.S. military build-up in 1968 began a period of serious political as well as socioeconomic difficulties, including a need to come to terms with the prospective U.S. withdrawal from Indochina. A short interval of democratization in 1969-1970 was succeeded by another military coup (November, 1971), after which a further period of economic difficulties and a growing tide of unrest culminated in the October, 1973 uprising. The largest demonstration in Thai history took place in Bangkok on October 13 (some 250,000 people), and a temporary retreat from power of the disorganized military-police establishment followed.[90]

The period between October, 1973 and October, 1976, when the generals reassumed control, was an extremely delicate one, with many forces contending for power. The U.S. role during these years, and in the bloody outcome, deserves close examination.

When the military was ousted from power in 1973, there existed a situation in some ways even less propitious for the success of democracy than that in Chile following the election of Allende. As with the Chilean case, there existed a very precarious balance of power between the political leadership nominally in control and the economic and military infrastructure which had at their disposal very effective means of vetoing government actions. And while in Chile there was some separation between the power structures of the economy and the military, in Thailand, the two were nearly identical.

But, if the conditions favoring democratic development were less than auspicious, the attempted changes were also less dramatic than in Chile. The government at no time attempted anything approaching a socialist program. Indeed, up until October, 1974, the country was ruled under the interim constitution of 1972, which was written by the generals, and the first free elections (which still excluded the Communists) were not held until the end of January, 1975.[91]

As might be expected, the economic situation under the new government was also anything but favorable. In a sense, the chickens of the war-based prosperity of the previous decade had come home to roost, to the disadvantage of the democratic government. The oil crisis and rise in energy prices also took their toll during the brief democratic interlude. The economic difficulties were exacerbated by a releasing of the pent-up grievances of the now legalized labor movement, whose strikes also inconvenienced and upset the middle class. Democracy brought with it a surge of cultural and intellectual ferment, in which personal behavior and open criticism of formerly sacrosanct cultural objects confused and disturbed many middle class citizens.[92] The business-controlled mass media made the most of strikes and cultural aberrations to stir up patriotic ardor and a longing for the simplicity of a bygone age. Thus economic and cultural factors helped reduce the base of democratic support among the population.

Significantly, during the democratic years two ultra-right wing movements appeared on the scene which were to prove important in the downfall of the civilian government. These were the Nawaphon movement and the Red Gaurs, both led by men closely linked to the U.S. military-intelligence establishment.

General Wallop Rojanawisut, one of the founders of both the Nawaphon movement and the Red Gaurs, was trained in psychological warfare in the United States and headed Thai military intelligence. The guiding force behind the Red Gaurs, Colonel Sudsai Hatsadinthon, was an officer in the CSOC (Communist Suppression Operations Command, later the Internal Security Operations Command [ISOC]), the chief counterinsurgency structure of the Thai military. He worked with the CIA in organizing Meo tribesmen from Laos into a counterrevolutionary force and he recruited into the Red Gaurs veterans of Thai forces that had fought in Vietnam. Both Nawaphon and the Red Gaurs were terrorist organizations using assassinations, beatings, threats of force, and disruptive tactics to break strikes, disperse demonstrations, destroy or intimidate any opposition media, bombing presses and killing or threatening publishers, journalists and newsdealers. They were remarkably successful, with a large part of the progressive media in Thailand stifled, while right wing papers and journals were untouched. All of this was done, along with other acts of violence, with police connivance or protection.[93]

Thus a new and open violence grew during this period, associated in large measure with the activities of these organized terrorist groups, and profoundly affecting the political process. In contrast with the peaceful elections of January, 1975, in which the left did rather well, the election of April, 1976 was violent and brutal, and the legal left was virtually eliminated—more than 40 people were killed, almost all of them students and leftists, including the secretary-general of the Socialist Party, and there were numerous fire bombings and other acts of terror. During the 1976 elections Nawaphon contributed financially to a number of rightist candidates, and backed the extreme-right party Thammathipatai, which did very poorly in the election. It was widely believed in Thailand that foreign, and mainly U.S. money flowed to some of these right wing groups and parties.[94] Despite the crushing electoral defeat of the ultra-right, however, its sponsors were about to resume uncontested control of the state.

The military establishment had a great deal to lose from the consolidation in power of a genuinely democratic order—it had become a huge corruption machine, operating and looting government enterprises, engaged in the massive shakedown system described above, and controlling the flow of U.S. military and economic aid, while siphoning a good part of it into its own pockets. U.S. and Japanese business did not like the prospects of democracy in Thailand either, with unions and strikes once more in evidence, and threats to such appurtenances of subfascism as favorable minerals concessions and low tax rates. And the U.S. military-intelligence establishment of course, faced a loss of access.

The battle lines become even clearer when it is recalled that these events occurred during a period of rapid deterioration in the U.S. position in Indochina. Thailand, having served as a strategic base for the U.S. military during the war, was still prized by the U.S. military for the Utapao naval base and the Ramesuan complex, the largest and most sophisticated U.S. electronic-intelligence installation outside of the U.S. and West Germany. Because the student-led democratic movement was calling for an elimination of the U.S. military presence in Thailand, it presented a direct obstacle to U.S. aims in the area, threatening the corrupt but "firm base" that the U.S. had enjoyed, compliments of the generals.

The government during the period of civilian rule, while itself somewhat paralyzed in its efforts at reform, was also doing things which made the fight against Communist guerrillas in the outlying provinces more difficult to pursue in the manner to which the army and police were accustomed. In March of 1975, the Interior Ministry revealed that its investigation of the Communist Suppression Operations Command and turned up a pattern of indiscriminate killing of suspects and in particular the summary execution of at least 70 people during 1970-1971 in Patthalung Province. These executions would not have been any more cause for notice than others previously, but for the fact that they seemed to mark a new style of killing in which the victims were first clubbed unconscious and then incinerated in oil drums to eliminate the evidence.[95]

In October, 1976, all the various forces acting to destabilize Thai democracy came to a head. The rightist elements, in an alliance with a fearful monarchy, were on the offensive with wild verbal attacks and increasingly numerous physical outrages.[96]The students were sitting-in at Thammasat University to protest the return to Thailand of Field Marshal Thanom Kittikachorn, former Prime Minister and dictator during the period of the largest U.S. military presence in Thailand. The border police (created by the CIA in 1951 and still closely linked with the CIA in fighting the guerrilla insurgents) and the Red Gaurs attacked the students, who were virtually unarmed. Sharpshooters, automatic weapons, and even an eight foot recoilless rifle were used in dislodging the students, rather than the usual and less violent tear gas and clubs. Forty or more students were killed and some were burned alive by the Red Gaurs. This fighting completely disabled the already fragmented student movement and the military coup which took place on October 6th was quite predictable.

The U.S. role in the 1976 overthrow of Thai democracy and the return to subfascist rule was clear and familiar in pattern. The establishment of a democratic government in late 1973 and early 1974 led to a sharp increase in military aid and a reduction in the modest economic aid, despite the troubled economic condition of Thailand. Just as in the case of Chile before the military coup, the intent was clearly hostile to the new democratic forces and supportive of the anti-democratic military-police establishment. In the years after 1973 the United States sent $150 million in military aid to Thailand, while economic aid fell from $39 million to $17 million in 1975. U.S. sales of military equipment in fiscal 1976 totaled $89.6 million, more than Thailand had purchased in the previous 25 years combined.[97]

It was indicated earlier that the neo-fascist terrorist organizations that played such an important role in disrupting the short-lived democratic system, the Red Gaurs and Nawaphon, were intimately connected with U.S. military-intelligence operations. Both organizations emerged out of the Communist Suppression Operations Command, the major anti-Communist, counterinsurgency organization set up and funded by the United States in 1965. The leaders of both terrorist organizations were affiliated with CSOC and had close earlier links with U.S. officials. CIA financing and organizational support to these terrorist organizations is widely alleged.[98] The CIA presence in Thailand had been substantial, with 100 operatives reported there in 1974. But as Flood has noted:

> Yet, to understand the October 6 rightwing military *coup,* and the subsequent repression, bookburning, and the like, it is not necessary to posit the overt presence of CIA officers directly manipulating events in Bangkok with walkie-talkies. It is only necessary to look at the cumulative effects of almost a quarter century of careful cultivation by the U.S. of an essentially fascist-minded, repressive, reactionary, privileged military elite, faced with a majority of farmers and laborers who have been deprived of the dignity of political, social or economic recognition. Given the "polarization" inherent in the situation, and the promotion by United States strategies of the rightwing military and police, a move by rightwing military to...displace civilian government was inevitable, with or without CIA direct manipulation.[99]

Flood's final assessment is worth quoting at some length:

> In the longer perspective, the entire Thai military and police structure is the creation of the United States. More specifically in reference to the recent bloody coup, the American-sponsored, -funded, -trained and -advised Internal Security Command—formerly the Communist Suppression Operations Command—has been the very embodiment of the American solution to the social problems of Asia: the counterinsurgency technique. Begun by a handful of CIA officers in the 1950s, pursued with thousands of Americans in a maze of the U.S. Defense Department agencies in Thailand in the '60s and early 70s, the counter-insurgency technique has revealed itself again in Thailand—as in South Korea, the Philippines, Indonesia, and the countries of Indochina until the end of the war, a technique to counter indigenous democracy, civilian sovereignty, human rights and social justice.
>
> The old altruistic illusions that the early technicians of counter-insurgency carried with them to Thailand have long since been stripped away. The ugly reality is that the intensive application of counter-insurgency techniques has produced in Thailand a political system markedly

> reminiscent of the civilian-military fascism of the '30s and '40s. It is to the shame of the United States that this system is a direct progeny of a quarter-century of American intervention, especially via the Central Intelligence Agency and the Department of Defense, in the destinies of the people of Thailand.[100]

In the 1973-1976 period of a weak democratic rule, terminated by a military coup, one searches in vain even for *verbal* support by the United States for the new democracy, for warnings to the powerful fascistic forces to restrain themselves, or for threats of any cut-off of aid or of other kinds of intervention in the event of an anti-democratic turnover. A pointless search, because the "land of the free," despite the Orwellian impression to the contrary, was the main sponsor of Thai subfascism after World War II and continued that pattern from 1973 up to the present. The benefits to the U.S. leadership from support of this series of bloody and corrupt tyrannies have been simple and decisive. For U.S. money and help in preserving their power and filling their pockets, this military clique has been willing to subordinate its foreign policy to that of the United States, serve as agent and errand boy, maintain an "open door" to U.S. economic interests, and allow the use of Thailand as a base for U.S. counterrevolutionary intervention in Southeast Asia.[101] Immediately following the Geneva Accords of 1954 the National Security Council laid out a plan for subversion throughout Southeast Asia, with Thailand "as the focal point of U.S. covert and psychological operations," including "covert operations on a large and effective scale" throughout Indochina, with the explicit intention of "making more difficult the control by the Viet Minh of North Vietnam."[102] Subsequently, it became the landlocked aircraft carrier for the U.S. wars in Vietnam and Laos, as well as a source of mercenaries, as already noted. The toleration level of U.S. leaders for graft, torture, and bloodbaths by "patriotic leaders" willing to defend their independence against Communist aggression by serving as a "firm base" for their sponsor's activities, is boundless.

The mass media have played their usual role in support of subfascism by the familiar devices: minimal coverage of the details of official Thai corruption and violence;[103] transmission of

Thai-U.S. official views of problems and issues as the almost exclusive form of "information";[104] and a simple refusal to probe beneath the surface of personalities and political shifts to expose the crucial U.S. role in creating, building, and shaping Thai militarism. A benevolent king, a great many generals, unruly students, an unstable political scene, some typically Asian corruption, a beautiful countryside, a traditionally friendly relationship between the United States and a Thailand whose freedom and independence the U.S. has been generously trying to protect—this is the pattern of images conveyed to the public by the U.S. media, and it is a masterpiece of deceptive propaganda.

4.3 Repacification in the Philippines

There is no better illustration of the promise that U.S. policy holds for Southeast Asia and the Third World in general than the case of the Philippines, the only official U.S. colony in Asia for half a century, and now still very much in the U.S. sphere of influence, one more militarized, repressive, and venal totalitarian free enterprise system, with the "haves" resorting once again to open violence to protect their interests against challenges from the "have-nots". After a brief interlude of post-World War II quasi-independence and CIA-manipulated democracy, the democratic facade was suspended under Marcos in 1972—without significant negative response from the United States[105]—and the standard client fascist model was put into place and given undeviating support by the Nixon, Ford and Carter administrations.

Filipino nationalists had declared their independence from Spain in 1898, only to be faced with an extended U.S. war of counterinsurgency, complete with massacres of civilians, burnings of villages, torture, and the other appurtenances of pacification. In those less cynical days U.S. commanders openly admitted their intention to turn resisting areas into a "howling wilderness."[106] The problem faced by the U.S. conquerors was well expressed by General J. Franklin Bell, who explained that "practically the entire population has been hostile to us at heart." Thus it was necessary to terrorize them into submission, keeping them "in such a state of anxiety and apprehension that living under such conditions will soon become unbearable" and their "burning desire for the war to cease" will ultimately "impel them to devote themselves in earnest to bringing about a real state of peace...[and]...to join hands with the Americans."[107] Hundreds of thousands of Filipinos were pacified permanently in this early exercise in winning hearts and minds.

Filipino nationalists, incidentally, knew very well what was to come when they attempted to defend their newly-won independence from U.S. forces dispatched—on direct orders from the Almighty Himself, as President McKinley explained—to secure this outpost for freedom in Asia. One wrote that the Filipinos

> have already accepted the arbitrament of war, and war is the worst condition conceivable, especially when waged by an Anglo-Saxon race which despises its opponent as an alien or inferior people. Yet the Filipinos accepted it with a full knowledge of its horror and of the sacrifices in life and property which they knew they would be called upon to make.[108]

The period of explicit colonial rule, lasting from 1898 to 1946 (with a brief World War II interregnum of Japanese occupation), was characterized by economic and political domination by U.S. administrators and a local and U.S.-based economic elite. The local elite was made up largely of major landholders whose interests were cemented to those of the United States by the privileged U.S. market position of Philippine sugar, though there was also a business class, partly independent but much of it servicing predominant U.S. economic interests. After the defeat of Japan in World War II, the Philippines were granted technical independence under the rule of a conservative oligarchy closely linked to the United States, with the pre-war colonial economy restored. The pre-1972 (pre-martial law) economy of the Philippines was one of extremely concentrated economic and political power, with a powerful landlord and business class (the famous "400" families) and enormous U.S. influence based on a nearly $2 billion investment and a network of business, financial and military linkages.[109]

The first president of the newly "independent" country was

Japanese collaborator Manuel Roxas, reinstated by General MacArthur under the pretext that he had been a double agent. The Philippine Communist Party (PKP), which had been in the forefront of the anti-Japanese guerrilla struggle, attempted "to enter the Philippine political arena legally through a front political party, the Democratic Alliance (DA)," but "failed, as DA-elected members of the Philippine Congress were denied their seats..."[110] The insurgency that followed was suppressed with extensive U.S. aid. This peasant rebellion had its roots in grievances and injustices that had become increasingly severe under U.S. colonial rule, and was a direct consequence of the violence and lawlessness of the elites linked to the U.S. colonial system and the brutal postwar repression of the anti-Japanese resistance forces by the United States, which lent its support to the Japanese collaborators among the landowning classes and devoted itself to destruction of the anti-Japanese resistance, very much as in Thailand, and for essentially the same reasons. Peasants turned to rebellion (stigmatized as "Communist terror") when very moderate demands were met with mounting force and violence by the United States and its local allies drawn from the wealthy elites.[111] As Jonathan Fast observed, "the Philippine counter-insurgency effort of the early 1950s served as a laboratory for later American involvement in Vietnam," where General Lansdale "tried to repeat his Philippine success with Ngo Dinh Diem."[112]

From 1946 to 1972 the economy of the Philippines expanded rapidly within its neo-colonial and dependency framework. The salient features of this "success" are described by van der Kroef: "declining real wage rates,[113] persistent extreme disparities in income levels, the seemingly unchecked power of private U.S. capital (especially in the context of the operations of a few Filipino family corporations)"; and "graft and corruption prevalent everywhere, but particularly in government, whose machinery of justice was felt to benefit only the rich."[114] The democratic facade of the Philippines was extremely brittle in this society dominated by external interests and a tiny and very wealthy elite, including the U.S. favorite Ferdinand Marcos.

A domestic crisis sharpened in the early 1970s, based fundamentally on the injustices of this exploitative elite-dominated society, but precipitated by a rising tide of nationalism, fueled both by hostility to the Vietnam War and by resentment at continued U.S. economic domination and further penetration. The ruling of the Supreme Court of the Philippines in 1972 that the United States could no longer maintain its privileged position in land ownership, and that U.S. citizens and corporations were subject to the general ban on foreign ownership of Philippine land, brought the situation to a head. Marcos declared martial law in September 1972, and followed this with widespread arrests of opposition figures and intellectuals, tight control of the press,[115] and "new constitutional proposals considerably more favorable to American business interests than leftist and more radical nationalist sentiment in the [Constitutional] Convention would have wanted."[116] Marcos "seemed eager to stay on the right side of the U.S. capital...He also seemed intent on expanding opportunities for the domestic Philippine business of a few powerful families whose links with foreign interests, and preponderant power in so many aspects of Philippine political life have long been viewed, particularly in PKP and NPA [New People's Army] circles, as major obstacles to all significant reforms"[117]—and rightly so.

When Marcos declared martial law in 1972 he announced a number of aims: reestablishing civil order, a crackdown on corruption, an intention to carry out major social reforms, and—more muted and passed along more quietly to foreign governments and business interests—an intent to improve the investment climate for business. Only the conservative and business-oriented objectives have been seriously pursued. Although Marcos spoke of leading a "revolution of the poor," this was cynical demagoguery—he has led a counterrevolution of a rich and expatriate elite. It was noted earlier that since 1972 corruption has not diminished in the least, but rather has shifted in composition of the looter class toward Marcos's family and friends.[118] His land reform has been insignificant, enabling perhaps 40,000 out of several million tenant families *to begin making payments* for land purchases from their landlords.[119] Wages have been controlled by martial law abridgments of labor rights to organize and strike,[120] and the operation of "natural forces" under totalitarian free enterprise conditions has exercised a further (and familiar) depressing influence on wages—in particular, the conversion of agricultural land to export and agribusiness has accelerated the displacement of rural labor and its flow into shanty-town suburbs. Since Marcos assumed the presidency in 1965 the real wages of blue collar and rural agricultural workers have fallen by one-third and middle class groups such as civil servants have also suffered major declines in real income.[121]

Social resources have gone heavily into beautifying Manila while the countryside, where over 85% of the population live, "has been committed to slumber in the 19th century," Wideman reports.[122] He adds that to impress foreign visitors the martial law government invested $608 million in 14 hotels and a convention center in Manila—all of them money losers—while over a quarter of the Manila population live in shanties and life in the rural areas is usually even more bleak. The allocation of resources between the military establishment and urgent social needs such as medical facilities has also been typically subfascist; there has been a huge military build-up since 1972, the armed forces quadrupling in size to 225,000 and military outlays also increasing by more than five fold (from $129 million in fiscal 1973 to $676 million in fiscal 1977). While military-police expenditures soar, in Eastern Visayas 85% of the population cannot afford to enter a hospital. According to public health officials, 37% of all doctors and 46% of all Philippine nurses work in Manila. Wideman reports further that although pneumonia and tuberculosis are the two major killers in the Philippines, there are no programs for their eradication. And despite the scarcity of health care in the rural areas, "Imelda Marcos, who was appointed Metro Manila governor by her husband the president, spent $50 million on a palatial Manila heart sanatorium (which is largely unused)."

The human rights-U.S. aid pattern is also familiar. Over 60,000 persons had been arrested under martial law by 1977, with the numbers detained at any one time necessarily obscure but running into the thousands. As late as December, 1975, Marcos asserted that "no one, but no one, has been tortured." But in fact torture has been "widespread and systematic" according to Amnesty International, and 88 individual torturers were identified by name by AI in 1976. The forms employed are the ones that have now been standardized throughout the empire, fantastically cruel and sadistic, and highly reminiscent of those we associate with Nazism:

prolonged beatings with fists, kicks and karate blows, beatings with a variety of contusive instruments—including rifle butts, heavy wooden clubs and family-sized soft drink bottles, the pounding of heads against walls or furniture (such as the edge of a filing cabinet), the burning of genitals and pubic hair with the flame of a cigarette lighter, *falanga* (beating on the soles of the feet) and the so-called "lying-on-air" torture, in which an individual is made to lie with his feet on one bed, his head on a second bed, with his body "lying-on-air" in between; the individual is then beaten or kicked whenever he lets his body fall or sag.

A particularly insidious pattern of interrogation/torture which emerges from the interviews is the use of "safe houses" as they are called—they are in fact torture centers which are used by the National Intelligence Service Agency or NISA. The following description...will give some idea of what has happened to martial law detainees taken to "safe houses."

"He was beaten with a wooden club with four flat surfaces and an inscription on it. The torturers concentrated on his thighs, lower legs and buttocks, but also struck his head, face, chest, stomach and back with the club. He vomited often during and after the beatings. His entire body grew swollen and areas of skin were stripped from his thighs. The scars continued to be painful when touched.

"The AI delegates found there were still two deep scars on his legs, a year and a half later, which were not completely healed. There were three scars on his legs from cigarette burns."

It should be noted that NISA is an intelligence agency answerable only to President Marcos and under the command of the President's personal head of security, General Fabian Ver.

There are other disturbing patterns of torture which emerge from the interviews. For example, a large number of detainees who were interrogated by the Metropolitan Command of the Philippines Constabulary...were sub-

> jected to torture by electro-shock...Two sisters in their early twenties, who were recently released without having been charged or tried after two years of detention, told us that they were subjected to approximately 45 minutes of electro-shock each, one sister being forced to watch the other. They described the ordeal as follows:
>
> "You can't help screaming—it makes you writhe all over...
>
> "We had hallucinations afterwards—we each lost five pounds from the torture sessions. We couldn't walk straight. We had burns on our hands. They didn't allow us to sleep for almost two nights running. We were threatened with rape from the very beginning."[123]

Mrs. Trinidad Herrera, a well-known community leader of Tondo, a huge squatter suburb of Manila, who has fought for the interests of the poor in opposition to "beautification" projects of Mrs. Marcos, which would have demolished several urban poor communities, was arrested by the regime and subjected to beatings and extensive electric shock tortures including applications to extremities and nipples in a "safe house." Upon release she was in a state of shock and unable to speak for five days. She was released in part because of a strenuous protest by the U.S. Department of State, which was responding to indignant outcries both within the Philippines and abroad. Which all goes to show that in a system of sponsored torture, the sponsor can occasionally demonstrate its essential humanity by such acts of grace.

The Herrera controversy was so intense that her torturers were actually brought to trial—and acquitted.[124] And their work continues unhindered except for momentary pauses on two occasions: (1) when aid to Marcos is under consideration by the U.S. Congress, and (2) when U.S. dignitaries such as Vice-President Mondale stop to visit on their journeys through the subfascist provinces.[125] For these occasions Marcos has mastered the art of making the verbal and tokenistic gestures necessary to placate an indulgent parent, a parent easily reassured on such secondary issues as a total suppression of democratic rights and systematic torture. He may announce a release of political prisoners (although none were admitted to exist previously), or he may proclaim and possibly even hold "demonstration elections,"[126] or he may issue bravados on "interference" and the need to renegotiate the terms of the agreement on U.S. bases in the Philippines. Marcos has little to worry about, however, as he knows from long experience. If he were to do something *serious*, such as expropriating U.S.-owned pineapple plantations, we would witness a less complacent U.S. response, less defensiveness with regard to Marcos, a reduced willingness to be taken in by gestures, and a deeper regard for human rights, not to speak of more forceful measures.

The Marcos regime has been sufficiently disturbed by international publicity and congressional reaction to its political prisoners and use of torture that it has moved to a more advanced subfascist process, namely, the use of unexplained "disappearances" and the police burial of dissidents allegedly killed in "fire fights" with the police and army.[127] By these improvements dissidents are killed and evidence of their torture is eliminated. Thus by the simple deployment of repression techniques used in other parts of the empire, dissidents can be dealt with more efficiently and the State Department can assert that torture "is on the decline."[128]

On the essentials—that is, creating a hospitable investment climate and, in the Philippines case, allowing U.S. occupation of major military base sites—Marcos has been entirely satisfactory, which is the main reason why his human rights violations will never be compellingly important and why U.S. leaders will always be impressed with "improvements" and Marcos' assurances that a better day lies immediately ahead. We saw earlier that Marcos quickly suspended the Supreme Court ruling against U.S. land ownership, and accommodated immediately to the primary condition for subfascist rule: namely, solidifying the external constituency by assuring U.S. business interests that their bidding will be done. *Business Week* noted that Marcos "has made it abundantly clear that he wants to help American business as much as domestic politics will allow."[129] All Marcos asks is a percentage of the take, which is standard practice in the empire; and as with the suspension of democracy and systematic torture this has been quite acceptable.

In fact, as we discussed earlier, repression and torture have been integral to the economic policies of subfascism as instruments for achieving passivity, "order," and "stability". In nationalistic Third World states, allowing multinationals to dominate the economy, to buy out or destroy domestic enterprises, to dispossess large numbers of peasants in a rapid development of export-oriented agriculture, and to implement the deflationary unemployment-generating policies required by the international banking fraternity—all these are not easily achieved within a democratic order. The collective conspiracy of a comprador-business elite, local military officers, and foreign economic and military interests normally cannot maintain "stability" without active or threatened terror. An officer of Manufacturers Hanover Trust bank, speaking of the Philippines, noted in 1976 that "in recent years, major social and political reforms [sic] have reduced the bottlenecks that hampered past efforts to achieve faster economic growth."[130] Since the only social and political reforms in recent years have been the implementation of the Marcos dictatorship and martial law regime, we have here an explicit translation of multinational business values into the concept of "reform" and desirable social and political structures for the Third World. It may throw some light on why the "human rights" crusade remains a dead letter within the U.S. sphere of influence.

In the case of the Philippines the two huge U.S. military installations at Subic Bay and Clark Air Force Base are also a factor influencing U.S. official reactions to human rights violations. The Pentagon wants these bases, and President Carter has been too weak to suffer the loss of face involved in abandoning them—although they have lost most of their value even for a "forward strategy,"[131] and Marcos uses them as an instrument of blackmail and to tie the United States more closely to his totalitarian regime. By holding up the United States for even greater ransom for their use, Marcos extracts more loot from the U.S. taxpayer (about $200 million a year) but also very cleverly conveys the impression of "independence" and of his willingness to stand up to his indulgent parent!

Marcos has provided the requisite terror and "stability" in the Philippines and, accordingly, he has been generously supported by the United States and its affiliated lending agencies. As human rights violations became truly massive under martial law, military aid from the U.S. doubled.[132] U.S. business, banks, and the IMF and World Bank have been greatly encouraged by Marcos' new order, and capital has poured in—foreign investment more than doubled on an annual average basis after 1972, and the external debt of the Philippines rose from $2.2 billion to $6 billion in 1977. The Philippines has become one of the largest borrowers from the international lending organizations, its loans having grown from $182.5 million in 1972 to $1.5 billion in 1976. The sharp increase in U.S. military and non-military aid is thus once more correlated with a major rise in violations of human rights, degradation of the economic and social condition of the majority of the population, *and* an improved investment climate.

The dominant elites of subfascism are fortunate also that the U.S. provides the best that money can buy in repression expertise and technology to help them keep their populations under control. Even before the constitutional convention was aborted by the Marcos coup of 1972, charges had been made that U.S.-AID and the CIA were training Philippine police under the public safety program "for eventual para-military and counterinsurgency operations as part of a global programme designed to militarize and 'mercenarize' the police forces of client states."[133] Between 1948 and 1968 more than $1.7 billion had been provided in U.S. economic and military grants and loans under the U.S. military assistance program, including more than $400 million in hardware.[134] Under the rubric of "technical assistance," U.S.-AID financed the Office of Public Safety (OPS), which was extensively involved "in reorganizing, funding, and training the Philippine police apparatus both in the Philippines and the U.S. from 1965 to September 21, 1972, the day martial law was declared."[135] In December, 1966, Frank Walton, fresh from service in Saigon, where "he oversaw the growth and large-scale reorganization of the South Vietnamese police force—all part of the overall CIA plan to dissolve the political infrastructure of the NLF"[136]—was installed as "Team Chief" for AID/OPS. He was assisted by a variety of U.S. officials with experience in Brazil, the Philippines, Ethiopia, and elsewhere, as well as by Philippine intelligence officers who had been trained by the CIA during the U.S.-backed suppression of the Huk insurgency "and had become resident experts on counter-intelligence operations in and around Saigon."[137] Walton's group submitted a report to USAID in February, 1967 which "served as the impetus for a drastic reorganization of the Philippine police apparatus and for a much enlarged and more involved U.S. Public Safety Division."[138] For fiscal year 1972-1973, the expanded Public Safety program was budgeted by the U.S. government at $3.9 million, a marked increase. Police are trained in the United States at CIA, FBI, army, and local police training centers, and in the Philippines at training academies which "were easily converted into detention camps to hold the large numbers of political prisoners" after martial law was declared.[139]

With increased U.S. involvement in internal security problems, the new program was patterned on the CORDS (Civil Operations and Revolutionary Development Support) program —the pacification program—in Vietnam. The new Philippines project was initially staffed by former CORDS officials from Vietnam headed by Thomas Rose, who was AID public administration chief in Saigon, and Richard Kriegel, former CORDS provincial adviser in Bindinh province. U.S. military units have been "involved in 'civic' operations in conjunction with the Filipino army that clearly had a relevance to internal security problems."[140] On July 12, 1973, William Sullivan was confirmed by the Senate for the post of Ambassador to the Philippines. Sullivan had been U.S. Ambassador in Laos from 1964 to 1969, where as Anthony Lewis remarks, he "played a decisive part in what must qualify as the most appalling episode of lawless cruelty in American history, the bombing of Laos"[141]—an episode which, incidentally, was initially supressed by the *New York Times* editors.[142] Sullivan has had a major role in organizing and coordinating U.S. subversive and military activities in Southeast Asia, and although his contributions to the people of Laos pale before those of murderous successor, G. McMurtrie Godley, who implemented the Nixon-Kissinger program, they nevertheless achieved considerable scale.[143] It is altogether appropriate that Sullivan should have been shifted to the Philippines just as Lansdale moved from the Philippines to Vietnam twenty years earlier, as part of the continuing effort to assist the people of Southeast Asia to remain in the Free World. The logical next step was to dispatch Sullivan to Iran, where he could convey Carter's messages of support to the Shah as his U.S.-armed troops machine-gunned demonstrators in the streets, another application of the famed "human rights" policy.

The resistance to Marcos's police state has grown slowly but persistently under the pressure of systematic abuse of the majority of the population, and there is good reason to suppose that U.S.-supplied weapons, counterinsurgency training and possibly even direct intervention will be needed sometime in the future to shore up a system that violates every principle of humanity. The Muslim Bangso Moro Army, which began large-scale fighting against the regular army in 1972, has been the most pressing internal threat to Marcos's rule. Its 20,000 person army is still resisting effectively after years of bloody encounters (over 5,000 government casualties, 60,000 civilians killed, a million refugees from Marcos's search-and-destroy). This struggle was based on a gradual accumulation of grievances by the Muslim population of the island of Mindanao, especially the continuous territorial encroachment by settlers, loggers, and agribusiness corporations, aided by Philippine Army pacification operations. A revolt was brewing on Mindanao in the 1960s, and it turned into a national rebellion in the early 1970s. Throughout the entire Philippines there is a growing National Democratic Front (NDF), begun in 1973 as a loosely organized coalition of many struggling resistance groups, covering many classes, organizations and strategies, united by a desire to end the "U.S.-Marcos dictatorship."[144] It includes the New Peoples Army (NPA), small but active on many islands, educating and encouraging passive and active guerrilla resistance and warfare in the countryside. The NPA is working a fertile field, since a substantial majority of the population is both rural and severely abused by Marcos's policies. The NDF also includes many members of the urban working class and sub-proletariat, banned from organizing and striking under Marcos regulations, but increasingly organizing and striking outside the law.[145] Large numbers of students, other members of the intelligentsia, and a great many religious workers are also properly included within the NDF. Marcos-U.S. force and threats of force have so far done their job in limiting the effectiveness of the NDF and in keeping the vast majority passive, but the latent hostility to the dictatorship bursts into the open when a little crevice of opportunity arises[146]—and suggests that the present regime may be sitting on a powder keg. All of this is reminiscent of the earlier peasant rebellion of 1946-1956.

There are still those who see U.S. actions in Vietnam as an aberration, a deviation from the disinterested concern and noble efforts that animate U.S. policy in Southeast Asia and elsewhere. This view of essential benevolence, in fact, has dominated scholarship, journalism, and school texts, with the aberration concept a necessary complement, providing an explanation for any ongoing exception. For many years the Philippines have stood as a neglected monument contradicting this conception of the fundamentals of U.S. foreign policy, from the brutal exercise in pacification at the turn of the century to the early post-World War II repression. As the groundwork is being laid in neocolonial economic and social conditions, aided by U.S.-financed and sponsored pacification techniques and policies, no one should be surprised if a renewed constructive bloodbath begins to unfold in that country. This is a system of injustice that daily sows the seeds of its own destruction. It may meet banker standards of worth, but it fails to meet any human criterion—as evidenced by its open reliance on violence and the denial of human rights to the vast bulk of the population. As in many parts of the empire, formerly conservative churches have been forced into open opposition by the sheer inhumanity of subfascist practice and the stripping away of other protective resources from a defenseless population.[147] It is a remarkable and central fact of modern history that the United States has sponsored and continues to support the subfascist state—its police-military arm, its torture, and its savagely exploitative economic policies—and has called forth in country after country a church response as the last refuge of abused majorities.[148]

4.4 The Dominican Republic: U.S. Model for Third World Development

In his *Stages of Economic Growth,* Walt W. Rostow describes a development process for Third World countries that come into our orbit: they become gradually like *us,* with advanced industrial technologies and democratic institutions. The Dominican Republic offers an earthy illustration of the reality of development processes under U.S. auspices. It is an especially apt and relevant case for this reason: with and after the invasion of 1965 the U.S. reasserted effective control over that small country and has thoroughly dominated its politics and economics. Given the absence of any threatening counterforces, we can say that in the Dominican Republic the flow of events surely must have been in conformity with the desires of the U.S. foreign policy leadership.

It will be recalled that the U.S. invaded the Dominican Republic in 1965 to prevent the displacement of the relatively benign fascist regime of Donald Reid Cabral by the Constitutionalist regime of Juan Bosch, who had been overthrown by a military coup in 1963—without eliciting any U.S. intervention to save *him* and his brief experiment in democratic government. The rationalization by Lyndon Johnson and his spokesmen, alleging an imminent threat of Communism, were convincingly shown by Theodore Draper and others to have been a hypocritical cover for a postive preference for fascism over a less reliable and less controllable democratic reformist government.[149] The invasion of 1965 reestablished a firm U.S. grip on the island. As Bosch put it in June, 1975, "This country is not pro-American, it is United States property."[150] What then have been the main characteristics of the Dominican model of Third World development, as seen in a country under close U.S. surveillance and control?

The first characteristic has been extensive and systematic terror. In the Dominican Republic, Guatemala, and Brazil, three client fascist systems that came into being with explicit U.S. connivance, by a strange coincidence para-military "death squads" quickly made their appearance and went on a rampage against political dissenters, petty criminals, and sometimes purely arbitrary victims. Amnesty International called special attention to "the numerous political assassinations carried out by Death Squads (such as the notorious *La Banda*) that have been openly tolerated and supported by the National Police. In 1970 it was alleged that there was one death or 'disappearance' every 34 hours."[51] In July, 1971, Norman Gall alleged that in the post-1965 era, the number of political murders in the Dominican Republic exceeded that of any comparable period under the monstrous Trujillo.[152] Gall noted further that

> The Santo Domingo newspaper *El Nacional* last December 30 filled a page and a half of newsprint with the details of 186 political murders and thirty disappearances during 1970. The Dominican terror resembles the current wave of political killings in Guatemala...in that the paramilitary death squads are organized by the armed forces and police, which in both cases over the years have been given heavy U.S. material and advisory support.

Gall went on to note that the essential function of political terror in the Dominican Republic has been to control the slum population, "which was the main force that defeated the Dominican military in the 1965 revolution." The *Wall Street Journal* reported on September 9, 1971 that "the conservative Catholic Church hierarchy has condemned the 'institutionalization' of terror." The *Journal* also claimed that the opinion was widespread in the Dominican Republic that the United States was behind the paramilitary death squads. Whether or not this specific allegation was true, the *Journal* observed that "the embassy has done nothing publicly to dissociate itself from the terror. The U.S. continues to provide substantial aid, training, equipment, and arms, to the Dominican police and army."

Since 1971 the rate of killing has slackened, but political assassinations continue and the incarceration and torture of political prisoners still plays a key role in maintaining stability. Amnesty International recently stated that "precise, detailed and consistent information...indicates that practices amounting to serious violations of human rights are still going on: the arbitrary arrest, kidnapping, and assassination of the regime's political opponents; the removal of certain political prisoners to isolation in provincial jails and military forts; deplorable prison conditions, ill-treatment and police brutality inflicted on many detainees...and the continued detention of prisoners once their sentences expire."[153]

The U.S. State Department, on the other hand, in its 1978 Human Rights Report to Congress, finds a "substantial reduction in incidents of military and police repression," a working "constitutional democracy," and "over a dozen political parties...officially recognized and freely active although the 1974 elections were marred by some incidents of military intervention on behalf of the President's reelection." On this last point, the Washington Office of Latin America notes that "the State Department demolishes its own argument. Official recognition means little and political parties are not really free if the military acts against them during an election. Harassment of opposition forces has not ceased, despite Balaguer's claim to have ordered the military to remain neutral. In the fall of 1977, as pre-election campaigning for 1978 was beginning, a local headquarters of the social democratic opposition party PRD was burned to the ground and a PRD official, Samuelo Santan Melo, was murdered."[154] Subsequently, of course, the military intervened more comprehensively to avert Balaguer's defeat in May, 1978, seizing the ballot boxes and arresting or driving underground many leaders of the PRD, before pressure from both the Dominican elite and the Carter administration eventually forced the military and Balaguer to allow a transfer of the presidency to Guzman. A wealthy landowner himself, Guzman would not have been running at all, and would not have been allowed to take office, if he had posed a threat of serious reform.[155] The military and its external sponsor assure that the new PRD operates within a very narrow boundary of policy actions.[156] All the more reason then for the State Department to be pleased with the progress of the Dominican Republic, to be reassured by the promises of its leaders, and to find that this client state deserves the funds still allocated to it for military assistance.[157]

A second characteristic of the Dominican Republic model is widespread venality. Alan Riding wrote in 1975 that "the blatant corruption of military and civilian sectors of the government is spreading bitterness among the urban masses, whose wages have been held down despite high inflation rates since 1960."[158] The military and police in this client state are numerous and well taken care of. According to Riding, one method whereby Balaguer retained control was "by openly allowing senior officials to enrich themselves. With official salaries of $700 a month, for example, most of the country's 37 generals live in huge modern houses, drive limousines, and own cattle ranches."

More recently, Jon Nordheimer wrote that

> Corruption among the generals is almost as legendary as is their ineptitude. In the first place there are about twice as many generals—around 40—as there should be for the size of the military forces. Generals are promoted on the basis of family, friendship and business connections...It is common knowledge that Lieut. Gen. Juan Beauchamps Javier, Secretary of State for the Armed Forces, owns a $300,000 yacht in partnership with a Dominican businessman and that Maj. Gen. Neit Nivar Siejas, the commander of the national police, is part owner of a major Santo Domingo hotel and gambling casino.[159]

A recent report to the Securities and Exchange Commission by Philip Morris showed: (1) a $16,000 payment to a Dominican tax official for a favorable tax ruling; (2) the payment of $120,000 to various Dominican legislators for passage of a law that would give Philip Morris a privileged position in the Virginia tobacco line; and (3) monthly payments of $1,000 by Philip Morris to Juan Balaguer himself.[160] The president of a presumably independent state taking payoffs from a private foreign business firm would seem rather sensational, but this passed off virtually unnoticed in the United States. Gulf & Western made $146,000 in "questionable" payments through foreign subsidiaries in 1976, and although the distribution of those payments was not revealed by the SEC, the usefulness of such a lubricant in the Dominican Republic and G & W's large place there rouses plausible suspicions.[161]

U.S. firms get business done in the Dominican Republic not only by payoffs but by putting important people on their payrolls and by building both personal and financial ties to the local elite. Thus in the mid-1970s the brother of the important Director of Tourism was a vice president of G & W's sugar-producing subsidiary in the Dominican Republic. G & W is also reported to have established "cordial relations" with General of the Police Tadeo Guerrero, who was active in the destruction of the last strong independent union in the sugar business.[162]

Gulf & Western is the largest private landowner and employer in the country, with some 8% of all arable land, mainly in sugar, owner of a large resort complex, and with investments in some 90 Dominican businesses. G & W's annual sales are larger than the

GNP of the Dominican Republic, and while it does not by itself control the country, its size, internal connections, and the background support of the external sponsor of Dominican subfascism, give the company a great deal of leverage and might even justify the designation of the Dominican Republic as a "company country."[163] Its rapid expansion within the Dominican Republic since 1967 has been a result, in part, of the great profitability of its sugar operations and an 18% ceiling on profit repatriation.[164]

A potential competitor to Gulf & Western's large seaside resort at La Romana, M. Wayne Fuller, ran into a steady series of obstacles in the early 1970s from the Tourism Office in importing supplies and obtaining tax concessions supposedly available to foreign enterprises. In April, 1975, a government decree was signed expropriating Fuller's beach-land property—for use as a public park—helped along possibly by the fact that the president of another G & W subsidiary was an advisor to the Dominican Republic Park Commission. This decree was rescinded when Fuller mobilized *his* forces, including various army officers and Balaguer himself.[165] In brief, foreign interests are exceedingly powerful as they curry and buy favor and mobilize their elite cadres, with whom they jointly dominate and loot this small dependency.

A third characteristic of the Dominican model has been a radical sweetening of conditions for foreign business and a strong reliance on foreign investment for national development. As in Greece under the Colonels' regime of 1967-1973, great stress has been placed on tourism and investments related to tourism (resort hotels, airport development). An Investment Incentives Law of 1968 removed any restrictions on foreign ownership, extended generous tax and duty exemptions to new investments, and guaranteed capital and profit repatriation. U.S. companies have swarmed into agriculture, food processing, mining, banking and hotel and resort complexes. In 1969 G & W became manager of a large tax-free zone adjacent to G & W's Cajuiles golf course. One of the many Dominican Republic ads in the *New York Times*—funded in good part by "contributions" from foreign companies in the country—notes that companies settling withing the G & W free zone "are given special duty free import and export privileges. They are granted a 10-year tax-free status." The reporter Michael

Flannery describes the G & W "free zone" in the following language:

> Shotgun-toting customs agents and national police man check points at entrances to the free zone, which is surrounded by a high chain-link fence topped with multiple strands of barbed wire...CNTD [National Confederation of Dominican Workers] and visiting officials of the AFL-CIO charged that the zone had the air of a "modern slave-labor camp." They said the carefully controlled access was designed not only to prevent smuggling, but to thwart efforts to organize the workers into unions that would force an improvement in conditions.[166]

A fourth characteristic of the Dominican Republic model, related to the preceding, is effective government pacification of the labor force, a crucial requirement for an appropriate "climate of investment." As noted above, the systematic police terror since 1965 has returned the large urban proletariat and sub-proletariat to the desired state of passivity, and the countryside has been more easily kept in line by periodic violence and threats. The Dominican Republic advertisement section in the *New York Times* of January 28, 1973, has a heading entitled "Industrialists Dream of Chances Like These," featuring the *low,* low wage rates, running between 25 and 50 cents an hour. The ad stresses the role of the *law* in fixing hours and wages and allowing the free import of foreign technicians.[167] There is no mention of any trade unions, but employers will properly read between the lines that unions have been broken and pacified (with the assistance of George Meany and the AFL-CIO). Of special interest is the regular use of government troops and police to break up independent unions. The agricultural union Sindicato Unido, which operated the fields now owned by G & W was broken by police action in 1966 and 1967, and a number of its leaders, including the union lawyer Guido Gil were arrested and killed by the forces of law and order.[168] Another major foreign enterprise, Falconbridge Nickel, also successfully broke a union with army and police assistance in 1970. A *Wall Street Journal* report of September 9, 1971 states that "when a union attempted to organize construction workers at a foreign-owned ferronickel mill project last year, Mr. Balaguer sent in the army to help straighten things out. While the soldiers kept order, the contractors fired 32 allegedly leftist leaders...The strike was broken in eight days." Matters had not changed much in the mid-70s. An *ad hoc* human rights group that visited the Dominican Republic in 1975 reported that "working people have been prevented by nearly every conceivable means from forming and joining trade union organizations."[169] A union organizing effort in the G & W free trade zone in the mid-1970s was broken with the help of the police in arresting, jailing, and deporting labor organizers, and with the use of "troops in full combat gear armed with submachine guns" to break up organizing meetings. Flannery states that

> Officials of the Dominican labor ministry told organizers that—contrary to the paper guarantees of the republic's laws—workers would not be allowed to form a union in the industrial free zone.[170]

On the matter of labor unions, the 1977 State Department Human Rights Report has the following "information": "Labor unions are permitted to function and numerous labor unions exist, including some associated with opposition parties, but under some government controls." That exhausts that topic.

In containing unions and rendering them docile the Dominican elite has had the steadfast support of the top echelons of the AFL-CIO, which has long cooperated closely with the CIA and international business firms in this unsavory operation. Its arm CONATRAL actually helped destroy the pro-labor Bosch regime in 1963 and has steadily supported its totalitarian and anti-labor successors.[171] Presumably their blind hatred of Communism and radicalism in general has led Meany and his close followers to sell out systematically the interests of labor in the Dominican Republic and in other U.S. satellites. Meany and some other labor bosses actually have a more direct interest in the pacification of labor in the Dominican Republic. Meany, his number two man Lane Kirkland, Alexander Barkan, director of COPE, the AFL-CIO political arm, and Edward J. Carlough, president of the sheet metal workers, all are stockholders in the 15,000 acre Punta Cana resort and plantation in the Dominican Republic. In order to clear the ground for this enterprise designed for the Beautiful People a large numbers of squatters were evicted by the army.[172]

A fifth characteristic of the Dominican model, following naturally from the preceding, is the sharp deterioration in the well-being of the bulk of the population. In serving the interests of a traditional and expatriate elite, the Dominican Republic has been turned into a tourist and industrial paradise, with a "25-cent-minimum wage rate and hard-working peaceful labor" [sic: translated, no threat of strikes from any independent unions], and with four tax free zones "filled with manufacturers of brushes, brassieres, batteries, electronic devices, wigs, undergarments, components and consumer goods."[173] The effects of the 1965 counterrevolution and the installation of the Dominican Republic model on income distribution and welfare were summarized by the *Wall Street Journal* (9 September 1971) as follows:

> The middle and upper classes are better off, as are the lower classes lucky enough to have jobs. But work is scarce; the poor are poorer and more numerous. "Per capita income is about the same as before 1965, but it's less equitably distributed," a foreign economic expert says. He estimates per capita income at $240—three times that of Haiti but half that of Cuba...Most of the 370 young women who work at La Romana earn 30 cents to 40 cents hour last year...Malnutrition is widespread. Says George B. Mathues, director of CARE in the Dominican Republic: "You see kids with swollen bellies all over the country, even here in Santo Domingo." Food production is hampered by semi-feudal land tenure. At last count, less than 1% of the farmers owned 47.5% of the land, while 82% farmed fewer than 10 acres...Land reform has moved with glacial speed...Most Dominican children don't go beyond the third grade; only one in five reaches the sixth grade.[174]

G & W acknowledged in 1978 that cane cutter money wages had not kept up with inflation in the years since 1966,[175] and there is other evidence to the same effect,[176] which suggests a probable further absolute fall in the real income of the majority and a further shift toward inequality in income shares. There is also evidence that the nutritional deficit of the Dominican majority is huge.[177] Michael Flannery cites a report which states that in 1972 "a mere 11 percent of Dominicans drink milk, 4 percent eat meat and 2 percent eat eggs. Fish are plentiful in the waters off the island, but draw better prices in other markets. So, few Dominicans include fish in their protein-poor diet."[178]

In the Dominican Republic we see the working out once again of the familiar repression-exploitation-trickle-down model of economic growth. The export-oriented agriculture is, as is common throughout the empire, displacing an already underemployed peasantry and rural work force, increasing the mass of dispossessed and malnourished. The unemployment rate has been extraordinarily high, on the order of 30%-40%.[179] The mass of the population has been entirely excluded from any opportunities for economic advancement, education, or political participation. The large majority as in Brazil, Indonesia, or the Philippines, is a cost to be minimized and a threat to be contained. The process of development observed here is acceptable on the assumption implicit throughout the empire—that only the welfare of the local and expatriate elites need be taken into account. The decline in the welfare of the majority, their exclusion from any power whatsoever, and the cultural degradation of the Dominican Republic, are obviously beside the point. "Stability" has been brought to the country, and from the perspective of U.S. investment opportunities, the Dominican Republic deserves the glowing description of a U.S. Embassy report describing it as a "little Brazil" and "one of the brightest spots in Latin America."

4.5 Latin America: Proliferating Subfascism

> "Friends and Fellow Christians, it is time that you realize that our continent is becoming one gigantic prison, and in some regions one vast cemetery...we—with the exception of Cuba—are trapped in the same system. We all move within one economic-political-military complex in which one finds committed [the] fabulous interests of [the] financial groups that dominate the life of your country and the creole oligarchies of our Latin American nations. Both groups, more allied today than ever, have held back

time after time the great transformations that our people need and desperately demand." (A Latin American Church group).[180]

"The dominant presence of this inevitable parameter—National Security—imposes the tremendous burden of an economy which is viscerally destructive to the normal expectations of development and welfare which move all peoples...Hence a new dilemma—Welfare or Security—previously pointed out by Goering in less just but highly suggestive terms: 'more guns, less butter.' In fact, there is no getting around the necessity of sacrificing Welfare to the benefit of Security when the latter is actually endangered. Those people who refuse to admit this have learned in the dust of defeat a well-deserved lesson." (A Brazilian General).[181]

4.5.1 The Nazi Parallel: The National Security State and the Churches

The two statements quoted above bring out some central features of modern Latin America. A close study of recent trends—including the specific totalitarian ideology of the generals, the system of ideological manipulation and terror, the diaspora, and the defensive response of the churches (and their harassment by the military juntas)—reveals startling similarities with patterns of thought and behavior under European fascism, especially under Nazism. Fascist ideology has flowed into Latin American directly and indirectly. Large numbers of Nazi refugees came to Latin America during and after World War II, and important ingredients of fascist ideology have been indirectly routed into that area through the U.S. military and intelligence establishment. Whatever the source, however, it has met a need of the local and foreign elites that dominate the area, and has been modified to meet their special requirements.

The ideology designated the "National Security Doctrine" (NSD) now prevails among the military elites that rule at least eight Latin American states—Argentina, Bolivia, Brazil, Chile, Ecuador, Paraguay, Peru, and Uruguay. The doctrine has three main elements:[182] (1) that the state is absolute and the individual is nothing;[183] (2) that every state is involved in permanent warfare, its present form being Communism versus the Free World;[184] and (3) that control over "subversion" is possible only through domination by the natural leadership in the struggle against subversion, namely the armed forces.[185] The first two elements of the NSD closely parallel Nazi ideology, which laid great stress on the organic Volkstaat and the deadly combat in process between the forces of good and evil (Bolshevism, Jewry). Geopolitics is also a favorite source of ideological nourishment to the Latin military elite, as it was for the Nazis. Nazi doctrine did not give primacy to the armed forces, although they were assigned an important place, but the Leader and the Party played an elite role. The special place of the armed forces in the NSD reflects in part the self-interested rationalization of the privileged and dominant military elite; it also represents the choice of vehicle by the colossus of the north, which has long invested in the military establishment as potentially "a major force for constructive social change in the American republics"[186] (Nelson Rockefeller).

An important ingredient of Nazi ideology, anti-Semitism, is absent from the NSD, although it has found a home with the military of certain countries (specifically, Argentina, where there has been a long anti-Semitic tradition). But the NSD also lacks any element of egalitarianism or notion of human community, both present in grotesquely perverted form in Nazi ideology, so that the Latin American version has been well adapted to justifying and institutionalizing extreme inequality and domination by a small elite. The NSD is not a doctrine with ugly potential consequences for specific minorities; it is one that fits the need for disregard and spoliation of the *majority*. The special place of army and police merely assures that the military elite will share in the spoliation along with the traditional elite group. It is, therefore, an appropriate doctrine for what we have been calling "subfascism."

Since the generals sponsoring the National Security Doctrine have been nurtured by and dependent on the U.S. military-intelligence establishment, and look to the United States as the heartland of anti-Communism and Freedom, it is little wonder that the economic doctrinal counterpart to the NSD is quite congenial to the interests of multinational business. The military juntas have adopted a "free enterprise—blind growth" model, on the alleged geopolitical rationale that growth means power, disregarding the fact that *dependent* growth means *foreign* power. Since profits equal investment equal growth equal power, it works out that state support for large interests—domestic and foreign—and neglect of the masses, is sound policy. We saw earlier that in the economics of client fascism, that is, National Security Economics, the welfare of the masses is no longer a system objective—the masses become a cost of goods sold, something to be minimized—so that although the military juntas sometimes speak of long run benefits trickling down to the lower orders, this is really an after-thought and is not to be taken too seriously.

Furthermore, since the world is one of good and evil, with "no room for comfortable neutralism" (Pinochet, echoing a familiar refrain of his U.S. mentor), and since free enterprise-growth-profits-USA are good, anybody challenging these concepts or their consequences is *ipso facto* a Communist-subversive-enemy. This is a logical deduction from NSD principles, and it is also clearly just what General Maxwell Taylor had in mind in telling the students of the police academy of the lessons of Vietnam and the need for anticipatory counter-subversion.[187] It also means that any resistance to business power and privilege in the interests of equity, or on the basis of an alternative view of desirable social ends or means, is a National Security and police problem. This applies to such organizations as peasant leagues, unions, student organizations or community or political groupings that might afford protection to the weak or threaten to become a political counterforce to elite domination. From the standpoint of the multinationals and latifundists, this is superb doctrine; reform is equated with subversion, the work force is kept in disarray by state power, and nothing stands in the way of organizing economic life in MNC-latifundist interests that can not be taken care of by a few well-placed bribes. As Nelson Rockefeller has said, in dealing with Latin American countries, for whom democracy "is a very subtle and difficult problem," we must be prepared to sacrifice some of our philosophical principles in the interest of helping "meet the basic needs of the people of the hemisphere."[188]

In Nazi Germany too, as in other totalitarian societies, a primary aim of the controlling leadership was the destruction of any organizational threat that might challenge the attainment of "state" ends; and unions, students and professional organizations, and community groups and political parties were infiltrated, harassed, destroyed, or brought under state control. The most powerful bases of organized resistance in Nazi Germany were the churches, which provided the "most active, most effective, and most consistent" opposition to Nazi terror.[189] The churches were so deeply rooted in their communities that it was difficult to attack them openly, although the Nazis tried from the beginning to undermine and destroy church authority. The churches were not only the first large organizations left intact that began to resist Hitlerism as organizations, "they also remained unique in this respect throughout the period from 1933 to 1945, although their resistance remained limited to certain issues and methods."[190] Throughout World War II one important segment of the Protestant Church (the Confessing Church) refused to pray for military victory, and by the war's end many hundreds of clergymen had died in concentration camps.[191]

The analogy here with Latin American experience is striking, although it has been diligently avoided in the mass media of the United States. The National Security States, like Hitler, have used informers and force to destroy or bring under state control all protective organizations of the working class, peasants, rural workers and sub-proletariat: a church group's description of Paraguay, where "the government's objective is to suppress any person or organization that strives to help those living in miserable poverty, that is to say 80% of the population,"[192] is widely applicable in the NSD world. This repression is not undertaken out of sadistic impulses. Rather, as the church throughout the empire now recognizes, "this whole universe of atomized workers, powerless and obliged to humiliate themselves," are kept in that condition for sound economic reasons, given the ends sought and the model of economic development employed by the military juntas.[193]

From the inception of this process, and especially since the Brazilian coup of 1964, the churches have been pressed into opposition to subfascism, just as under Nazism, as the last institutional refuge of the population against state terror and state-protected and state-sponsored exploitation. Initially, again in close analogy with Nazi experience, the coming into power of the

National Security State was greeted by the church in a country like Brazil with mixed feelings, and some positive expectations on the part of the more conservative church leaders. But subfascist processes steadily drove the church into a position of increasingly unified hostility, despite efforts by the military junta to alternatively threaten and attempt to bribe the church leaders into quiescence, if not support. Church opposition has been bothersome to the Brazilian junta, in part because the church remains a competing institutional power still providing a base of opposition and some protective cover for the pack animals (the 80% plus). Furthermore, the church and religion are part of the ceremonial apparatus of the Christian-West-Free World, and however little the generals may regard Christian principles, the symbols should be available for manipulation of the lower orders. But they have not been readily available, and the conflict between the churches and military juntas has escalated in Brazil and throughout the empire.

The reasons for the scope and strength of church resistance in Latin America and elsewhere include certain features of the churches themselves, such as the post-Vatican II internal discussions and subsequent democratization, and the institutional shift in church constituency and support. With the middle and upper classes—the traditional basis of support and personnel—gradually abandoning the church after World War II, the constituency of the church has gradually shifted to the 80% plus that is voiceless, powerless and outside the orbit of interest under subfascism. As the church has reached into the communities of the poor it has been obliged to *see* and *feel* the problems of this exploited mass, and the result has been a further democratization of the church, expressions of remorse at its elite supportive role in the past, and a new concern for meeting the needs of all people now: "The Holy Spirit is no longer a privilege of the hierarchy or of the religious; the Spirit does not only teach piety and obedience in the teaching of the church. The Spirit shows itself in the new martyrs, in the daring of the communities and their ministers, in the testimony given to the world by the humble and poor people."[194]

It is important to recognize that the dominant elements of the Catholic Church of Latin America were, and in important respects still are, quite conservative. It has been pushed into relatively unified and vigorous opposition against its desires and traditions, in large part by brutalities and injustice of a scale and severity that gave it no alternative.[195] The quality of the New Brazil that has evoked this church response can be illustrated by its treatment of abandoned children, vast numbers of whom wander and forage in the cities.[196] These children are regarded strictly as a police problem. Nothing is done *for* them, but they are periodically rounded up, put into police trucks, and transported to other Brazilian states, with a warning to stay away. If something positive is done for them, *this* is regarded as a menace. Lernoux reports that "in a recent typical case, a young teenager was arrested in Vitoria for trying to organize the city's abandoned children into a work cooperative. After he was beaten and tortured, the boy was sodomized in the local jail."[197]

The treatment of the mass of rural poor has been on the same humanistic plane. The military regime has encouraged and subsidized the shift to export crops such as soybeans and cattle, without the slighest concern, provision, or consideration for the (non-existent) opportunities for the millions of dispossessed:

> Their lands, houses and crops are wiped out by the savage growth of latifundia and big agribusiness. Their living and working conditions are becoming more difficult. In a tragic contradiction, in which the government economic favors multiply herds of cattle and enlarge plantations, the small laborer sees his family's food supply diminishing.[198]

Volkswagen, Tio Tinto Zinc, Swift Meat Packing, and others have been receiving tax write-offs to develop cattle ranches, while the indigenous people are written off in the process by their government.[199] Italy's Liquigas was allowed to buy six million acres of land in the heart of the territory of the Xavantas Indians, with 60 Indians killed in the eviction process.[200]

The state functions to prevent by force any defense of the rural majority and to allow the powerful to violate the already feeble law with impunity. A great many clergy have been brutalized for making the most elemental defenses of maltreated individuals. Although under Brazil's legal code peasants who have worked the land for 10 years or more are entitled to ownership rights, those rights are widely ignored and in any conflict are usually resolved by the force of the strong. In one contested case a land development company "simply bulldozed the village of Santa Teresinha off the map. When Father Francisco Jentel protested against the destruction of a health clinic built by the peasants, he was jailed and later sentenced to ten years in prison for 'inciting the people to revolt'."[201]

The Catholic Church has not been able to swallow passively the intensified post-1964 day-by-day spoliation of the Indians and peasantry. Bishop Dom Pedro Casadaliga has kept up a steady flow of denunciations of the policies of force, fraud and subsidization of rural dispossession by the military regime. He has exasperated the ranchers and military of Sao Felix by organizing peasant cooperatives, schools and health units and urging the peasants to "unite and know your legal rights."[202] The Bishop points out that there is only one private doctor in the prelature of Sao Felix, which covers 150,000 square kilometers, but the military regime still discourages church medical assistance efforts: "There used to be a nun nurse who worked in the hospital [the Santa Izabel Indian Hospital]. However, she was expelled and prohibited from taking care of Indians or *posseiros*. We opened a mobile health unit in Sao Felix which was closed by the Secretary of Health of Mato Grosso. Of the four mobile units of the region three are closed and the other is open only sporadically when a doctor of the army or air force is passing through."[203] Efforts to organize the peasantry, even for limited self-help activities, have been viewed with the deepest suspicion by the leaders of subfascism, and this form of subversion has led to the arrest, harassment and exile of numerous clergy in Brazil and elsewhere in the empire.

Bishop Casadaliga was the first of many Brazilian bishops to be subject to military interrogation. Many have suffered more severely. Dom Adriano Hipolito, the Bishop of Nova Iguazu, who has often denounced the Brazilian Anti-Communist Alliance (AAB) as a "bunch of thugs directed and protected by the police" was kidnapped by the AAB, beaten, stripped, painted red, and left lying on a deserted road.[204] And in October, 1976, Father Joao Brunier, who had gone to the police station with Bishop Casadaliga to protest the torture of two peasant women, was simply shot dead by a policeman (who was eventually "apprehended" and then "escaped"). Hundreds of priests and higher officials of the Latin American churches have been tortured, murdered or driven into exile. Six aides of Archbishop Camara have been murdered, and he is quite aware that only his international reputation has so far saved him from a similar fate.

The Latin American churches have been unified and radicalized by subfascist terror and exploitation. They have learned by bitter experience the roots and consequences of these processes. The Church in Brazil now points out frequently and with great clarity and courage that the National Security Doctrine is a cover for totalitarian violence against ordinary people and is a means of class warfare. It is interesting to see the church preaching with passion for the rights of the individual against a state created and supported by the heartland of "freedom"—"On the level of purpose, the State exists for persons. The person, as a subject of natural inalienable rights, is the origin, center and end of society...It is in this right that the power of authority of the state is based. All force practiced beyond and outside of this right is violence."[205] The church has also become more clear-eyed and explicit on the class bias and massive inhumanity of the development model of growth, and on the role of the U.S. and its military and economic interests in bringing into existence and sustaining the subfascist state. On the benefits of the Brazilian "miracle," one church document notes that

> Five percent (5 million out of 100 million) do attain something. But those who really have the advantage are the ones who are financing our "growth," those from abroad, the foreigners. If a bank will not extend credit without a guarantee of profit, much less will the foreigners finance our development and dispense with their profits. Our external debt amounts to about $10 billion.[206]

External interests not only sustain oppression by their support of the military governments; they are more directly in the picture as developers, expropriators and strike-breakers. Bishop Casadaliga claims that in Sao Felix where latifundias are frequently owned by MNCs, the foreign entities have fought his mild efforts more aggressively than the locals: "Of the attacks I have suffered the majority have been ordered by the administrators and technocrats of the multinational latifundios."[207] The Open Letter quoted at the beginning of this section is more passionate still in describing the sorrowful reality that has "demolished the image of 'the great democracy of the North'," including "the scandalous intervention of the United States in the installation and maintenance of military regimes" throughout Latin America; "the shameful Panamanian enclave with its military training centers" in which the murderers receive their higher education from U.S. instructors in techniques of "systematic persecution" and "scientifically perfected torture"; the activities of "the CIA and other agencies of penetration and espionage"; "the sometimes subtle and other times brazen domination and colonization practices" which have gradually eliminated the possibilities of independent economic development; and the "silent genocide, killing with hunger, with malnutrition, with tuberculosis the children of working families without resources."

The church-state struggle has become general in varying degrees throughout the expanding subfascist component of the empire. In Latin America, only in the few countries that retain a democratic order has an open conflict failed to emerge. In the now dominant terror states, including South Korea and the Philippines,[208] the clergy is under attack and is fighting back with the non-violent weapons at its disposal. It cannot be overstressed that while the church increasingly calls for major social changes, the vast bulk of its efforts have been directed toward the protection of the most elemental human rights—to vote, to have the laws enforced without favor, to be free from physical abuse, and to be able to organize, assemble, and petition for betterment. Most sinister for the leaders of subfascism is any sponsorship of organizational or self-help efforts that might give the underclasses not only a sense of personal dignity but also some notion that they have rights and might exercise some small modicum of power.

The hostility of the National Security States to church support for the majority has reached the level of cooperative efforts at intimidation. In the summer of 1976 a major church meeting in Ecuador was interrupted when "40 barbarians armed with machine guns, revolvers, and tear gas bombs burst in on us. None of us was allowed to touch any of our personal belongings, not even to put on a pair of socks. We were pushed at gunpoint into a waiting bus—80 of us crammed into a space meant for 50. We had no idea what was happening, and it was useless to ask those gangsters for an explanation."[209] The group, which included 15 foreign bishops and two foreign archbishops, was imprisoned overnight, and the foreign contingent was expelled the next day on the ground that it had been a "subversive meeting" (on subfascist principles, no doubt correct). One factor explaining the incident may have been the hostility to the host, Bishop Leonidas Proano, who had long been in conflict with the local ranchers over his defense of the ownership rights of the Indians. Church sources claim that a more potent factor was the increasingly close relations between Ecuador and the other subfascist states, particularly Brazil and Chile. At the time of the meeting 10 Chilean secret police were in Ecuador helping set up an intelligence and "security" network. The Chilean secret police arranged for a rock-throwing reception for the three Chilean bishops at the Santiago airport upon their return from Ecuador, and the Chilean press used the incident to demonstrate the Communist-subversive qualities of the bishops. The Chilean bishops concluded from their investigation of the episode that it had been a response to the pressures of "friendly governments" which had been applied to Ecuador.[210]

The conflict between the church and the state intensifies as subfascist abuse becomes a more integral component of the reigning system, the church responds, and the National Security State brooks no opposition: "If we don't subscribe to 'their Church,' we are subversive. But how can we accept a mentality that endorses torture and murder, that is so totally unchristian?"[211] And a Paraguayan priest says that "the bishops are arriving at a point where they must choose between their people and the military...It isn't a political choice between right and left but a humanitarian one. In Paraguay, for example, conservative and liberal bishops are united in their opposition to Alfredo Stroessner's regime. Even the military vicar signed the last pastoral letter denouncing government repression."[212] But the churches resist without the huge resources of the state, without access to the government controlled media, and without the power of physical coercion. On the international plane the churches also face the most formidable obstacle of all—namely, United States sponsorship and support for the National Security State. Thus economic and military aid flows to the military juntas and the United States protects them diplomatically, economically and militarily—militarily, of course, mainly against their own populations via counterinsurgency and police aid. The United States has actively cooperated in overthrowing reformers or radicals in democratic systems (Brazil, Chile), but it has never quite been able to throw its weight towards democracy and away from subfascist gangsters even when the gangsters have stood alone with their U.S.-trained militias and weapons against a unified population, as we witness in Nicaragua at the time of writing.

Because the National Security State is U.S.-sponsored and supported and meets U.S. criteria on the fundamentals, there is another important international consequence: the mass media in the United States play down and essentially suppress the evidence of the enormous inhumanities and institutionalized violence of these U.S. satellites. The *trial* of a single Soviet dissident, Anatol Shcharansky, received more newspaper space in 1978 than the several thousand official *murders* in Latin America during the same year, not to speak of the vast number of lesser events such as tortures and massive dispossession.[213] Information on Latin American horrors is readily available from church and other sources eager to tell the ghastly story, but—to put the matter baldly—the sponsors of class warfare under subfascism are hardly eager to focus attention on its victims. Just as in the case of warfare in Vietnam, both killing and ruthless exploitation at a distance are best done by proxy or through impersonal machinery, with eyes averted. The Free World establishment wisely chooses to focus on movements of the "gross national product" of Brazil, without too much attention to who gets what and *how*. The Free World media also concentrate on "terror," defined as we have seen so as to exclude official violence by definition[214]; and the media allow the world of subfascism to be viewed largely through the eyes of the torturers and U.S. officials and businessmen. U.S. power and interest have put a communications lid on the fate of the great majority of the population of Latin America under U.S.-sponsored subfascism. Thus the churches fight a lonely battle as the last institutional protection of the mass of the population, with the primary enemy an absentee ownership interest supported by a super-power. In Latin America it is widely recognized that the origin and preservation of the National Security State rests on U.S. support. It is the ultimate Orwellism that this same superpower is thought in the West to be fighting a noble battle for "human rights."

4.5.2 Notes on Some Insecurity States in Latin America

> Security, as a good of the nation, is incompatible with a permanent insecurity of the people. Insecurity is marked by arbitrary repressive measures without possibility of defense, compulsory internments, unexplainable disappearances, degrading processes and interrogation and acts of violence done in the easy bravery of clandestine terrorism and in frequent and almost total impunity. ("Christian Requirements of a Political Order," a charter produced by the 15th General Assembly of the National Conference of Brazilian Bishops, February 1977, reprinted in LADOC, Jan.-Feb. 1978.)

The Latin America horror chamber has been so extensively described by human rights organizations, refugees, priests, Latin American intellectuals, and others that we will make no effort here at a systematic review.[215] Such materials are accessible in books, reports and articles in journals, although these normally reach only a tiny segment of the population. The mass media spare the general populace such painful and unrewarding fare. Scattered information can be found in the mass media, but it is episodic, very sparse in relation to the human issues involved, and generally devoid of any indication of the systematic character of the reduction of Latin America to barbarism or its roots in U.S. support and global interests and policies.

The media also employ a number of other devices that assure sympathetic treatment of U.S.-sponsored subfascism. These include: reliance on the juntas themselves for information; an acceptance of their verbal statements as to objectives and good intentions[216]; a focus on alleged "improvements," on the "prolems" faced by the juntas, on the infighting among the "moderates" and "hardliners," on the unfortunate lack of control by the moderates (at the top) over the hardliners (who kill people); and an avoidance of details on their gory practices and victims. For example, in an article using all of these formulas, Joanne Omang of the *Washington Post* offers the following among a stream of clichés: "Videla has maintained the slow and stubbornly cautious pattern of decisions"; "Videla and the other junta officers have kept open their lines of communications with the country's various political elements, even though all political and union activities are officially suspended and many leaders are in jail" [communication is easier if you know just where they are]; "Everybody agrees that the junta knows what the problems are"; "Unions...are about to be granted organizational rights"; "The daily *La Opinion* estimated that leftist terrorists lost 4,000 persons in 1976."[217] The word "torture" does not appear in the article, nor figures on non-leftist non-terrorists killed (given the probable source of the 4,000, they are probably included in that figure), nor any details even on economic facts. Juan de Onis, who tops the field in the deployment of pro-junta clichés, notes that in Argentina "Many union delegates and clandestine activists [that is, people who, if in the open, would be shot] have been killed. This contributed to the human rights violations in question...," which must be admitted to be a fair inference.[218] Elsewhere, de Onis explains that "the military junta headed by Lieutenant General Jorge Rafael Videla, Commander in Chief of the army, has been unable to control the right-wing extremists, who are clearly linked to the military and police, despite the declared goal of the junta to exercise a monopoly of violence."[219] Since the "extremists" are "clearly linked" to the police and military, one obvious hypothesis is that they *are* controlled by their superior officers, who find it convenient for PR purposes to pretend to lack of control. De Onis does not consider this possibility.

As a further example, an AP Report in the *New York Times* (31 October 1976) discusses charges, from Amnesty International and Catholic sources, of torture, murder and other forms of repression in Argentina, Chile, Uruguay, Brazil, Paraguay, and Bolivia. The context is neither the number and plight of the victims nor the role in the atrocities of the "economic-political-military complex" described by religious leaders in Latin America, but rather the problem of how to cripple "leftist extremism," an effort which has unfortunately led many military leaders in Latin America to condone repressive practices—though some "called moderate, including General Jorge R. Videla, the President, are described as being committed to protecting human rights" but in the usual formula unable "to control unofficial repression by security agents." As a correspondent for *Le Monde* observes, "the Argentine military seem, in fact, to have distributed roles: some kill, the others distract the attention of the public with vague promises on the reestablishment of liberty and democracy."[220] Vague promises and allegations of a threat of "left-wing terrorism" are gratefully received by U.S. media and ideologists, looking eagerly for some basis for legitimizing constructive terror.

An Argentine editor is quoted in the AP report in support of the repression: "Those of us who want democracy are willing to pay any price to get it." His comment scarcely caricatures the general response among U.S. ideologists in the press and elsewhere. The occasional report in the U.S. press merely underscores its complicity in the spread of the plague of state terror in Latin America. The avoidance of any hint of U.S. responsibility is striking and consistent, and can only be compared with a (hypothetical) refusal to trace the system of Eastern Europe to its source in Moscow.[221]

A major target of the new Argentinian regime, not surprisingly, is the trade union movement, which has been effectively dismantled, while "according to Argentine labor sources, economic conditions for workers have never been worse," again, a typical concomitant of constructive terrorism.[222] U.S. business, however, is pleased with the militarized Argentina, which has not only been struggling to pacify the labor force, but has also applied deflationary policies of a draconian nature to arrange price-cost-budget values in accordance with the criteria and interests of the international financial community. The junta leaders have shown great deference to the bankers, meeting with them periodically to explain their policies and seek banker approval, much as if the bankers constituted the board of directors of a corporation called "Argentina."[223] The Economics Minister of Argentina, Jose Martinez de Hoz, is a free enterpriser perfectly in tune with the demands of international business, and a personal friend of David

Rockefeller, who addressed a group of bankers in New York at a screening of a promotional film on Argentina, explaining to them why Argentina was a new promised land:

> I have the impression that finally Argentina has a regime which understands the private enterprise system...Not since the Second World War has Argentina been presented with a combination of advantageous circumstances as it has now.[224]

The scale of state terror in Argentina since the military coup of March, 1976, is difficult to estimate. Jean-Pierre Clerc reports official figures of 8,500 missing, including 4,000 prisoners and presumably 4,500 killed, noting that a figure of 15,000 killed is widely accepted among Argentine journalists.[225] According to official reports, many have been killed in "combat," but Argentine dissidents are skeptical about the nature of this "combat". The Argentine writer and investigative reporter Rodolfo Walsh circulated an open letter to the junta documenting its crimes in March, 1977, in which he cited official figures from "combat" in 1976: 600 dead and 15 wounded, percentages "unheard of in even the most savage conflicts." He concluded, not unreasonably, that the "combats" are actually murder operations. He estimated that in the "savage reign of terror" since the coup 15,000 people are missing without trace, 10,000 are political prisoners, and tens of thousands are in exile, while the number of those tortured is unknown. Meanwhile, according to Walsh, real wages have been reduced by 60% in one year and food consumption has dropped by 40%, while "the only beneficiaries of your economic strategy are the old cattle-owning oligarchy, the new oligarchy of speculators, and a select group of international companies such as ITT, Exxon, U.S. Steel, and Siemens," to which the economics minister and his associates are "directly and personally linked."[226] Walsh was kidnapped the day after his letter appeared and has not been heard from since.

Amnesty International, a year after the coup, estimated that there were between 5,000-6,000 political prisoners and that "torture is widely and routinely practised," while some 2,000-5,000 people had disappeared without trace. Prisoners have been unofficially executed on the pretense of "attempting to escape."

Many reported to have been killed "in clashes with security forces" were in fact "known to have been abducted or even officially detained."[227]

In a subsequent report, AI estimated that "over 15,000 people have disappeared, and that 8-10,000 people are detained in official prisons" since the March, 1976 coup: "This does not include the secret detention camps where torture, terrible conditions and eventual execution are rampant." It also noted the sharp increase in violence after the coup and the declining living standards, and cited the definition of a "terrorist" offered by President Videlia: "a terrorist is not just someone with a gun or a bomb, but also someone who spreads ideas that are contrary to Western and Christian civilizations" (*London Times,* 4 January 1978). The General deserves high marks for honesty, at least.[228]

According to the same AI report, torture is carried out in Argentina at some 60 separate detention centers—presumably unbeknownst to the "moderate" head of state General Videla, or regrettably out of his powers of control; or perhaps the torture is moderate, or possibly systematic torture is consistent with moderation (reasonableness) if used for proper ends. So one might assume from the coverage of Argentine terror in the *New York Times*, for example. Men, women, and children have been tortured with the most brutal and sophisticated methods available in the empire. Patricia Erb, the 19 year old daughter of a U.S. Mennonite Missionary, was abducted in September, 1976, by armed men in civilian clothes, blindfolded, and eventually tortured, but released under foreign pressure. She gave the following account of what she had endured:

> The day after my abduction, I was conducted, as were many others, to rooms which we called the 'torture house.' There, men dressed in civilian clothes interrogated us, using torture 'when it was necessary' in attempts to extract confessions. This torture took various forms: beatings with clubs and fists, kicks, immersion in water or in fecal substance almost to the point of drowning, and the use of la picana (electric prod) which was applied to the most sensitive parts of the body, such as the mouth, eyes, nose, vagina, breast, penis, feet and hands, In order to cause

> greater pain, they would tie us down to a wire bed which carried an electric current and entangled wire between our fingers and toes, splashing water on us in order to increase the pain. These methods were aimed at forcing confessions of alleged activities, which in many cases were inventions of the military. Sometimes these methods were used merely as punishment.
>
> After these interrogations we were taken again to the 'barn,' where the rest of the prisoners were being held. They, in turn, were conducted to the interrogation rooms while the rest of us could hear their screaming and howling. They came back almost unconscious and moaning in great pain. Sometimes doctors would come and look after the worst injuries, such as broken bones, bleeding kidneys, etc. I am very sorry I can't remember the names of all the prisoners who were there with me. When I knew of the possibility of being freed, because of my nationality, I tried to memorize as many names as I could.[229]

The Argentine regime uses all the familiar devices of modern totalitarianism to improve its international image. In the *New Statesman* (6 October 1978), Christopher Hitchens describes the case of Jaime Dri, a member of the Argentine Parliament until 1976, who was arrested in 1977 and "locked up in the *Escuela Mecanica de Armada,* a naval centre much used for the practice of torture upon political prisoners, (one of Argentina's few growth industries)." Dri was given the number 49, and was told that "he was the fifth person to have the number 49, which gives you some idea of the total involved." In April, 1978, he and other prisoners were moved elsewhere and there was a flurry of activity as the *Escuela* was painted and decorated, "trustees were dressed up in naval uniform," etc. "Dri, together with other top-security prisoners, was stuffed into a backroom where he found himself sitting on a pile of electric torture devices. Afterwards a warden told them that this was all in aid of a gullible British journalist who was being 'shown round'. When Dri got out, and told this story, he didn't know that a few weeks later a laudatory piece about the *Escuela* had appeared in what is sometimes called a respected British newspaper." In short, the technique that had long been used by the Soviet Union to dupe sympathetic visitors from abroad.

With Argentina in the news after its victory in the world soccer matches that it hosted, the *New York Times* again accorded it a column by Juan de Onis.[230] "Argentina and its military government are facing problems that are more complex" than winning soccer matches, he observes. One of their problems is that while they have "an excess of force," they have no "political course other than repression." "This repression has made human rights another major problem." The problem was caused by "a rampant subversive movement," now destroyed "with at least 3,000 killed in five years of conflict" and 3,500 security prisoners in jails, in addition to 1,600 missing (compare Amnesty's estimate). As is characteristic of this kind of journalism, de Onis does not inquire into the origins of the "rampant subversive movement" that bears the ultimate responsibility, in his account, for the human rights problem. According to the historian Alain Rouquié, author of a massive study of military power and politics in Argentina, "the launching of the guerrilla movement properly speaking was provoked by the military coup of 1966," and its deeper origins are to be found in long-term social and economic injustice (interview with Jean-Pierre Clerc, *Le Monde,* 15 September 1978). But questions of this nature are generally foreign to the political analysis that dominates the U.S. media, just as little is said about the social and economic content of the military terror that exploits a "terrorist threat" as justification for imposing the economic programs of client subfascism. The military leaders, de Onis writes, "are well aware that this country's international reputation would improve if these prisoners were either tried or released," but the memory of terrorist acts by "the extremists is too recent" for the military to move in this direction. The economic situation has improved under the military regime, though workers' wages are at "the lowest level of purchasing power since 1970" (compare Boggs and McLellan, note 222). Another problem is that the United States might cut off military supplies and perhaps economic aid through international banks might be jeopardized. One must feel a twinge of sympathy for the problems faced by Argentina's military leaders.

The U.S. has cut military aid to Argentina and blocked some

commercial transactions, on grounds of human rights violations. But funding from international lending institutions has increased since the coup, including the World Bank, the Inter-American Development Bank, and the International Monetary Fund, in all of which the United States plays a major role; and private banks, mostly American, have undertaken extensive loans now that Argentina is more "credit worthy" with its new economic policies.[231] Most of the responsibility for the cuts in government aid is attributable to congressional pressure and legislation, over the protests of the Carter administration. The administration has striven mightily to maintain the friendly relationships with the Argentine junta, with Secretary of State Vance making a special trip to Buenos Aires and with strenuous efforts devoted to preserving some flow of both "security assistance" and military training aid. The Pentagon, in the words of one high ranking officer, is trying "to maintain the special relationship we have with the Argentine Armed Forces."[232] In short, an enormous efflorescence of subfascist torture and murder is capable of causing a liberal administration claiming devotion to human rights reluctantly to apply a small rap on its client's knuckles, while continuing quietly to facilitate a large expansion in its borrowings and assuring it of a continued supportive and special relationship.

The Argentine catastrophe mirrors the recent history of Brazil, Chile and Uruguay.[233] On Brazil, see above, chapter 2, section 1.1.5. U.S. involvement in the Chile coup, with its murderous and destructive aftermath, is too-well known to require discussion here.[234] As for Uruguay, Amnesty International concludes that "the scale and intensity of repression in Uruguay is probably the highest in Latin America."[235] Joe Eldredge, a former missionary who now heads the Washington Office on Latin America (sponsored by a coalition of religious and academic groups), writes that "with nearly one out of every 500 persons in jail or in concentration camps, Uruguay holds the dubious distinction of having, on a per capita basis, the highest number of political prisoners in the world," and he gives the rather common estimate that one-fourth of the population has fled.[236] The *Times* story on the AI report cited above (31 October 1976) summarizes the situation in Uruguay as follows:

> In Uruguay 12 to 25 people are estimated to have been tortured to death since 1972, when the Tupamaro urban guerrillas began to decline. One out of 500 of Uruguay's three million people is said to be either a political prisoner or a refugee.

In fact, in an AI news conference in New York on February 19, 1976, 24 "known deaths by torture" were announced (see note 235). The "one out of 500" figure is, no doubt, an error, referring just to political prisoners; the number of refugees is far higher. The *Times* report is typical in its vague reference to the unexplained "decline" of the Tupamaros, not to speak of their equally mysterious prior rise.[237] In a later report, *Times* Latin American correspondent Juan de Onis observes (29 June 1978) that Uruguay "was convulsed by a left-wing terrorist movement, called the Tupamaros," which was as violent as the Italian Red Brigades and even killed a U.S. police advisor, Dan Mitrione, in 1970, evoking a right wing reaction. The reason for the original "convulsion" is beyond inquiry.[238] One would not know from de Onis's account that there was a social and historical background for the emergence of the Tupamaros, or that Dan Mitrione was the chief adviser to police who were found by Uruguayan senators to be "systematically torturing suspected Tupamaros" (Langguth, p. 249), among other atrocities. De Onis reports that "tens of thousands of people have left Uruguay"[239] and that the United States has suspended military assistance and reduced economic aid; the indirect channels of U.S. aid are not mentioned. He cites a military officer, explaining the view of the current leadership: "We take pride in being the guiding light in the struggle of our Western Christian civilization against international Marxist sedition."

A great deal of information about Uruguay can be found in material that is not destined to reach the U.S. press; for example, from Uruguayan Senator Zelmar Michelini, who was kidnapped with another Uruguayan political figure in Argentina shortly after the March, 1976 coup and later found shot to death, apparently tortured.[240] Senator Michelini testified on Uruguayan repression before the Russell Tribunal in Rome in April, 1974.[241] He estimated the number of Uruguayans tortured at "more than 5,000," while over 40,000 people had been held as political prisoners. Accompanying testimony by victims recounts many cases. Michelini pointed out that comparative figures for the U.S. would be about 3,200,000 political prisoners and 400,000 torture victims. Citing Michelini's estimates, the noted Uruguayan author Eduardo Galeano adds that in an unpopulated and fertile land with a low birth rate, one fourth of the population is in exile, one part of the flight of the persecuted in Latin America which, as we have already remarked, bears comparison to the Nazi period in Europe.[242]

Though the *New York Times* reports on Uruguay make no note of the fact, the systematic and sophisticated use of torture in Uruguay, as elsewhere, seems to have developed as one central component of the U.S. aid program. Victims have reported that Dan Mitrione, who was involved in the escalation of torture in Uruguay, participated directly in torture sessions.[243] There is little doubt that local torturers were trained by the United States and use equipment supplied through the U.S. assistance program with the knowledge of their U.S. advisors, who are also responsible for coordinating the operations of police terrorists in Latin America. Summarizing his investigation of U.S. police operations in Latin America, Langguth writes:

> ...the main exporter of cold-war ideas, the principal source of the belief that dissent must be crushed by every means and any means, has been the United States. Our indoctrination of foreign troops provided a justification for torture in the jail cells of Latin America. First in the Inter-American Police Academy in Panama, then at the more ambitious International Police Academy in Washington, foreign policemen were taught that in the war against international communism they were "the first line of defense."...the U.S. training turned already conservative men into political reactionaries.[244]

The torture is no big deal: "A former U.S. police adviser I ran across in Latin America," Langguth remarks, "assured me that some prisoners did not feel pain." After the students have graduated and are ready to work, they can still benefit from the assistance of U.S. advisors and international coordination that becomes useful when, for example, Uruguayan dissidents are to be assassinated by "death squads" that operate with impunity in Argentina.

The students and their teachers may believe that their task is to stand as a bulwark against "international communism," but at a higher level of planning it is no doubt well understood that the torturers are the first line of defense against the erosion of the privileges of the owners and managers of the advanced industrial societies. The victims have few illusions, as has already been noted. See the "Open Letter to North American Christians," (p. 251-52). Galeano writes:

> The military in power in Uruguay, who are now a scandal for the U.S., were good students of the Pentagon course in the Panama Canal Zone. There they learned the techniques of repression and the art of governing; it is with American arms and advisors that they have set in motion the gearing up of crime and torture. The dictatorship has destroyed the unions and political parties, closed the newspapers and reviews, forbidden books and songs in the name of an "*ideology of national security*," which, in clear language, means "*ideology for the security of foreign investment*." Liberty for business, liberty for prices, liberty for trade: one throws the people in prison so that business will remain free.

On the same day that President Carter announced the end of military aid, Galeano notes, "the World Bank, controlled by the U.S., announced a new credit of $30 million for Uruguay, added to the $55 million granted in 1976." The International Monetary Fund, he reports, is now the principal creditor of the country and directs its political economy so as to reduce popular consumption, lower wages, and stimulate exports: "The machine has its laws." It is only in the United States that mention of such truisms is considered indecent, if they are even understood by journalists and political analysts.

The U.S. contribution to civilizing South America is of fairly recent vintage. Central America has a longer history as a beneficiary of U.S. humanitarianism, and its ongoing constructive bloodbaths may therefore serve as a still more revealing indication of the systematic and long-term nature of U.S. policy within the domains of its influence and control.

Consider Guatemala, which, Joe Eldredge writes, "must have been the leader in all Latin America in terms of ruthless repression of large segments of the population" in the 1970s, and where "the slaughter continues."[245] A mild reformist government that threatened the prerogatives of the United Fruit Company was overthrown by a CIA-backed coup in 1954, terminating efforts at desperately-needed agrarian reform, decimating the labor movement (reduced from 100,000 to 27,000; more than 200 union leaders were killed immediately after the coup) and setting off waves of right-wing violence that have claimed thousands of lives, many during a U.S.-sponsored counterinsurgency campaign in the mid-1960s. The 1954 coup, like others (cf. note 1, chapter 2), was regarded as a great success in the U.S., and some key facts have long been concealed by the press, which much preferred fantasies about a "Communist takeover" blocked by the Guatemalan people. The basic doctrine was laid down in a Senate Resolution of June 25, 1954, which found "strong evidence of intervention by the international Communist movement in the State of Guatemala, whereby government institutions have been infiltrated by Communist agents, weapons of war have been secretly shipped into that country, and the pattern of Communist conquest has become manifest"—essentially the charges levelled against Czechoslovakia, *mutatis mutandis,* by the Warsaw Pact nations in 1968.[246] Under-Secretary of State Spruille Braden, a member of a family with large Latin American mining interests, a consultant to United Fruit, and the leader of a Council on Foreign Relations study group on Latin America, explained the basic principle in more general terms in March, 1953:

> Because Communism is so blatantly an international and not an internal affair, its suppression, even by force, in an American country, by one or more of the other republics, would not constitute an intervention in the internal affairs of the former.[247]

Rather, such suppression would be an example of defense against "internal aggression," as later explained by Adlai Stevenson and others.[248]

Having been saved from "Communism" and restored to its position as a "showplace for democracy," Guatemala has loyally undertaken its proper role, effectively providing agricultural assistance to the United States while its people die of malnutrition and even sending large quantities of blood to the developed world, contributed by people with the greatest nutritional deficiencies, who have no other way to survive.[249] With the brutal disruption of the efforts at rural organization that were carried out during the reform period of 1944-54, the peasant population has been reduced to the conditions of penury and serfdom that formerly prevailed, though now, in keeping with the forms of a "modernizing" society, the earlier feudal techniques have been replaced. But as Roger Plant explains:

> Illegal methods of persuasion still have to be used—thus the growing number of contractors today—but the growing highland population, increased land parcelisation, and above all the appallingly inegalitarian land distribution and agrarian policies of the government have ensured that poverty and starvation provide a cheap labour force for the estates more successfully than did the legislation and brute force of the colonial and nineteenth-century periods.[250]

These factors do not enter into the "Human Rights" calculations of the United States. Thus the State Department Human Rights Reports note the problem posed for the Guatemalan government by the violence of the "Guerrilla Army of the Poor," explaining that "much of Guatemala's long history of violence is the result of bitter personal feuds, rural banditry, and smuggling"—nothing more (1977). The 1978 Report adds that the government is moving ahead with reform measures to alleviate rural poverty but does not regard the condition of virtual slavery resulting from the U.S.-backed coup of 1954 as a human rights problem. By the standards of Freedom House, Guatemala is "partly free." The 1978 Human Rights Report observes that "for the past two decades Guatemalan politics have been dominated by the military within a constitutional framework providing for regular elections and civilian control below the top level," but it is silent on the events that took place two decades ago or their impact on the peasantry, the vast majority of the population. For them, unofficial observers report that life "is still akin to that of the pre-1944 or even colonial days" with "the most spectacular inequality and injustice to be found anywhere in the world."[251]

The State Department is not alone in coyly evading the events of 1954 in Guatemala. Stephen Schlesinger points out in *The Nation* (28 October 1978) that "what strikes an observer immediately about the Guatemala affair is how history has over the years practically abandoned it. No book has ever explored it; no Senate committee has ever investigated it." The oversight is not accidental, but is rather part of a systematic pattern of avoiding topics that might provide some insight into U.S. foreign policy, thus eroding the image of benevolence tainted with occasional "tragic error." Documents obtained by Schlesinger under the Freedom of Information Act demonstrate why historians and journalists are wise to keep U.S. relations with Guatemala under wraps. The documents show that far from being an exile operation carried out with the connivance of the CIA, "the [1954] *Putsch* was conceived of and run at the highest levels of the American Government in closest cahoots with the United Fruit Company and under the overall direction of Secretary of State John Foster Dulles, backed by President Eisenhower."

U.S. concern over developments in Guatemala began shortly after the institution of democratic government in 1944. "Under the new regime," Schlesinger writes, "the Guatemalan Congress approved a mild labor code which forced United Fruit, among other employers, to improve the wretched working conditions of its peasants. While the code was being debated, the State Department began to dispatch warnings to the Guatemalan President at the behest of United Fruit." When the code was nevertheless passed, the United States began to pressure the Guatemalan government to eliminate "Communist sympathizers." Under Eisenhower, the State Department and the CIA were in the hands of the Dulles brothers, who had close links to major corporations and had no difficulty persuading Eisenhower "to press a secret war against Guatemala" when the reform democratic government threatened to expropriate unused land belonging to United Fruit, then the country's principal landowner. A State Department intelligence estimate of June 1953, written shortly after the expropriation of United Fruit land, proposed that the U.S. should arm the tyrannies in the vicinity of Guatemala, a signal to the Guatemalan military to get rid of President Arbenz. The U.S. Information Service (USIS) planted articles in Latin American newspapers "labeling certain Guatemalan officials as Communists" (according to the then acting director of USIS). By December 1953 U.S. Ambassador Peurifoy was suggesting a variety of familiar means "to make more difficult continuation of [Arbenz] regime in Guatemala." Efforts undertaken by the United States did not succeed. The conflict became public when Guatemala, unable to purchase arms from the United States, had a shipment sent from Czechoslovakia on a Swedish ship. The U.S. government leaked the discovery to the press, flew arms to Nicaragua, and secretly dispatched naval vessels to search "suspicious" ships bound for Guatemala, an act of gangsterism that led to internal protest by Under Secretary of State Robert Murphy who wrote in a memo to Dulles that it "should give stir to the bones of Admiral von Tirpitz" and other Nazi naval officers.

Meanwhile, the United States was carrying out a double-edged program: arming rebels waiting in Honduras and Nicaragua to invade Guatemala and disseminating anti-Guatemalan propaganda, with the aid of sympathetic journalists. United Fruit and other U.S. companies were kept advised of U.S. plans. When the CIA-backed "incursion" took place on June 18, 1954, U.S. muscle was employed at the UN to prevent France and Britain from accepting a Soviet proposal to dispatch a UN peace-keeping force. After the *Putsch*, Dulles wired Ambassador Peurifoy to arrange talks between the new regime and United Fruit and to have our man Castillo Armas, now in control, begin a round-up of "Communists," initiating the constructive bloodbath that has been underway ever since, with regular United States initiatives when required.

Dulles also tried to convince Castillo to deny the traditional right of asylum and require that "asylees" who could not be charged with crimes on some pretext be denied safe conduct unless they agreed to go to Russia or, if "considered relatively harmless," to remote countries. This was too much even for the U.S. subfascist client, who decided to honor the right of asylum, though he did proceed "to persecute hundreds of Guatemalans for all sorts of vague 'Communist' crimes" and "rescinded the Agrarian Reform laws, handed back all of United Fruit's seized land, and generally set up a reliable, ruthless authoritarian regime in which the United States could put its trust" (Schlesinger).

Much of what Schlesinger reports was known to those who choose to know. The evidence of plotting at the highest level and of direct contacts with United Fruit is new, and reveals, as does other commonly ignored documentation (e.g., the Pentagon Papers) that the various expressions of the systematic U.S. program of global counterrevolutionary intervention are not attributable, as liberal doctrine would have it, to an intelligence system that has somehow gotten out of hand (the "rogue elephant" hypothesis), but rather to deep-seated factors rooted in the domestic power structure, governmental and extra-governmental.

Sometimes it is recognized that the U.S. has made certain "errors" in Guatemala. For example, a staff memorandum prepared for the Senate Committee on Foreign Relations by Pat M. Holt describes the "fundamental problems" of Guatemala which have become more difficult to deal with since the U.S. "got into the bear trap by intervening to frustrate a process of social change," though "the problems were, indeed, on the way to some kind of solution when the United States stepped in to restore a semblance of the status quo ante." Since the United States intervened, "most (not all) observers affirm that the rich have gotten richer and the poor both poorer and more numerous," and the United States has become "politically identified with police terrorism" because, unaccountably, the U.S. police training program has somehow failed—"the teaching hasn't been absorbed" (another theory comes to mind). Meanwhile U.S. aid continues, evidence "of the wisdom of the adage that it's easier to get into a bear trap than to get out of it."[252] How painful are the burdens of international benefactors.

Nothing is said in the staff memorandum concerning the activities of U.S. corporations, which approximately doubled their direct investment in Guatemala in the 1960s, and have apparently found the new Guatemala good; for example, the International Nickel Company, which in partnership with the Hanna Mining Company (both largely U.S. owned) is preparing to exploit what appears to be one of the world's richest deposits of nickel.

Amnesty International published a report on Guatemala in December, 1976, estimating "the victims of covertly-sanctioned murders or disappearances...to number over 20,000" since 1966. "The vast majority of the 'disappeared,' when located, are found to have been the victims of violent death." Many were found "with signs of torture or mutilation along roadsides or in ravines, floating in plastic bags in lakes or rivers, or buried in mass graves in the countryside."[253]

The year 1966 marked "the beginnings of official 'counter-terror.' " AI cites a report in *Time* magazine (26 January 1968) where Colonel John Webber, U.S. military attaché during one of the campaigns (later assassinated by guerrillas), reportedly acknowledged that "it was his idea and at his instigation that the technique of counter-terror had been implemented by the Guatemalan Army in the Izabal areas."[254] In May, 1968 the Southern Command Forces of the United States conducted joint "training exercises" with Nicaraguan and Guatemalan armies in the Department of Izabal, officially designated as "Operation Hawk." U.S. Embassy officials in Guatemala claimed that the steady flow of military visitors from the United States was merely "routine," and according to Thomas and Marjorie Melville: "They also state that all the Guatemalan officials trained in Fort Gulick, all the special police hired with Alliance for Progress funds (3,500 in 1967 and 1968), and the 'model police programmes' developed by AID consultant Peter Costello and implemented with AID money, are no more that what is done by 'similar U.S. missions in various Latin American countries,' "[225] which is no doubt true.

The victims of "counter-terror" are primarily from the peasantry or urban poor, AI believes, but include as well petty criminals, members and leaders of opposition parties, trade unionists and journalists, students and teachers, leaders of peasant cooperatives, occasionally businessmen or functionaries. Reports of 149 murders of members of security forces and others are also cited. Evidence of torture is "almost exclusively limited to reports of the physical condition of corpses of 'disappeared' persons when discovered."[256] The Senate staff memorandum cited above (note 252) claims that the reason why "the corpses of alleged guerrillas are being found on roadsides instead of the bodies of live guerrillas being produced in court" is that the judiciary is intimidated by guerrillas. The Amnesty Report points out, however, that "the massive use of extrajudicial execution continued unchecked and actually widened following the virtual elimination of the organized guerrillas by 1968." The guerrilla movement itself evidently developed in response to the situation brought about by the 1954 coup.

More recent AI reports allege that political murder and "disappearances" continue. In February, 1978 a list of 113 cases was released covering the last quarter of 1977. There was "considerable evidence," AI reported, "that the highest levels of government tacitly condoned the continuing abductions and murders, especially of peasant farmers and of the urban poor."[257]

The AI reports have been covered in the U.S. press; the December, 1976 document is reported in the *New York Times* (12 December 1976), and the 1978 update merited 12 lines on p. 14 (23 February 1978). It was mentioned again in a story on the presidential elections (Alan Riding, 9 March 1978), which reported that "most Guatemalans seem surprisingly indifferent about the outcome." The surprise is perhaps mitigated by the discovery that the previous election was marked by "blatant electoral fraud...to insure General Laugerud's victory over a popular left-leaning candidate" and that "there were no leftist or reformist candidates for the presidency."

The number of Guatemalans murdered since 1966 is approximately equal to the 22,000 killed by the earthquake of February 4, 1976, when, in Guatemala City, "the poorest areas were destroyed, while the wealthy neighborhoods were almost unscathed."[258] The deaths are not simply attributable to the wrath of God. Dr. Gordon Bateman, an American surgeon who worked with victims, observed that "we simply don't have these kinds of medical conditions in the United States—this is another world." James P. Sterba, reporting his observations, comments that in Guatemala, "the normal conditions of ill health and inadequate shelter left the victims particularly vulnerable after their injuries." Many victims died because of lack of transportation facilities or simply lack of food: "many people here cannot afford to buy more than a day's supply of food at one time" and village markets often have only a day's supply because of lack of refrigeration or packaging. Even clean running water is a luxury to the majority of Guatemalans.

Sterba notes that many Americans, who were shocked by the effects of the earthquake, "would have been equally shocked by the human scene here had the earthquake never occurred."[259] One wonders how many of the earthquake victims might have been saved, had the United States not entered into the "bear trap" in 1954, aborting desperately needed reforms then in progress. This question is not raised in the *New York Times* reports.

Jonathan Dimbleby took up the forbidden theme, however, in the *New Statesman*. "It was the poor, whose houses were too weak to withstand the shock, who died in the earthquake," he comments. He then recounts the effects of the U.S. subversion of 1954: more than 50,000 children die from malnutrition every year "in a country which could easily feed not only its own population, but the people of at least two neighbouring countries—if only the army and the Americans had permitted the reforms to go ahead"; "starvation wages" and "squalor that should cause a world outcry"; "a nicely balanced combination of mass poverty and mass murder" while Guatemala's oligarchy and Western businessmen are enriched; U.S.-guided pacification programs with thousands of victims; "30,000 peasant graves [that] bear witness" to the truth expressed by the men of the death squads: "if you 'wish to remain alive and well' you should abandon your 'communist sympathies.' " The Indians, nearly 70% of the population, are "treated as though they belonged to another species; were it not for the fact that oppressor and oppressed cannot be distinguished by colour, Guatemala would enjoy the same international obloquy heaped on Rhodesia and South Africa. Yet, no one, least of all the United States, breathes a word."[260] Which is not to suggest that many words have been breathed in respectable circles with regard to Southern Africa, except in response to pressures arising out of (mainly) black concern, agitation, and threats at home and in Africa.

To the tens of thousands murdered and the many hundreds of thousands who simply die of malnutrition, disease and catastrophe in this constructive bloodbath, we may add the victims of agribusiness. Cotton yields in Guatemala "are the highest in the Western hemisphere and vast profits are made every year," in part because "the level of pesticide spraying is the highest in the world and little concern is shown for the people who live near the cotton fields," a permanent population of about 370,000 supplemented with some 600,000 Indian seasonal workers. The level of DDT in mothers' milk in Guatemala is the highest in the Western world, up to 185 times higher than the safe limit, according to one study. Some new pesticides used "are five times more lethal to humans than DDT." Meat rejected for shipment to the U.S. because of high DDT content is reportedly sold locally or in the Caribbean islands. "Because the victims of the spraying have little voice in Guatemalan politics, the use of pesticides is rarely discussed in the capital and so far the issue has not been raised in the campaign for the presidential elections next March"—perhaps another reason for the "surprising" apathy noted later by the same correspondent.[261]

As we write, the massacre continues. On May 29, 1978, Catholic Church workers reported 114 peasants killed by the army in an Indian village when Indians attempted to present a petition protesting the takeover of their land by wealthy landowners who have made them squatters. The Indians work "in serflike conditions on huge estates" or on tiny patches of land. Eighty percent of their children under five suffer from malnutrition, according to government statistics. State Department officials say privately that there are 25 to 30 unexplained political deaths every month, perpetrated by "people in the intimidation business who are officially tolerated."[262]

Amnesty International investigated the May 29 massacre, reporting that more that ten weeks later the wounded were still in army custody. It notes that details of the events of May 29 are confused, and cites sources that "state that the army ordered evacuation of houses around the temporary garrison [of troops that arrived three days before the planned demonstration against threatened eviction], warning the occupants of gunfire, and that present with the troops were landowners who had been in dispute with the Indians." AI has the names of 51 of the dead (the government reported 35 killed after "leftwing agitators incited more than 800 Indians to attack the troops and demand the forcible take-over of private farms"). A Guatemalan commission of inquiry including trade unionists and opposition groups reported that "within hours of the demonstration the army buried 68 people (including nine women and 10 children) in a mass grave at Panzos and that 46 seriously wounded people who died later were buried in a second mass grave" (including 10 women and eight children). AI goes on to report that killings, abductions and disappearances in this region have "increased dramatically during the past three years" and that these abuses " have coincided with the development of the petroleum and mineral resources of the region." Indians who have refused to evacuate the lands they have traditionally farmed, now coveted by non-Indian landholders attracted by the rise in property values and increased economic activities, "have frequently suffered the extra-legal violence of para-military death squads." The May 29 incident was "unusual in its nature, its scale, and in that official spokesmen sought to justify the killings." The usual pattern is "abduction, torture and murder of individual leaders... or single important families,"or burning of huts and crops, which the Indians attribute to "Guatemalan army troops working at the behest of local large landholders."[263]

Nicaragua has been another traditional "bear trap" for the United States; for well over 100 years, in this case. In July, 1854 "San Juan del Norte (Greytown) was destroyed to avenge an insult to the American Minister to Nicaragua."[264] From 1926-1933 U.S. marines fought a counterinsurgency operation that led to the takeover by the Somoza family, which has since ruled Nicaragua as its private fiefdom. But they are not the only beneficiaries of over a century of intervention. A two-page advertisement in the *Wall Street Journal* (31 May 1977), is headed "Nicaragua: An Investor's Dream Come True." The subheadings give the flavor: "American Chamber of Commerce Invites Investment in Nicaragua," "A Country Where Foreign Capital Is Nurtured; 'Yanquis' Feel at Home," "A Good Export Base," "Industrial Parks," "Great Opportunities,"etc. Here the U.S. investor will find "a good investment climate," "stability, peace and a prospering economy," and will even be provided by the U.S. Chamber of Commerce with "a comprehensive guide for setting up business in Nicaragua, to share its experiences with others and to explain this country's policies and practices in support of the Free Enterprise System." The U.S. Department of Commerce predicted that "Nicaragua will continue to enjoy political stability and a bright economic future," the report continues. There is absolute assurance of freedom of remittance on profits and capital, and no capital gains or dividend tax, as well as other incentives. There is also "low-cost abundant labor" which "takes pride in its task," with no compulsory union affiliation. Nicaraguans even like baseball. In short, a very *simpatico* country, "with a long tradition of cooperation and good feeling towards the people of the United States."

The vitality of the country was shown after the earthquake that took 30,000 lives and wiped out the capital city. "But immediately its dynamic young President, Anastasio Somoza Debayle, leaped into the ruins, worked alongside the 2.2 million Nicaraguans, and built a new economy—healthier and stronger than ever before." Somoza "believes in the Free Enterprise System," and needless to say, runs "a full-time program of improvements in the quality of life of the agriculturalist" and maintains "a calm, secure political climate" with "free elections."

A year later, the calm, secure political climate had reached the point where the *New York Times Magazine* featured an article entitled "National Mutiny in Nicaragua," describing how "almost every sector of the country—radicals and conservatives, rich and poor—is rising up against a dynastic dictatorship that can no longer count on the support of the United States" (a fact not uncorrelated with the disaffection among wealthy businessmen, who are so "dismayed by what [their spokesman considers] the brutality and corruption of General Somoza's dictatorship" that they conducted a two-week work stoppage to try to force his resignation, and this having failed, formed an Opposition Front that includes the guerrillas aimed at the overthrow of General Somoza).[265]

One reason for what Riding describes as "the 'betrayal' of the Somoza family by two of its oldest allies—the wealthy business elite and the United States Government," is the fantastic corruption. A case in point was the behavior of the dynamic young president who "leaped into the ruins" to build a new economy after the Managua earthquake. In fact, relief supplies were stolen by Somoza's cronies and the National Guardsmen who constitute his "private army." But "while scandalous, the looting of emergency supplies was modest compared to the way the Somoza family and its associates seized 'reconstruction' as an opportunity for further enrichment," relocating the "new" Managua on some land that happened to belong to—or was quickly bought up by—the

Somoza family. Using foreign assistance to develop needed facilities, the family was able to make quite a killing as land prices skyrocketed. It is the "unfair competition" by these masters of corruption that has "most upset Nicaragua's private sector," Riding reports. For a long time the Somozas have allowed their own and affiliated companies to import foreign goods duty free, enabling them to underprice their business competition, obliged to pay import taxes.[266]

As for the happy peasants and workers of the *Wall Street Journal* advertisement, Riding writes that "economic injustice seemed institutionalized" with a per capita income of $130 a year in the countryside; "Malnutrition was endemic throughout the country, infant mortality was high, and half of the adults were illiterate."[267] John Huey, writing in the *Wall Street Journal*, says that "A recent walk through a barrio in the colonial city of Leon—before it erupted into full-scale guerrilla warfare—reveals a degree of poverty and desperation that is startling, even by Latin American standards."[268]

But in the violence of 1978 the poor were not standing alone against Somoza, as national guardsmen "clubbed middle-class women in the streets during the recent national strike, and guerrillas swooped down from the mountains to attack the guardsmen."[269] It is "the all-out entry of the country's elite, private business leadership—largely educated at prestigious U.S. universities—into the struggle to depose him" that is most "troubling to Gen. Somoza," and to the U.S. elite that put him into power and has always supported him through these decades of atrocity and corruption. This "archetypal banana republic dictatorship," Huey writes, is likely to succumb to "the capitalists—fed up with corruption and abuse of power" rather than the "Communists" whom the regime blames for its troubles. True, Somoza still has plenty of muscle. He is supported by "the extremely loyal national guard," the sole army or police force, which "still is trained by the U.S. in the Panama Canal Zone." And as probably "Central America's wealthiest man" he might be able to make good his boast that "if I gave away my title and gave away my political connections, I'd still be the strongest man in the country." But many believe his days as U.S. agent in Nicaragua are numbered. "Leading opposition strategists are maintaining close contact with the Carter Administration," which is as much disturbed as are local businessmen by the unbelievable corruption which is blamed "for stifling foreign investment, despite a laissez-faire legal structure that should draw outside capital like flies to honey."

Another pillar of support for Somoza, the Roman Catholic Church, has also begun "pressuring the regime in earnest," Huey adds. The reason, in this case, includes "charges of murder and torture of priests and peasants believed to be collaborators" of the guerrillas—charges that the priests, who live with the peasants, know to be true, and know to extend far beyond "collaborators."

These "charges" have been discussed elsewhere. "According to church sources, hundreds of peasants have been executed or have simply disappeared in the provinces of Matagalpa and Zelaya, since the government stepped up its offensive against leftist guerrillas in the region two years ago. The sources said that many others had been tortured or raped and that their homes had been burned and their crops and property stolen by government troops."[270] Riding notes that Nicaragua was assigned $2.5 million in military sales credits for 1977 (but see note 288) and that the United States continues to maintain an 11-member military assistance group in Managua to advise the U.S.-trained Nicaraguan forces. Church sources also report mass executions and bombing of hamlets by National Guard aircraft, "a reign of terror in the region," in a message read from many pulpits throughout the country though excluded from the censored local press.[271] The same sources report that helicopters bring in bodies after mass killings for burial in mass graves, after which the land of the victims is divided up among "police judges," and also widespread torture. "Because of the repression, many cottages and hamlets in the area are now empty, their occupants having fled or been killed."

More detailed discussion of these atrocities appears elsewhere.[272] Kinzer, who points out that "Nicaragua is the only country which sends the entire annual graduating class of its military academy for a full year of training" at the U.S. Army School of the Americas in the Panama Canal Zone, reports that there have been "thousands of deaths in the countryside, where whole villages suspected of harboring guerrillas were destroyed" with "aerial bombings, summary executions and gruesome tortures." Many believe "that an ongoing American-backed 'peasant welfare' program is actually a cover for anti-guerrilla activities." Reporting from the scene of some of these anti-guerrilla campaigns, Lernoux describes "the awful consequences of U.S. intervention, in the freshly dug graves of peasant families that form a macabre chain across the northern rain forests of Zelaya and the neighboring departments...There is hardly a family in this terror-stricken region that has not suffered from a brutal campaign supported by the U.S. Government to destroy a band of left-wing guerrillas" estimated at about 50 in number. The guerrillas, largely middle and upper class in origin, have never enjoyed significant peasant support, she writes, though "the Nicaraguan military has wiped out whole districts on the convenient pretext of guerrilla collaboration." "Many of the massacres are the result of the National Guard's greed for the spoils of war, including land, cattle and women," extending the gradual dispossession of peasants by wealthy ranchers and others. The pastoral letter that described the peasant massacre also spoke of "the increasing concentration of land and wealth at the expense of humble peasants who have been dispossessed of their fields." Lernoux alleges that some 25,000 people have been killed in the 41-year reign of terror aided and abetted by Washington, now reaching a crescendo of violence.

Catholic priests speak of the "tremendous cynicism" in State Department rebuttals of criticism of the Somoza regime. Lernoux's own on-the-spot investigations reveal that U.S. military and economic aid programs are hardly more than a device for killing peasants, destroying community structures, providing data banks on the local population for the National Guard, establishing schools run by military informers, and so on.

The "long purgatory" has continued under U.S. auspices because the Somozas have been careful to acknowledge U.S. hegemony and their own dependent status and "special relationship," and to create the paradise for foreign investment described in the *Wall Street Journal* advertisement. It may now come to an end because the looting by Somoza and his cronies has reached proportions that have alienated most of the local elite and threatened foreign investment opportunities. If the history of the region is any guide, replacement of Somoza's purgatory by a "moderate" regime will simply reinstitute similar practices more effectively. Recall the history of the Dominican Republic, where a similar scene was enacted in 1961.[273]

The Nicaraguan bloodbath, in short, is in the process of transition from "constructive terror" to merely desultory and destabilizing bloodshed. The U.S. media have naturally been in a state of some confusion regarding Nicaraguan conditions. This is illustrated by two paired news stories in the *Washington Post*.[274] In the first, Goshko and DeYoung point out that Nicaragua

> has become a proving ground where the Carter administration is under a trial-and-error test of its ability to translate a concern for human rights into an effective instrument of U.S. foreign policy...Since Central America is a collection of client states heavily dependent on U.S. trade and aid, it would seem to be the perfect laboratory for the successful use of these tactics. But, as Washington has been finding out, what looks logical when spelled out in a position paper isn't really that easy in practice. That was vividly underscored last month by a pair of State Department decisions involving Nicaragua—decisions so outwardly confusing and contradictory that they seem to border on the bizarre. First, the Administration decided to move ahead with approval of a military-assistance agreement whose practical effects would be to strengthen the forces holding the reins of dictatorship in Nicaragua. Then it turned around and withheld a sizable chunk of nonmilitary aid whose purpose was to help ease the poverty in Nicaragua...In this instance...even the most astute State Department watchers were left bewildered about what had happened.

They proceed with an elaborate analysis of bureaucracy, inefficiency, etc. in an effort to unravel this grave mystery.

The mystery and bewilderment rest on the assumption that the U.S. aid program is intended to serve a humanitarian function in the world of subfascism, a fallacy obvious enough to the illiterate and uneducated Nicaraguan peasants, as we discover in DeYoung's accompanying story datelined Chinandega, Nicaragua.

DeYoung describes a group of families who "live in huts made, literally, of rubbish" in an empty railroad yard ("Atop a heap of old paper bags and plastic, a pregnant woman lay quietly moaning with pain from an evil-looking abscess on her leg" while " a small, mud-covered child sat in the dirt beside her, its head shiny with bald patches caused by malnutrition and disease," etc.) These peasants had been evicted along with dozens of other families by the Nicaraguan National Guard from their seaside village 50 miles away. "The peasants, and their sympathizers here and abroad, have protested their treatment to the Nicaraguan government and to U.S. officials who have expressed an interest in human rights. They expect little assistance from either." The peasants believe, curiously, that "it is the United States through its economic and military assistance, that provides the 'moral force' that backs oppression here." They blame their eviction on "the desire of Nicaragua's large landholders to acquire still more acreage on which to grow the high-priced, long-fibre cotton that is the country's chief export crop"—a process described above in neighboring Guatemala. The soldiers, the peasants report, came to their villages unannounced, loaded them on trucks and dumped them in the rail yard where they now live. The only "assistance" provided by the government is "the menacing nighttime presence of armed national guard troops who occasionally prowl the outskirts of their encampment." They are totally without income, except for the lucky few who can obtain occasional employment at $1.70 a day picking and cleaning cotton in surrounding plantations, exhibiting, no doubt, that "pride in their task" referred to in the *Wall Street Journal* advertisement. "Local and international human rights groups charge that these families are among thousands of peasants who have been uprooted from their homes by the national guard...on orders from the handful of wealthy families who own more than 50 percent of the country's cultivated land." Juan Molina, an opposition member of the Nicaraguan House of Deputies, said in an interview that the peasants would prefer non-violent measures, but by such a system they "can't fight what the United States gives (Somoza) in weapons and aid." De Young adds that "the U.S.-donated weapons were used last week to put down a brief revolt, led by leftist guerrillas, in which at least 35 persons were killed," noting that "the one thing all Nicaraguans, pro- and anti-Somoza, have in common is a healthy respect for the power and influence of the United States." Molina says that "I know that Carter has good intentions, but above all, he's a North American. A North American politician. We are a small country, and talking against the dictator suits U.S. purposes right now. But it means nothing here."

As for the peasants, they increasingly talk of "confrontation":

> So far, the peasants' campaign has not moved much beyond nighttime meetings at which they quietly strum guitars and sing songs they have written to the beat of protest. The songs, like those of a hundred such struggles that have come and gone in Latin America, speak of unity, of throwing off the landlords—and of an end to suffering.

If they proceed beyond songs, and go back to their villages, they will no longer be pathetic peasants but "left-wing terrorists," and they will meet the full force of the U.S.-backed military, while Western academics write lengthy tracts attempting to explain the strange rise of Communist terrorism that has become the curse of the twentieth century, embittering lives and sowing the seeds of totalitarianism when the elite is compelled to respond in order to preserve civilized values.

The "garbled rights message" perhaps became a little less garbled shortly after, when the U.S. resolved the "contradiction" by freeing aid to Nicaragua in what "some State Department sources call a bow to congressional supporters of Nicaraguan President Anastasio Somoza."[275] As the elite local opposition to Somoza increased, the U.S. government withheld implementation of the $2.5 million arms credits previously authorized, trimming "military assistance for Somoza's forces to only $150,000 in training grants," in addition to $160,000 "quietly released" for a Nicaraguan military hospital. As for the "humanitarian aid," it is likely to be as efficacious as previous gifts described by Lernoux and others:

> The peasants are used to seeing the trucks and material the U.S. government sends here, said one peasant leader. They know that when a sign goes up saying a road

> or building is a 'gift of the government and the people of the United States of America,' it means nothing for them.[276]

A new factor in the situation, not only in Nicaragua but elsewhere in Latin America as well, is that the U.S. subfascist clients now have access to arms from elsewhere, particularly Israel, which has itself been the beneficiary of unprecedented U.S. military assistance. The fact is occasionally noted in the press. Alan Riding points out that "according to well-placed sources, [President Somoza] added that he had the full support of Brazil and Israel, which over the last 18 months has replaced the United States as Nicaragua's main arms supplier."[277] This matter has been discussed outside of the United States, including Israel. A report in the Labor Party newspaper *Davar* (1 November 1978) discusses an article by Hugh O'Shaughnessy in the *London Observer* concerning alleged pressures on Israel by the United States and Mexico (which, according to the report, threatened to cut off oil supplies to Israel) to "end its supplying of weapons to the Government of General Somoza in Nicaragua." The *Davar* report also cites an article in the West German press which is reported to have identified Israel as one of the major suppliers of arms to Central America, including Nicaragua. The Israeli Foreign Ministry refused to comment, according to *Davar*. The issue of Israeli involvement with Latin American dictatorships received some attention in Israel after three Israeli generals visited Chile and Argentina (see Marcel Zohar, *Ha'aretz,* August 10, 1978, a report from Buenos Aires on the meetings of Israeli Generals with members of the military junta, discussing also Israeli arms sales to Argentina, alleged to be significant).

Columnist Smith Hempstone offers a sympathetic account of Israel's policy of arming Somoza to repress and slaughter the population of Nicaragua in the *Washington Post* Sunday supplement.[278] In the same journal, Hempstone has been irate over the alleged failure of Western opinion to express concern over the fate of victims of Cambodian atrocities (a standard pretense, as we shall see) and has expounded on the moral imperative of bearing witness—in the case of Communist atrocities.[279]

On August 22, 1978, Sandenista guerrillas captured the National Palace in the capital city of Managua. A national strike by businessmen began immediately after. In mid-September guerrillas seized major cities throughout the country in what the dictator called a replay of the Tet offensive of 1968. His response was not unlike that of the U.S. forces that occupied South Vietnam. City after city was "destroyed in order to save it." Thousands were killed in what the *Wall Street Journal* correspondent described as "a bloody war between lightly armed teenagers and National guardsmen."[280] Many were simply executed in towns that were retaken, reduced to rubble by the armaments so generously supplied by the U.S. government, and now by its allies.[281]

In an interview with the leader of the guerrilla group that captured the National Palace, Tad Szulc learned that the factor that immediately precipitated the action was President Carter's letter to Somoza praising him "while our people were being massacred by the dictatorship" ("Commander Zero"). To the guerrillas, the letter "meant support for Somoza, and we were determined to show Carter that Nicaraguans are ready to fight Somoza, the cancer of our country." A second factor may have been the "earlier administration decision to release aid funds to Nicaragua despite the Somoza repression [which] has already hurt the American image in liberal circles [in Latin America], to say nothing of the effect in leftist groups in the region." The guerrilla action was timed to coincide with the session of the Nicaraguan congress to approve a loan from the United States.[282]

Carter is a man who is loyal to his friends. Only a few weeks after his letter to Somoza, President Carter "telephoned the royal palace [in Iran] to express support for Shah Mohammed Reza Pahlevi, who faced the worst crisis of his 37-year reign."[283] This time, Carter's communication followed the machine-gunning of demonstrators' by the Shah's military forces, armed and trained in the United States, which took thousands of lives according to dissidents. To make sure that the message was clear, the world's leading exponent of Human Rights reemphasized it several times, for example in a statement to the Shah's son in Washington on October 31:

> "Our friendship and our alliance with Iran is one of our important bases on which our entire foreign policy

> depends," Carter told the young prince, who is undergoing training at the U.S. Air Force Academy. "We're thankful for this move toward democracy," Carter added, referring to the Shah's liberalization policies. "We know it is opposed by some who don't like democratic principles, but his progressive administration is very valuable, I think, to the entire Western world."[284]

It soon became clear even in the United States that those who allegedly "opposed democratic principles" and the Shah's "progressive administration" included virtually the entire population, no longer able to tolerate his U.S.-backed corruption and oppression. Exactly as in the case of Nicaragua, so in the case of Iran, Carter's explicit rejection of any concern for democracy or human rights helped to trigger the explosion.[285] And just as the United States began to search for some alternative to Somoza when the scale of internal opposition (crucially including business elements) reached such a level that he lost his usefulness, so also in Iran the United States finally backed off from the Shah and began to seek other means to ensure that the country can play its intended role in the U.S.-dominated global system.[286] Events in both Iran and Nicaragua in the fall of 1978 illustrate once again the consistent lesson of history: the United States will give massive support to the regimes of torturers and gangsters that it imposes by force and subversion as long as they are successful in maintaining the kind of "stability" that suits U.S. interests, in the manner that we have discussed (see chapter 3). But when popular resistance threatens this "stability," the U.S. government, never ceasing to proclaim its advocacy of democracy and human rights, will search for alternatives that will prevent the kinds of social and economic change that are perceived as harmful to the interests of those who dominate U.S. society, however beneficial they might be for the victims of U.S. power.

In Nicaragua, the September bloodbath indicated to Washington that its long-standing support for the Somoza dictatorship was no longer contributing to "stability". It therefore offered to "mediate" between Somoza and the broad-based opposition. But these efforts met with little immediate success. Alan Riding wrote from Managua that 10 weeks after the September slaughter "hope has given way to disappointment and anger" as "moderate and leftist opposition leaders are distressed by their growing conviction that Washington believes the country's deep crisis can be resolved by replacing the Somoza dictatorship with an equally conservative, though less brutal successor."[287] They are, in short, learning the lesson of history. The moderate and left opposition, Riding continues, "think Washington, fearing 'another Cuba,' is searching for stability rather than for social and economic change or even human rights—repeating, as they see it, American policy during its occupation of Nicaragua between 1912 and 1933, and its subsequent support for the Somoza family." Were the U.S. system of brainwashing under freedom not so effective, Riding might have perceived and gone on to explain that there have been and remain very powerful reasons, rooted in the U.S. socioeconomic system, for the long-term consistency of U.S. policy and the concern of the United States for the very specific form of "stability" on which we have commented repeatedly, not only in the case of Central America but wherever U.S. influence reaches. Nicaraguans are aware that the U.S. proposal "skims over social problems and ignores the guerrillas," and they are also no doubt aware of the reasons, which are inexpressible within the U.S. doctrinal system. They further "note that the Carter Administration was silent when the National Guard killed 3,000 people in crushing the September insurrection, but moved quickly to mediate when it recognized the popularity of the Sandinist guerrillas." And we strongly suspect that the "tens of thousands of Nicaraguans [who] are fighting for a new society as well as a new government" do not consider the behavior of the Carter Administration to be an odd and inexplicable deviation from traditional U.S. benevolence, but rather have a much better understanding of the forces working to block their efforts than do those in the U.S. media who occasionally report their disillusionment with U.S. tactics.

As the dust was settling in Nicaragua and people were returning to the ruins of their homes to bury the dead, thoughtful commentators in the United States attempted to assess what had taken place. John M. Goshko of the *Washington Post* explained that "the hope that Nicaragua could be moved gradually and peacefully toward democracy was dashed August 22 when a

guerrilla group dramatically attacked the nati
Managua and touched off the unrest that escalate
This episode reveals the limits of U.S. power an
that face a government that is deeply committed
human rights.[288] Foreign commentators saw the matter ...
somewhat different light. *Le Monde* noted editorially that the U.S. government, while insisting in a September statement that it "was not trying to get General Anastasio Somoza to step down," nevertheless was "beginning to distance itself from one of Latin America's bloodiest and longest lasting dictatorships," limiting itself to "cautious phrasemongering," however, though it is clear that "the dictator would have been highly vulnerable to a total suspension of U.S. aid, a practical embargo on arms shipments and an unequivocal condemnation of his ghoulish style of government. By refusing to take this decisive step, President Carter had seriously damaged the credibility of the stances he has often taken on behalf of human rights."[289] The "new inflection" in U.S. policy "is undoubtedly a reaction to the news coming out of Managua of savage and mindless atrocities committed by the Nicaraguan National Guard in many parts of the country" while "the United States did nothing whatever to stop the slaughter when there was still time":

> United States responsibility in this shocking business is all the greater since it created the situation in the first place. Changing it would in no way be interference in the internal affairs of a state like any other, but at most it would right a grave historic wrong the people of Nicaragua have paid for too dearly and which has profited a good many American firms far too handsomely.

Washington observers, however, prefer to lament the limits of U.S. power, which are selectively discovered when there is a problem of impeding a massacre by U.S.-armed forces of a friendly dictator—though the quandary in Washington is real enough, now that the business community is unified against Somoza. The *Manchester Guardian* meanwhile commiserated with President Carter because the Organization of American States (which "looks increasingly like a military dictators' club with the United States feebly protesting against tyranny from a

..ority position") refused "to investigate the well-documented ,trocities committed by the National Guard in Nicaragua," probably "a matter of grief to President Carter" with his well-known commitment to human rights. Nothing further is said about why the OAS looks increasingly like a military dictators' club, or how this relates to U.S. policy over many years.[290]

The Carter Administration would have liked Somoza to resign and be replaced by "moderates," but it did not openly call for his resignation or entirely withdraw support from him. This vacillation set the stage for Somoza's forceful suppression of a virtually unified Nicaraguan population and the death of thousands in September, 1978, again compliments of the U.S.-trained and -armed national guard. With U.S.-supplied helicopters and gunships and other sophisticated weaponry, Somoza demonstrated that U.S. counterinsurgency techniques may now permit pacification by proxy of a unified hostile population. Once again we have an impressive demonstration of Washington's devotion to human rights; in this case, we see subfacism in the last stages of decay, with mindless brutality and uncontrollable greed that bring even the vast bulk of the local business elite into an alliance with the left, while the liberal Carter is still unable to dissociate himself from the torture regime.

The story is much the same elsewhere, for example, in Bolivia, where a coup that overturned the first elections in 12 years followed by the reported arrest of at least 100 labor and student leaders and human rights activists inspired the State Department to comment that it would withhold judgment about the future of U.S. relations with Bolivia, "pending a clarification" of the new government's intentions.[291] Or in El Salvador, where a priest is quoted as saying that "the peasants live like serfs in Europe 400 years ago"[292]—if they are lucky enough to survive at all.

A report three years later describes the familiar pattern.[293] "Hopes of peaceful democratic change were dashed in elections in 1972 and again in February 1977, when the military government resorted to fraud to block moderately reformist opposition candidates for the presidency. In apparent response, three Marxist guerrilla organizations...have emerged since 1975 and have been responsible for a large number of killings, bombings and kidnappings," so that many "wealthy businessmen and farmers in El

Salvador are living in fear." And "after an increase in repression by the military government, militant labor and peasant leaders are also living in fear, many trying to hold together their organizations while in hiding, some having 'disappeared' or landed in jail" in a country in which, "perhaps more than in any other Latin American country, wealth...is concentrated in few hands, with successive military regimes either unwilling or too weak to contemplate even the modest social and land reforms that have taken place in other countries of the region." Particularly worrisome to the wealthy elite is "the growing militancy of the peasants—making up 60% of the population of five million—and the evident appeal of a new leftist organization called the Popular Revolutionary Bloc, which has united anti-government workers, peasants, students, teachers and urban squatters" since 1975 and is "closely linked with progressive sectors of the Roman Catholic Church." Church sources report many killings, arrests and disappearances in the preceding few months. Offensives against peasants by "a large government-run paramilitary organization" have also taken a heavy toll. The secretary-general of the Federation of Christian peasants and the Farm Workers Union alleges that "the government's aim is to destroy all popular organizations, but it is aiming most at the peasant groups because they are growing fastest. There is a lot of fear, but hunger and misery oblige people to keep on fighting despite the repression. The peasants are desperate." The government, meanwhile, portrays itself as "trapped between the extreme left and the extreme right," a major problem being that "the extreme left is using the popular organizations," according to the president's information secretary.

Meanwhile the State Department Human Rights reports assure us that although there has been violence in the universities "triggered by an announcement of higher tuition fees" and perhaps "some isolated instances...of actions perpetrated by government agents which could be considered repressive," matters are more or less in hand, and El Salvador is "partly free," according to Freedom House (1977). The 1978 report notes "an upsurge of terrorism by extremists of both left and right" and refers to charges that the paramilitary organization is responsible for "some abuses." But despite these possible abuses and such problems as "a highly skewed income" and overpopulation, things are improving and in fact by the end of 1977 "there seemed to be greater freedom to participate in the political process than earlier in the year."

As those notes indicate, an assiduous reader of the nation's press can obtain a picture of what is happening in Latin America as the continent becomes "one gigantic prison, and in some regions one vast cemetery," in the words of the "Open Letter" cited at the outset, though much is disguised or withheld and analysis of the systematic and pervasive character of U.S. influence and intervention and its obvious roots in a domestic socioeconomic structure is spectacularly lacking. A semi-rational approach to international affairs, which relates prevailing phenomena to the existing distribution of power, is restricted to enemies of the state, and is then often embroidered with convenient mythology. In the U.S. domains, such an approach is excluded as unthinkable, and we read only of the limits of U.S. power, the quandaries of the human rights administration, certain past errors that have long been overcome though their consequences still haunt us, and so on. If the press and academic scholarship were free of compelling ideological blinders, the story of the United States in Latin America would be at the core of study of U.S. international affairs, past and current. Given the substantial and often determining U.S. influence on the region, the current plague of benign and constructive terror would be the central concern of human rights activists. Such is very far from the case.

CHAPTER 5

Bloodbaths in Indochina: Constructive, Nefarious and Mythical

The sheer scope and intensity of the violence imposed on Indochina by the U.S. war machine forced a great deal of information into the public domain and consciousness. The public was, nevertheless, spared a full picture of the war's true nature, and was kept in a state of confusion by a steady flow of allegations of enemy terror, assertions of Washington's benevolent intentions, and the pretense that the enormous destruction of the civil societies of Indochina resulted from the fact that "war inevitably hurts many innocent people." Enough got through the propaganda filter, however, to open many eyes to the ugly reality and to shatter the complacent faith of large numbers of Americans in the competence, humanity, and integrity of their leaders.

In reconstructing the faith it has been necessary to expunge from many memories the brutalities and lies of the war, and to transform the historical record so as to obfuscate its causes, minimize the toll it exacted upon its victims, and discount its meaning and historic significance. Much progress has been made along these lines by a simple process of non-discussion and suppression, allowing the war to fade, except where anti-Communist points can be scored. The propagandists have proven their mettle already on the crucial issue of cause and intent; they have succeeded in wiping the record clean of the substantial documentary evidence of rational imperial planning that provided the framework for the U.S. interventions, interpreting them more comfortably in terms of neutral categories such as "error" or "ignorance" in a framework of concern for freedom. A renewed effort has also commenced to show that the policies of search-and-destroy, harassment-and-interdiction fire, and napalming and high level bombing of densely populated areas were really not intended to kill civilians.[1] Rather, as Sidney Hook had already emphasized back when the U.S. was blowing up villages "suspected" of harboring "terrorists,"[2] the resulting casualties were not "deliberate American atrocities" but merely "the unfortunate accidental loss of life incurred by the efforts of American military forces to help the South Vietnamese repel the incursions of North Vietnam and its partisans"; or in a later version, "unintended consequences of military action."[3]

In volume II, we will consider the process of historical reconstruction in the context of analysis of Western reactions to developments in postwar Indochina. Here we will only review very briefly some salient features of the U.S. onslaught, soon to be lost in the mist of obfuscation and deceit as the propaganda system turns to the tasks that lie ahead. We will restrict the discussion to South Vietnam[4] and will not make any effort to touch on more than a few issues and examples. We have written on the subject extensively elsewhere, as have many others.[5]

5.1 Constructive Bloodbaths in Vietnam

5.1.1 French and Diemist Bloodbaths

Although the only pre-1965 bloodbath recognized in official doctrine is that which occurred in North Vietnam during its land reform of the mid-50s, there were others. In 1946, without warning, the French bombarded Haiphong, killing an estimated 6000 civilians,[6] perhaps more than the number of victims of the well publicized North Vietnamese land reform episode (see section 5.2.2). But as part of the French recolonization effort, and with Vietnam of little interest to the American leadership, this bloodbath was ignored and has not been mentioned by U.S. official or non-official propagandists in their historical reconstructions of terror in Indochina.

Diem's bloodbaths also were impressive, but as they were in the service of anti-Communism and the preservation of our client, they fall into the constructive or benign categories. Under our tutelage, Diem began his own "search-and-destroy" operations in the mid- and late 1950s, and his prison camps and the torture chambers were filled and active. In 1956 the official figure for political prisoners in South Vietnam was fifteen to twenty thousand. Even Diem's friend and adviser, P.J. Honey, concluded on the basis of talks with former inmates, that the majority of these were "neither Communists nor pro-Communists."[7] The maltreatment and massacre of political prisoners was a regular practice during the Diem period, although these problems became much more acute in later years.[8] The 1958 massacre of prisoners in Diem's concentration camp Phu Loi led to such an outcry that P. J. Honey was dispatched to inquire into these events; according to Lacouture Honey could not verify more than twenty deaths at Phu Loi.[9]

"Pacification" as it developed from the earliest Diem period consisted in "killing, or arresting without either evidence or trials, large numbers of persons suspected of being Vietminh or 'rebels'."[10] This resulted in many small bloodbaths at the local level, plus larger ones associated with military expeditions carried out by Diem against the rural population. One former Vietminh resistance fighter gave the following account of the Diemist terror and bloodbath in his village:

> My village chief was a stranger to the village. He was very cruel. He hunted all the former members of the Communist Party during the Resistance to arrest and kill them. All told, he slaughtered fourteen Party members in my village. I saw him with my own eyes order the killing of two Party members in Mau Lam hamlet. They had their hands tied behind their backs and they were buried alive by the militia. I was scared to death.[11]

Another former resistance fighter in Central Vietnam claimed that

> in 1956, the local government of Quang Nam started a terrorist action against old Resistance members. About 10,000 persons of the Resistance Army were arrested, and a good many of them were slaughtered. I had to run for my life, and I stayed in the mountains until 1960. I lived with three others who came from my village. We got help from the tribal population there.[12]

The general mechanics of the larger bloodbaths were described by Joseph Buttinger, a former Diem supporter and advisor.[13]

> In June 1956 Diem organized two massive expeditions to the regions that were controlled by the Communists without the slightest use of force. His soldiers arrested tens of thousands of people...Hundreds, perhaps thousands of peasants were killed. Whole villages whose populations were not friendly to the government were destroyed by artillery. These facts were kept secret from the American people.[14]

According to Jeffrey Race, a former U.S. Army advisor in South Vietnam who had access to extensive documentation on recent Vietnamese history,

> ...the government terrorized far more than did the revolutionary movement—for example, by liquidations of former Vietminh, by artillery and ground attacks on "communist villages," and by roundups of "communist sympathizers." Yet it was just these tactics that led to the constantly increasing strength of the revolutionary movement in Long An from 1960 to 1965.[15]

During the period 1955-60 the Vietminh mission was political, and "though it used assassinations and kidnapping," according to the *Pentagon Papers* historian it "circumspectly avoided military operations."[16] A USMAAG report of July 1957 stated: "The Viet Cong guerrillas and propagandists...are still waging a grim battle for survival. In addition to an accelerated propaganda compaign, the Communists have been forming 'front' organizations...seeking to spread the theory of 'Peace and Coexistence.' "[17] On the other hand, Diem, at least through 1957, was having "marked success with fairly sophisticated pacification programs in the countryside."[18] In a precise analogy to his sponsor's pacification efforts of 1965-72, "By the end of 1956, the civic action component of the GVN pacification program had been cut back severely."[19] The Pentagon historian refers to "Diem's nearly paranoid preoccupation with security," which led to policies that "thoroughly terrified the Vietnamese peasants, and detracted significantly from the regime's popularity."[20]

According to the Pentagon historian, "No direct links have been established between Hanoi and perpetrators of rural violence."[21] The phrase "perpetrators of rural violence" is applied by the Pentagon historian only to the Vietminh, who admittedly were concentrating on political activities, and not to the Diem regime, which as he notes was conducting a policy of large-scale reprisals and violence, so extensive and undiscriminating as to be counter-productive. It is not difficult to establish "direct links" between Washington and perpetrators of the Diemist repression, incidentally. Once again it is clear that "constructive" bloodbaths can never involve "violence" for establishment propagandists and scholars; the word is reserved for those seeking social change in an illegitimate direction and under improper auspices.

Diem's extensive use of violence and reprisals against former Resistance fighters was in direct violation of the Geneva Accords (Article 14c), as was his refusal to abide by the election proviso.[22] The main reason for Diem's refusal to abide by this mode of settlement in 1955-56 was quite evident: the expatriate mandarin imported from the United States had minimal popular support and little hope of winning in a free election. (This sequence of events has not prevented the liberal establishment from claiming that our intervention in South Vietnam was to assure "self-determination".) Diem was a typical subfascist tyrant, compensating for lack of indigenous support with extra doses of terror. Violence is the natural mode of domination for those without local roots or any positive strategy for gaining support, in this instance the United States and its client regime. It is striking that irrespective of the facts, American officials and journalists throughout the succeeding struggle formulated the issues in terms of "control of the population" (how can we wrest areas from Viet Cong "control"?, etc.), projecting their own inability to conceive of "support" on the hated enemy, who was not so limited in either policies or programs that might yield political successes without violence.

Diem's immediate resort to violence was in marked contrast to the behavior of those designated in the *Pentagon Papers* as "perpetrators of rural violence;" we return below (5.2.1) to Race's detailed and well-documented study of how the Communist Party rejected the use of violence "even in self-defense, against the increasing repressiveness of the government" (p. 104), while winning popular support through its social programs, until driven by Diem's repression to resorting to force in order to survive. Wherever detailed studies have been carried out, the conclusions are rather similar.

As for the toll exacted among the South Vietnamese during the Diem period, there are no firm estimates. Bernard Fall reports figures, which he seems to regard as realistic, indicating a death toll of over 150,000 "Viet Cong" from 1957 to April 1965—that is, before the first North Vietnamese battalion was allegedly detected in the South. These South Vietnamese, in his words, had been fighting "under the crushing weight of American armor, napalm, jet bombers and, finally, vomiting gases."[23] These 150,000 (or whatever the actual numbers may be) have also never been counted among the victims of a pre-1965 "bloodbath." Rather, they were physically eliminated in a classic exercise of constructive violence, and are now being eliminated from the historical record in a no less classic exercise of a hegemonic system of ideology and propaganda.

5.1.2 The Overall U.S. Assault as the Primary Bloodbath

In a very real sense the overall U.S. effort in South Vietnam was a huge and deliberately imposed bloodbath. Military escalation was undertaken to offset the well-understood lack of any significant social and political base for the elite military faction supported by the United States. Despite occasional expressions of interest in the welfare and free choice of the South Vietnamese, the documents in the *Pentagon Papers* show that U.S. planners consistently regarded the impact of their decisions on the Vietnamese as a peripheral issue at most, more commonly as totally inconsequential. Nonintervention and an NLF takeover were unacceptable for reasons that had nothing to do with Vietnamese interests; they were based on an assumed adverse effect on our material and strategic interests. It was assumed that an American failure would be harmful to our prestige and would reduce the confidence of our satellite governments that we would protect them from the winds of change.[24] The Thai elite, for example, might "conclude that we simply could not be counted on" to help them in suppressing local insurgencies. What is more, there was the constant threat of a "demonstration effect" of real social and economic progress in China,[25] North Korea,[26] and North Vietnam.[27]

In spite of official reiterations of the alleged threat of Chinese and North Vietnamese "expansionism," it was recognized by U.S. policy makers that a unified Communist Vietnam probably would have limited ambitions itself, and would provide a barrier to any Chinese moves further South.[28] It is not the threat of military expansion that official documents cite as the justification for the huge assault on Vietnam. Rather, it was feared that by processes never spelled out in detail, "the rot [might] spread to Thailand"[29] and perhaps beyond. The "rot" can only be the Communist "ideological threat;" that is, the possibility of social and economic progress outside the framework of U.S. control and imperial interests, which must be fought by U.S. intervention against local Communist organizing or uprisings, whether or not any Communist armed attack is involved. This is the rot that might spread to Thailand and beyond, inspiring Communist-led nationalist movements. But no skillful ideologists would want such implications spelled out too clearly to themselves or to others. Consequently, the central factors involved remain vague, their place taken by rhetoric about aggression, threatened bloodbaths, and our interest in self-determination.

It is important to bear in mind that these concepts—in fact, even the terminology in which they were expressed—were not invented by Vietnam planners. Rather, they merely adopted a standard mechanism of proven effectiveness in mobilizing support for U.S. intervention. When Dean Acheson faced the problem of convincing the "leaders of Congress" (his quotes) to support the Truman Doctrine in February, 1947, he outlined the threat to them as follows:

> In the past eighteen months, I said, Soviet pressure on the Straits, on Iran, and on northern Greece had brought the Balkans to the point where a highly possible Soviet breakthrough might open three continents to Soviet penetration. Like apples in a barrel infected by one rotten one, the corruption of Greece would infect Iran and all to the east. It would also carry infection to Africa through Asia

> Minor and Egypt, and to Europe through Italy and France, already threatened by the strongest domestic Communist parties in Western Europe.[30]

As Acheson well knew, Soviet pressure on the Straits and Iran had been withdrawn already and Western control was firmly established. Further, there was no evidence of Soviet pressure on Northern Greece—on the contrary, Stalin was unsympathetic to the Greek guerrillas. Still the rot might spread unless the U.S. undertook to rescue the terrorist regime in Athens, and a "Soviet breakthrough" was a useful propaganda device with which to mobilize domestic support. Acheson was concerned with the more remote dominoes—the Middle East and the industrial societies that were subject to the "threat" of internal democratic politics that might bring Communist parties to power, thwarting U.S. intentions. Similarly in the case of Indochina, it was the potential exit from the Free World of Indonesia with its rich resources, and ultimately industrial Japan, that obsessed U.S. planners as they contemplated the threat of falling dominoes and rotting apples.

Gabriel Kolko comments accurately that "translated into concrete terms, the domino theory [previously invoked with regard to Greece and the Middle East, as he notes] was a counterrevolutionary doctrine which defined modern history as a movement of Third World and dependent nations—those with economic and strategic value to the United States or its capitalist associates—away from colonialism or capitalism and toward national revolution and forms of socialism."[31] In its specific application to Indochina, the falling dominoes led inexorably to Japan, the "superdomino" in the nightmare of the planners, investing their effort to prevent an unwelcome form of independence in Indochina with cosmic significance.[32] Again, mainstream scholarship is assiduously at work removing this no less unwelcome issue from the realm of discussion.

As the *Pentagon Papers* and other documentary evidence show beyond question, top-level U.S. planners never had any doubt that in backing French colonialism and later intervening directly they were placing themselves in opposition to the main currents of Vietnamese nationalism, though a show of rage about aggression directed from Moscow or "Peiping" was always considered necessary for public relations purposes, and was always saleable to the mass media and important segments of academic scholarship. Illusions about a unified International Communist movement responsible for events in Indochina were not only fostered by propagandists, but also came to be accepted doctrine among high level planners themselves, even surviving the China-Soviet schism that was apparent by the late 1950s. A similar mixture of pretense for the population and internal delusion was standard with regard to the situation in South Vietnam, as we can see from the account of the *Pentagon Papers* historians and the government documents they provide.[33]

The U.S. leadership knew that in Vietnam the "primary sources of Communist strength in the South remain indigenous," with a corresponding "ability to recruit locally;" and it was recognized that the NLF "enjoys some status as a nationalist movement," whereas the military government "is composed primarily of technicians" lacking in "positive support from various key segments of the populace" and determined "to remain the real power in South Vietnam" without any "interference from the civilians in the conduct of the war."[34] The experienced pacification chief, John Paul Vann, writing in 1965, puts the matter more brutally:

> A popular political base for the Government of South Vietnam does not now exist....The existing government is oriented toward the exploitation of the rural and lower class urban populations. It is, in fact, a continuation of the French colonial system of government with upper class Vietnamese replacing the French....The dissatisfaction of the agrarian population...is expressed largely through alliance with the NLF.[35]

It was thus well known to U.S. authorities in 1965, as before, that they were fighting a nationalist mass movement in the name of a corrupt oligarchy that lacked popular backing. The Vietnam War was fought to return this nationalist mass movement to that "measure of passivity and defeatism" identified by Pool as necessary for "stability" in the Third World (see chapter 3, note 5).

It must be brought under comprador-military control of the sort that the U.S. has imposed or supported in Brazil, the Dominican Republic, Guatemala, Bolivia, Thailand, etc. As we have noted, however, the power to rationalize self-interest is great, and some U.S. leaders may have been able to keep their minds from being cluttered with inconvenient facts. In so doing, they preserved the belief that because we were the "good guys" our purposes must be benign and democratic and must have some positive relationship to the interests of the South Vietnamese people. Even the evidence that we were directing a large part of our military effort to assaulting and uprooting the rural population of the South, already overwhelming before 1965, was easily assimilated into the Orwellian doctrine of "defense against aggression."

The decision to employ technologically advanced conventional weaponry against the southern countryside made a certain amount of sense on two assumptions: first, that the revolutionary forces were predominant in the rural areas, so that the war had to be a true anti-population war to force submission; and second, that the "demonstration effect" is important to U.S. interests, so that our job was to terrorize, kill and destroy in order to prove that revolution "doesn't pay." The first assumption was true in fact and must be assumed to have contributed to the gradual emergence of a full-fledged policy of search-and-destroy and unrestrained firepower, whatever the human consequences. The second assumption was evidently important in the thinking of high level U.S. planners and advisers and also contributed to the evolution of policy.[36]

The very terminology of the planners reflected these accurate perceptions, as is noted occasionally by the *Pentagon Papers* analysts. A U.S. official commented that "essentially, we are fighting Vietnam's birth rate," in accordance with Westmoreland's concept of a "meatgrinder" ("where we could kill large numbers of the enemy, but in the end do little better than hold our own," in the words of the *Pentagon Papers* historian). Some in the U.S. remained optimistic. Robert ("Blowtorch") Komer, who was in charge of the "other war," cheerfully reported in early 1967 that "we are grinding the enemy down by sheer weight and mass" in what he correctly perceived as a "revolutionary, largely political conflict," though he never drew the obvious conclusions that follow from these conjoined observations.[37] Komer went on to recommend, rationally enough from the point of view of a major war criminal, that the United States must "*step up refugee programs deliberately aimed at depriving the VC of a recruiting base*" (his emphasis). Thus the United States could deprive the enemy of what the Combined Campaign Plan 1967 identifies as its "greatest asset," namely, "the people."

In January 1966, the well-known humanitarian Robert McNamara, now a passionate spokesman for the world's poor in his capacity as head of the World Bank, introduced evidence in Congressional testimony on the success of air and artillery attacks, including B-52 raids ("the most devastating and frightening weapons used so far against the VC"), in forcing villagers "to move where they will be safe from such attacks...regardless of their attitude to the GVN." One can gain certain insight into the mentality of pro-war intellectuals from the fact that McNamara's evidence was reprinted in the pro-war journal *Vietnam Perspectives* (May 1966) to show how well things were going for our side. A month earlier, General Westmoreland had predicted "a tremendous increase in the number of refugees,"[38] an expectation that was soon fulfilled as a result of B-52 bombings and other tactics. Meanwhile other humanitarians (e.g., Leo Cherne, chairman of the International Rescue Committee) thoughtfully explained how refugees were fleeing from Communism. (See Volume II, chapter 6, for references).

The character of U.S. policy was also influenced by the gradual recognition of two additional facts: first, that the South Vietnamese victims of "pacification" were essentially voiceless, unable to reach U.S. or world opinion even as effectively as the North Vietnamese, with the result that the population being "saved" could be treated with virtually unrestrained violence. The second fact was that relevant U.S. sensitivities (i.e., those of politically significant numbers of people) were almost exclusively related to U.S. casualties and costs. Both of these considerations encouraged the development of an indiscriminate war of fire-power, a war of shooting first and making inquiries later; this would minimize U.S. casualties and have the spin-off benefit of more thoroughly terrorizing the population. The enhanced civilian casualties need not be reported—the enormous statistical service of the Pentagon always had difficulty dredging up anything credible on this one question—or such casualties could be reported as "enemy" or "Vietcong." Years of familiarity with this practice did not cause the news services to refrain from transmitting, as straight news, Saigon and Pentagon handouts on "enemy" casualties.

The retrospective judgment of the generals themselves on the accuracy of casualty reports makes interesting reading. General Douglas Kinnard published a study based on responses of Army Generals who had been commanders in Vietnam to a variety of questions, including one on the accuracy of "body counts." Only 26% of the respondents felt that body count figures were "within reason accurate." The query elicited such responses as these: "The immensity of the false reporting is a blot on the honor of the Army;" "They were grossly exaggerated by many units primarily because of the incredible interest shown by people like McNamara and Westmoreland;" "A fake—totally worthless;" "Gruesome—a ticket punching item;" "Often blatant lies."[39] Most generals felt that the body count was exaggerated, but that reaction must be coupled with a recognition that much of the air and artillery barrage was directed against targets where casualties would never be known or counted. Kinnard, for example, reports that when he returned to Vietnam in May, 1969 as Commanding General of II Field Force Artillery he discovered that targets were being selected at random in areas where nightime firing was authorized—quite substantial areas, as we know from other sources. Who might be killed by such random fire will never be known in the West. Reporters on the scene have made similar observations. Katsuichi Honda of *Asahi Shimbun*, perhaps the only pro-Western correspondent to have spent any time in the liberated areas of South Vietnam, described the incessant attacks on undefended villages by gunboats in the Mekong River and helicopter gunships "firing away at random at farmhouses:"

> They seemed to fire whimsically and in passing even though they were not being shot at from the ground nor could they identify the people as NLF. They did it impulsively for fun, using the farmers for targets as if in a hunting mood. They are hunting Asians...This whimsical

> firing would explain the reason why the surgical wards in every hospital in the towns of the Mekong Delta were full of wounded.[40]

In the Mekong Delta, there were virtually no North Vietnamese troops when Honda reported in the fall of 1967. The victims of these hunting trips were not listed in the "body counts" and are not included in any accounting of "bloodbaths".

Still other factors were involved in making the entire U.S. enterprise in Vietnam a huge bloodbath; faith in technological solutions, racism reinforced by the corruption of "our" Vietnamese and the helplessness of the victimized population, and the frustrations of war. But essentially the initial high level decision to bomb freely, to conduct search-and-destroy operations, and to fight a war against the rural population with virtually unlimited force were the source of the bloodbath. The essence of the U.S. war in "saving" South Vietnam was well expressed by a U.S. Marine, in a 1967 letter to Senator William Fulbright:

> I went to Vietnam, a hard charging Marine 2nd Lieutenant, sure that I had answered the plea of a victimized people in their struggle against communist aggression. That belief lasted about two weeks. Instead of fighting communist aggressors I found that 90% of the time our military actions were directed against the people of South Vietnam. These people had little sympathy or for that matter knowledge of the Saigon Government...We are engaged in a war in South Vietnam to pound a people into submission to a government that has little or no popular support among the real people of South Vietnam. By real people I mean all those Vietnamese people who aren't war profiteers or who have [not] sold out to their government or the United States because it was the easy and/or profitable thing to do.[41]

The immensity of the overall U.S. imposed bloodbath can be inferred to some degree from the sheer volume of ordnance employed, the nature of the weaponry, and the principles which governed their use. Through the end of 1971 over 3.9 million tons of bombs were dropped on South Vietnam from the air alone—

about double the total bomb tonnage used by the United States in all theaters during World War II—with ground ordnance also employed in historically unprecented volume.[42] A large fraction of the napalm used in Indochina was dropped in South Vietnam, an illustration of the abuse visited on the voiceless South Vietnamese (in protecting them from "aggression!") by the U.S. command in collaboration with its client government in Saigon. Over 90% of the air strikes in South Vietnam were classified officially as "interdiction",[43] which means bombing not carried out in support of specific ongoing military actions, but rather area bombing, frequently on a programmed basis, and attacks on "what are suspected" to be "enemy base camps," or sites from which a shot may have been fired.

One former military intelligence officer with the Americal Division in South Vietnam told a congressional subcommittee: "Every information report (IR) we wrote based on our sources' information was classified as (1) unverifiable and (2) usually reliable source... The unverified and in fact unverifiable information, nevertheless, was used regularly as input to artillery strikes, harassment and interdiction fire (H&I), B-52 and other air strikes, often on populated areas."[44] In the words of Army Chief of Staff General Johnson, "We have not enough information. We act with ruthlessness, like a steamroller, bombing extensive areas and not selected targets based on detailed intelligence."[45] This is an expression of indiscriminateness as a principle—deliberate, calculated and discriminate indiscriminateness—and it is a perfect complement to the other facets of a policy which was from the beginning semi-genocidal in purpose and method, resting in large part on the fact that the civilian population has been regarded as enemy or, at best, of no account.

The number of civilian casualties inflicted on South Vietnam is unknown, but is very likely underestimated by the Senate Subcommittee on Refugees at 400,000 dead, 900,000 wounded and 6.4 million turned into refugees.[46] Conservative as these figures are, however, they mean "that there is hardly a family in South Vietnam that has not suffered a death, injury or the anguish of abandoning an ancient homestead."[47]

That the overall U.S. assault on South Vietnam involved a

huge bloodbath can also be inferred from the nature of "pacification," both in general concept and in the details of implementation. We shall not here go into the general concept and the ways in which it was applied and was rapidly transformed into the wholesale killing and forced transfer of civilians.[48] We shall confine ourselves to an examination of three cases: a specific operation by U.S. forces over a brief time period; a series of atrocities perpetrated over a six or seven-year period by our South Korean mercenary allies, with the certain knowledge and tacit acceptance of U.S. authorities; and the Phoenix program of extra-legal "counter terror" against enemy civilians. These are by no means the only bloodbaths that typify the constructive mode, but they are offered as illustrative and deserving of greater attention.

5.1.3 Operation SPEEDY EXPRESS

The atrocities committed by Westmoreland's killing machine as it was "grinding the enemy down by sheer weight and mass" are readily discerned even in the bureaucratic prose of the *Pentagon Papers* and other government reports, but it was only after the Tet offensive of January-February 1968, when the *Pentagon Papers* record terminates, that the full force of U.S. power was launched against the defenseless population of South Vietnam. Operation SPEEDY EXPRESS, conducted in the first six months of 1969, was only one of many major pacification efforts. It is unusual primarily in that it was studied in detail by Alex Shimkin and Kevin Buckley,[49] who examined the military and hospital records of the operation and interviewed South Vietnamese inhabitants and pacification officials of the Mekong Delta province of Kien Hoa, the target of SPEEDY EXPRESS.

For many years, the province had been "almost totally controlled" by the NLF:

> For a long time there was little or no military activity in the Delta. The 9th Division [which carried out the operation] did not even arrive until the end of 1966. Front activities went far beyond fighting. The VC ran schools, hospitals and even businesses. A pacification study revealed that an NLF sugar cane cooperative for three villages in the Mo Cay district of Kien Hoa produced

> revenue in 1968 which exceeded the entire Saigon government budget that year for Kien Hoa.

There appear to have been no North Vietnamese units present. As late as January 22, 1968, Defense Secretary McNamara had testified before the Senate that "no regular North Vietnamese units" were engaged in the Delta,[50] and while some entered after the massive killing of NLF guerrillas and civilians during the Tet offensive and after, there is no indication in the reports that the "enemy" in Kien Hoa included units of the North Vietnamese army.

Despite the success of the NLF, the "aggressive military effort carried out by the U.S. 9th Infantry Division" had succeeded in establishing some degree of government control.[51] In the six months of SPEEDY EXPRESS, this control was significantly extended; "a total of some 120,000 people who had been living in VC controlled areas" came under government control. This result was achieved by application of the "awesome firepower" of the 9th Division, including air strikes using napalm, high explosives and anti-personnel bombs, B-52 bombing, and artillery shelling "around the clock" at a level that "it is impossible to reckon." Armed helicopters "scour[ed] the landscape from the air night and day," accounting for "many and perhaps most of the enemy kills." Buckley's *Newsweek* account describes the events as follows:

> All the evidence I gathered pointed to a clear conclusion: a staggering number of noncombatant civilians—perhaps as many as 5,000 according to one official—were killed by U.S. firepower to "pacify" Kien Hoa. The death toll there made the My Lai massacre look trifling by comparison...
>
> The Ninth Division put all it had into the operation. Eight thousand infantrymen scoured the heavily populated countryside, but contact with the elusive enemy was rare. Thus, in its pursuit of pacification, the division relied heavily on its 50 artillery pieces, 50 helicopters (many armed with rockets and mini-guns) and the deadly support lent by the Air Force. There were 3,381 tactical air strikes by fighter bombers during "Speedy Express"...
>
> "Death is our business and business is good," was the

slogan painted on one helicopter unit's quarters during the operation. And so it was. Cumulative statistics for "Speedy Express" show that 10,899 "enemy" were killed. In the month of March alone, "over 3,000 enemy troops were killed...which is the largest monthly total for any American division in the Vietnam War," said the division's official magazine. When asked to account for the enormous body counts, a division senior officer explained that helicopter gun crews often caught unarmed "enemy" in open fields. But Vietnamese repeatedly told me that those "enemy" were farmers gunned down while they worked in their rice fields...

There is overwhelming evidence that virtually all the Viet Cong were well armed. Simple civilians were, of course, not armed. And the enormous discrepancy between the body count [11,000] and the number of captured weapons [748] is hard to explain—except by the conclusion that many victims were unarmed innocent civilians...

The people who still live in pacified Kien Hoa all have vivid recollections of the devastation that American firepower brought to their lives in early 1969. Virtually every person to whom I spoke had suffered in some way. "There were 5,000 people in our village before 1969, but there were none in 1970," one village elder told me. "The Americans destroyed every house with artillery, air strikes, or by burning them down with cigarette lighters. About 100 people were killed by bombing, others were wounded and others became refugees. Many were children killed by concussion from the bombs which their small bodies could not withstand, even if they were hiding underground."

Other officials, including the village police chief, corroborated the man's testimony. I could not, of course, reach every village. But in each of the many places where I went, the testimony was the same: 100 killed here, 200 killed there. One old man summed up all the stories: "The Americans killed some VC but only a small number. But of civilians, there were a large number killed..."

Buckley's notes add further detail. In the single month of March, the Ben Tre hospital reported 343 people wounded by "friendly" fire as compared with 25 by "the enemy." And as a U.S. pacification official noted, "Many people who were wounded died on the way to the hospitals," or were treated elsewhere (at home, in VC hospitals or ARVN dispensaries). And, of course, unknown numbers were simply killed outright. Buckley's actual citation about the "perhaps as many as 5,000 deaths" is that of a senior pacification official who estimated that "at least 5,000" of those killed "were what we refer to as non-combatants"—to which we may add that the "combatants," who are considered fair game in most U.S. reporting and historical analysis, were of course also South Vietnamese attempting to resist the overwhelming power of a foreign enemy. (Do we exculpate the Nazis for the killing of Resistance fighters in Europe?)

Interviews in the "pacified" areas add to the grim picture. One medic reported that this hospital took care of at least 1,000 people in four villages in early 1969. "Without exception the people testified that most of the civilians had been killed by a relentless night and day barrage of rockets, shells, bombs and bullets from planes, artillery and helicopters." In one area of four villages, the population was reduced from 16,000 to 1,600—which raises some questions about the official figures of casualties, largely fantasy in any event. Every masonry house there was in ruins. Coconut groves were destroyed by defoliants. Villagers were arrested by U.S. troops, beaten by interrogators, and sent off to prison camps. The MACV location plots for B-52s show that the target center for one raid was precisely on the village of Loung Phu, near the village of Luong Hoa where the village elder cited above reported that every house was destroyed. Pounding from the air was "relentless". Helicopters chased and killed people working in fields. Survival was possible in deep trenches and bunkers, but even in bunkers children were killed by concussion, as noted in the *Newsweek* article.

An experienced U.S. official compared My Lai to the operations of the 9th Division:

> The actions of the 9th Division in inflicting civilian casualties were worse. The sum total of what the 9th did was overwhelming. In sum, the horror was worse than My

> Lai. But with the 9th, the civilian casualties came in dribbles and were pieced out over a long time. And most of them were inflicted from the air and at night. Also, they were sanctioned by the command's insistence on high body counts...The result was an inevitable outcome of the unit's command policy.

That command policy can be traced directly back to Westmoreland and his civilian overseers, and derives immediately from the conditions of a war against a civilian population, already outlined.

On the matter of My Lai, misleadingly regarded in the West as somehow particularly evil (or perhaps, a shocking exception), Buckley also has relevant comments. The My Lai massacre was one of many that took place during Operation WHEELER WALLAWA. In this campaign, over 10,000 enemy were reported killed, including the victims of My Lai, who were listed in the official body count. Buckley writes:

> An examination of that whole operation would have revealed the incident at My Lai to be a particularly gruesome application of a wider policy which had the same effect in many places at many times. Of course, the blame for that could not have been dumped on a stumblebum lieutenant. Calley was an aberration, but "Wheeler Wallawa" was not.

The real issue concerning this operation, Buckley and Shimkin cabled to the U.S. office of *Newsweek,* was not the "indiscriminate use of firepower," as is often alleged. Rather, "it is charges of quite discriminating use—as a matter of policy, in populated areas."

By the standards applied at the trials of Axis war criminals after World War II, the entire U.S. command and the civilian leadership would have been hanged for the execution of this policy of discriminating use of firepower. My Lai was indeed an aberration, but primarily in the matter of disclosure. Though the press concealed evidence of the massacre for over a year, the news broke through, largely because of the pressure of mass peace movement demonstrations. In the subsequent investigation by a military panel, it was discovered that a similar massacre had taken place only a few miles away at the village of My Khe. Consider the likely density of such massacres, given this accidental discovery.

Proceedings against the officer in charge at My Khe were dismissed on the grounds that he had carried out a perfectly normal operation in which a village was destroyed and its population forcibly relocated,[52] with close to a hundred people reported killed. The panel's decision to exonerate the officer tells us all we need to know about Operation WHEELER WALLAWA, and in fact, reveals more about the Vietnam War than a dozen books.

Earl Martin, a Mennonite volunteer in Vietnam who is fluent in Vietnamese, was living in Quang Ngai city near My Lai at the time of the massacre, in close and regular contact with many Vietnamese. He writes that "the tragedy at My Lai never was talked about in Quang Ngai as it was in the United States...in the succeeding months we never once heard specific mention of My Lai from any of our friends" apart from a vague reference from a young boy. "The primary reason we heard little about My Lai," he writes, "was that the Vietnamese were afraid to tell an American—or even another Vietnamese who might have been a secret police for the Saigon government—for fear they would be accused of being *than-cong*, Communist sympathizers." He writes of the "tremendous pressure to cover up such atrocities," in the Saigon zones just as in the United States, though for different reasons, and discusses other "similar killings" that he heard about only years later from villagers near Quang Ngai, for example, a massacre at Truong Khanh where some Americans were killed when they triggered a mine and in retaliation "the troops stormed the hamlet, which was occupied mostly by old people, women and children," going from house to house, killing everyone they found, in the end, 62 villagers. The people of the village were broom makers. When they were dead, Martin was told by a friend, "the troops put the bodies on a pile, covered them with broom-straw and set them on fire." How many other incidents of this kind took place the West will never know, and in fact does not much care.[53]

Returning to SPEEDY EXPRESS, *Newsweek* reported that although John Paul Vann found that SPEEDY EXPRESS had alienated the population (a profound discovery), the Army command considered its work well done. After all, "the 'land rush' succeeded. Government troops moved into the ravaged countryside in the wake of the bombardments, set up outposts and established Saigon's dominance of Kien Hoa"—a notable victory for "our Vietnamese."

Operation SPEEDY EXPRESS was regarded by the Army as a "stunning success." Lauding the Commanding General on the occasion of his promotion, General Creighton Abrams spoke of "the great admiration I have for the performance of the 9th Division and especially the superb leadership and brilliant operational concepts you have given the Division." "You personify the military professional at his best in devotion and service to God and country," Abrams rhapsodized, referring specifically to the "magnificent" performance of the 9th Division, its "unparalleled and unequaled performance." During Operation SPEEDY EXPRESS, for example. On another occasion, when awarding him the Legion of Merit, Abrams referred to George Patton III, one of the men best noted for converting "pacification" into plain massacre, as "one of my finest young commanders."[54]

While the 9th Division was at work in the field, others were doing their job at home. One well-known behaviorial scientist who had long deplored the emotionalism of critics of the war and the inadequacy of their empirical data penned the following observations as Operation SPEEDY EXPRESS ground on: "The only sense in which [we have demolished the society of Vietnam] is the sense in which every modernizing country abandons reactionary traditionalism."[55]

SPEEDY EXPRESS, as noted, was unusual in that it was investigated and publicly reported, not in the fact that it occurred. Most of our information about comparable operations is derived by accident, when U.S. observers happened to make an effort to find out what had happened (the same is true of My Lai, incidentally). For this reason, something is known about U.S. operations at the same time in areas where Quaker relief groups were operating, for example, Operation BOLD MARINER in January 1969. In the course of this campaign, some 12,000 peasants (including, it seems, the remnants of My Lai) were driven from their homes in the Batangan Peninsula after having lived in caves and bunkers for months in an effort to survive constant bombardment,[56] and were then shipped to a waterless camp near Quang Ngai over which floated a banner which said, "We thank you for liberating us from communist terror." After the population was forcibly removed, the land was levelled with artillery barrages and bombing and then cleared by "Rome Plows," one of the most destructive weapons in the U.S. campaigns of ecocide in Vietnam. Since the dikes protecting rice paddies from the sea had been bombed, it was impossible to grow rice; rice purchased elsewhere was confiscated, according to inhabitants, since the population was regarded as sympathetic to the enemy and likely to give them rice. As of April 1971, the dike—which had been purposely destroyed to deny food to the enemy—had not been repaired. Refugees who returned lived under guard in camps surrounded by ten-foot rows of bamboo, from which they might look over the flooded paddies to the hills were their huts had been, now a ruin of bomb fragments, mines, unexploded artillery shells and B-52 craters nearly 20-feet deep.[57] All of this, just another episode in which this "modernizing country abandons reactionary traditionalism" under the guidance of its benevolent big brother.

In one of the postwar efforts to diminish the significance and scale of the U.S. war in Vietnam, historian Guenter Lewy, describing the "spectacular" results of operation SPEEDY EXPRESS, writes that "the assertion of Kevin P. Buckley of *Newsweek* that perhaps close to half of the more than 10,000 killed in Operation SPEEDY EXPRESS were noncombatants remains unsubstantiated... "[58] The assertion was not Buckley's; he cited it from a high U.S. pacification official. But it is true that it remains "unsubstantiated," as does the official record of 10,899 dead, which is, of course, an ugly joke, down to the last digit. The U.S. command had no idea how many people were killed by their B-52 and helicopter gunship attacks or the artillery barrage, napalm and anti-personnel weapons. Perhaps 5,000 "noncombatants" were killed, or perhaps some other number. An honest review of the matter would at least have mentioned some of what Buckley and Shimkin discovered concerning civilian casualties in their detailed investigation, and would have considered the significance of the operation, casualties aside, under the circumstances just reviewed. Lewy, however, prefers to keep to official sources, merely expressing some skepticism as to whether what he calls "the amazing results of Operation SPEEDY EXPRESS" should "be accepted at face value," avoiding the question of what is implied by this successful operation of "pacification" in an area where South Vietnamese had successfully resisted the U.S. invasion.

5.1.4 The 43-Plus My Lais of the South Korean Mercenaries

South Korean mercenary forces were contracted for and brought into South Vietnam by the Johnson Administration in 1965, and they remained there into 1973.[59] News reports in 1965 and 1966 described these South Korean forces as "fierce" and "effective," but only in January, 1970 was it disclosed publicly that their effectiveness rested on a policy of deliberate murder of South Vietnamese civilians. At that time it was reported that they had carried out a policy of simply shooting one of ten civilians in villages which they occupied.[60]

Not until 1972, however, did the scale of South Korean civilian murders become public knowledge (although still of little interest to the mass media—these murders fall into the "constructive" category).[61] Two Vietnamese-speaking Quakers, Diane and Michael Jones, carried out an intensive study of a portion of the area that had been occupied by the South Koreans for half a decade. To summarize their findings:

(a) The South Korean "rented soldiers," as the South Vietnamese describe them, committed a whole series of My Lai-scale massacres. Twelve separate massacres of 100 or more civilians were uncovered in the Jones's study. These soldiers carried out dozens of other massacres of twenty or more unarmed civilians, plus innumerable isolated killings, robberies, rapes, tortures, and devastation of land and personal property. The aggregate number of known murders by the South Koreans clearly runs into many thousands; and the Joneses examined only a part of the territory "pacified" by these "allied" forces.

(b) The bulk of the victims of these slaughters were women, children and old people, as draft-age males had either joined the NLF, had been recruited into the Saigon army, or were in hiding.

(c) These mass murders were carried out in part, but only in part, as reprisals for attacks on the South Korean forces or as a warning against such attacks.[62] Briefly, the civilians of the entire area covered by the South Koreans served as hostages; if any casualties

were taken by these mercenaries, as by an exploding mine, they often would go to the nearest village and shoot twenty, or 120, unarmed civilians. This policy is similar to that employed by the Nazis, but South Korean hostage murders of civilians were relatively more extensive and undiscriminating than those perpetrated by the Nazis in Western Europe during World War II.
(d) These mass murders were carried out over an extended time period, and into 1972, with knowledge by U.S. authorities.[63] There is no evidence that U.S. officials made any effort to discourage this form of "pacification" or that any disciplinary action was ever taken in response to these frequent and sustained atrocities. In fact, there is reason to believe the South Korean policy of deliberate murder of civilians was not merely known and tolerated but was looked upon with favor by some U.S. authorities. Frank Baldwin, of Columbia University's East Asia Institute, reports that the Korean policy was "an open secret in Korea for several years." U.S. officials admitted to Baldwin that these accounts were true, "sometimes with regret, but usually with admiration."[64]
(e) In its request for $134 million for fiscal 1973 to support the continued presence of South Korean troops in Vietnam (raising the 1966-73 total to $1.76 billion), the DOD pointed out to Congress that South Korean troops "protect" an important section of South Vietnam. It is a fact that South Koreans "protected" and gave "security"[65] to people in South Vietnam in precisely the Orwellian-official U.S. sense in which Nixon, Westmoreland and the pacification program in general did the same.[66]

The acceptability of this form of pacification, and the now well established and consistent propensity of U.S. forces and each of their "allies"—not merely South Koreans[67]—to carry out systematic acts of violence against South Vietnamese civilians, suggest that such atrocities and bloodbaths were "built in" to the U.S. effort and mission; they constituted an integral part of the task of "pacifying" a poor, virtually defenseless, but stubbornly uncooperative, foreign population.

5.1.5 Phoenix: A Case Study of Indiscriminate "Selective" Terror

With unlimited resources available for killing, one option fitfully pursued by the U.S. invaders of Vietnam—supplementing bombing, search-and-destroy and the organization of forces of mercenaries—was selective "counter-terror."[68] If the NLF had a political infrastructure that was important to its success, and if their own terror responding to that of the Saigon political machine effectively had made a shambles of the latter, why not duplicate and better their program of selective force? By doing so we would, as in providing them with the South Koreans and the U.S. Ninth Division, help "to protect the Vietnamese people against terrorism" (to quote William Colby),[69] and thus bring "security" to the peasantry, threatened by the terror employed by their relatives among the NLF cadre.

Phoenix was a late-comer on the stage of selective counter-terror. It points up the ease with which U.S. programs were absorbed into (and added further corrupting impetus to) a system of rackets and indiscriminate torture and killings, and the willingness of the U.S. political-military bureaucracy actively to support and rationalize the most outlandish and brutal systems of terror. The defense of this degenerate program by Komer, Colby, Sullivan and other U.S. officials is also noteworthy in the quality of the rationalizations offered for U.S.-planned and financed bloodbaths.[70]

The immediate predecessor[71] of the Phoenix program was the Intelligence Coordination and Exploitation (ICEX) programs initiated in mid-1967,[72] under the direction of Westmoreland and Komer, and involving CIA, U.S. civilian and military personnel, and the Saigon military-intelligence-police apparatus. Early internal directives describe the Phoenix program as a U.S. effort of advice, support, and assistance to the Saigon Phung Hoang program. Later modifications delete reference to "Phoenix" and refer merely to the Saigon Phung Hoang program, in line with the approach of "keep[ing] the GVN foremost in the picture presented to its own people and the world at large."[73] On March 4, 1968, the U.S. Secretary of Defense recommended that "Operation Phoenix which is targetted [sic] against the Viet Cong must be pursued more vigorously in closer liaison with the U.S." while "Vietnamese armed forces should be devoted to anti-infrastructure activities on a priority basis."[74]

After Westmoreland's and Komer's ICEX became Phoenix, the coordinated U.S.-Saigon intelligence-military-police program succeeded in "neutralizing"[75] some 84,000 "Viet Cong infrastructure," with 21,000 killed, according to one set of reported official figures.[76] The Saigon government claims that under Phoenix, 40,994 suspected enemy civilians were killed, from its inception in August, 1968 through the middle of 1971.[77] Just who these victims were is not entirely clear to William E. Colby, former head of Civil Operations and Rural Development [sic] Support Program (CORDS), later head of the CIA and now a respected figure on the campus and community lecture circuit. Colby told a Congressional Committee that he had "never been highly satisfied with the accuracies of our intelligence efforts on the Vietcong infrastructure," conceding that "larger numbers" than the thousand suggested to him by Congressman Reid "might have been improperly identified" as Vietcong Infrastructure in the course of Phoenix operations.[78] However, he assured the Committee that things are steadily "improving" (everyone's favorite word), and while we have not yet reached perfect due process or comprehensive knowledge of VC Infrastructure, Phoenix has actually improved the quality of U.S.-Saigon counter-terror by its deep concern with accurate intelligence and its dedication to "stern justice."[79] Most of the Vietnamese killed, Colby (like Sullivan) assured the Committee, were killed "as members of military units or while fighting off arrest."[80] Conveniently these dead enemy have usually had incriminating documents on their person to permit identification. ("What they are identified from is from documents on the body after a fire fight.")[81] Thus although things are not perfect, South Vietnam is not the "pretty wild place" it was at one period "when the government was very unstable." Though there are "unjustifiable abuses," "in collaboration with the Vietnamese authorities we have moved to stop that sort of nonsense."[82]

Colby's suggestions that intelligence concerning VC Infrastructure had improved, that such intelligence had been relevant to Phoenix operations, and that deaths had occurred mainly in combat were contradicted by substantial nonofficial testimony on the subject. The program initially was motivated by the belief that U.S. forces were developing much valuable information that was not being put to use.[83] Actually, much of this intelligence was unverified and unverifiable even in the best of circumstances. And Komer and his colleagues were aware of the fact that the "primary interest" of Saigon officials "is money,"[84] with the potential, therefore, that a counter-terror program using Saigon machinery would be corrupt, indiscriminate, and ineffective, except for the "spinoff" from mass terror. Potential corruption would be further heightened under a body quota system, which was quickly installed and subsequently enlarged with specific prize money of $11,000 offered for a live VCI and half that for a dead one. Corruption would be maximized by using dubious personnel to carry out the assassinations. And, in fact, assassinations were carried out regularly by former criminals or former Communists recruited and paid by the CIA, by CIA-directed teams drawn from ethnic minorities, U.S. military men, and Nationalist Chinese and Thai mercenaries. A U.S. IVS volunteer reports picking up two hitchhikers in the Mekong Delta, former criminals, who told him that by bringing in a few bodies now and then and collecting the bounty, they could live handsomely.[85]

The quota system was applied at many levels. Michael J. Uhl, a former military intelligence (MI) officer, testified that a Phoenix MI team "measured its success...not only by its 'body count' and 'kill ratio' but by the number of CD's [civil detainees] it had captured...All CD's, because of this command pressure...were listed as VCI. To my knowledge, not one of these people ever freely admitted being a cadre member. And again, contrary to Colby's statement, most of our CD's were women and children..."[86] Quotas were also fixed for local officials in an effort to produce "results" on a wider front; and as one U.S. adviser noted, "They will meet every quota that's established for them."[87]

Torture, a long-standing policy of the Saigon regime, was greatly encouraged by quotas and rewards for neutralizing "Vietcong Infrastructure." A sardonic saying favored by the Saigon police was: "If they are innocent beat them until they become guilty."[88] According to Uhl, "Not only was there no due process... but fully all detainees were brutalized and many were literally tortured."[89] A woman interviewed by Tom Fox after her release from a Saigon interrogation center in July, 1972 claimed that more than 90% of those arrested and taken to the center were subjected to torture.[90] K. Barton Osborn, who served in a covert program of intelligence in Vietnam, not only testified to a wide variety of forms of torture used by U.S. and Saigon personnel, but also made the startling claim that "I never knew an individual to be detained as a VC suspect who ever lived through an interrogation in a year and a half, and that included quite a number of individuals."[91]

By mid-1971, when the Saigon government had reported over 40,000 eliminated, the pacification program was being accelerated with "top priority" reportedly being given to neutralization of the VC political apparatus, at a reported cost of over $1 billion to the U.S. and an undisclosed amount to the Saigon government.[92] A rare statistic for April, 1971 reveals that in that month, of 2,000 "neutralized" more than 40 percent were assassinated.[93] According to British journalist Richard West, a U.S. intelligence officer assigned to the Phoenix program stated that when he arrived in his district, he was given a list of 200 names of people who were to be killed; when he left six months later, 260 had been killed, but none of those on his list.[94]

In some respects the Phoenix system was biased in favor of the NLF and its cadres and against the ordinary citizen. The former were more elusive and better able to defend themselves and sometimes established a modus vivendi with local officials. But Phoenix was "widely used to arrest and detail[sic] non-Communist dissidents," according to Theodore Jacqueney, a former AID and CORDS employee in Vietnam.[95] The Phoenix program also reportedly served for personal vendettas or for obtaining cash rewards for producing bodies. Meeting quotas was always possible in Free Vietnam by simply committing violence against the defenseless.

A system of terror-run-amok was facilitated by the incompetence and chronic irrelevance of the "intelligence" system that Colby claimed to be "improving" and which gave him hopes of "stern justice." According to Michael Uhl, Colby's claim of increasingly adequate intelligence as a basis for the huge number of Phoenix victims simply reflects Colby's "general lack of understanding of what is actually going on in the field."[96] According to Uhl, the MI groups in South Vietnam never had the capacity to do such a major intelligence job. "A mammoth task such as this would greatly tax even our resourceful FBI, where we have none of the vast cross-cultural problems to contend with." In the reality of practice:

> We had no way of determining the background of these sources, nor their motivation for providing American units with information. No American in the team spoke or understood Vietnamese well enough to independently debrief any "contact"....Our paid sources could easily have been either provocateurs or opportunists with a score to settle. Every information report (IR) we wrote based on our sources' information was classified as (1) unverifiable and (2) usually reliable source. As to the first, it speaks for itself; the second, in most cases was pure rationale for the existence of the program.
> The unverified and in fact unverifiable information, nevertheless, was used regularly as input to artillery strikes, harassment and interdiction fire (H & I), B52 and other air strikes, often on populated areas.[97]

Osborne testified that the Phoenix bureaucracy unofficially encouraged killing on the spot rather than going through the required administrative procedure:

> After all, it was a big problem that had to be dealt with expediently. This was the mentality. This carries a semi-official or semi-illegal program to the logical conclusion that I described here. It became a sterile depersonalized murder program...There was no cross-check; there was no investigation; there were no second options. And certainly not whatever official modus operandi had been described as a triple reporting system for verification. There was no verification and there was no discrimination.[98]

The indiscriminateness of the Phoenix murders was so blatant that in 1970 one senior AID advisor of the Danang City Advisory Group told Jacqueney that he refused ever to set foot in the Provincial Interrogation Center again, because "war crimes are going on there."[99] A UPI report of November, 1971 cites another U.S. adviser, who claims that local officials in the Delta decided simply to kill outright 80% of their "suspects," but U.S. advisers were able to convince them that the proportion should be reduced to 50%.[100] This is the "selective counter-terror" by which the United States and its clients brought "security" to the peasants.[101]

For all its lack of discrimination in selection of victims, the Phoenix program and other techniques of "pacification" were not without impact on the Southern resistance movement. In fact, they may have been so successful as to guarantee North Vietnamese dominance over the wreckage left by the U.S. war. We return to this topic in Volume II, chapter 1.

5.1.6 The Last Years of the Thieu Regime

As the war ground to a bloody end, the Saigon system of counterrevolutionary "stabilization" continued to function with new atrocities. The end product of "Vietnamization"was a centralized, corrupt, and exceptionally brutal police state. It became the ultimate satellite—the pure negative, built on anti-Communism, violence, and external sustenance. The base of the Thieu regime was a huge foreign-organized and -financed military and police apparatus; the population under its control was increasingly brutalized and "pacified" as enemy.

With U.S. "know-how" placed in the hands of the most fanatic and vicious elements of the dying order in South Vietnam, the modes and scope of torture and systematic police violence in the Thieu state reached new heights.[102] Electrical and water torture, the ripping out of fingernails, enforced drinking of solutions of powdered lime, the driving of nails into prisoners' bones (kneecaps or ankles), beatings ending in death, became *standard operating procedure* in the Thieu prisons.[103] In Quang Ngai, for example, Dr. Marjorie Nelson saw "dozens of patients who had coughed up, vomited, or urinated blood after being beaten about the chest, back and stomach."[104] In another AFSC report: "A 17 year old boy, near death, had been unable to urinate for four days and was in extreme pain. After treatment by a Quaker doctor, we were informed that the prisoner had been tortured by electrical charges to his genital organs. A young girl had seizures, stared into space and exhibited symptoms of loss of memory. She said she had been forced to drink a lime solution many times while being interrogated."[105]

Following the release of ten students from Thieu's jails, these students put themselves on display in a college laboratory. One of them was in a state of semi-shock and was still being fed dextrose intravenously. His fingernails were blackened as a result of pins and slivers of wood being inserted under them. His hearing had been impaired by soapy water having been poured into his ears. Luu Hoang Thao, Deputy Chairman of the Van Hanh Student Association, described what happened to him after his arrest, as follows:

> For the first three days, the police beat me continuously. They didn't ask me any questions or to sign anything. They just beat my knee caps and neck with their billy clubs. Then they beat me with chair legs. When a chair leg broke, they took another one. I was beaten until I was unconscious. When I regained consciousness, they beat me again. Finally, after three days, they asked me to sign a paper they had already written. They read the paper but would not let me see it. I wouldn't sign it, so they beat me some more.
>
> They put pins under my fingernails. They attached electrodes to my ears, my tongue and my penis. They forced soapy water into my mouth, tramping on my stomach when it became bloated with water. They then hung me from the ceiling and extinguished lighted cigarettes in my nipples and penis.[106]

In a 1972 study of the treatment of prisoners in South Vietnam, the Quaker term from Quang Ngai reported that there had been a further increase in torture in that stricken province.[107] Ngo Cong Duc (former Catholic deputy and president of the Saigon publishers association and now returned to Vietnam as publisher of the journal *Tin Sung*) claimed that the typical prisoner in South Vietnam "undergoes three torture sessions at the arresting agency," with the most brutal designed to force the divulgence of names.[108] The evidence that was streaming in from all over the Thieu state indicated that it was probably the torture capital of the world.

Under Vietnamization the previously tenuous rule of law was terminated completely; the other side of the coin was the rise and triumph of essentially unrestrained police powers to seize, imprison, and molest. We have already quoted former military intelligence officer Michael Uhl, who pointed out that large numbers of detainees, the majority women and children, were "captured" in repeated dragnet operation, "and whatever looked good in the catch, regardless of evidence, was classified as VCI...Not only was there no due process" applied to these prisoners, "fully all detainees were brutalized and many were literally tortured."[109] In 1972 arrests were proceeding at an estimated rate of 14,000 to 15,000 persons per month.[110] The victims of this process had no protection in the U.S.-Thieu state, especially if they were ordinary citizens seized in countryside villages.

The breakdown of anything resembling a "legal system" was paralleled by a huge increase in the numbers of police. The National Police Force, which was only one of a dozen agencies legally authorized to make arrests, was enlarged from 16,000 in 1963, to 88,000 in 1969; under Vietnamization the numbers rose to 122,000 in 1972. Concurrently, a pervasive police-intelligence network spread throughout South Vietnam.

A police state is a prison state, and the Thieu state may have led all others (even Indonesia) in the number of political prisoners. Over 200 national prisons and hundreds of local jails in South Vietnam housed a prisoner population that many estimated at over 200,000.[111] A great many of these prisoners were middle-of-the-road students, clergy, intellectuals, and labor leaders who showed some interest in political affairs and therefore constituted a threat to the leaders of the police state. One should add that the prisoners were drawn from that sector of the population that was more favorably treated by the U.S.-Saigon system; those beyond its reach were subjected to the full rigors of mechanized war. Under Vietnamization the Thieu government engaged in a determined effort to destroy any non-Communist opposition to its rule, largely by means of intimidation and violence. The vast repressive machinery of the Thieu regime was employed to a great extent against these center elements, which it properly regarded as threatening to its rule. The degeneration of this state was so extreme that a great many subjects of police terror were essentially "random" victims—brutalized as a matter of course once they fell into police hands (as in the dragnet seizures described by Uhl, above).

Many of the maltreated were victims of attempts at shakedowns. Staff of the American Friends Service Committee reported speaking with a young woman who had been imprisoned and tortured for rejecting the advances of an ARVN officer who had friends in the police.[112] And many arrests had payoffs in bribes from the families of the imprisoned, solicited or offered with knowledge that these might be useful in reducing the severity of tortures to be applied.[111]

As the threat of a political settlement became manifest in 1972-73, the repression intensified. The reason was simple. The Saigon diplomatic representative in Phnom Penh in 1959 told a reporter: "You must understand that we in Saigon are desperate men. We are a government of desperadoes."[114] True enough, though Diem was an authentic nationalist and relatively benign in comparison with the collaborationist regimes that followed as the U.S. intervention grew to full-scale war against rural South Vietnam where the vast majority of the population had lived. The desperation stemmed in part from the fact that, as each successive U.S. client found, terror does not build popular support, but on the contrary, generates more "Communists," or at best leaves demoralization and apathy. More violence was always required to give the people "security". Thus, after many years of U.S.-sponsored protective terror, Thieu acknowledged to Saigon officials in January, 1973 his continued inability to compete with the Communists *on a purely political basis:* "If we let things go the population may vote for the Communists, who know how to make propaganda."[115] The occasion was the signing of the peace agreements that were to establish parallel and equivalent authorities in South Vietnam (Thieu and the PRG) which were to reach a peaceful political settlement. But Thieu did not have to fear that the United States would help expedite any such arrangement. Recognizing no less than Thieu the hopelessness of political competition,[116] the U.S. government unilaterally rescinded these provisions.

But even the *possibility* of political competition sent shivers through the Thieu government. In June, 1972 several thousand persons were arrested and shipped to Con Son island, many of them "merely relatives of political suspects" and many of them women and children.[117] George Hunter reported that

> special Branch Police swooped down on houses all over South Vietnam and arrested anyone under the remotest

> suspicion of being 'left wing'...The government has a blacklist of suspects, but I understand that wives, mothers and fathers—anyone with the slimmest association with those on it are being caught in the net.[118]

Another roundup took place during the period of the threat of a Peace Agreement in October and November of 1972. On November 9, Hoang Duc Nha (Thieu's closest adviser) announced to a group of Vietnamese journalists the seizure of over 40,000 "Communists" over the previous two-week period, thanks to a vast network of police.[119] The mammoth scale of arrests to which Free Vietnam had been accustomed was sharply intensified, at just the time that Thieu and Nixon were theoretically readying themselves to sign an agreement committing them to a policy of national reconciliation.

After the agreements were signed, measures were taken that laid the basis for imprisonments with the potential of simple extermination—whether realized or not, it is hard to determine. In an official telegram sent by the Commander in Chief of Thieu's police and the Saigon head of Phoenix on April 5, 1973, police and other arresting agents were advised as follows on the proper classification of detainees:

> Do not use the expression "condemned communist or communist agent." Write only: "Disturbs the peace."[120]

Disturbers of the peace might be regarded as common criminals; a Communist agent would be a political prisoner covered by the January 27th Agreement. This practice was supplemented by the reclassification of current prisoners to common-law status. For example, Mme. Ngo Ba Thanh, president of the Saigon-based Women's Committee Struggling for the Right to Live, with a law degree from Columbia University, was among those transferred to a prison for common-law criminals in Bien Hoa Province. Documents from inside the prisons alleged that prison authorities incited common-law prisoners to provoke and even to kill reclassified political prisoners.[121]

Another technique used by the Thieu government was the alleged release of political prisoners, not to the PRG and DRV as stipulated in the January Agreements, but at large within South

Vietnam. In early February, Thieu announced the release of 40,000 prisoners, with no specifics as to names and places of release.[122] The media failed to perceive the most significant aspect of this action, portrayed as a magnanimous act although in technical violation of the Agreements. The crucial point missed was that, by this device, prisoners who were murdered could be alleged to have been "released" and thus no longer a Thieu responsibility.[123] Previously, families of prisoners held at Phu Quoc whose terms had expired were informed of the prisoners' release, yet these individuals had disappeared.[124]

Accelerated mistreatment of political prisoners was also reported as the threat of peace mounted, including further sharp reductions in the rice ration (which had already been reduced severely in January, 1972), the practice of mingling healthy prisoners with others in advanced stages of contagious diseases such as tuberculosis—another happy innovation in pacification—and direct physical violence.[125] Jean-Pierre Debris, who had recently been released from Chi Hoa prison, wrote that "the aim of the Thieu regime is to break the prisoners physically so that they will never be able to take any part in national life again...The conditions under which thousands are held is critical and becoming more dramatic at the present time."[126]

Finally, reports of the direct killing of prisoners began filtering through with increased frequency. The two French prisoners released in December reported that just prior to their departure "there were massive deportations to the Paulo Condor [Con Son] camp," the scene of numerous reported atrocities in the past. They speculated that their sudden release might have been motivated by concern that they might witness what they expected would then take place, "a liquidation operation which might begin in the prisons."[127] Amnesty International cited "evidence that selective elimination of oppostion members had begun" in the prisons, and a report that 300 prisoners being moved from Con Son to the mainland were killed.[128] On Sunday, March 25, NBC Monitor News transmitted a report from the Swedish office of Amnesty International that observers had sighted thousands of bodies in prison uniforms floating in the area off South Vietnam. The PRG and DRV reported a steady stream of killings and disappearances, impossible to verify but frequently specific as to place, and hardly to be ruled out in the light of processes then at work in the Thieu state.

Although it was sometimes said that the Thieu government was "a coalition of the extreme Right" (a description by the pro-Thieu *Saigon Daily News)*, this characterization was rejected by informed Vietnamese, who preferred the term "Mafia" to describe the Thieu coalition; they pointed to the huge thievery, the common involvement in the heroin trade, and the long and parasitic dependence of this tiny faction on a foreign power for survival. The repressive character of the Thieu state epitomized the long-term incapacity of the Diem regime and its increasingly militarized successors to respond to grievances except by violence. With Thieu the blend of egotism, fanatical anti-Communism and a life of professional military service under foreign sponsorship brought repression and police state violence to a new level of refinement.

The U.S. role in the police repression apparatus of the Thieu state was straightforward. In the broadest sense, the long U.S. intervention was the only reason that a Thieu-type regime could exist in the first place; more specifically, the U.S. financed, advised, provided technological improvements and afforded a public relations cover for the direct instruments of terror. From the time of Diem the United States placed great weight on the police and intelligence; the funding and advising of the prison-police-intelligence ensemble of South Vietnam began at once, as the United States entered the scene directly after the Geneva Accords of 1954. A spokesperson for AID told Congress:

> AID and its predecessor agencies have supported public safety programs [essentially police] in Vietnam since 1955...AID's task has been to assist the National Police in recruiting, training and organizing a force for the maintenance of law and order.[129]

AID provided police specialists to train Saigon's police and advise them at all levels, and to work in Thieu's "Public Safety" programs. Over $100 million was spent on Public Safety in Vietnam from 1968 through 1971.[130] The Provincial Interrogation Centers, which were reported by Americans on the scene to have uniformly employed torture, were funded directly by the United States.[131] The pacification programs in general, including Phoenix, were paid for by the United States, at a cost estimated conservatively at about $5 billion for the period 1968-71.[132] AID put more money into South Vietnamese prisons than schools, and even after the discovery and notoriety of Tiger Cages, it funded the construction of additional Tiger Cages for Con Son prison, even smaller than those already located on the island.[133]

Advice was also continuous, extending both to general strategy and specific tactics. William Colby indicated: "The function of U.S. advice and support was to *initiate* and support a Vietnamese effort which can be taken up and maintained by the Vietnamese alone...[and] a considerable degree of advice and support of the GVN pacification program has come from the U.S. side over the years." In later years, in addition to Phoenix, U.S. advice and funds went toward

> provision of commodity and advisory support for a police force of 108,000 men by the end of Fiscal 1971;...assisting the National Identity Registration Program (N.I.R.P.) to register more than 12,000,000 persons 15 years of age and over by the end of 1971; continuing to provide basic and specialized training for approximately 40,000 police annually; providing technical assistance to the police detention system, including planning and supervision of the construction of facilities for an additional 8,000 inmates during 1970; and helping to achieve a major increase in the number of police presently working at the village level.[135]

Advice included the introduction of Western technology to improve Third World "security". Some examples are mentioned in the AID statement quoted above. Another illustration was provided by a former prisoner in the Con Son Tiger Cages, who reported on the ingenuity of U.S. advisers in improving the technique of torture.[136]

It is not in question that the United States played the decisive role in the evolution of South Vietnamese political life from 1955-75. U.S. authorities did not merely accommodate to events thrust upon them from the outside; as adviser, controller of the purse strings, and occupying power, the United States had critical leverage, which it exercised time and again to make specific choices. The character of the Thieu regime reflected a series of consistent decisions made in Washington, and expressed a preference and choice as to the nature of a client state that is not confined to South Vietnam. The Saigon authorities, in general, went along with U.S. advice, partly because of their proclivities, partly because they were dependents, but also because each new policy innovation meant an additional inflow of cash which the Saigon leadership knew could be absorbed readily into the existing system of corruption.

In addition to funding, advising and providing the equipment and know-how, the United States provided a moral cover for the Thieu state. This resulted in part from the fact that the United States is a democracy; its officials pretend that democracy and an open society are among its serious objectives in intervening. Thus moderate scholars and others determined to think well of the United States have found it possible to employ the argument from long-run benefit. This mystification was furthered by the constant reference of U.S. officials to "encouraging developments" in their client police states, and to the fact of "our working with the Vietnamese government," which is making "very substantial strides" toward eliminating the unjustifiable abuses that we all recognize and are doing our level best to eradicate.[137]

The apologetics include more or less continuous lying, especially at the higher levels of officialdom, as when Colby and Sullivan suggested that many of the 21,000 or 41,000 killings under Phoenix might be combat deaths. Or in Colby's constant reference to pacification as a program for the "defense of the people" against somebody else's terror. Or the statement of Randolph Berkeley, chief of the Corrections and Detention Division of AID: "Generally speaking we have found the Vietnamese very light in their punishment."[138] Or the statement of Frank E. Walton, Director of the AID Public Safety Program, that Con Son prison is "like a Boy Scout Recreational Camp."[139] The same Frank Walton who denied any knowledge of the Tiger Cages in 1970 signed a report dated October 1, 1963, which stated that:

> In Con Son II, some of the hardcore communists keep preaching the 'party' line, so these 'Reds' are sent to the Tiger Cages in Con Son I where they are isolated from all

> others for months at a time. This confinement may also include rice without salt and water—the United States prisons' equivalent of bread and water. It may include immobilization—the prisoner is bolted to the floor, handcuffed to a bar or rod, or leg irons with the chain through an eyebolt, or around a bar or rod.[140]

The Paris Agreements of January, 1973 brought no reprieve to the suffering people of South Vietnam. As already noted, the United States announced at once that it would disregard the central provisos of the Agreements it had signed in Paris and proceeded to do so, a fact effectively concealed by the press. (See Volume II, chapter 1). The Thieu Regime, as always a creature of the United States, persisted in the sole program that it was equipped to conduct: violence and terror. The evidence is voluminous. We will give only one illustrative example as the appendix to this chapter, a discussion of the activities of the U.S.-Thieu regime after the January, 1973 ceasefire, presented by two U.S. relief workers in Quang Ngai Province. In the next volume, we will turn to the subsequent history. Here we only emphasize the obvious: the many years of U.S. savagery in South Vietnam devastated the land, tore the society to tatters, decimated both the popular resistance and the non-Communist opposition, and left a legacy of horror that may never be overcome and will certainly have bitter consequences for many years, long after the true story of the U.S. war has been excised from history and safely forgotten in the West. But those elements in United States society and political life that could impose such suffering on South Vietnam and the rest of Indochina will not hesitate to organize another constructive bloodbath if needed to save people elsewhere from any foolish attempt to exit from the Free World.

5.2 Nefarious and Mythical Bloodbaths

5.2.1 Revolutionary Terror in Theory and Practice

The Vietnamese revolutionaries shed considerable blood over the years in individual acts of terror, some deliberate and calculated, others reflecting sporadic breakdowns in the discipline of cadres under enormous pressure, along with occasional sheer vengeance killing. There are very few authenticated cases, however, in which the insurgents killed significant numbers of unarmed civilians in deliberate acts of mass murder.[141] This appears to have been a result of a long-standing revolutionary philosophy and strategy, their relationship to the underlying population and superior discipline.

Despite the widely held belief to the contrary, a product of decades of officially inspired propaganda, the Vietnamese revolutionary movement always gave force and violence a lower rating in the spectrum of *means* than did the Diem government and its successors or their U.S. sponsors. This was in close accord with classical Maoist principles of revolutionary organization, strategy and behavior. The NLF view in early 1960 was:

> Armed activities only fulfill a supporting role for the political struggle movement. It is impossible to substitute armed forces and armed struggle for political forces and political struggle. Formerly we erred in slighting the role of armed activity. Today we must push armed activity to the right degree, but at the same time we must not abuse or rely excessively on armed activity.[142]

Douglas Pike, the official United States government authority on the NLF, confirmed the great weight given by it to the political struggle as opposed to "violence":

> It maintained that its contest with the GVN and the United States should be fought out at the political level and that the use of massed military might was itself illegitimate. Thus one of the NLF's unspoken, and largely unsuccessful, purposes was to use the struggle movement before the onlooking world to force the GVN and the United States to play the game according to its rules: The battle was to be organizational or quasi-political, the battleground was to be the minds and loyalties of the rural Vietnamese, the weapons were to be ideas;...and all force was automatically condemned as terror or repression.[143]

The United States and the Diem regime would not play by the rules of any such game, and as Pike states, in the end "armed combat was a GVN-imposed requirement; the NFL was obliged to use counterforce to survive."[144]

According to Jeffrey Race, before 1960 the South Vietnamese

revolutionaries carried out an official policy of "non-violence" which led to a serious decimation of their ranks, as violence was monopolized almost entirely by the U.S.-sponsored Diem regime. Race contends:

> By adopting an almost entirely defensive role during this period and by allowing the government to be the first to employ violence, the Party—at great cost—allowed the government to pursue the conflict in increasingly violent terms, through its relentless reprisal against any opposition, its use of torture, and particularly after May 1959, through the psychological impact in the rural areas of the proclamation of Law 10/59.[145]

The idea that the success of the Vietnam revolutionaries was based on "terrorizing" the population is shown by Race to be a serious misperception; in fact, it was the Saigon government, sponsored and advised by the United States, that in the end helped destroy itself by its inability to respond to problems and threats except by terror. Race's discussion is worth quoting at length:

> The lessons of Long An are that violence can destroy, but cannot build; violence may explain the cooperation of a few individuals, but it cannot explain the cooperation of a whole social class, for this would involve us in the contradiction of "Who is to coerce the coercers?" Such logic leads inevitably to the absurd picture of the revolutionary leader in his jungle base, "coercing" millions of terrorized individuals throughout the country[146]...The history of events in Long An also indicates that violence will work against the user, unless he has already preempted a large part of the population and then limits his acts of violence to a sharply defined minority. In fact, this is exactly what happened in the case of the government: far from being bound by any commitments to legality or humane principles, the government terrorized far more than did the revolutionary movement...[and] *it was just these tactics that led to the constantly increasing strength of the revolutionary movement in Long An from 1960 to 1965.*[147]

Race indicates that official Communist executions "actually were the consequence of extensive investigation and approval by higher authority." Furthermore, many careless executions during the resistance prior to 1954 had had adverse effects on the Party, so that after it became stronger it "exercised much tighter control over the procedures for approving executions..."[148] This concern for the secondary effects of unjust executions sharply contrasted with the policies of the Saigon regimes under U.S. sponsorship, and even more with the policies of the United States itself from 1965-75.

Race's study shows how the Communist Party's refusal to authorize violence "except in limited circumstances...even in self-defense, against the increasing repressiveness of the government," while at the same time it was gaining support through its constructive programs, gave rise to an "anomaly"; "the revolutionary organization [was] being ground down while the revolutionary potential was increasing."[149] In response to angry demands from southern Party members who were being decimated by U.S.-Diem terror, a May 1959 decision in Hanoi authorized the use of violence to support the political struggle.[150] From this point on the threat of terror was "equalized" and violence was no longer a government monopoly. In the province near Saigon that Race studied intensively (Long An), the result was that the revolutionary forces quickly became dominant while the government apparatus and its armed forces dissolved without violent conflict, undermined by Party propaganda and disappearing from the scene.[151] The revolutionary potential had become a reality. By late 1964 parts of the province were declared a free strike zone and by early 1965, when the full-scale U.S. invasion took place, "revolutionary forces had gained victory in nearly all the rural areas of Long An."[152] As for the "North Vietnamese aggressors," their first units entered the province at the time of the 1968 Tet offensive.[153]

Revolutionary success in Vietnam both in theory and practice was based primarily on understanding and trying to meet the needs of the masses. Race noted that government officials were aware of the fact that "communist cadres are close to the people, while ours are not."[154] Yet they appeared to be unaware of the reasons, which he believes were traceable to a recruitment pattern for government office that systematically "denied advancement to those from majority elements of the rural population." The reasons also were related to a total failure on the part of the government to meet the real needs of the rural masses, in contrast with the revolutionary forces who "offered concrete and practical solutions to the daily problems of substantial segments of the rural population..."[155] A movement geared to winning support from the rural masses is not likely to resort to bloodbaths among the rural population. A government recruiting wholly from an elite minority centered in the cities and admittedly "out of touch" with its own people, dependent on a foreign power for its existence and sustenance, generously supplied with weapons of mass destruction by its foreign sponsor—this type of government could well be expected to try to "pacify" its own people and to rely on its foreign protector to do so more effectively, while both speak of their objective as "protecting" the rural masses from "revolutionary terror."

Numerous cases of atrocities have been attributed to the NLF or DRV,[156] and several were nurtured by U.S. government propaganda as cornerstones of the justification for United States intervention. We focus briefly on the two most important mythical bloodbaths:[157] that associated with the North Vietnamese land reform of the mid-1950s, and the Hue massacres of 1968.

5.2.2 Land Reform in the Mid-Fifties

In an address on November 3, 1969, President Nixon spoke of the DRV Communists having murdered more than 50,000 people following their takeover in the North in the 1950s. Six months later, in a speech given on April 30, 1970 he raised the ante to "hundreds of thousands" who had been exposed in 1954 to the "slaughter and savagery" of the DRV leadership. Then, one week later, on May 8, 1970, apparently in some panic at the public's response to his invasion of Cambodia, Mr. Nixon invoked the image of "millions" of civilians who would be massacred if the North Vietnamese were ever to descend into South Vietnam. Subsequently, in the calm of a press interview on April 16, 1971, President Nixon reported that "a half a million, by conservative estimates...were murdered or otherwise exterminated by the North Vietnamese."

It is obvious that a credibility problem exists with periodic variations in numbers of alleged victims, but there are three elements in this particular bloodbath myth worthy of discussion.

First, whatever the numbers involved in the DRV land reform abuses, they had little or nothing to do with retaliatory action for collaboration with the French. Even in the sources relied on by official propagandists, the intended victims were identified primarily as landlords being punished for alleged past offenses against their dependent tenants, rather than wartime collaborators. Thus the attempts to use this episode as proof of a probable bloodbath in retaliation for collaboration with the U.S. or noncooperation during the continuing fighting was somewhat strained.

Second, the North Vietnamese leadership was upset by the abuses in the land reform, publicly acknowledged its errors, punished many officials who had carried out or permitted injustices, and implemented administrative reforms to prevent recurrences. In brief, the DRV leadership showed a capacity to respond to abuses and keep in touch with rural interests and needs.[158] It was a "bitter truth" for Professor Samuel Huntington that the "relative political stability" of North Vietnam, in contrast with the South, rested on the fact that "the organization of the Communist party reaches out into the rural areas and provides a channel for communication of rural grievances to the center and for control of the countryside by the government."[159] What Huntington missed is that the DRV and NLF leadership were not prevented by class interest, as were the successive regimes in Saigon, from responding constructively to rural grievances. In the South, as Jeffrey Race points out, even when the reactionary elites came into possession of captured documents that stressed rural grievances which the insurgents felt they could capitalize on (and for which *they* offered programs) "the government did not develop appropriate policies to head off the exploitation of the issues enumerated in the document."[160]

Third, and perhaps most important for present purposes, the basic sources for the larger estimates of killings in the North Vietnamese land reform were persons affiliated with the CIA or the Saigon Propaganda Ministry. According to a Vietnamese Catholic now living in France, Colonel Nguyen Van Chau, head of the Central Psychological War Service for the Saigon Army from 1956 to 1962, the "bloodbath" figures for the land reform were "100% fabricated" by the intelligence services of Saigon. According to Colonel Chau, a systematic campaign of vilification by the use of forged documents was carried out during the mid-1950s to justify Diem's refusal to negotiate with Hanoi in preparation for the unheld unifying elections originally scheduled for 1956. According to Chau the forging of documents was assisted by U.S. and British intelligence agencies, who helped gather authentic documents that permitted a plausible foundation to be laid for the forgeries, which "were distributed to various political groups and to groups of writers and artists, who used the false documents to carry out the propaganda campaign."[161]

The primary source of information on the land reform for many years was the work of Hoang Van Chi, formerly a substantial landholder in North Vietnam, and employed and subsidized by the Saigon Ministry of Information, CIA, and other official U.S. sources for many years.[162] D. Gareth Porter undertook the first close analysis of his work and demonstrated that Chi's conclusions were based on a series of falsehoods, nonexistent documents, and slanted and deceptive translations of real documents. For example, Chi stated that the DRV authorities fixed a minimum quota of three landlords to be *executed* in each village, when in fact they placed an *upper* limit of three who could be *denounced and tried,* not executed.[163] In another passage Chi quotes Giap as saying, "Worse still, torture came to be regarded as normal practice during Party reorganization," when in fact Giap actually said: "Even coercion was used in carrying out party reorganization." Other passages cited by Chi as evidence of a plan for a "deliberate excess of terror" were shown by Porter to be "simply cases of slanted translation for a propaganda purpose."[164]

His estimate of 700,000, or 5% of the population of North Vietnam, as victims of the land reform, Chi eventually conceded to be merely a "guess," based largely on experience in his own village where ten of 200 persons died, although only one was literally executed.[165] This admission came after Porter had made Chi's falsifications public. Given Chi's proven willingness to lie, his figure of ten deaths attributable to the land reform can hardly be taken at face value, but his extrapolation of this sample to the entirety of North Vietnam, which even Chi explicitly recognized as nonhomogeneous, is not even worth discussing.[166] Although scientifically worthless, and surely fabricated for propaganda purposes, Chi's "guess" served well for many years in providing authoritative and "conservative" estimates, not only for political leaders and their media conduits, but even for serious students of the war. Bernard Fall was taken in by Chi, and Frances FitzGerald in her influential *Fire in the Lake* followed Fall in giving a "conservative estimate" that "some fifty thousand people of all economic stations were killed" in the course of the land reform.[167] Because of their reputations as opponents of the war, Fall and FitzGerald played an especially important role in the perpetration of a myth that still flourishes in its third decade of life.[168]

On the basis of an analysis of official figures and credible documents, plus an estimate made by the Diem government itself in 1959, Porter concluded that a realistic range of executions taking place during the land reform would be between 800 and 2500.[169]

The North Vietnamese land reform has been subjected to a more recent and exhaustive study by Edwin E. Moise.[170] To Porter's "negative" argument, based largely on his demonstration that "the documentary evidence for the bloodbath theory seems to have been a fabrication almost in its entirety," Moise adds "some positive evidence": namely, he points out that Saigon propaganda contained little about land reform until Saigon had learned from international press agency dispatches in 1956 of the North Vietnamese discussions of errors and failures. Even Hoang Van Chi, in 1955 interviews, did not make any accusations about atrocities; "It was only in later years that his memories began to alter," that is after the United States and the Saigon regime learned about the land reform problems from the discussion in the Hanoi press, which, Moise writes, was "extremely informative" and "sometimes extraordinarily candid in discussing errors and failures." After a detailed discussion of sources, Moise concludes that "allowing for these uncertainties, it seems reasonable to estimate that the total number of people executed during the land reform was probably in the vicinity of 5,000, and almost certainly between 3,000 and 15,000, and that the slaughter of tens of thousands of innocent victims, often described in anti-Communist propaganda, never took place." These victims, Moise concludes, were not killed in the course of a government program of retribution and murder but rather were victims of "paranoid distrust of the exploiting classes," lack of experience on the part of poorly-trained cadres, and the problems inherent in attempting to engage poor peasants and agricultural workers directly in a leadership role. "One of the most extraordinary things about the land reform," he writes, "was the fact that its errors were not covered up, or blamed on a few scapegoats, after it was over," but were publicly admitted by the government and party which "corrected them to the extent possible." "Economically, the land reform had succeeded"; land was given to peasants who lacked it and agricultural production rose rapidly, overcoming the severe food shortages and famine of earlier years, and thus saving many lives. Subsequent steps towards cooperatives proceeded "without any significant amount of violence," largely on the basis of persuasion.

However one may choose to evaluate these efforts at social reform in the countryside under harsh conditions and in the aftermath of a bitter war, the picture is radically different from what has filtered through journalism and scholarship to the Western reader and continues to be repeated today as proof of Communist barbarism. We might point out, finally, that the indiscriminate massacre in the single operation SPEEDY EXPRESS claimed as many victims as the land reform that has served U.S. propaganda for so many years, and that the perpetrators of this massacre, which was quite clearly a direct expression of high level policy aimed at systematic destruction and murder, were not punished or condemned but rather were honored for their crimes.

5.2.3 The Hue Massacre of 1968

The essential claim of the myth of the Hue massacre (see note 157) is that during their month-long occupation of Hue at the time of the Tet Offensive of 1968, NLF and North Vietnamese forces deliberately, according to an advance plan and "blacklist," rounded up and murdered thousands of civilians, either because they worked for the government or represented "class enemies." The basic documentation supporting the myth consists of a report issued by the Saigon government in April 1968, a captured document made public by the U.S. Mission in November 1969, and a long analysis published in 1970 by USIS employee Douglas Pike. Both the Saigon and Pike reports should have aroused suspicions on the basis of their source, their tone, and their role in an extended propaganda campaign, timed in the latter case to reduce the impact of the My Lai massacre. But, even more important, the substance of these documents does not withstand scrutiny.[171]

As in the case of the land reform bloodbath myth just discussed, official estimates of alleged NLF-DRV killings of civilians at Hue escalated sharply in response to domestic political contingencies, in this case, in the fall of 1969, coincident with the Nixon administration's attempt to offset the effects of the October and November surge of organized peace activity and to counteract the exposure of the My Lai massacre in November 1969. Shortly after the Tet offensive itself, Police Chief Doan Cong Lap of Hue estimated the number of NLF-DRV killings at about 200,[172] and the mass grave of local officials and prominent citizens allegedly found by the Mayor of Hue contained 300 bodies. (The authenticity of these numbers and responsibility for these bodies is debatable, as is discussed below.) In a report issued in late April 1968 by the propaganda arm of the Saigon government, it was claimed that about one thousand executions had been carried out by the Communists in and around Hue, and that nearly half of the victims had been buried alive. Since the story was ignored, the U.S. embassy put out the same report the following week, and this time it was headlined in U.S. papers. The story was not questioned, despite the fact that no Western journalist had ever been taken to see the grave sites when the bodies were uncovered. On the contrary, French photographer Marc Riboud was repeatedly denied permission to see one of the sites where the Province Chief claimed 300 civilian government workers had been executed by the Communists. When he was finally taken by helicopter to the alleged site, the pilot refused to land, claiming the area was "insecure."[173]

AFSC staff people in Hue were also unable to confirm the reports of mass graves, though they reported many civilians shot and killed during the reconquest of the city.[174]

Len Ackland, an IVS worker in Hue in 1967 who returned in April 1968 to investigate, was informed by U.S. and Vietnamese officials that about 700 Vietnamese were killed by the Viet Cong, an estimate generally supported by his detailed investigations, which also indicate that the killings were primarily by local NLF forces during the last stages of the bloody month-long battle as they were retreating.[175] Richard West, who was in Hue shortly after the battle, estimated "several hundred Vietnamese and a handful of foreigners" killed by Communists and speculated that victims of My Lai-style massacres by the U.S.-ARVN forces might have been among those buried in the mass graves.[176]

In the fall of 1969 a "captured document" was discovered that had been mysteriously sitting unnoticed in the official files for 19 months, in which the enemy allegedly "admitted" having killed 2,748 persons during the Hue campaign. This document is the main foundation on which the myth of the Hue massacre was constructed. At the time it was released to the press, in November 1969, Douglas Pike was in Saigon to push the Hue massacre story, at the request of Ambassador Ellsworth Bunker. Pike, an expert media manipulator, recognized that American reporters love "documents," so he produced documents. He also knew that virtually none of these journalists understood Vietnamese, so that documents could be translated and reconstructed to conform with the requirements of a massacre. He also knew that few journalists would challenge his veracity and independently assess and develop evidence, despite the long record of official duplicity on Vietnam and the coincidence of this new document with official public relations needs of the moment[177]—the My Lai story had broken, and organized peace activity in the fall of 1969 was intense. Pike was correct on this point also, and the few indications of skepticism by foreign reporters were not allowed to interfere with the institutionalization of the official version.

The newly captured document and its interpretation by a well-known official propagandist were thus promptly accepted without question by many reporters (e.g., Don Oberdorfer, in his book *Tet*). Frances FitzGerald swallowed completely the official tale that "the Front and the North Vietnamese forces murdered some three thousand civilians" in their month of terror at Hue in 1968, and she took at face value all Saigon allegations of grave findings as well as the "piecing [of] various bits of evidence together" by Douglas Pike.[178] In the hysterical propaganda effusions of Robert Thompson, the number of people executed by the Communists was escalated to 5,700, and we learn that "in captured documents they gloated over these figures and only complained that they had not killed enough."[179] No documents were identified, nor was any explanation advanced for such odd behavior. Senator William Saxbe insisted on no less than 7,000 murdered by "North Vietnamese," considerably more than the total number reported killed from all causes during this period in Hue (*Congressional Record,* May 3, 1972).

Thus, in the fall of 1969 the press in general once again headlined the refurbished story, quoting from the captured document: "We eliminated 1,892 administrative personnel, 39 policemen, 790 tyrants, 6 captains, 2 first lieutenants, 20 second lieutenants and many noncommissioned officers." This sentence and document were accepted as confirmation of the U.S.-Saigon version of what had taken place, despite the fact that nowhere in the document is it claimed or even suggested that any civilians had been *executed.* Furthermore, the quoted sentence was taken out of the context of the document as a whole, which had nothing to do with the punishment of individuals, but was rather a low-level report, describing the military victory of the NLF in a particular district of Hue. But the press was too interested in reaffirming the cruelty of the Viet Cong to pay attention to such fine distinctions.

In manipulating this document for propaganda purposes, the Vietnamese word "diet" was translated as "eliminate," which implies killing, although the word was used by the NLF in the military sense of putting out of action (killing, wounding, capturing, or inducing to surrender or defect). If the NLF had intended to describe plain killing or deliberate executions, they would have used any number of Vietnamese terms, but not "diet". The government propaganda version also disregarded the fact that the 2748 figure clearly included estimated numbers of enemy troops killed and wounded in combat. This deception was facilitated by mistranslating the word "te" as "administrative personnel" in the version circulated to journalists when, in fact, according to a standard North Vietnamese dictionary it has the broader meaning of "puppet personnel," which would include both civilian administrators and the military. The propaganda operation also produced a list of fifteen categories of "enemies of the people" allegedly targeted for liquidation, when the documents in question never used the quoted phrase and suggested only that those categories of people should be carefully "watched". Those targeted for repression, let alone liquidation, were in completely different categories.[180] Finally, it was claimed that the NLF had blacklists for execution which included "selected non-official and natural leaders of the community, chiefly educators and religionists," when in fact the testimony of Hue's chief of secret police contradicts this. According to the latter, the only names on the list of those to be executed immediately were the officers of the secret police of Hue. Other lists were of those who were to be "reeducated".[181] Porter states that no captured document has yet been produced which suggests that the NLF and DRV had any intention of executing any civilians. Porter claims further that the general strategy of the NLF conveyed in the documents, and misrepresented by Douglas Pike and his associates, was to try to mobilize and gain support from the masses, organized religious groups, and even ordinary policemen.[182]

The documents uniformly attest to an NLF policy of attempting to rally large numbers with minimum reprisals. Furthermore, the killings that did take place occurred after the NLF realized that it would have to evacuate the city, then under a massive U.S. attack, and during that evacuation. In Porter's words:

> The real lesson of Hue, therefore, is that in circumstances of peace and full political control, the basic Communist policy toward those associated with the Saigon regime would be one of no reprisals, with the exception of key personnel in Saigon's repressive apparatus (and even in these cases, officials can redeem themselves at the last moment by abandoning resistance to the revolutionary forces).[183]

This lesson, the opposite of that which the U.S.-Saigon propaganda machines succeeded in conveying, gains plausibility in view of the events of postwar Vietnam (see volume II, chapters 1 and 4). There is no credible evidence that the behavior of the victors resembles that of the gloating butchers who "only complained that they had not killed enough." In fact, the long-predicted bloodbath in Vietnam did not materialize.

Apart from the "captured documents," the most persuasive

support for the alleged massacre came from the finding of mass graves—but this evidence is as unconvincing as the managed documents. A fundamental difficulty arises from the fact that large numbers of civilians were killed in the U.S.-Saigon recapture of Hue by the massive and indiscriminate use of firepower. David Douglas Duncan, the famous combat photographer, said of the recapture that it was a "total effort to root out and kill every enemy soldier. The mind reels at the carnage, cost and ruthlessness of it all."[184] Another distinguished photographer, Philip Jones Griffiths, wrote that most of the victims "were killed by the most hysterical use of American firepower ever seen" and were then designated "as the victims of a Communist massacre."[185] Robert Shaplen wrote at the time: "Nothing I saw during the Korean War, or in the Vietnam War so far has been as terrible, in terms of destruction and despair, as what I saw in Hue."[186] Of Hue's 17,134 houses, 9,776 were completely destroyed and 3,169 more were officially classified as "seriously damaged." The initial official South Vietnamese estimate of the number of civilians killed in the fighting during the bloody reconquest was 3,776.[187] Townsend Hoopes, Undersecretary of the Air Force at the time, stated that in the recapture effort 80% of the buildings were reduced to rubble, and that "in the smashed ruins lay 2,000 dead civilians..."[188] The Hoopes and Saigon numbers exceed the highest estimates of NLF-DRV killings, including official ones, that are not demonstrable propaganda fabrications. According to Oberdorfer, the U.S. Marines put "Communist losses" at more than 5000, while Hoopes states that the city was captured by a Communist force of 1,000, many of whom escaped—suggesting again that most of those killed were civilian victims of U.S. firepower.

Some of the civilian casualties of this U.S. assault were buried in mass graves by NLF personnel alongside their own casualties (according to NLF-DRV sources), and a large number of civilians were bulldozed into mass graves by the "allies".[189] The NLF claim to have buried 2000 victims of the bombardment in mass graves.[190] Oberdorfer says that 2800 "victims of the occupation" were discovered in mass graves, but he gives no reason for believing that these were victims of the NLF-DRV "political slaughter" rather than people killed in the U.S. bombardment. He seems to have relied entirely on the assertions of the Ministries of

Propaganda. Fox Butterfield, in the *New York Times* of 11 April 1975, even places all 3,000 bodies in a single grave! Samuel A. Adams, a former analyst with the CIA, wrote in the *Wall Street Journal* of March 26, 1975, that "South Vietnamese and Communist estimates of the dead coincide almost exactly. Saigon says it dug up some 2,800 bodies; a Viet Cong police report puts the number at about 3,000." There are no known "police reports" that say any such thing; and it apparently never occurred to Adams that the 2,800 figure might have been adjusted to the needs of the mistranslated document.

An interesting feature of the mass graves, as noted earlier, is that independent journalists were never allowed to be present at their opening, and that they had difficulty locating their precise whereabouts despite repeated requests.[191] One of the authors spoke with a United States Marine present at the first publicized grand opening, who claims that the reporters present were carefully hand-picked reliables, that the bodies were not available for inspection, and that he observed tracks and scour marks indicative of the use of bulldozers (which the DRV and NLF did not possess).[192] Perhaps the only Western physician to have examined the graves, the Canadian Dr. Alje Vennema, found that the number of victims in the grave sites he examined were inflated in the U.S.-Saigon count by over sevenfold, totaling only 68 instead of the officially claimed 477; that most of them had wounds and appeared to be victims of the fighting, and that most of the bodies he saw were clothed in military uniforms.[193]

Little attention has been paid to the possibility that massacre victims at Hue may have been killed neither by the NLF-DRV nor U.S. firepower, but rather by the returning Saigon military and political police. Many NLF sympathizers "surfaced" during the Tet offensive, cooperated in the provisional government formed by the revolutionaries in Hue, or otherwise revealed their support for the NLF. With the retreat of the NLF and DRV forces from Hue in 1968 many cadres and supporters were left in a vulnerable position as potential victims of Saigon retribution. Evidence has come to light that large-scale retaliatory killing may have taken place in Hue by the Saigon forces *after* its recapture. In a graphic description, Italian journalist Oriana Fallaci, citing a French priest from Hue, concluded that: "Altogether, there have been

1,100 killed [after 'liberation' by Saigon forces]. Mostly students, university teachers, priests. Intellectuals and religious people at Hue have never hidden their sympathy for the NLF."[194]

One of the U.S. reporters who entered Hue immediately after the U.S. Marines had recaptured part of it was John Lengel of AP. He filed a report on February 10 concerned primarily with the extensive war damage, and then added the following intriguing comment:

> But few seasoned observers see the devastation of Hue backfiring on the communists. They see as the greatest hope a massive and instant program of restoration underlined by a careful psychological warfare program pinning the blame on the communists.
> It is hard, however, to imagine expertise on such a broad scale in this land.[195]

It seems quite possible that the "seasoned observers" whom Lengel cites gave the matter some further thought, and that contrary to his speculation, there was sufficient psywar expertise to manage the media—never very difficult for the government—and to "pin the blame on the communists." That seems, at least, a very reasonable speculation given the information now available, and one that gains credibility from the early reaction of "seasoned observers" to the havoc wrought by the U.S. forces reconquering the city.

In any case, given the very confused state of events and evidence plus the total unreliability of U.S.-Saigon "proofs," at a minimum it can be said that the NLF-DRV "bloodbath" at Hue was constructed on flimsy evidence indeed. It seems quite likely that U.S. firepower "saving" the Vietnamese killed many more civilians than did the NLF and DRV. It is also not unlikely that political killings by the Saigon authorities exceeded any massacres by the NLF and DRV at Hue. Porter's analysis of the NLF documents used by U.S.-Saigon propagandists suggests that mass political killings were neither contemplated nor consistent with revolutionary strategy at Hue. The evidence indicates that "the vast majority of policemen, civil servants, and soldiers were initially on 'reeducation' rather than on liquidation lists, but the number of killings mounted as the military pressure on the NLF and North Vietnamese mounted."[196] It is also of interest here, as in the land reform case, that the retreating Front forces "were severely criticized by their superiors for excesses which 'hurt the revolution'."[197] We have not yet heard of any such self-criticism coming from U.S. and Saigon superiors for their more extensive killings at Hue.

As noted earlier, the apparent absence of retributory killings in postwar Vietnam is suggestive of where the truth may lie on the question of the Hue massacre. The Pike-Thompson version led to forecasts which have been refuted by history. Nonetheless the force of the U.S. propaganda machine and U.S. influence are such that the Hue massacre (by the Communists!) is still an institutionalized truth, not only in the United States but overseas as well. For example, Michel Tatu of *Le Monde* has taken the Pike version as established truth. And in his letter proposing Sakharov for the 1973 Nobel Peace Prize, Aleksandr Solzhenitsyn also refers to "the bestial mass killing in Hue" as "reliably proved"—and we can be sure he is not referring to the nearly 4,000 civilians mentioned by the Saigon authorities themselves, most of whom were buried in the rubble created by U.S. firepower.

We have discussed several of the more blatant exercises of the U.S.-Saigon propaganda machines, but it must be emphasized that even their day-to-day reports, which constituted the great mass of information about Indochina, should have been treated with comparable skepticism. On the rare occasions when competent reporters made serious investigations, the information presented by U.S. and Saigon sources turned out to be no less tainted. The Japanese reporter Katsuichi Honda once undertook to investigate the weekly report of the General Information Bureau of the U.S. Army in Saigon entitled "Terrorist Activities by Viet Cong." Pursuing "one isolated case" that interested him, he discovered

> that not only was amazingly brutal and persistent terrorism occurring regularly, it was actually being shielded from public scrutiny by Saigon's "information control." It soon appeared that the murders were not done by the National Liberation Front at all. There were, it seemed, innumerable "terrible facts" which had been secretly hushed up behind the scenes of the intensifying Vietnam War.[198]

In the case in question, he discovered that the assassination of five Buddhist student volunteers, officially victims of Viet Cong terror, had apparently been carried out by government forces. In another case, "drunken soldiers of the Government army quarreling among themselves threw grenades, and some civilian bystanders were killed," the case again being reported "as another instance of 'Viet Cong terrorism'."

In other cases, the facts have emerged only by accident. To mention one particularly grotesque example, the camp where the remnants of the My Lai massacre had been relocated was largely destroyed by ARVN air and artillery bombardment in the spring of 1972. The destruction was attributed routinely to Viet Cong terror. The truth was revealed by Quaker service workers in the area.[199]

These examples point up the fact that in the instances in question the official reports were lies and deceptions, and in some cases were converted into official myths; the more important conclusion is that official sources in general have extremely limited credibility. They raise questions, but provide no reliable answers.

Appendix: Indochina—Quang Ngai Province Five Months After the Peace Agreement: Arrests, Tortures, Artillery Fire Continue as Before the Ceasefire, by Jane and David Barton

[Jane and David Barton had worked for two years in the hospitals of Quang Ngai Province in central Vietnam at the time they wrote the report presented below. In this sector as in others, the ceasefire and the accords ratified in January, 1973 scarcely changed the lives of the population. The prisons remained full, the police continued to torture, the U.S. continued to finance and "advise" those who directed the system of camps and prisons.]

Since the ceasefire agreements, the Saigon government continues to detain, to arrest, to interrogate, and to torture a large number of civilians in Quang Ngai. At present there are about two thousand political prisoners in the province. At the Provincial Interrogation Center, there are more than a thousand; a thousand are in the prison of Quang Ngai and hundreds of others are in the eight district detention centers. During two years time, we have encountered hundreds of detainees. We have never seen a single prisoner arrested for a criminal offense. The detainees of Quang Ngai wear labels giving name and registration number; often the words "political prisoner" are written. At least 90% of these prisoners are political prisoners and not prisoners of war.

Since the January agreements, the number of prisoners has remained constant. The majority of the persons arrested before January have not been released. One example: Phan Thi Thi, a woman sixty-seven years old, was incarcerated on 17 November 1972 in the district of Mo Duc; she had transported 1 kilogram of rice into a zone considered "low security." She was taken to the police headquarters of Mo Duc, interrogated, beaten, tortured. During this session, her brain was affected and half her body is paralyzed. The first time that we saw her, in the prisoners' section of the hospital, she was lying on sheets of cardboard. She was naked, and under her a hole was cut out for her relief. She was greatly weakened, weighed about 35 kilos (77 pounds), and the other prisoners fed her.[1] After the signing of the accords, the police took her to the district capital to interrogate her again, in spite of her paralysis and although she was hardly able to speak. After repeated requests, we were able to "transfer her temporarily" to the Quang Ngai hospital, but on April 14, when her health had become critical to the point that she was placed in an intensive care ward, the police refused to release her. Phan Thi Thi remains incarcerated.

This is also the case for women who have been imprisoned for much longer periods. Huynh Thi Tuyet, a thirty-six-year-old woman, was arrested in March 1967. She says that she was taken with other villagers by the army close to her village, in the district of Son Tinh. Many other villagers were freed because the soldiers had had enough of watching the group of "prisoners", but, she says, she was taken together with 18 persons, including a child of 7 and a man of 59, to the prison of Quang Ngai, where she remains ever since, without knowing of what she is accused. Marjorie Nelson, an American doctor, has examined her several times. Huynh Thi Tuyet continues to consider herself a forgotten prisoner who may remain so for a long time to come. Here are some other cases: Ho Thi Nhung, thirty-six-year-old woman, mother of a baby a few weeks old, suffering from respiratory difficulties; Phan Suong, 49, victim of advanced tuberculosis and pneumonia; Trinh Thi Cung, a young woman of 18, suffering from venereal disease after having been raped six times by men of the Saigon Army; Nguyen Thi Nuoi, a woman of 42, with cancer of the lymphatic passages.

Torture by Electricity

The authorities customarily take the "suspects" from the detention center to the interrogation center, a building located in the middle of the detention complex; there they are interrogated and often tortured. The situation has not changed at all since January. We were able to prove this by means of medical examinations, interviews, direct testimony of the prisoners, and also by means of X-rays and photographs. Phan Thi Nguyet, a nineteen-year-old woman, found herself in the interrogation center and in prison six months before the agreements. The police wanted to know whether her father, who left for the DRV when she was 9, had communicated with her, since rumor had it that he had returned to the sector. Nguyet was tortured on eight occasions before the accords; after the signing, she was taken from the prison back to the interrogation center where she was tortured by electricity; she was made to swallow soapy water and was beaten four times between the 2nd of February and the 23 of March. Her nervous system was affected and her left leg is paralyzed.

Several people arrested after the ceasefire have told us their stories. We encountered a woman, Nguyen Thi Sanh, on March 6, in the prisoners' section of the hospital. Her body was swollen all over and had black and blue marks; she was immobilized on her bed, her eyes swollen and almost shut. She is a native of Duc My, district of Mo Duc. Four days earlier, she left her house to go to the fields; the village chief stopped her, accusing her of wanting to make contact with soldiers of the P.R.G. She answered that she herself, her six children and her husband—a lieutenant of the Saigon Army—had fled the communists six times, but the village chief ordered the police to interrogate her and beat her. She was severely beaten at the district center and sent to the Provincial Interrogation Center, but she arrived there in such a state that she was hospitalized. At this time she is in the Quang Ngai Interrogation Center.

Lam is twelve. He was arrested after the ceasefire and sent to the Interrogation Center. When the police apprehended him, he carried two vials of penicillin in his pocket; he was accused of carrying medicine to the P.R.G. He now remains at the Interrogation Center; still, the authorities know that his father is a nurse at the Quang Ngai hospital. His father has stated to the police that Lam was carrying the medicine to a sick aunt.

Loc is seventeen. He is a student. He was arrested by the military police and incarcerated at the Provincial Interrogation Center. Yet his identification papers were in order and he is too young to serve under a flag. The police gave him the choice between enrolling or remaining in the interrogation center for one year, at which time he will be old enough to become a soldier. All of these acts occurred after the ceasefire.

Since January, the Saigon government has scarcely demonstrated a spirit of reconciliation. The festival of Tet came shortly after the signing of the accords. The government authorities of Quang Ngai clearly showed their intentions in the instructions published regarding family reunions. Trucks equipped with loudspeakers announced to the inhabitants that if members of their families who worked for the P.R.G. or the Northerners attempted to return home for the festival, the neighbors should beat them to death.

Harsh measures were taken by the police and the army in order to strictly control and limit movements of the population.[2] Once again, it was announced by loudspeakers mounted on trucks to the tens of thousands of refugees of the provincial capital and vicinity that it was forbidden on penalty of death by gunfire to go onto the ancestral lands and into ancestral homes. Since the signing of the accords, no movement has been authorized between zones.

Thousands of Shells

On May 1st, Nguyen Quy, a grandfather 74 years old, deaf and nearly blind, was arrested and imprisoned in the detention center of Son Tinh. We learned this from a person who worked at the hospital. His house was located in the region of My Lai (scene of one of the most "famous" massacres); almost a year ago, fighting was going on there. He sought refuge with his ten-year-old granddaughter on the island of Ly Son. After that, he decided to return to the mainland and pay a visit to friends in the camp for refugees from the My Lai region. The refugee camp is made of tents set up on a sandy point of the Tra-Khuc river, just outside of Quang Ngai. On his arrival, he was arrested by the police, who did not believe his story; they took him away, leaving his granddaughter alone and in tears in the camp. Friends came to ask us to help him. The chief of the "special police" (in fact specialized in torture) of the district of Son Tinh declared that the old man presented a potential danger, since he might have stayed in a zone that had come under the control of the P.R.G. Although he had valid identification papers and had worked for the government in the past, it was necessary to interrogate him. It took us four weeks of constant efforts to have him freed.

At the "rehabilitation" center of the provincial hospital, more wounded have been admitted since the ceasefire than during the same period last year. Most of the wounds are attributed to Saigon artillery shells, to exchanges of fire and to mines. Almost every evening since the ceasefire, we have heard government artillery. A U.S. diplomat told us that at Hue, the Saigon forces fire thousands of shells every week because "the more they fire, the more the Americans replace their ammunitions."

Human Mine Detectors

Liem is a little girl of twelve, a native of Mo Duc; Phong is a boy of 10, a native of Son Tinh; both of them are paraplegics because they were wounded by shells that fell near their home one night in February. Le Nam is 50; his right leg had to be amputated above the knee; on February 24, he was working in his rice paddy several hundred meters from a P.R.G. flag when a helicopter of the Saigon Army fired at him several times. On February 7, on the 5th day of Tet, a man of 70 named Vinh left the Binh Son district refugee camp early in the morning to cultivate his sweet potatoes. Both his legs were cut off by a government army mine that had been set the night before and not deactivated. On February 15, Buoi, a 14-year old boy, lost his left leg below the knee in a grenade explosion.

We also received first-hand reports from persons from the Batangan peninsula who were forced at gunpoint to lower a P.R.G. flag. Luckily, this time, the ground was not mined, but the Saigon soldiers told the people that they were using them as mine detectors. The story was told to us by Tran Lam, 57 years old, a native of Phu Quy. The incident, he told us, took place on March 27. Tran Lam was going from the market of Binh Son towards Binh Duc. He told the soldiers that he was old and did not want to die; the soldiers laughed out loud and said they were young and that he had to die for them...

We also want to say that the United States must be held responsible for these injuries after the ceasefire, for these incarcerations, for the repressive system in which the refugees are held and which the U.S. has been financing for years, while Americans advise the Saigon personnel. We hope that the ceasefire will be respected, that all the prisoners will be released, and that the Vietnamese will be able to return to the land of their ancestors. Then, if the killing stops, if the prisoners are set free, if the peasants return to their land, the Vietnamese will finally have the possibility of freely determining the future of their country.

NOTES

Frontispiece

1. Countries are included on the Frontispiece diagram on the following criteria: (a) that they have been classified as using torture "on an administrative basis" or as "an essential mode of governance" in the Amnesty International (AI) *Report on Torture* (U.S. edition, Farrar, Straus and Giroux, 1975), or in other AI reports on specific countries; (b) that there is other reasonably authentic evidence of extensive torture in the 1970s, with cumulative numbers tortured probably in excess of 500, and with torture carried out on a systematic basis in multiple detention centers. There are ambiguities in the concept of torture and in the notion of torture on an administrative basis. The data are also imperfect. But we see no reason to believe that there are any net biases that should call into question the fundamental drift of facts described in this chart (whose roots are discussed in Chapter 2, section 2.1.2). Amnesty International's global concern for political prisoners and their maltreatment has made it the subject of abuse and criticism for alleged bias by a variety of ideologues and special interest groups. For several from the West, and a vigorous AI response, see the following: "Amnesty's Odd Man In," editorial *New York Times* (14 December 1978); Stephen Miller, "Politics and Amnesty International," *Commentary*, March 1978; Andrew Blane, "The Individual in the Cell: A Rebuttal to 'Politics and Amnesty International'," *Matchbox*, Winter 1979.

The parent-client relationship is one of superiority-inferiority, dominance-subordination, and control-dependency. It arises commonly from sheer economic-military strength and interest by one power relative to its neighbors, and the relationship often emerges without the overt use of force. Among the 26 planets, for a substantial number the governments were installed by direct or indirect action of the sun; and for all of them the sun is recognized to be the friendly superpower within whose orbit the planets move, protected from external or internal threats by the military and economic might of the sun. We have limited the number of planets to cases of countries basking in the sun's orbit that have also received significant flows of direct economic and military aid. South Africa is excluded immediately on grounds of the absence of such aid, but its ties to Great Britain and its strength and relative independence would disqualify it from planetary status in any event.

2. Data for the filiation lines connecting the sun with the planets were taken from the following: military aid, 1946-1975, from A.I.D., *U.S. Overseas Loans and Grants and Assistance from International Organizations*, 1976 ed.; number of client military trained in the United States, 1950-1975, from "The Pentagon's Proteges, U.S. Training Programs For Foreign Military Personnel," *NACLA's Latin America & Empire Report,* January 1976, p. 28; and police aid or training to clients, from Michael T. Klare, *Supplying Repression*, Field Foundation, December, 1977, pp. 20-21.

Preface

1. The principal sources for this account of the suppression are affidavits supplied to the authors by the publisher and associate publisher of Warner Modular Publications, Inc.
2. See Chapter 2, section 2.2, and Volume II, Chapter 4.

3. For a more general discussion of mass media choices and bases of selection see chapter 2, section 2.0.
4. Herbert Mitgang, "Nixon Book Dispute Erupts at Meeting," *New York Times* (28 May 1978) p. 16.

1 Introduction: Summary of Major Findings and Conclusions

1. See, for example, Andrei D. Sakharov, "Human Rights: A Common Goal," *Wall Street Journal* (27 June 1978); also Valery Chalidze, "Human Rights: A Policy of Honor," *Wall Street Journal* (8 April 1977). According to Chalidze, "A state does not initiate aggression with a declaration of war; it begins by persecuting its own citizens' honest and lawful behavior. After its critics are silenced, a government can prepare international aggression, whip up a war psychosis among its citizens and secretly increase military expenditures at the expense of social needs."
2. See M.J. Crozier, S.P. Huntington, and Joji Watanuki, *The Crisis of Democracy: Report on the Governability of Democracies to the Trilateral Commission,* NYU Press, 1975. For discussion, see N. Chomsky, "*Human Rights" and American Foreign Policy*, Spokesman, 1978.
3. See especially Richard A. Falk, *The Vietnam War and International Law*, Princeton University Press, 1968, 2 vols.
4. See Seymour M. Hersh, *Chemical and Biological Warfare*, Bobbs-Merrill, 1968; Eric Prokosch, "Conventional Killers," *The New Republic*, 1 November 1969; AFSC-Narmic, *Weapons for Counter-Insurgency*, 1970; Prokosch, *The Simple Art of Murder: Anti-Personnel Weapons and their Development*, AFSC-Narmic, 1972.
5. See below, chapter 4, section 4.
6. The deep involvement of the U.S. government in the overthrow of the last democratic government of Brazil is discussed in detail in A.J. Langguth, *Hidden Terrors*, Pantheon, 1978, pp. 38-116 and in Jan K. Black, *United States Penetration of Brazil,* University of Pennsylvania Press, 1977, passim. Some of the key facts are as follows: the U.S. government not only knew of the plotting but probably helped to coordinate it and to persuade key military personnel to join the conspiracy. It never informed the legally established government of the plots, and never considered trying to talk the military out of carrying out the coup. The official U.S. worry was only that the coup might fail, and the United States was not only ready with standby arrangements for aid, but assured coup plotters of our intervention in their favor if trouble arose. The Sixth Fleet was standing offshore at the time of the coup. A great many of the Brazilian military had been trained in the United States, and their links with U.S. intelligence and military personnel were extensive and warm. The U.S.-trained elements of the Brazil military predominated in the conspiracy. The CIA had pervaded Brazil with informers and paid propagandists, and had engaged in extensive bribing in Brazilian elections. A state investigation of CIA bribery was cut short by the coup. While collaborating intimately in a real anti-democratic coup, cold war liberals like Ambassador Lincoln Gordon seem to have convinced themselves that Goulart and the Communists were an imminent threat to democracy. Goulart may have been a threat to U.S. economic interests, for which the embassy is the *de facto* representative, but the threat to democracy was a myth that conveniently helped justify U.S. subversion.
7. See below, chapter 2, sections 1.1, 1.4, and 1.5.

8. See below, chapter 2, section 1.
9. Langguth, *op. cit.*, p. 251.
10. *Ibid.*, pp. 225-26.
11. *Ibid.* Langguth cites a number of other examples as well, as have U.S. personnel who were directly involved in such programs; see chapter 5, sections 1.5, and 1.6.
12. See below, section 14.
13. See below, "Notes on Some Insecurity States in Latin America," chapter 4, section 5.2. Also the corresponding definition of "security" as applied to "pacified" populations, chapter 5, note 66.
14. Black, *op. cit.*, p. 6.
15. *Ibid.*, p. 11.
16. "New Wounds on Both Sides in the Battle of Terrorism," *New York Times* (25 June 1978).
17. See "Free Photography," *New Statesman*, 29 September 1978, describing how over 600 Namibians, most of them children and old people, were killed by bombing by French-built Mirage jets and by paratroopers transported by U.S.-built Hercules troop carriers. The official South African explanation that Kassinga was a SWAPO military base "was a lie," as discovered by foreign journalists who visited shortly after. Rather, "The massacre was planned with brutal cynicism to forestall a breakthrough in negotiations with the UN which might lead to fair and free elections in Namibia." South Africa hoped that this murderous attack would provoke SWAPO to break negotiations, so that the guerrillas could be portrayed as "intransigents" while Vorster gained "much-needed international sympathy." "Vorster must have known it would not be worth risking such a crude ploy unless he could expect only the shallowest of coverage from the Western press." He was not disappointed. The article notes that the mainstream British press offered "little coverage" and refused even to publish photos supplied by AP. In the United States as well the media virtually suppressed this butchery. On the background, see Christopher Hitchens, "Namibia—The Birth of a Nation," *New Statesman*, 3 November 1978; *Fellowship*, May 1977.
18. Haynes Johnson, "Terrorism: It's the crime of our times," *Philadelphia Inquirer* (13 March 1977).
19. Or, at least, their "excesses," though regrettable and offensive to high-minded and civilized Westerners, are nevertheless understandable under the unfortunate circumstances created by "terrorism."

This process of thrusting a frightening symbol before the public, and simultaneously assuring them that their government is busily engaged in dealing with the problem, is an example of political action in which "a semblance of reality is created, and facts that do not fit are screened out of it. Conformity and satisfaction with the basic order are the keynotes; and the acting out of what is to be believed is a psychologically effective mode of instilling conviction and fixing patterns of future behavior." Murray Edelman, *The Symbolic Uses of Politics*, University of Illinois, 1964, p. 17.
20. For an example of the brainwashing effect of media on willing victims, see the remarks by *Encounter*'s columnist *R* (G. Rees), *Encounter*, December 1976, describing the period when the thesis that universities (as part of an evil society) must be destroyed "rang across every campus in the United States, and libraries were burned, and universities wrecked"—all in his fevered imagination, needless to say. On the role of the U.S. government in inspiring terrorist acts by students

and others through the use of provocateurs, see Dave Dellinger, *More Power Than We Know*, Doubleday, 1976; introduction to N.Blackstock, ed., *Cointelpro,* Vintage, 1976. See these references and also M. Halperin et al., *The Lawless State,* Penguin, 1976, for some discussion of FBI terrorism during this period, which vastly exceeded anything attributable to the student movement.

21. Within peace movement circles, the role of the government in fomenting violence was well-known long before it reached the attention of Senate inquiries. It was standard practice, from the earliest stage, to be wary of individuals who were calling for violent acts on the assumption, often verified later, that they were government agents.

22. Farrar, Straus and Giroux, 1975, pp. 184-85.

23. *Ibid.*, p. 7.

24. *Ibid.*, p.191.

25. *Ibid.*

26. *The Amnesty International Report*, 1975-1976, p. 84.

27. *Ibid.*

28. *Report on Torture*, pp. 206-7. For many more gruesome descriptions, see the Appendix: "Special Report on Chile," by Rose Styron.

29. For further discussion, see chapter 2 and chapter 4, section 5.2.

30. Hugo Neira, "Guerre Totale contre les Elites en Amerique Latine," *Le Monde diplomatique*, January 1977.

31. *The Amnesty International Report*, 1975-1976, p. 84.

32. See chapter 4, section 5.

33. See chapter 4, section 5.1.

34. International Movement of Catholic Intellectuals and Professionals, "Voice From Northeastern Brazil To III Conference of Bishops," Mexico, November 1977, reprinted in LADOC (Latin America Document Service), May-June 1978, p. 15.

35. "Turning Point in Brazil," 2 June 1965.

36. The review by Tom Buckley (27 December 1978) of the ABC documentary shown that evening neatly encapsulates many of the standard maneuvers of propagandists on both sides of the iron curtain. We return to it in section 7. Its main characteristic is distress at the very airing of the subject of torture in U.S. client states. There is not a word of sympathy for the victims of these little tyrannies, let alone any recognition of the U.S. role, but only outrage over the fact that ABC has engaged in this "simpleminded" exercise.

37. Quoted in Reza Baraheni, "Persia Today: No Magic Carpet Rides," *Matchbox* (Amnesty International), Fall 1976.

38. Quoted in *ibid.*

39. William A. Dorman and Ehsan Omad, "Reporting Iran the Shah's Way," *Columbia Journalism Review*, January-February 1979.

40. See Reza Baraheni, *The Crowned Cannibals: Writings on Repression in Iran*, Vintage, 1976; Bahman Nirumand, *Iran, the New Imperialism in Action*, Monthly Review, 1969. The chief CIA analyst on Iran from 1968-73, Jesse Leaf, stated that the practice of torture by the SAVAK was well-known to the CIA and that "a senior C.I.A. official was involved in instructing officials in the Savak on torture techniques.... The C.I.A.'s torture seminars, Mr. Leaf said, 'were based on German torture techniques from World War II'." Seymour M. Hersh, "Ex-Analyst Says C.I.A. Rejected Warning on Shah," *New York Times* (7 January 1979). On the corruption, see chapter 2, p. 64.

41. Of the non-industrialized countries, Iran has been the largest purchaser of military equipment in the world, buying over $18 billion in arms from the United States alone, 1950-1977. "Defense" spending increased tenfold from 1971 to 1975. See Cynthia Arnson, Stephen Daggett, and Michael Klare, "Background Information on the Crisis in Iran," Institute for Policy Studies, Washington, D.C., December 1978.

42. As it became more obvious that the Shah's regime was seriously threatened, the veil began to lift slightly. Thus, Youssef M. Ibrahim reported from Teheran in the *New York Times* (4 December 1978) that "the fear of torture, prison, arbitrary arrest, and the ubiquitous presence of Savak seems overwhelming," and describes the torture of political detainees and the horrible conditions of life for the masses of people driven to urban slums by what is called in the West the Shah's "progressive" land reform program, including people who work a 13-hour day, live in miserable huts, waste away from disease—but also ask the reporter to leave them alone, because "we don't want to attract attention," for obvious reasons. The continuing torture of prisoners is discussed away from the U.S. media mainstream by Alexander Cockburn and James Ridgeway, *Village Voice* (4 December 1978), reporting the experiences of a recently released British prisoner (from the *International Herald Tribune*). The same authors discuss the actual impact of the Shah's "agricultural reforms," citing the well-known French agronomist René Dumont, an adviser to the Shah who became "appalled" when he discovered that "the reforms were a farce" that drove the peasants from the land which was then taken over by agribusiness, much of the land becoming desert, with the effect that "large numbers of the Iranian people face starvation" (*Village Voice*, 20 November 1978). For further discussion, see Thierry Brun and René Dumont, "Imperial Pretensions and Agricultural Dependence," MERIP Reports No. 71, October 1978. One rarely reads commentary on these matters in the mainstream press, but see the letter by Iran specialist Richard Cottam (*Washington Post*, 2 October 1978), responding to some absurd commentary by Joseph Kraft and outlining the progressive destruction of agriculture, real income decline for most Iranians, and the massive waste of resources on weapons and consumption for the newly rich. On SAVAK and other Iranian government activity in the United States (surveillance, subversion of Congress and universities, use of provocateurs, etc.), surely with the cooperation of the U.S. government, see Gregory F. Rose, "The Shah's Secret Police Are Here," *New York*, 18 September 1978.

43. Cited by James A. Bill, "Iran and the Crisis of '78," *Foreign Affairs*, Winter, 1978-79. Moderate opposition groups, according to Bill, were "stunned and embittered by Carter's performance" and "turned more sharply than ever away from the United States." While Western propaganda pretends that it was Carter's advocacy of human rights that laid the basis for the explosive events in Iran in 1978, the fact of the matter is that it was his clarity in *rejecting* any concern for human rights that gave an impetus to these developments. Much the same was true in Nicaragua, as Carter's expressed support for Somoza contributed to setting off the uprising of August-September, 1978. See chapter 4, section 5.2. See also notes 80 and 88, this chapter.

44. See *New Statesman,* 29 September 1978, citing new shipments of supplies for crowd control (insert in the *Nation*, 21 October 1978, Michael Klare, "Iranian Quagmire"). See also *Internews International Bulletin*, 20 November 1978, on "anti-riot" gear sent to the Shah after the declaration of martial law and the

massacres of September 1978, and the plan to send a U.S. army team to train the Shah's army in riot control.
45. Walter Laqueur, "Trouble for the Shah," *New Republic*, 23 September 1978. The same journal also featured an hysterical article by Robert Moss explaining events in Iran as basically a Soviet plot (2 December 1978).
46. In chapter 3 and 4 we will give a number of examples. See the 13 reports on individual countries discussed by the State Department prepared under the direction of the Coalition on Human Rights and the Coalition for a New Foreign and Military Policy, reproduced in the Congressional Record, 5 April 1978, pp. H 2507-2518. These reports show in great detail the extent to which the State Department role amounts to apologetics for client terror. Typical is the statement by the Office of Haitian Refugee Concerns of the National Council of Churches, which claims that the section on Haiti consists largely of "generalized statements of improvements based either on flagrant misrepresentation or outright omission of facts that have been presented to the State Department by our office and by others." They cite the repeated use of words like "apparently" and "appear" with respect to alleged improvements (the infamous Fort Dimanche prison is "reportedly" being replaced by a modern facility, etc.).

But even more instructive in the glossing over of such problems is the experience of the eleven opponents of the government exiled in 1977, to whom the State Department makes several references. Several of these men had been abroad and had returned under the "national reconciliation" program begun by Duvalier in 1972. The report notes the reconciliation program but does not point out that these men were rearrested and held without charges upon their return. All eleven then became part of a group of 105 who were released in September, 1977 and, according to the State Department, were "presented to the press and the diplomatic corps at the time of their release." *Not* reported is the fact that the eleven who were to be exiled had been withdrawn from their cells the previous March and given six months of intensive medical treatment to prepare them for international inspection. Despite this precaution by the Haitian government *all eleven* were hospitalized again in Jamaica within a week of their release, an event which was covered widely in the Jamaican press.

On the treatment of "boat people" from Haiti, see Volume II, chapter 3.
47. Richard H. Rovere, "Letter from Washington," *New Yorker*, 29 April 1974. He continues: "but our withdrawal has contributed no more than did our original intervention to the stability of the region..." The idea that the U.S. intervention to prevent the victory of the Indochinese revolutionaries was intended, or might be conceived, as a contribution to "stability" is the kind of drivel that one expects from such sources.
48. "Deliverance," *Washington Post* (30 April 1975).
49. See Volume II, chapter 1, and on "the last days," see Frank Snepp, *Decent Interval*, Random House, 1977. But see note 12 of Volume II, chapter 1, on Snepp's account.
50. One exception was the effort of the CIA to eliminate Trujillo, who was not only becoming something of an embarrassment, but perhaps even more important had gone too far in taking over the economic opportunities of the country as his private domain. Military regimes that have "radical" or "populist" flavor, as in Peru, may also find themselves a target for U.S. intrigue and "destabilization".

51. For a discussion of the remarkably close parallel between the Khrushchev and Brezhnev doctrines, and the antecedent Eisenhower and Johnson doctrines, respectively, which may well have contributed to the choice of rhetoric, see Thomas M. Franck and Edward Weisband, *Word Politics: Verbal Strategy Among the Superpowers,* Oxford University Press, 1971.
52. See chapter 5.
53. This may be an understatement of the disproportion; the ratio of firepower expended was closer to 500 to 1, and U.S. firepower was consistently used against civilian targets, as in the saturation bombing and "free fire zones" in populated regions or in random "harassment and interdiction" fire by artillery. Cf. General Douglas Kinnard, *The War Managers*, Univ. Press of New England, 1977, p. 47n., for one of many examples. See p. 310. NLF violence was far slighter in scale as well as more selective in character. See Edward S. Herman, *Atrocities in Vietnam,* Pilgrim Press, 1970, for discussion and evidence.
54. One reason why this happened is that "live" coverage in Vietnam was invariably a portrayal of U.S. actions, since those of the enemy were not accessible on the same basis to U.S. media. Despite controlled displays of U.S. actions, with so many of them destructive it was not easy to maintain an image of beneficence.
55. Some propagandists have not been satisfied with real or manufactured atrocities in postwar Indochina, so that we find such flights of rhetoric as those of Sidney Hook, who writes: "It is indisputably true that in every collectivist economy in the world today political despotism prevails, exercising a terror unexampled in its nature by anything known in previous history." That is, it is "indisputably true" that the terror that prevails today in Hungary and Poland exceeds that of Nazi Germany. Reprinted from the *New York Times* in *Encounter*, February 1978.
56. The term "Khmer Rouge" was coined by Sihanouk as a defamatory appellation for the guerrilla and peasant movements that he was attempting to suppress in the 1960s, often with great brutality and violence. It has become standard in the West, so much so that we too will use it, with misgivings. Comparably, the term "Viet Cong" was created by the U.S.-Saigon propaganda services, and also became standard in Western commentary, though even those initially supportive of the U.S. client regime in the South (e.g., Joseph Buttinger) recognized that the "Viet Cong" were simply the Viet Minh reconstituted to defend themselves against the terrorism of the U.S.-Saigon regime. Similarly, the term "South Vietnamese" was used by the propaganda services, and adopted without question by the submissive intelligentsia of the West, to refer to the tiny elite placed in power by the United States, which even the U.S. command treated with contempt.
57. See Ian Black, "Peace or no peace, Israel will still need cheap Arab labour," *New Statesman*, 28 September 1978, for a rare discussion, not matched in the United States, to our knowledge.
58. See chapter 4, section 1. As we shall see, it is not unusual in the Free Press to place the blame for the massacre on the victims.
59. See chapter 3, section 4.4.
60. See chapter 4, note 224.
61. The word "negligible" may be too generous. In response to this charge in a letter by the present authors, the Executive Director of the CDM wrote an indignant denial to the *New York Times* (letter, 9 August 1978) which failed to

cite even a single example to the contrary. It is also intriguing to read his effort to interpret the charge against CDM—which, as his letter reveals, is fully accurate—as an expression of "indifference to truth and to the suffering of Soviet victims" on the part of the present authors. Comparably, someone who criticized a Russian party hack for focusing his attention on human rights abuses in the West could be denounced for his "indifference to the suffering of the Chileans and Vietnamese." Compare also the *New York Times* critique of the ABC documentary, already discussed, with its effort to shift attention to the Communist enemy.

62. For illustrations, see chapter 2, sections 1.4 and 1.5.

63. The absence of official censorship allows room for sometimes vigorous debate among the substantial interests, and fringe and dissident elements are at least allowed to exist and argue, mainly among themselves, but occasionally penetrating to the consciousness of decision-makers, especially on matters of irrational behavior in relationship to establishment objectives.

64. The phenomenon has long been familiar. In a study conducted for the group of historians who enlisted in the service of the U.S. government in World War I (cf. Volume II, chapter 2, section 1), Victor S. Clark concluded that the "voluntary co-operation of the newspaper publishers of America resulted in a more effective standardization of the information and arguments presented to the American people, than existed under the nominally strict military control exercised in Germany." ("The German Press and the War," *Historical Outlook*, November 1919, cited by Carol S. Gruber, *Mars and Minerva: World War I and the Uses of the Higher Learning in America*, Louisiana State University Press, 1975, p. 140.) The same has often been true since. Given the general community of interest among the Western powers with regard to the Third World, one is not surprised to find, for example, that the media in Great Britain tended to view the Vietnam War pretty much through U.S. eyes. See *The British Press and Vietnam*, Indochina Solidarity Conference, July 1973. See also, Alex Carey, "The ennobling of the Vietnam war," unpublished, June 1978, for analysis of parts of a remarkable BBC TV "retrospective" on the war, which exhibits a degree of subservience to the U.S. propaganda system beyond what would be tolerated even by U.S. commercial TV, an interesting example of cultural colonization.

65. On the nature and quality of this ideology among the Brazilian military, see Black, *op. cit.*, pp. 190, 195.

66. For extensive evidence, see *ibid.*, pp. 188-199, and 210-222. On the longstanding strong current of extreme rightwing tendencies within the U.S. military establishment, see Fred Cook, "The Ultras," *Nation*, 30 June 1962.

67. State ownership has continued to play an important though usually declining role in some of these states, based to a great extent on inertia and on the usefulness of state enterprise for more direct looting. See chapter 4, sections 1 and 2.

68. On the concept of "security" as its usage has developed in the West, see p. 5; also chapter 5, note 66.

69. Cited in Black, *op. cit.*, p. 160.

70. Taylor Branch, "The Letelier Investigation," *New York Times Magazine*, 16 July 1978.

71. Black, *op. cit.*, quoting U.S. General Robert W. Porter, p. 211.

72. On the Letelier-Moffitt murders, see Saul Landau, *They Educated The Crows*, Transnational Institute, 1978. See also note 70.

73. See also note 42, above.

74. Black, *op. cit.*, p. 73, note 34.
75. See the Nixon eulogies in *ibid.*, p. 55.
76. Quoted in Black, *op. cit.*, p. 55, from the *Jornal do Brasil,* 4 February 1972.
77. See chapter 2, section 2.2. Also Volume II, chapter 1, section 1.
78. Not entirely, however. For example, Jean and Simonne Lacouture point out that after "the reconquest and unification of Vietnam by Vietnamese citizens" in April 1975, there was no bloody revenge. The Vietnamese revolutionaries did not follow the example of "their French, Russian or Chinese predecessors. Not to kill is a great virtue; one seems to ignore that a bit too easily." "They are probably the first victors in a civil war (embittered and aggravated by two foreign interventions) who have not unleashed any operation of massive reprisal." Furthermore, "the Vietnamese *maquisards*, more honorable than their French comrades of 1944," did not humiliate the hundreds of thousands of prostitutes created by the American invasion. (*Vietnam: voyage à travers une victoire,* Seuil, 1976, pp. 7, 11, 110-12).

The Lacoutures' book is a record of their visit to Vietnam in April-May 1976. Though highly critical of the Vietnamese revolution—so much as to elicit a sharp rejoinder in the Vietnamese press—it was nevertheless sympathetic and balanced, and did not fail to describe the horrendous residue of thirty years of imperial violence. It was unable to find a U.S. publisher, and its very existence was denied in the U.S. press, as we shall see in Volume II, chapter 4. Jean Lacouture, a distinguished commentator on Vietnam with decades of experience in the country, is treated very differently when his message is more palatable to imperial tastes, as we shall see in Volume II, chapter 6.

79. For Western precedents, considered highly moral in contrast to the barbarous behavior of the Vietnamese, see Volume II, chapter 2, section 2.
80. Congress has barred aid (let alone reparations) to seven countries: Cuba, Angola, Mozambique, Uganda, Vietnam, Cambodia, and Laos. U.S. representatives to international financial institutions have been instructed to vote against aid to these countries, which are unique as "violators of human rights" (and by sheer coincidence, are also—apart from Uganda— countries which have recently freed themselves from the U.S.-dominated global system). In the case of Uganda, furthermore, the sanctions are *pro forma*, as we shall see. In contrast, proposals to bar aid to Nicaragua and South Korea, for example, because of human rights violations, were explicitly rejected, while Carter asked for—and received—authorization to continue arms aid to the Marcos dictatorship (Richard Burt, "Carter Asks For No Cut in Arms Aid to Marcos Despite Negative Human-Rights Report," *New York Times*, 6 February 1978); it is expected that the 1979 fiscal year will surpass the preceding year's total of $36 million despite massive human rights violations. The government has also made it clear that there is no intention "to link its massive arms sales to Iran with the issue of human rights" (Joe Alex Morris, *Los Angeles Times - Boston Globe*, 14 May 1977), naturally enough, since as Mr. Carter observed, "there is no leader with whom I have a deeper sense of personal gratitude and personal friendship" than the Shah, who received "no lecturing on the question of human rights" but only "a sympathetic ear" for a request for hundreds of advanced jet fighters (Geoffrey Godsell, *Christian Science Monitor*, 2 March 1978). See pp. 14f; see also William Branigan, "Vance Indicates Rights Issue, Iranian Arms Are Not Linked," *Washington Post* (14 May 1977).

It is a real tribute to the propaganda system that the press can still refer to a "human rights campaign"—with occasional qualifications: e.g., "The Administration has been put in the embarrassing position of trying to check the zeal of some lawmakers who say they want to translate President Carter's words into action." (Clyde Farnsworth, *New York Times*, 19 June 1977, citing also a study that shows how the World Bank, the Inter-American Development Bank and the International Monetary Fund, with U.S. acquiescence and support, were increasing aid to the worst human rights violators.)

81. "The reader may have noticed that I never called the South Vietnamese dictatorships from Diem to Thieu fascist. There is a good historical reason for this: no matter how totalitarian some of the dictatorships are which the U.S. still supports around the world, they should be called fascist only if, in gaining power and at least temporarily maintaining it they can rely on—in addition to political terror—some organized mass support, something possessed by Mussolini, Hitler, and even Franco, but not by any of the South Vietnamese regimes." Joseph Buttinger, *Vietnam: The Unforgettable Tragedy*, Horizon, 1977, p. 165. Other close observers were less reticent. General Lansdale, one of the chief U.S. specialists in subversion and counterrevolutionary intervention in Vietnam and elsewhere in the 1950s and 1960s, did not hesitate to describe the Diem regime that he backed as "fascistic" (cf. U.S. Department of Defense, *United States - Vietnam Relations, 1945-67*, book 2, IV, A.5, tab 4, p. 66 (the government edition of the *Pentagon Papers*).

82. Louis P. Kubicka, "From the Plain of Jars," *Progressive*, March 1978. See Volume II, chapter 5.

83. But curiously this is not true of the Viet Cong—who seem "eight feet tall" as they devise ingenious strategies to defeat American power and construct jungle laboratories, etc. Cf. John Mecklin, *Mission in Torment*, Doubleday, 1965, pp. 76f.

84. These insights are expressed by Townsend Hoopes, Undersecretary of the Air Force and a critic of the war after 1968, and William Pfaff, liberal-in-residence at the Hudson Institute. See Pfaff, *Condemned to Freedom,* Random House, 1971, a close paraphrase (with no acknowledgment) of Hoopes, *Limits of Intervention*, David McKay, 1969, where Pfaff is mentioned. It is unclear who deserves the credit for these deep thoughts. Cf. Chomsky, *At War With Asia*, (p. 297f.) and *For Reasons of State* (p. 94f.) for precise attribution and for additional examples and discussion, from these and other sources.

85. See Philip Shabecoff, "Murder Verdict Eased in Vietnam," *New York Times*, 31 March 1970. While the *New York Times* and other Establishment journals repeatedly expressed their outrage over the uncivilized behavior of the barbarians we faced in Vietnam, their own reporters casually documented U.S. war crimes without notice or comment. See Seymour Melman, ed., *In the Name of America*, Turnpike, 1968—well before the full-force of U.S. "pacification" was unleashed. To cite just one subsequent example, Malcolm Browne, quoting an official who describes May, 1972 B-52 strikes as "the most lucrative raids made at any time during the war," reports blandly that "every single bomb crater is surrounded with bodies, wrecked equipment and dazed and bleeding people. At one such hole there were 40 or 50 men, all in green North Vietnamese uniforms but without their weapons, lying around in an obvious state of shock. We sent in helicopter gunships, which quickly put them out of their misery" (*New York Times*, 6 May 1972). This was, needless to say, in express defiance of the laws of war to which the

Times editors expressed their solemn devotion when deploring the treatment of pilots captured while bombing North Vietnamese villages.
86. "A Craving For Rights," 31 January 1977.
87. Volume II, chapter 3, for reference and discussion.
88. See above for examples from December 1977 through the fall of 1978, repeated with continuing fervor through the fall 1978 crisis. As demonstrations against the Shah reached a peak of intensity at the year's end, "A State Department spokesman, Hodding Carter, yesterday reiterated Washington's backing for the monarch, saying the United States supports the shah 'in his efforts to promote stability'." Robert H. Reid, AP, "Rioters paralyze Tehran," *Boston Globe* (27 December 1978).
89. *Internews International Bulletin*, 20 November 1978.
90. Martin Woollacott, "Egypt's forces now without a role," *Manchester Guardian Weekly*, 15 October 1978. See also Thomas W. Lippman, "Display of Egypt's War Machine Hints at New Role," *Washington Post* (7 October 1978); John Cooley, "U.S. arms boost to Egypt, Israel awaits peace gains," *Christian Science Monitor* (12 October 1978); Ned Temko, "Egypt stepping forward to halt Soviets in Mideast," *ibid.* (6 December 1978). The main thrust of these and similar reports is that the Egyptian army is being reconstructed by the United States as an African strike force rather than a force designed for desert warfare. On the close relation between U.S. support for Israel and perceived Israeli success in upholding U.S. interests, see N. Chomsky, "Armageddon Is Well Located," *Nation*, 22 July 1977. It will be interesting to see whether the policy with regard to Egypt will be modified in the light of the collapse of the U.S. position in Iran.
91. See "Terror—Argentina Style," *Matchbox*, Winter 1977; Geoff Rips, "Argentina: Gilding the Monster," USLA *Reporter*, 30 November 1978, citing a special appeal from Amnesty International who reports that "disappearances" are again on the increase after some cosmetic touches timed to coincide with the World Soccer Cup.
92. See Rips, *ibid.*; also the report of the Coalition for a New Foreign and Military Policy, cited in the USLA *Reporter*, 30 November 1978; Karen DeYoung and Charles A.Krause, "Our Mixed Signals On Human Rights In Argentina," *Washington Post* (29 October 1978).
93. *Ibid.* See also James Nelson Goodsell, "US takes a friendlier attitude toward Argentina," *Christian Science Monitor* (14 November 1978). Noting that the administration "was forced to buckle under to business and trade considerations, letting its public human-rights policy go by the board," Goodsell remarks: "This does not mean that Washington will not privately continue to nudge the Videla government behind the scenes on human rights. But it means that as a public issue, human rights is certainly going to take a less important role than in the past." Given its actual role in the past, this "less important role" will approach zero.
94. Charles A. Krause, "Argentine Describes 'Excruciating' Pain of Torture," *Washington Post* (29 October 1978).
95. Eric Bourne, "Czech dissident attacks Carter rights pressure," *Christian Science Monitor* (6 February 1978).
96. Edward Walsh, "President to Remain Firm in Human Rights Campaign," *Washington Post* (3 June 1977). See Chomsky, *'Human Rights' and American Foreign Policy*, chapter 2, for discussion.
97. See chapter 3, section 4.4.

2 The CIA-Pentagon Archipelago

1. While we will speak of the "Brazilianization" of the Third World under U.S. aegis, we do not want to be understood as suggesting that the process began in 1964 with the U.S.-backed coup that installed the Brazilian generals in power, but merely that that coup and its totalitarian free enterprise aftermath have been warmly admired and considered worthy of emulation, maybe even in the United States (see p. 28). An earlier Latin American model is Guatemala (see chapter 4, section 5.2), and there are many still earlier precedents in Latin America and the Far East. The CIA effort in Guatemala in 1954 was no doubt stimulated in part by its earlier success in overthrowing the nationalist government in Iran and reinstalling the Shah in 1953. (Cf. David Wise and Thomas B. Ross, *The Invisible Government,* Bantam, 1964, pp. 116-121.) This achievement was highly praised in the United States. The *New York Times*, for example, explained in an editorial of August 6, 1954 that "underdeveloped countries with rich resources now have an object lesson in the heavy cost that must be paid by one of their number which goes berserk with fanatical nationalism." In later interventions, as in Vietnam, this "demonstration effect" was also much lauded.

Anyone inclined to regard such interventions as a post-World War II phenomenon might turn to the list of "Instances of the Use of United States Armed Forces Abroad, 1798-1945," containing over 200 entries, presented to Senate committees considering U.S. problems in Cuba by Secretary of State Rusk to show that there is ample precedent for intervention without congressional authorization. Hearings, "Situation in Cuba," Committee on Foreign Relations and Committee on Armed Services, U.S. Senate, 87th Congress, Second Session, (17 September 1962), pp. 82-87.

2. Not only has liberalism contributed to the cold war anti-Communist ideology, but liberals were active leaders in the initiation of counter-insurgency and preventive subversion. The Vietnam war and the spread of military juntas in the American sphere of interest is to a considerable degree a product of cold war liberalism. Lobe points out that "the Kennedy Administration was infatuated with counter-insurgency theory and attempted to press this theory onto the practice and policies of Washington bureaucracies...Attorney-General Robert Kennedy was the energizing force in the Special Group (CI), and it was he who propelled this body to recommend police aid to friendly Third World governments." Thomas Lobe, *United States National Security Policy and Aid to the Thailand Police,* University of Denver Monograph Series in World Affairs, Vol. 14, Bk. 2, 1977, pp. 5, 7. Langguth adds that "at no time did any of its members question the C-I Group's goals. As one participant recalled, 'We knew we were acting from damn good motives' "—in their mood of chauvinist arrogance, the Kennedy liberals were untroubled by the fact that their imperial predecessors had characteristically adopted a similar pose. (A.J. Langguth, *Hidden Terrors,* Pantheon, 1978, p. 50). Langguth describes in detail how the same group of Kennedy liberals engineered the overthrow of Brazilian democracy and its replacement with the subfascist regime that still rules, after President Goulart had

refused Robert Kennedy's admonition to end his flirtation with "romantic left-wing causes" (Langguth, p. 99). Particularly striking is his account of the great glee in Washington when Ambassador Lincoln Gordon returned after the successful military coup, the ninth case in which a military junta had replaced an elected government in Brazil since Kennedy was elected president, as General Andrew O'Meara reminded congressmen, adding that the Brazilian coup "saved that country from an immediate dictatorship." Meanwhile the director of the AIFLD, which merged the talents of the AFL-CIO and the CIA, boasted of their role in instituting the new military dictatorship, and Robert Kennedy, though "still grieving over the murder of his brother," nevertheless "found cheer in the events in Brazil," saying: "Well, Goulart got what was coming to him. Too bad he didn't follow the advice we gave him when I was down there." Langguth, pp. 115-16.

The general attitude is expressed very well by William P. Bundy, referring to the origins and development of the CIA: to many in government, he wrote, "the preservation of liberal values, for America and other nations, required the use of the full range of U.S. power, including if necessary its more shady applications," even if this might involve "ambiguity". Foreword to Douglas S. Blaufarb, *The Counter-Insurgency Era,* Free Press, 1977, p. x. Note that these words were written well after the ugly record could no longer be concealed.

3. Three-year comparisons were used except where data were unavailable or other political events intervened to require a two-year horizon.

4. One is the overall trend factor—if aid is going up in general, avoidance of bias may require deflating to the trend line. Such an adjustment does not alter the findings presented here.

5. On the valuable contribution of the Korean mercenaries to "security" in Vietnam, see below, chapter 5, section 1.4.

6. The origination, funding, and staffing of these institutions provide even more definitive evidence of U.S. dominance. See Teresa Hayter, *Aid As Imperialism,* Penguin, 1971; Michael Tanzer, *The Political Economy of International Oil and the Underdeveloped Countries,* Beacon, 1969, chapter 8.

7. There are eight countries common to Tables 1 and 2; Table 2 includes Ethiopia and Argentina, whereas Table 1 has instead Guatemala and the Dominican Republic.

8. *Supplying Repression*, Field Foundation, December 1977, p. 10. Italics in original. Table 2 is reproduced, with permission, from this work, p. 9.

9. Joanne Omang, "Latin American Left, Right Say U.S. Militarized Continent," *Washington Post* (11 April 1977).

10. Black, *United States Penetration of Brazil*, pp. 220-22.

11. *Ibid.*, pp. 96, 170; Jeffrey Stein, "Grad School For Juntas," *Nation*, 21 May 1977.

12. "A frank Minister of Foreign Relations in the mid-1960s startled even the subservient Brazilian press with his declaration, 'What's good for the United States is good for Brazil'." E. Bradford Burns, "Brazil: The Imitative Society," *Nation*, 10 July 1976.

13. *Op. cit.*, p. 23.

14. "Torture, an Official Way of Life," *New York Times* (4 August 1974).

15. *Washington Post* (9 May 1977). On torture in Israel, see the *London Sunday Times* (19 June 1977), reporting the results of a 5-month investigation by the

Insight team that produced evidence of torture of Arab prisoners so widespread and systematic that "it appears to be sanctioned at some level as deliberate policy," perhaps "to persuade Arabs in occupied territories that it is least painful to behave passively." This report was bitterly attacked in the United States, though the *Sunday Times* study itself, which is confirmed from many other sources, was barely reported. Two of the journalists who conducted the study, Paul Eddy and Peter Gillman, added substantial information on their procedures and discoveries and on the reaction to them in testimony before the United Nations, 6-7 September 1977; see the report of the Special Political Committee, Thirty-second session, Agenda item 57, UN General Assembly, Report of the Special Committee to Investigate Israeli Practices Affecting the Human Rights of the Population of the Occupied Territories, A/SPC/32/L.12, 11 November 1977. Mr. Eddy informs us that the *London Times* Insight team report was offered to both the *New York Times* and the *Washington Post* but was rejected.

16. Holmes Brown, Don Luce, *Hostages of War, Saigon's Political Prisoners*, Indochina Mobile Education Project, 1973, pp. 62-63.

17. "U.S.-Iran Ties Strong but Controversial," *New York Times* (9 July 1978). See also chapter 1, note 40, on direct CIA involvement in torture.

18. Black, *op. cit.* p. 146.

19. *Ibid.*, pp. 141-43; Langguth, *op. cit.*, pp. 162-65.

20. *Op. cit.*, p. 81.

21. John Stockwell, *In Search of Enemies*, Norton, 1978, p. 172.

22. *Alleged Assassination Plots Involving Foreign Leaders,* Interim Report of Select Senate Committee on Intelligence Activities, 20 November 1975, pp. 71-109.

23. See Volume II, chapter 5, and references cited there.

24. See below, section 2.2, this chapter.

25. Black, *op. cit.*, pp. 59-110.

26. *Ibid.*, p. 129.

27. See chapter 4, note 5.

28. Agee, *Inside the Company*, Stonehill, 1975, pp. 361-62.

29. Black, *op. cit.*, pp. 111-124. See note 2.

30. *Ibid.*, pp. 129, 155.

31. Stockwell, *op. cit.*, pp. 185-190.

32. Cf. note 1. We stress again the *systematic* character of CIA and other forms of U.S. intervention abroad. By the 1960s, the official definition of covert action was "any clandestine activity designed to influence foreign governments, events, organizations or persons in support of United States foreign policy." The major victims have been weaker, primarily Third World countries seeking a measure of independence, and there can be no doubt that covert action programs of the CIA have been a major factor in the deterioration of human rights throughout much of the world, including subversion of democratic elections, press manipulation, and direct export of violence. When subversion succeeds, some of the major terror organizations of the world (e.g., Iran's SAVAK, South Korea's KCIA, Chile's DINA, the Greek CIA subsidiary under the fascist colonels—all noted for their ruthlessness, brutality and venality) have been installed with U.S. assistance; a minor aspect of their efforts is intimidation and control of residents in the United States, tolerated by the U.S. government in part to ensure that CIA agents will not be harassed in the parent country. There have been a number of

important books reviewing a range of CIA activities, among them Agee, *op. cit.*; Victor Marchetti and John D. Marks, *The CIA and the Cult of Intelligence*, Knopf, 1974; Howard Frazier, ed., *Uncloaking the CIA*, Free Press, 1978; *The Pike Report*, Spokesman, 1977, and the secret report of the House Select Committee on Intelligence headed by Congressman Otis Pike, published in the *Village Voice* (16,23 February 1976). For a brief summary of CIA activities, see "CIA's Covert Operations vs. Human Rights," Center for National Security Studies, 122 Maryland Avenue, N.E., Washington, D.C.

33. See especially Langguth, *op. cit.*, pp. 99-100; Black, *op. cit.*, pp. 39-41.

34. Black, *op. cit.*, pp. 100-107.

35. J. Levinson and J. de Onis, *The Alliance That Lost Its Way*, Quadrangle, 1970, p. 89.

36. "Helms Tells of Using Top U.S. Businessmen," *Washington Post* (11 March 1974). A discussion of Ashland Oil's report on corporate payments noted that $98,968 of CIA payments to Ashland wound up in the company's own slush funds: "One speculation was that the money was CIA salary for its agents using overseas Ashland jobs as a cover." "What Ashland Oil said about itself," *Business Week*, 12 July 1975.

37. Black, *op. cit.*, p. 87.

38. The latter case is an interesting one. While described by the compliant U.S. press as "Cuban subversion," following the government's lead, the secret arms cache in Venezuela is regarded with some skepticism by former CIA agent Joseph Smith, in a book written to support the CIA after Agee's critical study had appeared (Joseph Smith, *Portrait of a Cold Warrior*, Putnam, 1976, p. 382). Smith believes that the cache may have been a CIA job to meet the requirements of John F. Kennedy's anti-Castro crusade, which he was pressuring to make into a Latin American cause just before his assassination.

Arthur M. Schlesinger described the "great cache of weapons" found in Venezuela as "unquestionably Cuban in origin and provenance, secreted for terrorists at a point along the Caribbean coast," sure proof of the "central threat" posed by Castro to freedom in the Americas. U.S. terrorism aimed at Cuba is not discussed. *A Thousand Days*, Houghton Mifflin, 1965; Fawcett reprinting, 1967, pp. 713-14.

39. *American Banker*, 28 November 1975, p. 13. For another banker's expression of delight in the Marcos suspension of political democracy in the Philippines, see chapter 4, p. 238.

40. "Philippines: A government that needs U.S. business," *Business Week*, 4 November 1972.

41. "Marginalization" is a term used extensively in Church documents in Latin America to describe the condition of the vast majority of the population, but neither the term nor its content has yet penetrated the Judeo-Christian conscience or the media of North America. In the terminology of economics, the concept can be expressed as follows: in the social welfare function of the subfascist leadership, the lowest 90% of the population does not appear as a maximand (i.e., a value to the maximized). On the contrary, the underlying population—Veblen's suggestive phrase—appears in the economic calculations of this elite as a cost and threat.

42. International Movement of Catholic Intellectuals and Professionals, "Voice From Northeastern Brazil to III Conference of Bishops," Mexico, November 1977, reprinted in *LADOC*, May-June 1978, p. 15.

43. See Eduardo Galeano, "The De-Nationalization of Brazilian Industry," *Monthly Review*, December 1969.
44. *Latin American Economic Report*, January 1976, p. 9.
45. U.S. investment in Brazil grew from $323 million in 1946 to about $2.5 billion in 1972, although at the latter date it was only one-third of all foreign capital invested there. See Richard S. Newfarmer and Willard F. Mueller, *Multinational Corporations in Brazil and Mexico: Structural Sources of Economic and Noneconomic Power*, Report to the Subcommittee on Multinational Corporations of the Senate Committee on Foreign Relations, 94th Congress, 1st Session, August 1975, p. 148.
46. Henry Kamm, "Philippine Democracy, an American Legacy, Has Crumbled," *New York Times* (1 March 1977). What "crumbled" was, in any event, a short-lived facade, constantly manipulated by the U.S. (cf. Smith, *op. cit.*) and meaningless for most of the population. (See chapter 4, section 3.)
47. Bernard Wideman, "Dominating The Pineapple Trade," *Far Eastern Economic Review*, 8 July 1974; also, for Bataan, interviews by AFSC staff.
48. Shelton H. Davis, *Victims of the Miracle*, Cambridge, 1977, chapter 8; also the two Church documents of 1973, "Marginalization of a People" and "I Have Heard the Cry of My People."
49. Stephen Sansweet, "Captive Workers: Prisoners in Colombia Are Working for Units of U.S. Multinationals," *Wall Street Journal* (20 May 1975).
50. "The Marginalization of a People, The Cry of the Churches," 6 May 1973. This document was not allowed to circulate in Brazil, and the lay publisher and several of his co-workers were arrested, charged, and heavily fined for printing this "subversive" document. It has received negligible attention in the U.S. as well, by self-censorship rather than direct censorship as in Brazil.
51. 9 August 1976.
52. Black, *op. cit.*, pp. 239-240.
53. 28 April 1975.
54. David Felix, "Economic Development: Takeoffs Into Unsustained Growth," *Social Research*, Summer 1969, p. 267.
55. "I Have Heard the Cry of My People," a powerful statement signed by 18 Catholic bishops of Northeast Brazil, 6 May 1973, discussed widely abroad, but again, not in the United States.
56. Marvine Howe, "Brazil's Inflation Said to Halve Real Income of Poor in Decade," *New York Times* (14 December 1974).
57. Black, *op. cit.*, pp. 241, 246.
58. Stanford, 1973, p. vii.
59. *Ibid.*, pp. 178-79.
60. *Ibid.*, pp. 165, 169, 170.
61. Quoted in Gabriel Kolko, *The Politics of War*, Random House, 1970, p. 214.
62. *Ibid.*, p. 229.
63. *Ibid.*, p. 230.
64. "By American choice" in a very literal sense: According to General Khanh, "On January, 1964 Wilson [his U.S. advisor] told me a coup d'etat was planned in Saigon and that I was to become President.... On 8 February 1964 I took over as Premier." Interview with the German magazine *Stern*, reprinted in *Los Angeles New Advocate* (1-15 April 1972).

It is interesting to contrast the official disavowals of any "arrogant" attempts to influence client governments, with the matter-of-fact assumption by U.S. officials that *they* determine who rules in these client states, as disclosed in internal governmental documents. General Taylor, in a briefing of 27 November 1964, for example, speaks with assurance about our "establishing some reasonably satisfactory government" in South Vietnam; and that if not satisfied with the way things are going, "we could try again with another civilian government....Another alternative would be to *invite back* a military dictatorship on the model of that headed of late by General Khanh." (*Pentagon Papers*, Gravel Edition, III, p. 669; emphasis added.)

Taylor, in fact, expressed his contempt for his Vietnamese puppets quite openly on the public record as well. Thus, he describes Diem's "unexpected resistance" to the U.S. demand for direct participation in civil administration, and adds: "On the chance that Diem might continue to be intransigent, the old search for a possible replacement for him was resumed in State." Later he speaks of "the impetuosity of Diem's American critics and our opposition to ousting him without a replacement in sight." When General Khanh began to lose his shaky political base, "the question was: If not Khanh, who? This time there was again the possibility that 'Big' Minh might do. He had been behaving quite well...." Taylor's attitudes are perhaps no more astonishing than the fact that he is willing to voice them in public. See *Swords and Plowshares*, Norton, 1972, pp. 248, 294, 322.

65. *New York Herald Tribune* (3 February 1964). The evidence available suggests that Khanh's exit was as much a matter of internal Vietnamese politics as his rise to power. While he was technically removed by the Vietnamese generals and shipped out to "indefinite exile," this followed a message to the generals from Ambassador Taylor "that the U.S. government had lost confidence in Khanh and could not work with him" in accordance with his plans, which seemed to the U.S. mission to amount "to a dangerous Khanh-Buddhist alliance which might eventually lead to an unfriendly government with which we could not work" (Taylor, *op. cit.*, pp. 334f.).

66. *Civilian Casualty and Refugee Problems in South Vietnam*, Findings and Recommendations, Subcommittee on Refugees, Senate Judiciary Committee, U.S. Senate, 90th Congress, 2nd Session, 9 May 1969, p. 36.

67. See Noam Chomsky and Edward S. Herman, "Saigon's Corruption Crisis: The Search for an Honest Quisling," *Ramparts*, December 1974-January 1975.

68. "Philippines: A government that needs U.S. business," *Business Week*, 4 November 1972.

69. See the three part series in the *New York Times* by Fox Butterfield, "Power of Philippine Ruler Growing," (1 January 1977); "Marcos Facing Criticism May End $1 Billion Westinghouse Contract," (14 January 1977); "Manila Inner Circle Gains Under Marcos," (15 January 1977). (See chapter 4, section 3.)

70. Daniel Kirk, "The Bold Words of Kim," *New York Times Magazine* (7 January 1973), p. 56.

71. "Yes, yes, it's graft. But don't fight." *New York Times* (24 February 1977).

72. "Exporting Military-Economic Development—America and the Overthrow of Sukarno, 1965-67," in Malcolm Caldwell, ed., *Ten Years' Military Terror in Indonesia*, Spokesman, 1975, p. 219.

73. Michael T. Kaufman, "Zaire: A Mobutu Fiefdom Where Fortunes Shift Quickly," *New York Times* (3 June 1978).

74. John Stockwell, former chief of the CIA Angola Task Force, pointed out in his letter of resignation from the CIA that the decision of the Angolan

government to permit "Zairian exiles to invade the Shaba province of Zaire" could hardly have been a surprise: "I myself warned the Interagency Working Group in October, 1975 that the Zairian invasion of northern Angola would be answered by the introduction of large numbers of Cuban troops...and would invite an eventual retaliatory invasion of Zaire from Angola" *Washington Post* (10 April 1977). The background was conveniently forgotten when the predicted retaliation took place. Carter's attempt to make the Cubans the villains of the piece was inept and dishonest demagoguery, reminiscent of Johnson's effort to have the U.S. embassy in Santo Domingo scout up some names of Communists to provide a rationale for the U.S. invasion. As for Angola itself, Stockwell states that the United States moved into Angola before the USSR and intervened steadily (and ineptly) thereafter. *In Search of Enemies*, pp. 66-67 and passim. Stockwell also notes that subsequent Cuban intervention was consistent with its ideology and international stance, while ours, as was so often the case, "was a direct contradiction of our public policies [more accurately, the proclaimed public policies], making it essential that we keep the American public [and also the Congress] from knowing the truth" (p. 171).

75. Stockwell, *op. cit.*, p. 246.

76. According to Eric Pace, "In Iran, It's Alms to the Poor and the Rich," *New York Times* (26 September 1976), section F.

77. See Robert Graham, "The Pahlavi Foundation," *Nation*, 9 December 1978.

78. See Fred Cook, "The Billion Dollar Mystery," *Nation*, 12 April 1965.

79. Reportedly helped along by the display in front of the Royal Court, by the wife of the Commander-in-Chief of the Royal Navy, of a diamond valued at more than a million dollars. See Eric Rouleau, "Iran—Myths and Realities," *Le Monde* (3-4 October 1976).

80. *Ibid.*

81. Flora Lewis, "Shah of Iran Forbids Royal Family To Make Profits on Business Deals," *New York Times* (4 July 1978).

82. Black, *op. cit.*, pp. 86-90.

83. This was also true in Guatemala, Iran, Brazil, Chile, the Dominican Republic, Zaire, Indonesia, and elsewhere.

84. Malcolm Browne, *The New Face of War,* Bobbs-Merrill, 1965, p. 211. See further below, chapter 5.

85. This is the effective meaning of Communism for the neo-fascist elites that the United States has sponsored in Latin America and elsewhere. (See below, chapter 4, section 5.1.)

86. Entirely outside of the club is, of course, the majority of the population, terrorized into passivity in the interest of "the club elite," and clearly irrelevant except as a cheap labor force or threat to "stability."

87. Stephen Sansweet and William Blundell, "On the Give: For U.S. Firms Abroad Bribery Can Often Be Routine Business Cost," *Wall Street Journal* (9 May 1975).

88. The Brazilian military began to feed on itself in the 1970s. "Twenty percent of the field officers had been removed from their posts for ideological deviation by 1973, and in 1975 eleven army officers were arrested for 'studying literature from the Portuguese Armed Forces Movement'." Black, *op. cit.*, p. 247.

89. Human slavery also lasted quite a long time in the Western democracies, not to speak of vicious exploitation, imported cheap labor, and other admirable

practices, which still are prevalent.

90. William McNeill, *The Rise of the West*, Chicago, 1963, pp. 256-57.

91. *Security Agreements and Commitments Abroad.* Report to the Senate Foreign Relations Committee, 21 December 1970, p. 3.

92. The United States was, in fact, bombing the only major rail connection between southwestern China and the rest of China, which happened to pass through Vietnam near Hanoi. The dispatch of Chinese technicians to help restore rail service was offered in the U.S. press as another example of Chinese aggressiveness. As we now know, official U.S. policy enunciated in 1954 involved a readiness to use force against China if China was regarded by the U.S. leadership as the "external source" of local subversion or rebellion in Southeast Asia. For discussion of the relevant documents, see Chomsky, *For Reasons of State*, Pantheon, 1973, p. 100f.

93. See note 22 above.

94. Drew Fethersten and John Cummings, "Canadian Says U.S. Paid Him $5,000 to Infect Cuban Poultry," *Washington Post (Newsday)* (21 March 1977), p. A18; this report states that "The major details of the Canadian's story have been confirmed by sources within and outside the American intelligence community." Fethersten and Cummings, "CIA tied to Cuba's '71 pig fever outbreak," *Boston Globe (Newsday)* (9 January 1977): "With at least the tacit backing of Central Intelligence Agency officials, operatives linked to anti-Castro terrorists introduced African swine fever virus into Cuba in 1971. Six weeks later an outbreak of the disease forced the slaughter of 500,000 pigs to prevent a nationwide animal epidemic." This "was the first and only time the disease has hit the Western Hemisphere" and "was labeled the 'most alarming event' of 1971 by the United Nations Food and Agricultural Organization." All production of pork came to a halt for several months. "A U.S. intelligence source said in an interview that he was given the virus in a sealed, unmarked container" at Ft. Gulick, the U.S. Army and CIA base in the Panama Canal Zone. See also UPI, "CIA reportedly tried to dry up Cuban crop," *Boston Globe* (27 June 1976), reporting the allegation by a former Pentagon researcher that the CIA and the Pentagon seeded clouds "to try to dry up the Cuban sugar crop in 1969 and 1970" (denied by the Pentagon; cf. *Globe*, 28 June 1976). On the background, see Taylor Branch and George Crile III, "The Kennedy Vendetta, How the CIA waged a silent war against Cuba," *Harper's*, August 1975, reporting attempts as late as 1964 by the CIA, under the original orders of President Kennedy, to land weapons and destroy oil refineries, railroad bridges, sugar mills and other targets, many successfully attacked.

95. David Binder, "Carter Says Cubans May Leave Angola, Is Receptive on Ties," *New York Times* (17 February 1977).

96. It is, for example, no surprise that the *Washington Post* (24 February 1978) can feature (in a special box) a letter to the editor from a reader who writes:

> I wasn't all that bothered when it turned out that the CIA had tried to poison Lumumba's toothpaste and contaminate Castro's diving suit with itching powder. The cold war always seemed to be a humorless comedy of errors anyway...[But I]...find it disconcerting to read that within the space of several weeks the CIA has published two contradictory estimates of Saudi Arabia's capacity to produce oil.

97. For discussion of media handling of the Cambodia issue, and the factual context, see Volume II, chapter 6.

98. See the discussion of East Timor in chapter 3, section 5.4.
99. See especially the discussion below of the press treatment of human rights issues in Indonesia, Thailand, and the numerous subfascist clients of the U.S. in Latin America in chapters 3 and 4. We turn to the media treatment of the Communist states in Volume II.
100. Terror and repression are real enough, but the terms, in Free World jargon, are typically used to include, for example, the suffering of those who are starving in regions where farming is next to impossible because draught animals have been killed by bombing, the land is littered with lethal unexploded ordnance and cratered by saturation bombing, and much of the labor force has been killed, injured or disabled by malnutrition and disease. Particularly in the case of Cambodia, the U.S. bombing from 1969, the U.S.-ARVN invasion of 1970, and the ferocious bombing of 1973, at a time when it was surely understood in Washington that the war in Cambodia was lost, have large-scale (and predicted) effects with regard to starvation, disease, and retribution killings. (See Volume II, chapter 6, for details.)
101. If they deviate ever so slightly, they face serious problems. To cite one example, consider *Business Week*'s report (30 August 1976) that the *New York Times* has "slid precipitously to the left and has become stridently antibusiness in tone, ignoring the fact that the *Times* itself is a business—and one with very serious problems" (the concept of the *Times* sliding to the left, precipitously or even perceptibly, is so ludicrous as to suggest that irony was intended until one realizes how remarkably skewed the general spectrum of opinion is in the United States as compared with other industrial democracies). One example of "the paper's political swing to the left" was an editorial recommending an increase in taxes on business to help overcome the city's financial problems. " 'Something like that,' muses a Wall Street analyst, 'could put the *Times* right out of business'." How? An accompanying remark supplies part of the answer: "Following a *Times* series on medical incompetence," a magazine run by the parent company "lost $500,000 in pharmaceutical advertising." In short, the *Times* had better remember that it too is a business. On the impact of these warnings, see James Aronson, "The *Times* is a-changing," *In These Times,* 2 March 1977. Such overt pressures to prevent even the most minuscule departure from right-wing orthodoxy are rare, because the necessity rarely arises; but the threat is ever-present. For similar reasons,corporate managers need not be admonished that their role is to maximize profits.
102. Eric Barnouw, *The Sponsor,* Oxford, 1978, pp. 127, 119.
103. "Where are you Mr. Chairman," *Chief Executive Magazine,* July-September 1977.
104. Barnouw describes the commercial failure of an NBC weekly on ecology, "In Which We Live," launched in May 1970 to depict various environmental hazards. It was abruptly ended the following month, having failed to attract much advertising, although ecology was then a hot topic for shows and commercials. Barnouw comments: "Since their [commercials and companies] message was one of reassurance, they apparently did not regard an NBC documentary series focusing on problems as a suitable vehicle" (*op. cit.*, p. 135).
105. See Edward J. Epstein, *News From Nowhere,* Random House, 1973, pp. 72-75.
106. See chapter 3, section 4.4.
107. Thus Anthony Lewis joins with William Buckley in deploring the nastiness

of the Soviets, the need to bring pressure on them, the foolishness of Andrew Young in drawing comparisons to the United States, etc. Liberals who join the chorus of protest over the Shcharansky-Ginzburg trials do not, however, note how curious it is to focus such unique attention on the plight of Russian dissidents in a world where literally thousands are incarcerated, tortured, or assassinated without even the mockery of a trial in the U.S. client states. Comparisons of the Shcharansky trial with that of David Truong and Ronald Humphries have been sparse indeed considering the important similarities between them. Another similar case that was ignored—or worse—is that of Sami Esmail, a U.S. citizen who had the temerity to try to visit his dying father in Ramallah in the occupied West Bank. He was arrested by Israeli police and during "interrogation" produced a "confession" (under duress, he alleges). On the basis of this "confession," he was sentenced to 15 months in prison just prior to the Shcharansky-Ginzburg trials that aroused such indignation in the U.S. The crime extracted from him by the Israeli interrogators was to have visited Libya and taken part in "terrorist training" and to have been a member of an Arab guerrilla organization. He was also charged with having worked with Palestinian groups in the United States. No act of any kind was alleged. The court president "said the sentence had to be sufficient to act as a deterrent in view of attempts by Palestinian organizations to recruit supporters on American campuses" (*New York Times* 13 June 1978). None of this arouses any protest in the U.S. mainstream, where all sorts of punitive actions are urged against the Soviets but not against the recipient of about half of total U.S. military aid. Rather, it elicits the kind of apologetics that one recalls from the worst days of Stalinism; cf. Monroe H. Freedman and Alan M. Dershowitz, *New York Times* (2 June 1978)—neatly timed to appear just before the conviction. Worse yet, *New York Times* editorialists conclude on the authority of these apologists that the trial was "eminently fair" (11 June 1978); and in a spirit of collegiality, the *Washington Post* reported on May 29 that the two law professors "witnessed the trial and thought it was fair," sure proof, since they are "well-known for their civil libertarian views" (in fact, Dershowitz in particular is well-known for his scandalous and often libelous attacks on political prisoners in Israel and on Israeli civil libertarians, including quite outrageous falsehoods; but it is true that he is a civil libertarian on domestic issues, exactly as was true of his Stalinist counterparts). Not content with a "news report," the *Post* also devoted an editorial to the conclusions of the two "civil libertarians" (5 June 1978), and another news story on June 8 referring to the Freedman-Dershowitz report, which was hailed by the Israeli press as well. The *Post* cites a *Jerusalem Post* editorial: "a fuller vindication of Israel's system of justice...would be hard to imagine."

The fact that Esmail "confessed" should come as no surprise. Observers have noted a remarkably high rate of confessions by Arab prisoners under interrogation. Asked to explain this curious fact, Israeli Supreme Court Justice Moshe Etzioni said in London: "The Arabs in any case—if they are arrested—do not take much time before they confess. It's part of their nature" (*Amnesty International Newsletter*, September 1977). Nothing here to disturb well-known civil libertarians.

108. For some discussion of the propagandistic use of this gambit, see chapter 5, section 2. See also Edward S. Herman, *Atrocities in Vietnam*, Pilgrim, 1970, chapter 4; and Tran Van Dinh, "Fear of a Bloodbath," *New Republic*, 6 December 1969.

109. For example, John P. Roche, a long-time liberal apologist for U.S. aggression in Indochina, now writes: "I only regret the government of the United States repudiated its objectives and created the present Asian Auschwitz in Indochina." The "objectives" to which he is referring are explicitly those of 1967, i.e., to maintain U.S. control over South Vietnam (or in official translation: the "independence" of South Vietnam). Thus Roche is asserting that South Vietnam is an "Asian Auschwitz." The facts are as relevant to this distinguished thinker, now acting dean of the Fletcher School of Law and Diplomacy of Tufts University, as they have always been in the past.

The occasion for Roche's remarks was the disclosure by Richard Dudman that Roche had connived with Lyndon Johnson in 1967 to organize an allegedly independent prestigious pro-war group, with the White House role hidden. This chicanery not only served their political purposes, but also allowed the acting dean of the School of Law and Diplomacy to defraud the government by obtaining some $200,000 in tax-deductible contributions on the pretense that the purpose of the group that was secretly organized and sponsored by the government was "to make inquiry into the nonpartisan fundamentals of American foreign policy and to conduct educational activities in connection therewith; and to promote and contribute to a broad-based, nonpartisan public debate about Vietnam and related matters"—which would, as secret documents disclose, include only people who "share the same fundamental [pro-war] outlook." The White House lied outright about its role. Roche has no comment on any of this, except to say that the committee "was a first-rate outfit organized in a good cause," namely, to prevent the Asian Auschwitz which has since been "created by the United States in South Vietnam. *Nation*, 23 December 1978.

110. "Signing 100,000 Death Warrants," *Wall Street Journal* (26 March 1975). Hosmer wrote that "one could expect a 'bloodbath' of very large proportions," with hardly fewer than 100,000 executions and possibly many more if the Vietcong "fostered" the kind of grass roots violence characteristic of the North Vietnamese land reform. Stephen P. Hosmer, *Viet Cong Repression and Its Implications for the Future* (Rand), 1970, pp. 117, 122. The forecast was erroneous, as was the suggestion that the DRV "fostered" grass roots violence in the land reform period (see chapter 5, section 2.2). Grass roots violence was indeed fostered in Indonesia and Chile; it is interesting to see how often propagandists transfer to the enemy the uglier features of their own state.

111. Max Lerner, "flaps and rights," *New York Post* (4 February 1977).

112. For discussion of these matters see N. Chomsky, *American Power and the New Mandarins*, Pantheon, 1969; *For Reasons of State*, Pantheon, 1973; *"Human Rights" and American Foreign Policy*, Spokesman, 1978. During the late 1960s, under the impact of the peace movement and the student movement, ideological controls were somewhat relaxed, but as these pressures waned, they are being reinstituted, though not quite with the earlier effectiveness, since the consequences of the slightly greater openness of the intervening period are difficult to erase completely.

113. See Thomas C. Cochran, *Business in American Life: a History,* McGraw-Hill, 1972, especially chapter 19. Also see Alex Carey and Trudy Korber, *Propaganda and Democracy in America*, forthcoming. On the educational system, see Joel H. Spring, *Education and the Rise of the Corporate State*, Beacon, 1972.

3 Benign Terror

1. See chapter 1, note 53.
2. See chapter 5, sections 1.1, 2.1.
3. *Fiscal Year 1970 AID Report to the Ambassador*, p. 35.
4. *New York Times* (20 December 1967).
5. To use the classic language of Ithiel de Sola Pool on the requirements for the maintenance of order on a world-wide scale, in "The Public and the Polity," (in Pool, ed.), *Contemporary Political Science: Toward Empirical Theory*, McGraw Hill, 1967, p. 26.
6. "Stability" is used almost invariably by U.S. officials in an Orwellian sense, synonymous with a set of economic and political arrangements satisfactory to U.S. imperial interests. Thus for the period 1949-69 Thailand represented "stability," China a source of "instability".
7. In the case of Brazil, for example, "A hard policy of domestic repression has apoliticized national life making it practically impossible for the lower classes to become socially conscious of their plight or to organize for change." Agostino Bono, "Unjolly Green Giant," *Commonweal*, 2 February 1973. They need change desperately, however. See "Torture, murder, hunger in Brazil," *The Guardian* (Manchester) (19 May 1973).
8. Walter Laqueur, *Terrorism*, Little, Brown, 1977, p. 7.
9. *Ibid.* pp. 183-84.
10. We rely here on the account by A.J. Langguth, *Hidden Terrors*, Pantheon, 1978, chapter 6. Quotes are from Langguth.
11. J. Bowyer Bell, "Terrorist scripts and live-action spectaculars," *Columbia Journalism Review*, May-June 1978.
12. J. Anthony Lukas, *Don't Shoot—We Are Your Children!*, Random House, 1971.
13. Apologetics for torture among the U.S. intelligentsia are, of course, already implicit in their support and cover-up for the torture regimes in the U.S. sphere of influence; we refer here to explicit justification for torture.
14. One might inquire into the question how the state that is so abjectly served by the *New Republic* has chosen to answer this question, in its own internal practice. Its Prime Minister is the former leader of a terrorist group that was responsible for a long series of atrocities: bombs in Arab market places, blowing up buildings, massacres by armed thugs in villages, etc. The Speaker of the Knesset was a commander of the group that assassinated UN Mediator Folke Bernadotte among other atrocities. The recently appointed Secretary-General of the Jewish Agency is a man who murdered several dozen Arab civilians under guard in an undefended Lebanese village during the land-clearing operations of October 1948 — he was sentenced to 7 years in prison but quickly amnestied, then granted a second amnesty which "denies the punishment and the charge as well," and later granted a lawyer's license by the Israeli Legal Council on grounds that his act carried "no stigma." *Al-Hamishmar* (3 March 1978).
15. Seth Kaplan, "Torture Tempest," *New Republic*, 23 July 1977. On the

London Sunday Times report, see chapter 2, note 15; see also chapter 2, note 107.
16. There are exceptions. For the early stages, see particularly Yehoshua Porath, *The Palestinian Arab National Movement: 1929-1939*, Frank Cass, 1977, the second volume of an outstanding study by an Israeli scholar that discusses the sources of the 1936-39 rebellion, largely involving poorer sectors in regions of heavy Jewish colonization, after all other measures for redress of grievances had failed. See also David Hirst, *The Gun and the Olive Branch*, Harcourt, Barce, Jovanovich, 1977; Kenneth Love, *Suez: The Twice-Fought War*, McGraw-Hill, 1969.
17. "The Argentine situation concerning human rights," September 1978.
18. Jeffrey A. Tannenbaum, "The Terrorists: For World's Alienated, Violence Often Reaps Political Recognition," *Wall Street Journal* (4 January 1977).
19. See "Rightist Terror Stirs Argentina," 29 August 1976, and "Argentina's Terror: Army Is Ahead," 2 January 1977. (See also chapter 4, section 5.)
20. T.D. Allman, *Far Eastern Economic Review*, 7 May 1970.
21. Charles Meyer, *Derrière le souirire Khmer*, Plon, 1971, p. 405. Meyer, a long-time French resident of Cambodia and advisor to Sihanouk, remained for a time after the March 1970 coup. His book was never published in the United States, nor was it reviewed, in striking contrast to the treatment of French studies of Cambodian atrocities. (See Volume II, chapter 6.)
22. The 1969 bombings were kept "secret" in the United States until mid-1973 in part through the complicity of the press. (See Volume II, chapter 6.) But they were known, at least to a degree. Cf. Chomsky, *At War with Asia*, Pantheon, 1970, pp. 122-23.
23. Nixon Press Conference, 12 November 1971, *New York Times* (13 November 1971).
24. See Volume II, chapter 6.
25. *Ibid.*
26. The "aggression from the North" thesis of the Johnson administration, for example, was devastated quickly by analyses of the White Paper of 1965, two of the best being I.F. Stone, "A Reply to the White Paper," *I.F. Stone's Weekly* (8 March 1965), and the editors of *The New Republic*, "White Paper on Vietnam" (13 March 1965). None of these made a dent on the typical editorial, news article, column, or presentation of Administration handouts, however. Even after the *Pentagon Papers* release, which vindicated the hardest of hard-line dove analyses of aggression (locating it firmly in Washington, D.C.), the mythical truth held firm. (See chapter 5; and also Volume II, chapter 1.)
27. The Hue massacre, which was subject to early and effective challenge as a propaganda fabrication, was almost uniformly portrayed in the mass media as firmly established truth. The better papers would *occasionally* allow critics of the myth a few paragraphs of space for rebuttal, but on pages reserved for opinion. The government-approved version, in contrast, was presented on pages devoted to "news," i.e., "fact." (See chapter 5, section 2.3.)
28. Sidney Hook, "The Knight of the Double Standard," *The Humanist* (January 1971).
29. In reviewing the impact of the war, Wendell S. Merrick and James N. Wallace concede that "a great many Vietnamese suffered terribly," but note judiciously that "these effects of war would have occurred with or without Americans being here." *U.S. News and World Report* (2 April 1973).

30. William F. Buckley, Jr. *Boston Globe* (23 April 1973).
31. See Vietnam Veterans Against the War, eds., *Winter Soldier Investigation*, Beacon Press, 1972; *The Dellums Committee Hearing on War Crimes in Vietnam*, Vintage, 1972; James S. Kunen, *Standard Operating Procedure*, Avon, 1971; D. Thorne and G. Butler, eds., *The New Soldier*, Collier, 1971; James Duffett, ed., *Against the Crime of Silence, Proceedings of the Russell International War Crimes Tribunal*, O'Hare Books, 1968.
32. *Far Eastern Economic Review*, 26 March 1973. On torture in the Saigon prisons, see Holmes Brown and Don Luce, *Hostages of War*, Indochina Mobile Education Project, 1973. (See chapter 5, section 1.)
33. *New York Times* editorial (8 April 1973). The *New York Times* meanwhile blandly reported U.S. violations of the Geneva Conventions without notice or comment. (See chapter 1, note 85.)
34. On the interesting concept of "internal aggression," which refers to activities by local forces against governments placed in power by the United States and its allies, see Noam Chomsky, *For Reasons of State*, Pantheon, 1973, pp. 114ff.
35. Quoted in Jan K. Black, *United States Penetration of Brazil*, University of Pennsylvania, 1977, p. 143.
36. Frederick Nunn, "Military Professionalism and Professional Militarism in Brazil, 1870-1970," *Journal of Latin American Studies*, vol. 4, n. 1 (1972), quoted in Black, *op. cit.*, p. 194. On this issue, see further Black, pp. 179-199.
37. "The Marginalization of A People, The Cry of the Churches," signed by Six Brazilian Church Bishops and Archbishops, 6 May 1973. IDOC, *International Documentation*, no. 65, p. 59.
38. Bishop Dom Pedro Casaldaliga, "The Gospel Is My Weapon," 12 October 1975, *Latin America Press* (6 November 1975).
39. "I Have Heard the Cry of my People," a statement signed by 18 Catholic religious leaders of Northeast Brazil, 6 May 1973, IDOC translation and reprint, p. 43.
40. E. Bradford Burns, "Brazil: The Imitative Society," *The Nation*, 10 July 1972, quoted in Black, *op. cit.*, p. 261.
41. Konrad Kellen, "1971 and Beyond: The View From Hanoi," Rand Corporation (June 1971), pp. 14-15.
42. The flavor of "our" South Vietnam may be captured, however, in the finding by one former AID employee: "I have personally witnessed poor urban people literally quaking with fear when I questioned them about the activity of the secret police in a post election campaign. One poor fisherman in Da Nang, animated and talkative in complaining about economic conditions, clammed up in near terror when queried about the police...." Theodore Jacqueney, Hearings before Subcommittee of House Committee on Government Operations, *U.S. Assistance Programs in Vietnam* (July-August 1971), p. 251.
43. Cf. *For Reasons of State*, p. 96.
44. Bernard Fall, *Street Without Joy*, Stackpole, 1967, p. 373. Fall is often regarded as an opponent of the U.S. intervention in Vietnam. This is inaccurate. He was a bitter anti-Communist and a strong supporter of the goals of the U.S. intervention, though he was later to be appalled at the methods used, and feared that Vietnam would not survive this terroristic onslaught. The simple answer he gives in the text fails to come to grips with *why* the West systematically gravitated to regimes without popular support.

45. John P. Lewis, *New York Times*, Op-Ed, (9 December 1971).
46. *New York Times* (9 January 1972).
47. On this matter see the illuminating analysis by Eqbal Ahmad, "Notes on South Asia in Crisis," *Bulletin of the Concerned Asian Scholars* (1972), vol. 4, no. 1.
48. "Purely internal" is also used by U.S. officials in an Orwellian sense, meaning not so threatening to our perceived interests as to demand intervention. Thus the Pakistan instance, or the case of Thailand where "the general tendency of most Americans [sic] was to declare that the ruthless suppression of political opposition by the military leaders [who, as we will see, were a product and on the payroll of the U.S.] was a purely internal affair." Frank C. Darling, *Thailand and the United States,* Public Affairs Press, 1965, p. 129; for some years Darling was a CIA analyst specializing in Southeast Asia, Thailand in particular. In contrast, the NLF's "aggression" in South Vietnam was clearly an "external affair".
49. *New York Times* (9 January 1972).
50. The quotation, from a government official who followed internal cable reports from Burundi, is taken from Michael Bowen, Gary Freedman, Kay Miller and Roger Morris, *Passing By, The United States and Genocide in Burundi,* 1972, Carnegie Endowment for International Peace (undated), p. 5. This document is referred to hereafter as *Passing By*. The Hutu constituted 85 percent of the population of Burundi, but have been ruled by the fourteen percent Tutsi minority since the 16th century.
51. Quoted from *Passing By*, p. 6.
52. On 14 July 1973 the *New York Times* brought up the subject again in a front page article by Charles Mohr entitled "Exiles Keeping Strife in Burundi Alive." As suggested by the title itself, the article starts out with, and features heavily, the subversive activities of "militant Hutu refugees" allegedly trying to overthrow "the predominantly Tutsi Government." A "major factor" in the Burundi tragedy is the "passionately militant Hutu students in exile," who have disturbed the "relative quiet in recent days after a serious out-break of incidents [sic] in mid-May in which, it is said, thousands of Hutus were slain." Later in the article Mohr discussed further the number of Hutus killed, but finds the matter inconclusive (Tutsis were killed also), and passes on quickly to the disruptive behavior of the Hutu students and refugees. According to the Carnegie study the Burundi government itself admitted to 80,000 casualties, and "the State Department had authoritative intelligence that the death toll in Burundi was two to three times that number." *Op. cit.*, p. 22.
53. See the 23 June 1972 hearings on the confirmation of Robert L. Yost, excerpted in *Passing By*, pp. 35-37.
54. *Ibid.*, p. 27.
55. *Ibid.*, pp. 13-17.
56. *Ibid.*, pp. 17-19, 31-33.
57. *Ibid.*, p. 24.
58. *Ibid.*, p. 26.
59. In Richard Arens, ed., *Genocide in Paraguay*, Temple University Press, 1976. Unless otherwise indicated, references below (through note 67) are to articles in this collection.
60. The leading Paraguayan specialist on the Indians, Professor Miguel Chase Sardi, who had worked courageously to defend them and make their plight

known, was imprisoned in December 1975, terminating the Indian aid project that he had headed. He and others arrested were tortured. Asked if the U.S. government could call a halt to the torture, the State Department responded that no steps could be taken.

61. The term "Guayakí," meaning something like "rabid rat," is used as a term of racist contempt for the Aché. See Mark Münzel's article in the Arens collection. The reservation to which the Aché have been driven to die is called the "National Guayaki Colony." It is, Wolf comments, not really a reservation or even a prison, but "an extermination camp."

62. Richard Arens, "Death Camps in Paraguay," *Inquiry*, 2 January 1978. This article was based on a personal visit to Paraguay by Arens in August and September 1977.

63. This Director of Indian Affairs was subsequently identified in eye-witness affidavits filed by Arens for the Aché in the UN as trafficking in female slaves — but although Arens addressed a UN Subcommittee on this subject on behalf of the British Anti-Slavery Society, the only media interest in the matter was in Western Europe.

64. Even an offer by Arens to underwrite the hospital costs of one dying child with a widespread cancer that had been ignored by reservation officials for 18 months could not prevent the child's removal from the hospital within a few days by the reservation authorities. See "Death Camps in Paraguay."

65. *Ibid.*

66. *Ibid.*

67. The curious role of the International League for Human Rights also deserves some comment. Though quite willing to organize press conferences on human rights violations attributed to enemies of the United States (e.g., Vietnam), the League has refused to do so in the case of the Paraguayan Indians. Richard Arens, a member of the League's board of directors, has exerted strenous but vain efforts to induce the League to overcome its reticence in this regard. The League ignored the condemnation of Paraguay for the mistreatment and enslavement of the Indians by the Inter-American Commission for Human Rights in June 1977, and while under Arens's prodding it requested and obtained a place on the UN agenda for consideration of abuse of the Indians, no publicity was given this development. Had the League pressed the issue prior to the last Congressional appropriations bill, Paraguay might have been deprived of aid. The State Department, however, supported the Paraguayan appropriations and in fact used League documents in support of its position. (We are indebted to Richard Arens for this information.) League press conferences on Vietnam also comport well with U.S. policy. It is perhaps non-coincidental that the State Department is usually represented at meetings of the board of the League and that its former Executive-Director, Roberta Cohen, is now an employee of the State Department.

The relations of the League to U.S. government policy deserve a closer study, in our view. It is striking, for example, to compare the way in which the League treats evidence concerning alleged repression and atrocities in Vietnam or Russia and statements by officials of these enemy regimes, with its treatment of the prime recipient of U.S. aid, Israel. For a detailed commentary on the latter topic, see "Noam Chomsky on International League for Human Rights: And Israeli Human Rights Violations," *Palestine Human Rights Bulletin*, no. 2, pp. 1-5, 30 August 1977. To cite only one instance, the International League disaffiliated its Israeli branch when the Israeli government attempted to take it over in an effort so clumsy that it was blocked by an Israeli Court that expressed extraordinary hostility to the Israeli affiliate. Despite repeated appeals, the League has refused to reverse this action, which is on a par with disaffiliation of a Russian branch on the sole grounds that it comes under state attack.

68. Amnesty International *Report on Torture*, 1974, p. 216.

69. *Human Rights Reports*, prepared by The Department of State, submitted to the Subcommittee on Foreign Assistance of the Committee on Foreign Relations, U.S. Senate, March 1977, Government Printing Office, Washington, 1977; *Country Reports on Human Rights Practices*, Report submitted to the Committee on International Relations, U.S. House of Representatives and Committee on Foreign Relations, U.S. Senate, by The Department of State, 3 February 1978, Government Printing Office, 1978.

70. Robert J. Smith and Bartomeu Melia, " Genocide of Aché-Guayaki?," *Survival International Supplement*, June 1978, p. 12.

71. Arens in his discussions with U.S. embassy personnel in Asuncion came away with the clear impression that the embassy staff saw Stroessner as a vital element of stability in South America and that there had been no change from the policies of past administrations in supporting Stroessner as a "friend".

72. Penny Lernoux, "Apartheid Sails West: White Africans in Latin America," *Nation*, 23 September 1978.

73. While these charges are common in Latin America, we know of no evidence to support them. The real problems are much deeper, relating to the missionary role, conscious or inadvertent, in preparing the ground for the kind of "assimilation" of the Indians that often leads to destructive or even genocidal consequences. See *Christian Mission for the Empire*, NACLA, December 1973, for discussion; and Søren Hvalkof and Peter Aaby, eds. *God is an American: The Work of the Summer Institute of Linguistics*, in preparation, for extensive study of this topic.

In an interview in the cited NACLA study, Doug Hostetter, formerly a Mennonite missionary in Vietnam, notes CIA efforts to use Wycliffe (SIL) missionaries, which were rebuffed, though he reports that missionaries often intentionally or casually gave information to the CIA ("An Insider's Story: Religious Agencies in Vietnam"). See Volume II, chapter 4 for some comment on the role of the church in Indochina.

74. See chapter 4, section 5. From the earliest stages of colonization, religion has served as a cloak for pillage, torture and massacre. See Hans Koning, *Columbus: His Enterprise*, Monthly Review Press, 1976.

75. Cited from *Translation*, October-December 1971, in Laurie Hart, "Story of the Wycliffe Translators: Pacifying the Last Frontiers," in *Christian Mission for the Empire.*

76. *Washington Post* (12 September 1978). Kraft is thinking specifically of Iran, where so far the "supersleuths" whose dangerous influence so worries Kraft have not prevented the country from virtually sinking into the sea under the weight of U.S. armaments, and where the application of "human rights principles" could not be discerned with an electron microscope. But it is never too early to issue a warning, reaffirmed, the same day, by the *Post* editorial.

77. Shelton H. Davis, *Victims of the Miracle*, Cambridge University Press, 1977, p. xi. Davis is an anthropologist who has taught in Brazil and done ethnographic

work elsewhere in Latin America, and was a founder of the documentation and information center INDIGENA which is concerned with native Americans.

78. One might add that attempts to seek protection for victims of torture evoke similar consequences — for the fortunate, trials rather than death squads. As we write, trials are beginning before a military court for nine civilians accused "of leaking information in 1969 on torture in Brazilian prisons." The information merits nine lines in the *Boston Globe* (1 October 1978). The Shcharansky-Ginzburg trials in the USSR, in contrast, were a major international incident only a few months earlier. (See chapter 1, section 9.)

79. Pp. 156-57, cited by Davis from the *Los Angeles Times* (5 April 1973).

80. For background, see Helen Hill, *The Timor Story*, Timor Information Service, 183 Gertrude Street, Fitzroy, Vic., 3065, Australia, second edition, undated, running through 1975. The story is carried forward in James S. Dunn, *East Timor — from Portuguese Colonialism to Indonesian Incorporation,* Parliament of Australia, the Parliamentary Library, Legislative Research Service, 14 September 1977; henceforth: *Dunn Report*. There is an illuminating study concentrating primarily on the crucial period before the Indonesian invasion by Jill Jolliffe: *East Timor: Nationalism and Colonialism*, University of Queensland Press (Australia), 1978; Prentice-Hall. Jolliffe was one of the few Western journalists in East Timor from September 1975 until December 2, when Australians were evacuated because of the impending Indonesian invasion. See also Richard W. Franke, *East Timor: The Hidden War*, East Timor Defense Committee, P.O.Box 251, Old Chelsea Station, New York, N.Y. 10010, second edition, December 1976; and *Decolonization*, publication of the United Nations Department of Political Affairs, Trusteeship and Decolonization, No. 7, August 1976, *Issue on East Timor*. For a rare if not unique review in the U.S. media, see Arnold S. Kohen, "Human Rights in Indonesia," *Nation*, 26 November 1977. See also *Indonesian Intervention in East Timor: A Chronology*, updated edition, 10 April 1977, East Timor Information and Research Project and Cornell East Timor Association, 410 Stewart Ave., Ithaca, N.Y. 14850. Important information and documents also appear in Marcel Roger, *Timor Oriental*, L'Harmattan, Paris, 1977.

See also the hearings of the Fraser subcommittee: *Human Rights in East Timor and the Question of the Use of U.S. Equipment by the Indonesian Armed Forces*, 23 March 1977—henceforth, *March Hearings*; *Human Rights in East Timor*, 28 June and 19 July 1977 — henceforth, *June-July Hearings; U.S. Policy on Human Rights and Military Assistance: Overview and Indonesia*, 15 February 1978 — henceforth, *February 1978 Hearings*. These were hearings before the Subcommittee on International Organizations of the Committee on International Relations, chaired by Rep. Donald M. Fraser, whose record throughout was consistently honorable, in marked contrast to most of his colleagues.

We are very much indebted to Kohen, Franke, Sue Nichterlein, Richard Tanter, and the information groups in the U.S. and Australia for access to material on East Timor. Their dedicated and futile efforts merely highlight the complicity of the media in the West, specifically the United States, in ongoing atrocities.

81. Shepard Forman, Professor of Anthropology at the University of Michigan, who lived with mountain people in Timor in 1973-74, *June-July Hearings*, p. 15.

82. *Ibid.*, pp. 18f. Corroborative testimony appears in the same hearings from Elizabeth Traube, professor at Wesleyan University, who spent 2 years in other

mountain areas of East Timor from 1972 to 1974.
83. *Ibid.*, p. 30.
84. *Decolonization*, p. 9, citing "observers" and UN and Australian studies. Much the same is reported quite generally. See the sources cited in note 80.
85. Robin Osborne, *Australian*, 26 February 1975, cited by Jolliffe, p. 90.
86. *Decolonization*, p. 10. Dunn notes that most of the FRETILIN leaders "remained devout practising Catholics"; he refers to the party as "populist Catholic" (*March Hearings*, p. 27). He also points out that "from the outset they were at pains to dissociate the party from communist ideology and movements" (*Dunn Report*, p. 26), a point stressed by all informed observers, relevant here only because of Indonesian claims to the contrary, commonly repeated in the U.S. press, as we will see.
87. *Decolonization*, p. 11. Again, this judgment seems unanimous apart from Indonesian propaganda.
88. Apologists have pointed out that collaboration with the Japanese was not untypical among Third World nationalists, but this claim, while accurate, is irrelevant here, given the Timorese resistance to the Japanese conquest and the massive Japanese atrocities. It is quite appropriate to describe Araújo as a collaborator in Japanese war crimes.
89. The Deputy Governor of this "Provisional Government," his immediate subordinate, was Lopes da Cruz, "the only UDT leader regarded as reliable by the Indonesians," who had in fact been placed under house arrest by other UDT leaders "for his virulently pro-Indonesian views" in August 1975 (Jolliffe, p. 272). He was later to be cited as an authority by the *New York Times*. (See pp. 169-70.)
90. *Decolonization*, p. 19. Dunn, who headed the Australian team, gives slightly lower estimates.
91. Quoted by Hill, *op. cit.*, p. 11, from an Australian TV interview with the pilot.
92. There is no reference to the fact that the only doctor had been forced to leave by the Portuguese at gunpoint, so FRETILIN sources claim, according to Stone.
93. Here is another example of *New York Times* editing. In his original story, Stone describes both the UDT and FRETILIN. "Where the UDT appears to draw its support from the better-educated and more comfortably situated classes, Fretilin has consistently sought its ideology and symbols from the people." The *New York Times* edits as follows: the UDT "appears to draw support from the better-educated and more well-to-do people in the Portuguese territory." The reference to FRETILIN is deleted, and of course the *New York Times* spares its readers the obscene word "classes".
94. On the nature and character of these programs, which were bringing "a number of important changes in the patterns of village life," see Jolliffe, pp. 100f. She suggests that FRETILIN was coming to identify itself as a "black nationalist movement" at this time (p. 116), and that it was much influenced by developments in Portuguese Africa.
95. *New York Times* (12 August 1975).
96. *Ibid.* Indonesian aspirations were widely recognized. A *London Times* editorial (4 November 1975) noted that "The Indonesians expect Timor to fall into their lap" and predicted that if FRETILIN declared independence and the Portuguese accept it then the Indonesians "would probably mount their own liberation movement." Months earlier, the *Economist* had reported that "General Suharto and his advisers are reported to be seriously considering a military takeover of Portuguese Timor," expecting that "Indonesia would not be seriously

affected by any international odium that might follow" (15 March 1975) — an apt assessment of Western commitment to freedom and self-determination. In the United States, the *Christian Science Monitor* carried a report on 24 April 1975 ("Indonesia eyes Portuguese colony") commenting that if a FRETILIN government were to be established "then some observers expect the Indonesians to waste little time in launching a military assault on the Portuguese colony." There was no lack of similar predictions, which places the pretense of ignorance on the part of U.S. officials in an interesting light.

97. *February 1978 Hearings*, p. 78. Anderson is a specialist on Indonesia and Southeast Asia at Cornell University. Some speculate that elements in the Portuguese administration may also have had a hand in the coup. See Forman's speculation in his Congressional testimony (*July Hearings*, p. 19) that the UDT coup was "hatched within the whitewashed walls of the colonial administration itself."

98. *Dunn Report*, pp. 65-66. Dunn had been Australian consul in Portuguese Timor in 1962-64.

99. This was also noted by Stone, *op. cit.*, who remarks that one of the prisoners who was beaten was a FRETILIN prisoner.

100. Cited from the Security Council record (S/PV. 1909) in *Decolonization,* p. 24.

101. The letter is reproduced in Jolliffe, p. 66; Roger, p. 27.

102. *Dunn Report*, pp. 37-38.

103. *Ibid.*, pp. 72ff. One of the Timorese who participated in the attack, José Martins (President of the right-wing KOTA party), later reported that about 1200 Indonesian troops (six companies) were involved in the attack, supported by tanks. Jolliffe, p. 284.

104. Their reports, and also reports in *Le Monde*, 30 November-1 December, and the *Economist*, 6 December, are cited in *Decolonization*, p. 28. We return to the U.S. press directly.

105. Jolliffe, pp. 177, 186, 201ff. See also *Dunn Report.*

106. Melbourne *Age*, 26 November 1975.

107. Jolliffe, pp. 226-27. A detailed report on the pre-invasion period by David Scott of the Australian aid mission appears in Sue Nichterlein, "The struggle for East Timor: 1976," unpublished ms., 1 June 1977.

108. *June-July Hearings*, p. 37.

109. *Tempo*, 8 July 1978. Reprinted in *Tapol*, November 1978. *Tapol* is the journal of the U.S. Campaign for the Release of Indonesian Political Prisoners, P.O. Box 609, Montclair, N.J. 07042.

110. On Australian intelligence information, see Christopher Sweeney, *Manchester Guardian,* (10 January 1978) reporting from Sydney. On the Australian government cover-up, see Andrew Clark, *National Times* (Australia) (5-10 January 1976).

111. Bruce Juddery, Canberra *Times* (31 May 1976). An accompanying report states that "from late 1974 the Government, or at least the then Prime Minister, Mr Whitlam, was being given reports of Indonesian operations intended to result in the incorporation of East Timor."

112. See Lee Lescaze, "U.S. Stopped Aid to Indonesia in '75 Over E. Timor Repression," *Washington Post* (18 March 1977); Reuters, "U.S. Briefly Halted Aid to Jakarta Because of Takeover of East Timor," *New York Times* (18 March

1977). Both of the cited headlines are false.

113. *February 1978 Hearings*, p. 36-37. We omit Anderson's footnote references documenting these statements.

114. *Ibid.*, p. 59. The facts were reported by Lenny Siegel, "U.S. officials deny deception on aid," *In These Times* (26 April-2 May 1978). The mainstream press seems to have shown no interest in the matter.

115. *February 1978 Hearings*, pp. 60-61.

116. Jacqui Chagnon, "East Timor and the Congress," *Tapol*, 15 April 1977. Chagnon was a member of the Human Rights office of Clergy and Laity Concerned.

117. At that early point in the Indonesian aggression the *Times* did not yet quite have its signals straight. Thus, on 28 December 1975, it published a Reuters dispatch from Darwin, Australia, reporting correctly that FRETILIN had "abandoned the territory's capital, Dili, to invading Indonesian troops on December 7," along with an AFP dispatch from Jakarta citing an official Indonesian press agency report "that pro-Indonesian forces had advanced to a line 12 miles south of Dili." The "pro-Indonesian forces" were, of course, the Indonesian army. If they had advanced 12 miles from the capital by December 27, when this dispatch was filed from Jakarta, they plainly had not seized the entire territory on December 7 as the *Times* had been claiming. The Reuters dispatch cited a radio message from FRETILIN stating, according to the *Times*, that "About 15,000 Indonesian-supported troops are advancing in eastern Timor on mountain strongholds" of FRETILIN. It is highly unlikely that this radio message referred to "Indonesian-supported troops" and no one with the vaguest familiarity with the situation believes that there were 15,000 such troops. No doubt the radio message referred to 15,000 *Indonesian* troops and the *Times* did a bit of re-editing, in its customary way.

According to Australian intelligence sources, the Indonesians landed an additional 15,000-20,000 troops on Christmas Day, 25 December 1975. See Jolliffe, p. 268.

118. State Department spokesman Robert B. Oakley at the *March Hearings*, p. 16, one of many statements to this effect before and since.

119. The Indonesian government, not surprisingly, agrees with its U.S. sponsor. The Fourth committee of the UN General Assembly agreed to hear testimony from one of the authors in November 1978 on Indonesian aggression and the services rendered it by the U.S. government and press, over the opposition of the representative of Indonesia, who said "it would serve no useful purpose." United Nations Press Release, GA/T/2269, 30 November 1978, referring to the decision to grant a hearing to N. Chomsky (document A/C.4/33/7 Add.3). See also *Inquiry*, January 1979.

120. John Hamilton, "Timor toll not the issue: US," Melbourne *Herald* (7 April 1977).

121. On the terms under which Indonesia is willing to accept such assistance, see p. 197-98.

122. Michael Leifer, "Indonesia and the incorporation of East Timor," *The World Today*, September 1976.

123. *New York Times*, "Strife-Torn Timor, Short of Food, Asks World Help," special to the *Times* (15 September 1975).

124. Andelman, "Jakarta Strives to Keep Foreign Aid; More U.S. Arms and Other Help Due," Jakarta, *New York Times* (26 November 1975).

125. November 9, our emphasis. There was in fact no civil war raging, contrary to Indonesian propaganda and its New York outlet. The statement about the five foreigners is also false. The bodies of the five journalists had been identified in propaganda broadcasts of the Indonesian collaborators as "Australian communists" by late October; cf. Jolliffe, p. 234f. (See note 157, this chapter.)

126. On the selectivity of Western humanitarianism in this regard, see Volume II, chapter 3.

127. Letter, *Far Eastern Economic Review*, 11 November 1977. On the floor of Congress, Burke has explained that "virulent Marxism" was spreading through East Timor in 1974 in a local struggle "in which inevitably the Government of Indonesia had to involve itself. However, by the time matters were put to rights by the Indonesians and their supporters in East Timor the situation had become a catspaw of Communist conspiracy, designed to embarrass and weaken the Government of Indonesia, erode the necessary and peaceful ties between Indonesia and Australia, and finally, to embarrass the current conservative government in Australia." The House of Representatives itself "has been involved" in this deplorable attempt by "elevating the relatively insignificant question of East Timor to an attention it does not altogether deserve"; "by having hearings and suggesting the legitimacy of an independent East Timor, the remnants of the Fretilin forces are encouraged to continue killing other Timorese and Indonesians," as resistance forces in France were encouraged to continue killing other Frenchmen and Germans by allied propaganda during World War II. *Congressional Record*-House, 20 July 1977.

128. *June-July Hearings*, p. 7. The visit by Meyner and Rep. William F. Goodling elicited some acid comment in the Australian press. Noel Hawken offered Rep. Meyner his "Simple-minded Soul Award for 1977" for her report of the "welcoming crowds" and general tranquillity. Noel Hawken, "Smile, Helen, you're on credulity camera," Melbourne *Herald* (27 April 1977). As for her colleague, Hawken reports that his views, "as he returned to Jakarta, were diamond clear. The Indonesian take-over was the best thing and should have been carried out three months earlier." Hawken is presumably referring to Goodling's statement quoted in the Indonesian press: "I deeply regret that Indonesia did not act three months earlier. Such a step would have prevented much of the bloodshed." Canberra *Times* (14 April 1977). See the report of Goodling's statements from Jakarta in the Melbourne *Age* (14 April 1977). Elizabeth Traube also dismisses the local response to the congressional delegation, noting that such "obligatory throngs of welcomers" were also customarily convened by the Portuguese authorities and regarded as "necessary nuisances" by the populations (*June-July Hearings*, pp. 22-23).

Hawken concludes that because of Australian complicity, we can never again "honestly speak up as a 'freedom-loving nation', dedicated to the freedom of other peoples"—a statement that is applicable with far greater force to the United States, where it has yet to be voiced in the press.

129. *June-July Hearings*, p. 62.

130. *March Hearings*, p. 1.

131. *June-July Hearings*, p. 72. The response by the State Department representative is an incoherent evasion that defies summary and would be pointless to quote.

132. *June-July Hearings*, p. 59.

133. Cited by Franke, *op. cit.*, p. 42, from *Foreign Assistance Act of 1968, Hearings,* House Foreign Affairs Committee, p. 706.
134. *June-July Hearings*, p. 61. The reference to "the fighting that was going on" is disingenuous. There was fighting, because the Indonesian army was carrying out clandestine military actions against East Timor, the civil war having ended in September. Referring to allegations of loss of life in a wave of violence "from August to December, prior to Indonesian intervention" (Richard Holbrooke, Assistant Secretary of State for East Asian and Pacific Affairs, *March Hearings*, p. 6), Dunn remarks that the official was "seemingly ignorant of the fact that there was no fighting between the Timorese from mid-September onwards" (*Dunn Report,* p. 129). Holbrooke also seemed unaware of Indonesian military intervention from September, 1975.
135. As already noted, Australian intelligence was well aware of the impending invasion, and the press had been reporting its likelihood for some time. The *Washington Post* ran a story on 30 November 1975 stating that "Indonesia is preparing to intervene militarily to overturn yesterday's declaration of independence by a leftist nationalist group in Portuguese East Timor, a high government official said today" (John Saar, "Jakarta Set to Use Force to Overturn Timor Independence," citing Gen. Ali Murtopo, deputy chief of Indonesia's intellignece agency and a senior adviser to President Suharto). The *New York Times* reported on December 5 that Foreign Minister Malik told pro-Indonesian Timorese "that the situation had gone beyond diplomacy and could be resolved only on the battlefield" (David Andelman, "President Ford's Stop Today: Indonesia, one of Asia's Richest Yet Poorest Countries"). Andelman reports that Malik's statement "puzzled American officials" because of its "stridency" and timing, just before President Ford's visit. Normal diplomacy would require cooperating in the pretense that the United States does not know about such things, the regular stance of government witnesses in the Congressional Hearings.
136. *March Hearings*, pp. 5, 10.
137. UPI, Lisbon, "Indonesia seizes E. Timor city," *Boston Globe* (8 December 1975). Note that this report, from Lisbon, states accurately that Indonesia captured Dili, not East Timor, as the *New York Times* falsely reported. The report is primarily devoted to Portugal's breaking diplomatic relations with Indonesia.
138. *Los Angeles Times* (7 December 1975). See also *Christian Science Monitor* (28 January 1976). The Ford and Kissinger reactions appear to have been effectively suppressed in the media, apart from these references.
139. Laurie Oakes, Melbourne *Sun* (1 May 1976). See also the *Dunn Report*, p. 44.
140. Ross Waby, *Australian* (22 January 1976) reporting from New York.
141. Most of the relevant UN Documents are cited in *Decolonization*. The text of the December 1976 resolution appears in the *Dunn Report*, Appendix IV.
142. The text of the cablegram appears in the *New York Times* (28 January 1976).
143. *June-July Hearings*, p. 57.
144. Paul Hofmann, "U.N. Calls on Indonesia to Leave Eastern Timor," 23 April 1976.
145. Frederic A. Moritz, *Christian Science Monitor* (8 December 1977).
146. Cf. Jolliffe, pp. 267, 276.

147. Offered as a "rough guess" by Robert Oakley, Deputy Assistant Secretary of State for East Asian and Pacific Affairs, *March Hearings*, p. 8; the context suggests that Oakley may also be including Indonesian casualties, which he states, "certainly were fairly heavy," in this total. On the demoralizing effect of the war for the Indonesian invaders, see Jolliffe, p. 300. Oakley also claims that most of the violence ended in March 1976.

148. On the ridiculous character of the Timorese "ratification" of integration, see Forman, *op. cit.*, pp. 12f.; Jolliffe, p. 289. Forman adds that "the Indonesians have largely ignored world opinion on the East Timor matter to date because of our government's acquiescence" (p. 35). See also *Dunn Report*, p. 104; *Decolonization*, pp. 37-38.

149. Allen S. Nanes, Specialist in U.S. Foreign Policy, Congressional Research Service, Library of Congress, entitled "The U.S. Position on Recognizing Forced Annexation of Territory," 1 June 1977; Appendix to *June-July Hearings*. Morocco's King Hassan was in Washington in mid-November 1978 to request an additional $100 million worth of U.S. counterinsurgency equipment to fight the Polisario guerrillas, who at the same time were cooling their heels at the United Nations, hoping to testify on Moroccan aggression in the former Spanish Sahara (not that one would know this from the U.S. mass media). As we write, the Carter administration is deliberating, unwilling to alienate Algeria, with which the United States had trade relations amounting to over $3.5 billion in the preceding year. Meanwhile, "Northrop Corp., the giant military contractor, is plunging ahead with plans to develop a $200 million electronic surveillance network to help Morocco pinpoint Polisario guerrillas in the Western Sahara. Three of the U.S. experts devising this system are retired Air Force generals who developed a massive sensor network in Vietnam." *Internews International Bulletin* (P.O.Box 4400, Berkeley, California 94704), 20 November 1978.

150. *June-July Hearings*, p. 53.

151. *Ibid.*, pp. 61-62. Australia's conservative government has similar scruples — with regard to the Baltic states. David A. Andelman reports from Canberra that the Fraser government "is reported preparing to inform Moscow that Australia does not recognize the incorporation of Estonia, Latvia and Lithuania into the Soviet Union." *New York Times* (18 December 1975). The same government, however, has given *de facto* recognition to Indonesian aggression in East Timor and has also sought to lend its assistance, e.g., by blocking FRETILIN communications to the outside world through Darwin.

152. But not total silence. The *Washington Post* commented editorially on "The Indonesian annexation of East Timor," describing it as "a depressing example of international double standards." The editorial observed almost correctly that Indonesian intervention began in October 1975 followed by the December invasion, "backed up by the sort of military paraphernalia the US used to employ in Vietnam." It also noted the "sickening reports of thousands of civilians dying in massacres" as "the whole episode has been treated as fait accompli" and pointed out that "the need to keep about 20,000 troops to fight considerably smaller guerrilla forces gives the lie to this propaganda" that the "forcible act of integration" is "an act of free choice." "Integration without choice," editorial, *Washington Post* (23 May 1976) on the occasion of the announcement by the head of the Indonesian client regime that full integration would take place shortly.

153. *March Hearings*, pp. 19f.

154. *February 1978 Hearings*, pp. 39-40.
155. *Ibid.*, p. 73, our emphasis.
156. "Australia's Rift with Indonesians over Timor Troubles U.S.," 2 May 1976.
157. On the killing of the five journalists, see Jolliffe, pp. 234f. and 283f. The evidence appears persuasive that they were killed by the Indonesian forces, and then identified as "communists." See also *Dunn Report*, p. 77f. Also Dunn's testimony in the *March Hearings*. See also Hill, *op. cit.* Martin's account was covered in the Australian press; see Graeme Beaton, "Timor deaths 'hidden'," *Australian* (29 April 1976) reporting from New York. Beaton reports that Martins, official spokesman on Timor affairs for the Indonesian government until his defection, arrived in Balibó two hours after the Australians were killed and conducted an on-the-spot investigation which, he claims, provides documentary evidence that the Australians were killed "in cold blood" and that Indonesian reports were a "cover-up." Martins alleged that he was required to sign fabricated reports almost under threat of death. See Jolliffe, pp. 283f., for further details. Two U.S. representatives of the American Friends Service Committee, Russell and Irene Johnson, were informed by reliable sources in Jakarta that the journalists were killed by Indonesian commandos dispatched for the purpose.
158. The reference to "a very Asian answer" is typical of Western journalistic racism.
159. Dunn, *March Hearings*, pp. 26ff.
160. Their numbers, according to the refugee reports, are far less than the State Department claims. In this as in other respects the U.S. State Department keeps closely to the Indonesian propaganda line. In general, as we have seen, one major feature of this progaganda is to exaggerate the severity of the civil war and its consequences, so as to mask the U.S.-backed Indonesian atrocities.
161. Cf. Jolliffe, p. 279, for discussion of the contents of some of these letters, which were smuggled to Darwin in January 1976 and describe wholesale murder and pillage.
162. *March Hearings*, pp. 12-13.
163. Marvine Howe, "Portugal Refugees Face Bleak Winter," *New York Times* (24 October 1976).
164. See Volume II for many examples.
165. See note 89, this chapter.
166. The 15 February 1976 *Times* story was cited by Franck in his testimony at the *June-July Hearings* (pp. 68, 57).
167. John Sharkey, "House to Probe Charge Indonesians Killed 100,000 on Timor," *Washington Post* (13 March 1977).
168. Bernard Gwertzman, *New York Times* (13 March 1977).
169. "Charge 100,000 slain in East Timor," AP, Canberra, *Ithaca Journal* (28 February 1977). This AP report does not appear to have been considered worthy of publication by the national media.
170. See note 202, this chapter, for further details. Gwertzman, in the report cited in note 168, stated that 56 Australian parliamentarians (the number was actually 95) had urged President Carter "to take action over the alleged human rights violations."
171. Richard Dudman, "American Aid to Indonesia Ignores Human Rights Abuses," *St. Louis Post-Dispatch* (1 January 1978).
172. *June-July Hearings*, p. 31.

173. *Ibid.*, p. 38.
174. *Ibid.*, p. 69.
175. Australian Broadcasting Commission, A.M. Program, 1 April 1977. We rely on a transcript provided by a reliable source.
176. The reference to "civil war" expresses the Indonesian claim that there were no Indonesian armed forces involved, but only "volunteers" assisting anti-FRETILIN Timorese who were being oppressed and massacred. Despite occasional genuflections, these claims are dismissed out of hand by Western governments and international bodies, as by independent observers. See, for example, the record of UN resolutions reviewed above. The Western press has been quite willing to present these absurd claims as fact, however, as we have seen.
177. See chapter 4, section 1, for Sudomo's statement shortly before the State Department version appeared in *Human Rights and U.S. Policy: Argentina, Haiti, Indonesia, Iran, Peru, and the Philippines*, Reports submitted to the Committee on International Relations, U.S. House of Representatives, by the Department of State, 31 December 1976, Government Printing Office, Washington D.C., 1976.
178. Russell Skelton, "Indons Killed 60,000: Report," Melbourne *Age* (19 November 1976). The report is undoubtedly the same one from which Dunn quoted the estimates transmitted by the Indonesian church officials.
179. Michael Richardson, "Timor: One year later — Fretilin's alive and kicking," Melbourne *Age* (8 December 1976).
180. The document was printed in part in Commonwealth of Australia, Parliamentary Debates, Senate, 17 March 1977, p. 319, introduced by Senator Gietzelt. It had already appeared in full in the *Tribune* (1 December 1976) (Communist), where the anti-FRETILIN contents are noted.
181. The talk of "volunteers" and "pro-Indonesian forces" is only for foreign consumption. (See note 176, this chapter.)
182. Bram Alexander, "100,000 killed by Indons in Timor: Report," *Sun News Pictorial,* 17 January 1977.
183. Parts were published in Australia: John Hurst, "god hasnt forsaken Timor," *Nation Review*, 12-18 January 1978.
184. *March Hearings*, p. 8. Recall also that the State Department estimated at the very same time that only 200,000 of the 650,000 population were in areas administered by Indonesia. (See p. 162.)
185. In his Congressional testimony of 15 February 1978 (p. 58; see note 80, this chapter), Benedict Anderson noted other apparent violations of U.S. law, specifically, the supply to Indonesia of military aid considerably in excess of what is permitted by law to countries that violate principles of the United Nations. Since "even the State Department has accepted the fact that Indonesia has not allowed the East Timorese to have self-determination, and that is clearly a United Nations principle," it follows that the law has been violated. Anderson remarks: "It seems to me that this kind of calmly overturning or ignoring of American statutes is something very worrying and it concerns me very much. It is this evidence of what goes on in our Government that alarms me at least as much as what goes on in Indonesia," a point worth making when one thinks of the global impact of United States policy, quite apart from its implications with regard to U.S. democracy.
186. "'Religious war' in Timor, says Liberal MP," Canberra *Times* (25 March 1978).

187. The letter was reported in the *Internews International Bulletin* (30 January 1978). Substantial excerpts appear in the *Guardian*, New York (15 February 1978). In short, it was not inaccessible to enterprising journalists.
188. Canberra *Times* (14 February 1978). Extracts reprinted in *East Timor News*, Bulletin of the East Timor Agency, 232 Castlereagh St., Sydney, NSW, 2000.
189. For an important exception, see the testimony by the two anthropologists who worked with the mountain tribesmen in the *June-July Hearings*, cited above. Like all other informed observers, they credit the accounts of Indonesian atrocities and dismiss the Indonesian claims to local support.
190. This one point is incorrect, Jolliffe notes, according to intelligence sources that place the Indonesian troop level at 14,000, "although this may be a too conservative estimate." The *Financial Review* (Australia), 8 October 1976, estimated that "pacification of East Timor is being carried out by an Indonesian army of nearly 40,000 men, according to informed estimates."
191. See pp. 191-93, this chapter.
192. *Dunn Report*, p. 97.
193. Cf. Volume II, chapter 6, for an account of his honors for these journalistic achievements, a Pulitzer Prize, bestowed over the heads of the jury just at the time of this penetrating report. (See note 198, this chapter.)
194. Cf. Jolliffe, p. 287, citing José Martins, who was directly involved as an Indonesian collaborator.
195. Press reporting from Vietnam as well as such material as the *Pentagon Papers* continually referred to Vietnamese "xenophobia," which always posed serious difficulties for the U.S. liberators. The sheer stupidity of imperial propagandists over the years really is quite difficult to believe. (See section 3 for some examples from the Kennedy Administration.)
196. Reuters, Jakarta, "Collapse Forecast for the Revolt of East Timor," *San Francisco Chronicle* (18 October 1978).
197. Letter to Arnold Kohen, dated 3 July 1978.
198. Henry Kamm, "Guerrillas in Timor Still Fight Indonesia," *New York Times,* (19 April 1978). The *Times* refused to publish a letter by Arnold Kohen (see note 80, this chapter) objecting to some of the more obvious falsehoods in Kamm's report, and noting Kamm's curious failure even to mention allegations of genocide — particularly striking, given that the bulk of his reporting is concerned with precisely this issue — from "enemy territory," however. Kamm's report was the subject of appropriate derision by Alexander Cockburn, *Village Voice* (8 May 1978).
199. Cf. Jolliffe, pp. 291-92.
200. Cited in *Timor Information Service*, October 1978 (Australia) from the *Review of International Affairs*, 5-20 August 1978.
201. See, for example, Keith Martin, "Shipping ban on Indonesia to stay," Sydney *Morning Herald* (25 February 1977) reporting that "the ban by Australian maritime unions on Indonesian shipping seems likely to remain in force." The ban was imposed in November 1975 just prior to the Indonesian invasion, which was known to be imminent despite feigned State Department "ignorance." Most unions "favoured retaining the ban as a continuing expression of protest against the Timor invasion," rejecting the interest of Australia in wheat sales to Indonesia. See Hill, pp. 14-15, on union opposition to the Indonesian invasion and

business support for it. Also Jolliffe, pp. 294-95. There has apparently been considerable internal union conflict on this issue.

202. The letter is reprinted in full in Hansard, *op. cit.*, p. 321; cf. note 180, this chapter. According to Senator Gietzelt, who introduced it into the record, it was signed by 95 members of Parliament, the majority from Government parties, constituting a majority of the Australian Parliament. It applauded Carter's concern for human rights in the USSR and Uganda and urged him to approach Indonesia on the matter of East Timor, apparently without irony.

203. We return to this matter in Volume II. In contrast, the U.S. press has recognized "responsible" opposition to the U.S. war on grounds of excessive cost and failure, the kind of opposition expressed in regard to Nazi aggression by thoughtful Germans after Stalingrad.

204. Newcastle *Morning Herald* (6 April 1977).

205. Michael Hodgman, "Timor appeasement must end," *Australian* (21 February 1977).

206. Reuters, "30,000 deaths," *Manchester Guardian* (14 September 1978), a 33-word item that did not reach the United States, to our knowledge.

207. The letter appears as Appendix 2 in the *March Hearings.*

208. The letter, dated 29 April 1976, is reproduced in full in *Timor Information Service*, 6 May 1976, Australia. As noted above, Martins was the official spokesman on Timor affairs for the Indonesian government.

209. Cf. Jolliffe, pp. 282f. for further details.

210. *March Hearings*, 52ff.

211. Interview translated in FBIS, Indonesia, IV, 28 September 1978, N1-N2, from *l'Humanité*, Paris, 18 September 1978. The context indicates that by the word translated as "casualties," Alkatiri meant "deaths."

212. George McArthur, "Indonesia Anxious to Replace Decrepit Arms," reporting from Jakarta, *IHT*, 5 December 1977, reprinted from the *Los Angeles Times.* McArthur states that "the Indonesians generally have avoided using U.S. equipment to spare Washington's sensibilities, but a lot of U.S. equipment nevertheless is being used." This statement, perhaps, reflects the same logic that enabled him to say that the Indonesian Communist Party subjected the country to a huge massacre in the mid-1960s, and that the "attempted Communist coup...failed in a national bloodbath...." (See chapter 4, section 4.1., p. 216.)

213. This is a constant pretense in the media. In fact, arms sales have boomed under Carter, as the press also reports. See, e.g., George C. Wilson, "Arms Sales Record Set in Fiscal 1978," *Washington Post* (3 October 1978), reporting that "the United States sold a record amount of military weapons and services to foreign nations in the fiscal year just ended, according to Pentagon figures released yesterday." On sales to Indonesia, see note 235, this chapter.

214. Terence Smith, "Mondale is a Nonexpert Who Matters," *New York Times*, Week in Review (14 May 1978). No mention of East Timor appears in this account, though that is where these planes are likely to be used. (But see note 223.) Representatives Donald Fraser and Helen Meyner wrote a letter on 22 June 1978 to Secretary of State Cyrus Vance expressing their reservations over the projected sale of A-4 aircraft to Indonesia, noting that these would be "particularly useful in East Timor" for air to ground attack. They questioned the State Department's claim that these aircraft would be used primarily for training purposes. The response by Douglas Bennet of the State Department (15 August 1978) assured

them that "the Indonesian Government has no intention of using the A-4 aircraft in East Timor" (he also noted, interestingly, that the U.S. government is not "sanguine over the prospects for a peaceful resolution of the fighting between Fretilin and the Indonesian Government," as of August 1978; recall previous claims that the fighting is essentially over). This is a standard pretense by the governments that are taking part in the slaughter in East Timor. Thus, the State Department representative, Robert Oakley, testified in the *February 1978 Hearings*, when asked by Rep. Fraser about the sale of F-5E and F-5F jet warplaces to Indonesia: "So far as I know, sir, there is no intention on the part of Indonesia to use them....But this is something on which we cannot be categoric....I do not believe that the supply of one squadron of F-5E's to replace a squadron of F-86E's is going to have any impact on the situation in East Timor, sir," though he agreed with Fraser's comment that "F-86E's are nearing the end of their life" (p. 67). Later he added that "the arms which we are supplying now," including attack aircraft, "are not as best I know, destined for East Timor, although, as I said, we can't give a guarantee to this effect" (p. 73). But we'll give them the planes anyway, trusting our Indonesian friends.

215. *East Timor Information Bulletin*, 40 Concannon Road, London SW2, May 1978.

216. R.-P. Paringaux, "La France envisage de livrer divers armements a l'Indonesie," *Le Monde* (14 September 1978).

217. We return to this matter in Volume II, chapter 4.

218. In Volume II, chapter 6, we will consider in some detail the evidence that has been produced by those who speak in these terms.

219. See Roger, *op. cit.*, p. 77, for quotes and references, specifically, to *La Croix*, 23 June 1976, an article by Christian Rudel.

220. Tom Uren, then Deputy Leader of the Opposition, Parliamentary Debates (Australia), 17 November 1976, Representatives, 282s.

221. Lauries Oakes, Melbourne *Sun* (17 November 1976).

222. Technically, the answer is "yes." In the early days of the Indonesian invasion—when, as already noted, proper news control had not yet been fully established (see note 117, this chapter)—the *New York Times* did publish tiny items based on radio communications of the forces resisting what the *Times* itself recognized as blatant aggression. See "500 Reported Killed," (9 December 1975); "Indonesian Attack in Timor Reported," (27 December 1975); "Broadcast from Timor Says Pro-Indonesian Forces Advance," (28 December 1975); "Burning of Food Alleged in Timor," (4 January 1976). The first of these is from Lisbon, the last three from Darwin, Australia. These exceptions, which a serious theory of the Free Press would treat as statistical error, show that it is not beyond the technical capacity of the Free Press to report the news of the world, were it to choose to do so; a fact which is obvious in any event.

On the December 28 dispatch, see note 117, this chapter. Note that the headline cited, with its reference to "Pro-Indonesian Forces," almost certainly involves a *Times* editorial fabrication, which appears as well in the report itself.

223. On 1 December 1977, Amnesty International released a criticism of Indonesia for refusing to allow the Red Cross to visit East Timor. It received no press coverage. The *Australian* (11 May 1978) reports that Indonesia "has agreed to allow relief teams, including the International Red Cross, into East Timor for the first time since it was taken over in July, 1976." The information comes from sources close to Vice-President Mondale, and allegedly Indonesia's "decision" is a

consequence of Mondale's discussions in Jakarta in which he was so impressed with Indonesia's leap forward in the Human Rights field that he exerted unusual efforts to obtain planes for them to use in their annihilation of simple mountain people in Timor. The reference is interesting; it shows that behind the mask of silence, the U.S. government is not as ignorant as it pretends. As we write, the International Red Cross has not been admitted, nor have journalists been permitted anything but a highly restricted glimpse. We assume that the A-4 ground attack bombers have been or will be delivered, however. It should all be good for a few laughs over coffee and Danish at the Friday breakfast. (See p. 191, this chapter.)

224. For example the Reuters report of 18 October 1978 in the *San Francisco Chronicle* cited above (see note 196, this chapter) states that "one sign of FRETILIN's deteriorating strength can be seen in the fact that a radio station run by the guerrillas—a small portable transmitter—has not been heard for several months." The report is false. Despite the efforts of Indonesia and Australia to stop communications, radio transmissions from FRETILIN were being received through November 1978. One may perhaps also question the conclusion supported by the false premise.

In a statement prepared for delivery before the Fourth Committee of the UN General Assembly, November 1978, Jill Jolliffe cites a radio broadcast of November 28.

225. "CIA Said to Aid Indonesia Units in East Timor," *International Herald Tribune* (20 June 1978).

226. Richard Carleton, "Brainwash follows the bloodbath," *London Observer* (31 July 1977); "Timor—and a story of massacre," "The place of death in Timor," Melbourne *Age* (10-11 August 1977); the version the *Age* has is considerably more detailed.

227. David Jenkins, "Timor's arithmetic of despair," *Far Eastern Economic Review*, 29 September 1978.

228. Sydney *Morning Herald* (11 September 1978).

229. Jill Jolliffe's paraphrase in her prepared testimony for the Fourth Committee of the General Assembly. (See note 224, this chapter.)

230. *Ibid.* Recall that Dili was the one place where there may have been some initial willingness to accept Indonesian "integration," prior to the invasion. Recall also the description of the situation in Dili by the Indonesian Church officials, who report that two-thirds of its original 30,000 people want to leave for Portugal while others are with FRETILIN in the mountains.

231. See p. 177 and note 177, this chapter, for the first of these.

232. *Country Reports on Human Rights Practices*, p. 235. (See note 69, this chapter.)

233. *Human Rights Conditions in Selected Countries and the U.S. Response*, prepared for the Subcommittee on International Organizations of the Committee on International Relations, U.S. House of Representatives, by the Foreign Affairs and National Defense Division, Congressional Research Service, Library of Congress, 25 July 1978, U.S. Government Printing Office, 1978, pp. 103-104.

234. Seth Lipsky and Raphael Pura, "Indonesia: Testing time for the 'New Order', " *Foreign Affairs*, Fall, 1978.

235. The diligent reader of the press might have been able to recall the story by Ann Crittenden, *New York Times* (17 July 1977) reporting "a recently completed and detailed analysis of American foreign aid to eight developing countries"

which notes that "the Carter Administration has requested a sizable increase in military assistance to Indonesia in the 1978 fiscal year, in spite of that country's invasion in 1975 of the neighboring island of East Timor, which it still occupies" in defiance of UN resolutions and "charges that 30,000 to 100,000 political prisoners have been held [in Indonesia] for years without trial," after the bloodbath of the 1960s.

236. The official Indonesian figure for total detainees since the Communists were crushed in 1965 is 750,000. (See p. 208, this chapter.) Note also the lack of comment on the 12-year delay in releasing these "thousands." This is rectified elsewhere. Thus on 30 October 1977, the *Times* remarks ("Topics") that "hundreds of thousands of Indonesians were arrested after an aborted left-wing coup in 1965" (the U.S. government and media version; cf. chapter 4, section 1 on the facts) and that "tens of thousands remain in indefinite detention without even a trial," most of them classified in "'Category B,' meaning that while they are believed to have been *indirectly* involved in the 1965 coup attempt, there is not sufficient evidence for court." This seems excessive to the *Times* editorialists, who comment: "Twelve years in prison are surely enough for that offense." That is, twelve years in prison seems to suffice for the "offense" of being "believed to have been indirectly involved" in a coup attempt that appears to have been a propaganda fabrication in the first place.

237. Mark Baker, "Iran war kills 9000," Melbourne *Age* (24 April 1978).

238. Richard W. Franke, review of *The Rule of the Sword: The Story of West Irian*, by Nonie Sharp, Kibble Books, 1977; BCAS, vol. 10, no. 1, 1978.

4 Constructive Terror

1. The Orwellian twists and turns of Western usage of these words in the interests of a workable double standard is discussed above, chapter 3, section 1.

2. Peter Dale Scott, "Exporting Military-Economic Development: America and the Overthrow of Sukarno, 1965-67," in Malcolm Caldwell, ed., *Ten Years' Military Terror in Indonesia,* Spokesman Books, 1975, p. 209.

3. As C.L. Sulzberger noted, "From an American viewpoint, this represents a positive achievement"; "As the Shadow Lengthens," *New York Times* (3 December 1965). He refers only to the generals' coup. The associated bloodbath, already well under way, he does not even find worthy of mention.

4. James Reston's article featuring Indonesia, in which there is no mention of mass murder, was titled "A Gleam of Light," *New York Times* (19 June 1966).

The changes are referred to as "significant" and "hopeful," with Indonesia no longer controlled by people "fiercely hostile to the United States." See also the "moderate scholars" statement discussed on p. 86.

5. The model may well have been quite explicit. In a study of CIA psychological warfare leading to the coup in which Allende was deposed and murdered, Fred Landis points out that the CIA concocted a document purporting to reveal a leftist plot to murder Chilean military officers—the pretext used by the Indonesian generals to launch their mass murder—while the CIA-backed press ran headlines to the same effect. Meanwhile, "hundreds of leftist leaders received a card 'Djakarta is approaching' " as did military officers, while a CIA agent directed right-wing groups "to paint this same slogan in red all over Santiago." Fred Landis, "Psychological Warfare in Chile: The CIA Makes Headlines," *Liberation*, March-April 1975. See also Scott, *op. cit.*

6. Scott, *op. cit.*, p. 247; Malcolm Caldwell in Selden, ed., *Remaking Asia,* Pantheon, 1973, p. 48. The leaders seem to have been an anti-corruption and populist group, reacting against the frozen hierarchical structure of the military establishment and the massive looting by the top echelons. See Ben Anderson, "Last Days of Indonesia's Suharto?" in *Southeast Asia Chronicle,* No. 62, July-August, 1978, pp. 2-3. For a broad account suggesting some PKI involvement, but giving little credence to PKI initiative or domination, see Harold Crouch, *The Army and Politics in Indonesia,* Cornell University Press, 1978, chapter 4.

7. Crouch, *op. cit.*, pp. 34, 48-49.

8. Scott, *op. cit.*, cites RAND memoranda by Indonesia specialist Guy Pauker who feared in 1964 that the Indonesian anti-Communist forces "would probably lack the ruthlessness that made it possible for the Nazis to suppress the Communist Party of Germany" in 1933, since they "are weaker than the Nazis, not only in numbers and in mass support, but also in unity, discipline, and leadership." But, as he explained four years later, "The assassination of the six army generals by the September 30 Movement elicited the ruthlessness that I had not anticipated a year earlier and resulted in the death of large numbers of Communist cadres."

9. Roger Hilsman, *To Move A Nation*, Doubleday, New York, 1967, p. 377. Before the 1965 coup over 4,000 Indonesian officers had been trained in the U.S. and a substantial proportion of Indonesian weapons were made in the U.S. See also Ruth McVey, "The Post Revolutionary Transformation of the Indonesian Army, II," *Indonesia*, April 1972, p. 169. Before October 1965 the USSR was a major supplier of heavy equipment to the Indonesian navy and air force. It was displaced after the coup, and the U.S. became virtually sole supplier of the Indonesian armed forces.

10. "Lest We Forget," in Caldwell, *Ten Years' Military Terror*, p. 14.

11. *Ibid.*, pp. 15-17.

12. Amnesty International, *Indonesia*, AI, 1977, p. 21.

13. "Lest We Forget," *op. cit.*, pp. 14-15.

14. "Indonesian Communism Since the 1965 Coup," *Pacific Affairs*, Spring 1970, pp. 35-36.

15. *Ibid.*, p. 52.

16. *Ibid.*, p. 56.

17. AI, *Indonesia*, p. 22.

18. "Jakarta Says Most Political Prisoners Will Be Free in '79," *New York Times* (12 April 1978).

19. Ernest Utrecht, "The Indonesian Army as an Instrument of Repression," *Journal of Contemporary Asia,* March 1972.
20. AI, *Indonesia*, p. 13.
21. *Ibid.*, pp. 41, 44.
22. *Ibid.*, p. 46.
23. *Ibid.*, p. 9.
24. *Ibid.*, p. 76.
25. Jacques Decornoy, "Des dizaines de milliers de personnes sont internees sans grand espoir d'etre jugees un jour," *Le Monde* (11 November 1972).
26. Richard Robison, "Toward a Class Analysis of the Indonesian Military State," *Indonesia*, April 1978, p. 24, n. 23.
27. *Ibid.*, p. 21.
28. Anderson, *op. cit.*, p. 13.
29. "Indonesia: Why foreign investors are scared," *Business Week*, 18 April 1977.
30. David Andelman, "Indonesia Opens Inquiry on Charge of Huge Payoffs in Satellite Project," *New York Times* (4 February 1977).
31. Burt Schorr, "Indonesia Restaurant Shows How Firms Can Succumb to Threat to Foreign Stakes," *Wall Street Journal* (13 October 1977). Schorr quotes one restaurant critic saying: "Obviously somebody spent a lot of time (and money) putting it all together." Schorr says: "Somebody did spend a lot of money on the Ramayana: more than 50 companies and individuals that either were doing business in Indonesia or hoped to. Altogether, they bought more than $1 million of stock in Ramayana's parent company after some not-so-subtle arm-twisting by officials of...Pertamina, which organized the adventure in dining."
32. *Ibid.*
33. Robison, *op. cit.*, pp. 28-29.
34. *Ibid.*, pp. 31-32.
35. *Ibid.*, pp. 32.
36. Crouch, *op. cit.*, pp. 287-88.
37. Ingrid Palmer, "The Economy, 1965-1975," in Caldwell, *op. cit.*, p. 148.
38. Crouch, *op. cit.*, p. 269.
39. Barry Newman, " 'Sticky Handshakes' Are Coming Unglued A Bit in Indonesia," *Wall Street Journal* (8 December 1977).
40. *Ibid.*
41. Anderson, *op. cit.*, pp. 8-9.
42. "Some indication of this scale is suggested by the recent criminal conviction of a middle-level provincial official of the National Supply Board for the embezzlement of $19 million." *Ibid.*, p. 9.
43. *Ibid.*
44. Andelman, *op. cit.* (note 30).
45. David A. Andelman, "Indonesia Is One of the Richest and Poorest Countries in Asia," *New York Times* (5 December 1975).
46. Robison, *op. cit.*, p. 33.
47. *Ibid.*, p. 37.
48. Barry Newman, "Slowed Development and Huge Debts are Pertamina's Legacy to Indonesia," *Wall Street Journal* (11 February 1977). Only a few years previously, *Fortune* had written an accolade to General Sutowo and Pertamina for his understanding of the need to be very nice to foreign oil companies. While

pointing out that some critics "have accused him of milking the company," *Fortune* swallowed at face value Sutowo's denials. See Louis Kraar, "Oil and Nationalism Mix Beautifully in Indonesia," *Fortune*, July 1973, pp. 99ff.

49. Newman, *op. cit.*

50. See chapter 3, section 4.4, for a discussion of the material results of Mondale's pleasure over the improvement in the human rights situation: namely, Mondale's personal intervention to obtain A/4 attack bombers that can be put to use to murder the population of East Timor, while the accompanying Indonesian promise to allow entry to the International Red Cross was conveniently forgotten by all concerned as soon as the state visit was completed. See p. 191-92 and chapter 3, note 223.

51. The Pentagon is reasonably pleased with the satellite status of Indonesia, but it is far from happy with the abysmal performance of the Indonesian military in its now three year old unsuccessful war of aggression in East Timor. (See chapter 3, section 4.4.)

52. According to a study by Joel Rocamora, "Political Prisoners and the Army Regime in Indonesia," Cornell University, June 1970, p. 1.

53. "It is authoritatively estimated that 10% to 15% of the total cost of bank-financed projects in Indonesia is dissipated through 'leakage'." Barry Newman, "Missing the Mark: In Indonesia Attempts By World Bank to Aid Poor Often Go Astray," *Wall Street Journal* (10 November 1977).

54. Don Moser, "Where the rivers ran crimson," *Life*, 1 July 1966; cited by Landis, *op. cit.*

55. George McArthur, "Teng's successes in SE Asia," *Los Angeles Times-Boston Globe* (15 November 1978).

56. George McArthur, "Indonesia Anxious to Replace Decrepit Arms," *International Herald Tribune* (5 December 1977), reprinted from the *Los Angeles Times*. On the contents of this quite significant report from Jakarta, see chapter 3, section 4.4., p. 191.

57. These moderate scholars not only use a double standard—with violence in the interest of opposition to social change justified by a set of nationalistic rationalizations—they also show themselves to be incompetent scholars, or propagandists, or both. As already noted, the U.S.-Diem forces always gave violence a higher priority on the spectrum of means for effecting or opposing change than did the NLF, and up until 1960 the NLF used minimal violence. They were *not* "committed to the thesis that violence was the best means of effecting change;" but Diem and his advisors never were able to make a serious and sustained effort at any course other than counterrevolutionary violence. (See chapter 5, sections 1.1, 2.1)

58. *New York Times* (6 July 1966).

59. *U.S. News and World Report*, 27 November 1972.

60. See the reviews by Coral Bell and B. Anderson in the *China Quarterly*, No. 28, October-December 1966, pp. 140-43.

61. Frank C. Darling, *Thailand and the United States*, Public Affairs Press, 1965, p. 65. For some years Darling was a CIA analyst specializing in Thailand.

62. *Ibid.*, p. 169.

63. Testimony of Leonard Unger, in Senate Foreign Relations Committee Hearings on U.S. Security Agreements and Commitments Abroad, *Kingdom of Thailand* (1969), p. 613. Hereafter, *Thailand*.

64. Darling, *op. cit.*, p. 111.

65. *Ibid.*, p. 106.
66. *Ibid.*, p. 138.
67. "And we are trying to preserve, trying to help them preserve, their independence." Ambassador Unger, *Thailand*, p. 859.
68. *Thailand*, p. 639.
69. *Ibid.*, p. 648.
70. *Ibid.*, p. 611.
71. *Ibid.*, p. 613.
72. *Ibid.*
73. Myrdal, *Asian Drama*, Pantheon, 1968, vol. I, p. 486.
74. Darling, *op. cit.*, p. 74.
75. *Ibid.*, p. 117.
76. *Thailand*, p. 748.
77. David A. Andelman, "Thai Business Chiefs Still Uneasy in Wake of Military Coup," *New York Times* (17 October 1976).
78. *Ibid.*
79. Darling, *op. cit.*, p. 168.
80. *Ibid.*, p. 128.
81. *Ibid.*, p. 82.
82. This is reminiscent of the Thieu technique of allegedly "releasing prisoners," not to the PRG as required in the January 1973 agreement, but into the population at large. (See chapter 5, section 1.6.) This device was thought by some to have been a mechanism for covering up the murder of political prisoners.
83. *Ibid.*, p. 169.
84. *Ibid.*, p. 114.
85. See especially, Thomas Lobe, *United States National Security Policy and Aid To The Thailand Police*, University of Denver Monograph Series in World Affairs, vol. 14, no. 2, 1977, pp. 19-25.
86. E. Thadeus Flood, *The United States and the Military Coup in Thailand: A Background Study*, Indochina Resource Center, 1976, pp. 1-2.
87. *Ibid.*, p. 2.
88. *Ibid.*
89. Lobe, *op. cit.*, pp. 47-48.
90. "The U.S. Role in Thai Society," in "Military Coup in Thailand," *Indochina Chronicle*, January-February 1977, pp. 6-7.
91. *Thailand Fact Sheet* (1932-1976), Southeast Asian Specialists at Cornell University, 18 October 1976, pp. 7-8.
92. See especially, Ben Anderson, "Withdrawal Symptoms: Social and Cultural Aspects of the October 6 Coup," *Bulletin of Concerned Asian Scholars*, October 1977, pp. 16-19.
93. Flood, *op. cit.*, pp. 5-7; *Thailand Fact Sheet*, pp. 8-10.
94. On U.S. involvement, see also Don Luce, "Thailand: How the U.S. Engineered A Coup," *Win*, 21 October 1976; Harvey Wasserman, "Thailand on the Tide of Reaction," *The Nation*, 30 October 1976; David and Susan Morell, "Thailand and the U.S.," *New York Times* (Op.-Ed.) (22 November 1976).
95. *Thailand Fact Sheet*, p. 8.
96. Both media fabrications and agents provacateurs played a significant role in counterrevolutionary activity in Thailand. The major pre-coup fabrication is

described by Anderson as follows:

> Some days earlier [prior to the coup on 6 October 1976], on September 24, two workers at Nakhon Pathom, putting up posters protesting former dictator Thanom's re-entry into Siam under the cloak of monkhood, were beaten to death by some local policemen and their corpses hanged. Two days before the coup, a radical student troupe staged a dramatic re-enactment of the murder in the Bo Tree courtyard of Thammasat University as part of a nationwide campaign for Thanom's expulsion. The rabid right wing newspaper *Dao Sayam* touched up photographs of the performance in such a way as to suggest that one of the actors "strangled" had been made up to look like the crown prince. In a coordinated maneuver, the Armored Division Radio broadcast the slander, urged the citizenry to buy copies of *Dao Sayam*, and demanded retribution for this "cruel attack" on the royal family. From this stemmed the lynch-mobs that paved the way for the military takeover. ("Withdrawal Symptoms...," *op. cit.*)

97. Luce, *op. cit.*; "U.S. Role in Thai Society," p. 9, n.1.
98. See Luce, Susan and David Morell, and Flood, *op. cit.*
99. Flood, p. 4.
100. *Ibid.*, p. 7.
101. Ambassador Gauss wrote to Cordell Hull during World War II that Chiang Kai-Shek had reminded him that "In the matter of world problems, China is disposed to follow our lead...." Department of State, *Relations With China*, p. 561. Chiang's state, though deeply corrupt and unstable, therefore held out a great potential for becoming "the principal stabilizing factor in the Far East," *Yalta Papers*, p. 353. Cited by Gabriel Kolko, *Politics of War*, Random House, 1968, p. 221.
102. National Security Council; 5429/2 (20 August 1954). U.S. Department of Defense, United States — Vietnam Relations, 1945-67, Book 10, pp. 731ff., Government Printing Office, 1971. (This is the government edition of the Pentagon Papers.)
103. An exception in its detail on Thai corruption is the Andelman article cited in note 77, this chapter, but even this article completely avoids any analysis of U.S. involvement and responsibility, or the economic consequences of military shakedowns and intervention (either efficiency or income distribution effects). The article conveys a resigned flavor of objective recognition of inevitable forces, avoiding any trace of the moral indignation that is standard in news stories dealing with official enemies.
104. An early illustration is a 1966 report by Peter Braestrup, "U.S. Helps Thailand at Village Level in Effort to Thwart Reds," *New York Times* (27 December 1966), which conveys the straight U.S. propaganda line that while Bangkok had been engaged only in suppression in the villages up to now, with U.S. aid there was a new thrust toward winning hearts and minds. Corruption appears only in quotes, as a Communist allegation. The nature and quality of the political and social order and the U.S. role are completely ignored.
105. "The U.S. has maintained an official silence on developments here during the past five months, and, for better or worse, this silence is widely viewed, among both friends and foes of Marcos, as signifying U.S. support for the president and his policies." Peter Kann, "Marcos's Manila: 'Smiling Martial Law' Leaves Most Filipinos Carrying On as Usual," *Wall Street Journal* (12 March 1973).

106. General "Jake" Smith. Cited in Teodoro A. Agoncillo and Oscar M. Alfonso, *History of the Filipino People*, Malaya Books, 1967, p. 272.
107. Cited by Jonathan Fast, "Crisis in the Philippines," *New Left Review* (March-April, 1973), p. 75, from Moorfield Storey and Julian Codman, *Secretary Root's Records: Marked Severities in Philippine Warfare*, Chicago, 1902, pp. 116, 71-73. For similar observations from U.S. War Department records, see Chomsky, *American Power and the New Mandarins,* Pantheon, 1969, chapter 3, pp. 252-53.
108. Sixto Lopez, "The Philippine Problem: a proposition for a solution," *The Outlook*, 13 April 1901.
109. Bernard Wideman, "The Philippines: Five Years of Martial Law," *Ampo: Japan-Asia Quarterly Review,* July-November 1977, p. 69.
110. Justus M. van der Kroef, "Communism and Reform in the Philippines," *Pacific Affairs,* Spring, 1973, p. 31.
111. For an account of the postwar peasant rebellion, which has been clouded for years in one of the more successful propaganda campaigns, see Benedict J. Kerkvliet, *The Huk Rebellion: A Study of Peasant Revolt in the Philippines*, University of California Press, 1977.
112. Fast, *op. cit.*, pp. 85-86.
113. "Real wage rates of Philippine skilled workers dropped [1955 is 100] from 89.2 in 1969 to 74.9 at the end of the first half of 1971; the rates for unskilled workers fell in the same period from 100.0 to 90.4." Van der Kroef, *op. cit.*, p. 41.
114. The last item is Van der Kroef's summary of one of the findings of the 1970 Agbayani House Sub-Committee Report, *ibid.*, p. 39.
115. Ownership of the main elements of the press, radio and TV quickly passed into the hands of Marcos, his family and associates, after the declaration of martial law. *Ibid.*, p. 58.
116. *Ibid.*, p. 30.
117. *Ibid.*, pp. 52-53.
118. See chapter 2, pp. 62.
119. Wideman, *op. cit.*, p. 64. The methods of classification of land eligible for reform has tended to accelerate conversion to intensive uses qualifying for exemption, with further displacement effects.
120. There have been strikes even under martial law, but thousands of workers have been detained by the military in strike-breaking efforts, and there can be no question but that the number and effectiveness of strikes has been greatly reduced.
121. Wideman, *op. cit.*, p. 69.
122. *Ibid.*
123. Tom Jones, "Philippines Report," *Matchbox (Amnesty International),* Winter, 1977, p. 13.
124. This is quite reasonable since Marcos bears direct responsibility for the system of torture. And Marcos's masters in the background, such as McNamara (as head of the World Bank), Nixon, Ford, Carter, and their top advisers complete the circle of responsibility in the same fashion as Johnson-Rusk-Nixon-Kissinger did for the multitude of Mylais in Vietnam.
125. Such visits as Mondale's are, of course, a big political plus for the rulers of the provinces, acknowledging the importance of the province and the supportive link to the tyrant. The *New York Times* noted that "there was, to be sure, the

requisite 'candid and constructive' chat with Mr. Marcos, who was reportedly told that if the Philippines did not shape up on human rights, strained relations could result. But before flying off, Mr. Mondale left his host a going away present, signing four rural aid agreements worth $41 million." "Tread Not on Us, Filipino Answer On Human Rights," *New York Times* (7 May 1978). It would be interesting to know what was said that was "constructive." Even more interesting would be Mondale's conception of human rights conditions in the Philippines, if any, that could alter our continuing solid support of that police state. (See note 50 on Mondale's contributions to human rights as he passed through Jakarta.)

126. The demonstration election technique was in regular use during the U.S. occupation of South Vietnam, where, as in the Philippines, it was geared strictly to the needs of the external power. In a 1968 volume by one of the authors, the concept was defined as follows: "A circus performed in a client state to reassure the populace of the intervening country that their intrusion is well received." (Edward S. Herman, *The Great Society Dictionary*, Philadelphia, 1968, p. 11) George Kahin recently described the last elections in the Philippines as "strongly influenced by senior American foreign policy officials who apparently hoped that such an exercise would help improve the deteriorating image Marcos had developed abroad as a consequence of 5½ years of martial law...It must be understood that this election was conducted primarily for a foreign audience, the American Congress in particular." Kahin went on to point out the incongruity for an allegedly human rights-oriented administration "that so far it has indicated no audible concern over the fact that within less than 2 hours of the close of the polls on April 7, Marcos ordered troops and police to round up a number of the key 21 opposition candidates, people who had had the courage to run against him and his wife in metropolitan Manila." *Human Rights in the Philippines: Recent Developments*, Hearings Before the Subcommittee on International Organizations of the House Committee on International Relations, 95th Congress, 2nd Session, 27 April 1978, p. 5.

127. This new technique is discussed in many of the expatriate journals such as *Ang Katipunan* ("Victims of Liquidation? Many Political Prisoners Missing," 27 July - 10 August 1977, p. 12) and the *Philippine Liberation Courier* ("Political Prisoners Missing," 10 February 1978, p. 6). As described by George Kahin:

> ...beginning a little over a year ago, a new and rapidly increasing tactic has been introduced, referred to by the Philippine army as "salvaging," a process wherein the torture continues but most of the physical evidence is removed.
>
> This calls for the removal of the person who has been tortured, in most cases—one of the most knowledgeable sources estimated about 90 percent of the time—removed through out-right killing. Now, the killings, of course, help insure the disappearance of the often quite indelible marks of torture.
>
> A frequent pattern of these so-called salvage operations is for the Government to announce that in a fire-fight, alleged or real, with forces of the pro-Communist insurgents the bodies of one or more who disappeared after torture had been found and then, of course, conveniently buried.
>
> Thereby the Government secures two objectives: It "proves" that the missing person had, as the Government alleges, Communist or subversive connections because of the context in which the body was

found, and it hides the physical evidence of the previous torture. (Testimony before the Subcommittee on Intergovernmental Organizations of the House Committee on International Relations, 27 April 1978, p. 6.)
128. *Ibid.*
129. "Philippines: A government that needs U.S. business," *Business Week*, 4 November 1972.
130. Donald McCouch (Vice President of MHT), "As Lenders See It, Philippines Excels in Managing Debt," *American Banker*, 21 September 1976, p. 10A.
131. For a good discussion of the dispensability of the Philippine bases, see George Kahin's article in the *Washington Post* (27 August 1978), reprinted in the *Congressional Record* ("Philippine Bases Reconsidered"), 8 September 1978, pp. S14841-4.
132. See Table 1, chapter 2.
133. *Far Eastern Economic Review* (5 August 1972), p. 13; cited by Van der Kroef, *op. cit.*, p. 51.
134. *Ibid.*, pp. 51-52.
135. Geoffrey Arlin, "The Organisers," *Far Eastern Economic Review*, 2 July 1973.
136. Walton was subsequently reassigned to Iran, "his capacity there being what it was in Saigon and Manila: the creation and strengthening of the civil police in order to 'protect' the people from any anti-Government movements." *Ibid.*
137. *Ibid.*
138. *Ibid.*
139. *Ibid.*
140. Tad Szulc, "The Moveable War," *New Republic,* 12 May 1973.
141. "Another Senate Test," *New York Times* (9 July 1973).
142. See Volume II, chapters 4 and 5.
143. For some details, see Chomsky, *At War with Asia*, Pantheon, 1970, chapter 4 and *For Reasons of State,* Pantheon, 1973, chapter 2 and references cited there. For a Laotian view, see Fred Branfman, ed., *Voices from the Plain of Jars,* Harper, 1972.
144. The program of the NDF and a discussion of its constituency and growth is given in "Preparing For Revolution, The United Front in the Philippines," *Southeast Asia Chronicle*, No. 62, May-June 1978.
145. *Ibid.*, pp. 8-9.
146. Thus, on the eve of the demonstration election of April 7, 1978, hundreds of thousands of people in Manila turned out—"workers and upper class matrons, students and soldiers, young and old, housewives and taxi drivers, bar hostesses and stockbrokers—poured into the streets shouting, banging pots and pans, honking car horns, exploding firecrackers, singing, marching through the streets in demonstration of support for the opposition *Laban* (Fight) Party. For three hours, the people shouted their anger, frustration and hatred for the Marcos regime. *Laban* organizers had called for a 15-minute demonstration." *Ibid.*, p. 2.

This is reminiscent of Greece on November 3, 1968. The last legally elected Greek Prime Minister, George Papandreou, died on November 1, 1968, and the junta of Colonels, by then in power for 18 months, could hardly prevent a public funeral for this notable. One month previously the junta had "won" a completely fraudulent and meaningless referendum. The funeral of November 3 brought out a crowd of 500,000 mourners into the streets of Athens, who in the safety of overwhelming numbers made very clear their contempt and hatred for the U.S.-sponsored client fascist regime of Greece. It was a moment of truth for the junta and for those outside Greece who wanted to see.

147. See Joseph Lelyveld, "Church in Philippines Becoming A Focus of Opposition to Marcos," *New York Times* (18 October 1973); "Manila Presses Its Drive on Liberal Catholics With Arrests and Closing of Radio Stations," *New York Times* (28 November 1976); Richard Deats, "Christian Resistance Intensifies in the Philippines," *Social Questions Bulletin,* The Methodist Federation For Social Action, March-April 1975.

148. See section 4.5. of this chapter.

149. Johnson put out a search for Communists in the Dominican Republic *after* the decision to invade had already been made, in order to provide the touch of acceptability that an honest admission of an intent to prevent a modestly independent democracy would not have given him. In their hasty mustering up of a list of "Communists," the Embassy in Santo Domingo included a number of small children and deceased individuals. See Theodore Draper, *The Dominican Revolt: A Case Study in American Policy*, Commentary, 1968; Jerome Slater, *The United States and the Dominican Revolution*, Harper, 1971.

150. Alan Riding, "Balaguer and His Firm Ally, the U.S., Are Targets of Dominican Unrest," *New York Times* (6 June 1975).

151. AI, *Report on Torture*, pp. 211-212.

152. Norman Gall, "Santo Domingo: The Politics of Terror," *New York Review of Books*, 22 July 1971.

153. AI, *Annual Report* for 1977, p. 138.

154. Coalition for Human Rights, *Congressional Record*, 5 April 1978, H 2511.

155. The PRD ran on a vague platform that promised improved health programs, a larger educational budget, and mild land reform. But under the pressures of the military and economic elites Guzman gradually backed away from the mildly threatening aspects of his program and also promised to send abroad for a year the PRD's black Secretary General, Jose Francisco Pena Gomez, one of the few top level holdovers from the far more reformist PRD of the Bosch era. While Guzman was backtracking on his reformism,

> At the same time, Balaguer successfully maneuvered 40 measures—including new military statutes—through a lame duck legislature that will significantly limit Guzman's freedom of action. Civil courts will no longer have jurisdiction over members of the armed forces, and the military will have the power to decide which Dominican citizens living abroad (some in exile) can return home. In addition, under pressure from Balaguer, the Electoral Commission gave four contested Senate seats to his right-wing Revolutionary Party, assuring it a majority in that body. All legislation has to be approved by both houses....[All judges in the Republic are appointed by the Senate, including the Chief Justice of the Supreme Court, who would become President if Guzman or the Vice President were deposed.] Under the new legislative constraints and the continuing strength of a vigilant military, it seems unlikely the new government will change much in the Dominican Republic.

Elizabeth Farnsworth, "U.S. Endorses Dominican Election: New President Has Little Room to Maneuver," *International Bulletin*, 28 August 1978.

156. The PRD moved steadily to the right following the 1965 invasion, with important leaders killed or exiled, and with Bosch himself leaving the party in 1973 to form a new party. It has become more and more a party of the mildest sorts of reform, under the leadership of increasingly respectable men of wealth with close ties to foreign corporations and representatives of foreign powers. Philip Wheaton notes that Jacob Majluta, the vice presidential candidate, is an economist-businessman with long-standing ties to foreign companies and to Sacha Volman, a key CIA-labor operative in the Dominican Republic, now a labor adviser to Falconbridge Nickel. George Blanco, who ran on the PRD ticket as Senator for Santo Domingo, serves as a lawyer for a number of multinationals. "Dominican Republic Elections," NACLA *Report on the Americas*, vol. XII, July-August 1978, pp. 39-41.

157. We have noted elsewhere that in its search for justifications for military support of terror states, the State Department grasps at resounding promises, and the leaders of subfascism are very obliging on this point. As the Washington Office on Latin America points out in regard to the State Department treatment of the Dominican Republic:

> The report admits that Amnesty was critical of human rights practices in the Dominican Republic in 1977. It goes on to cite "*regrets*" by Balaguer, his "*signing*" of the American Human Rights Convention, and his "*agreement*" to invite Amnesty to visit the country, an invitation which was later rescinded. In other words, the State Department accepts Balaguer's verbal promises rather than looking at actual evidence as a means of countering the Amnesty report. Balaguer is playing the game of endorsing the campaign for human rights in order to whitewash the actual violations. (Coalition For Human Rights, *Congressional Record*, 5 April 1978, H 2511.)

158. See note 150, this chapter.

159. "A Reporter's Notebook: For the Dominicans the Elections Is a Test of a Shaky Democracy," *New York Times* (27 May 1978).

160. Deborah Sue Yaeger, "Internal Philip Morris Filings Outline Payoffs by Dominican Republic Affiliate," *Wall Street Journal* (28 December 1976).

161. "Gulf & Western In The Dominican Republic: II," *CIC Brief*, November-December 1976, p. 3D.

162. "Gulf & Western In The Dominican Republic," *CIC Brief*, October 1975, p. 3C.

163. The phrase is attributed to "some cynics" in Alan Riding, "The Caribbean Role of G & W," *New York Times* (24 June 1974).

164. Of the eight divisions of G & W's conglomerate operations, the food and agricultural products group in 1974 accounted for 6% of total revenues but 26% ($58 million) of operating income. Most of that profitability came from G & W's Dominican sugar operations. See "Gulf & Western In the Dominican Republic," *CIC Brief*, October 1975.

165. Stanley Penn, "Angry Investor Thinks Gulf & Western Is Trying to Block His Dominican Resort," *Wall Street Journal* (1 June 1976).

166. "An Employer's Paradise: America's sweatshop in the sun," *Chicago Sun-Times* (26 March 1978).

167. In its Report No. 3 on *Gulf & Western In the Dominican Republic*, dated May 1968, G & W notes that "Wage scales in the Free Zone are established by the

Dominican Republic's Secretariat of Labor...." At the time the report was written the minimum wage in the Free Zone was 55¢ an hour according to G & W (p. 53), 34¢ an hour according to Michael Flannery.

168. In its 1978 report on Dominican Operations G & W stresses the fact that it was a successor to South Puerto Rico Sugar Company (SPR), which still controlled operations at the time of the strike-breaking. G & W contends that the SPR management was "imperious" and that there was "chronic neglect of employees, wages, working conditions and health care." An example of imperiousness was the fact that "At 5 p.m. every day the city water supply was shut off so SPR executives could water their lawns" (p. 29). This practice was stopped immediately, and G & W contends that radical changes took place otherwise, but no independent union yet exists and wages are low. Wages are hard to measure, but G & W acknowledges that real wages per ton of sugar cane cut fell between 1966-78 (p. 61). It claims that free housing, medical services and subsidized food that it now provides make a big difference, however, and that its wages are well above those paid in government sugar operations.

169. "U.S. team denounced Balaguer, Jesuit accuses U.S. government of 'aid'," *National Catholic Reporter* (3 October 1975).

170. Michael Flannery, "Dominican guns keep unions out," *Chicago Sun-Times* (27 March 1978).

171. The lower echelons, visiting the Dominican Republic, have bitterly criticized the repression of the unions (*ibid.*), a consequence of the U.S. policy that is aided consistently by their AFL-CIO superiors. On the role of the AFL-CIO and CONATRAL in undermining the Bosch regime, see Suzanne Bodenheimer, "The AFL-CIO In Latin America," *The Dominican Republic: A Case Study, Viet-Report*, September-October 1967.

172. Jonathan Kwitny, "Strange Bedfellows From Labor, Business Own Dominican Resort," *Wall Street Journal* (25 May 1973).

173. An advertisement in the *Wall Street Journal* (25 January 1974), p. 9.

174. See further the items cited above, notes 166-170.

175. See note 168, this chapter.

176. The October 1975 *CIC Brief* on Gulf & Western quotes a June 1975 U.S. Embassy (Santo Domingo) document on economic trends as indicating that wages have not been keeping up with prices.

177. See the discussion in "Gulf & Western In The Dominican Republic," *CIC Brief*, November-December 1976, p. 3B.

178. "An Employer's Paradise..."

179. See the discussion in "Gulf & Western In The Dominican Republic," *CIC Brief*, November-December 1976, p. 3B.

180. "Open Letter to North American Christians" (signed by a number of religious leaders of Latin America, sent to the American National Council of Churches), reprinted in *Fellowship*, journal of the Fellowship of Reconciliation, September 1977.

181. Statement of General Golbery de Couto e Silva, member of the Brazilian government and chief aide to the President. Quoted in *IDOC Monthly Bulletin*, January-February 1977, p. 6. (IDOC abbreviates International Documentation; the Bulletin is a Catholic Church-affiliated service that publishes documents of international interest.)

182. See "Jose Comblin on National Security Doctrine," a summary of the work

of the leading author on this subject, with annotated bibliography, *IDOC Monthly Bulletin*, January-February 1977, pp. 3-9.
183. "The nation is absolute or it is nothing. A nation can accept no limitations of its absolute power." (Silva, *op. cit.*, p. 3.)
184. "For many it is difficult to admit that the world is living in a situation of permanent warfare." Col. Baciagalupo (Chile), quoted in *ibid.*, p. 4.
185. "The Third World's armed forces are the only social organization that is cohesive, capable and efficient enough to cope with the socio-economic problems of the underdeveloped countries." Major Claudio Lopez Silva (Chile), quoted in *ibid.*
186. *Rockefeller Report on the Americas*, Quadrangle, 1969, p. 32.
187. See p. 100.
188. *Rockefeller Report on the Americas*, p. 58.
189. Frederick O. Bonkovsky, "The German State and Protestant Elites," in Franklin H. Littell and Hubert Locke, eds., *The German Church Struggle and the Holocaust*, Wayne State University, 1974, p. 136.
190. Peter Hoffman, "Problems of Resistance in National Socialist Germany," in *ibid.*, p. 99.
191. Bonkovsky, *op. cit.*, p. 143.
192. This is a statement of members of a mission to Paraguay of the U.S. Disciples of Christ, quoted in Penny Lernoux, *Notes on a Revolutionary Church: Human Rights in Latin America*, Alicia Patterson Foundation, February 1978, p. 55.
193. See the church statement quoted earlier on the relationship between "security" and the development model, p. 54.
194. "Voice From Northeastern Brazil to III Conference of Bishops," November 1977, *LADOC*, May-June 1978, p. 9.
195. We will not review here the internal conflicts over these issues in the Catholic Church, which are far from resolution. As we have seen, the role of the churches in Latin America is complex and often destructive, to this day. (See chapter 3, section 5.3.)
196. Lernoux gives an estimate of 3.5 million; *op. cit.*, p. 41.
197. *Ibid.*, p. 40.
198. "For Justice and Liberation," (published in Brazil by 20 lay organizations of Sao Paulo, 18 September 1977), reprinted as "Brazilian Lay People Decry Persecution of the Church," *Latinamerica Press* (20 October 1977).
199. Lernoux, *op. cit.*, p. 46.
200. *Ibid.*
201. *Ibid.*, p. 45.
202. *Ibid.*
203. Bishop Casadaliga, "The Gospel Is My Weapon," *Latinamerica Press* (6 November 1975).
204. Lernoux, *op. cit.*, p. 47.
205. "Christian Requirements of a Political Order," presented by the Brazilian Bishops in Itaica, Sao Paulo, 17 February 1977, reprinted in *LADOC*, January-February 1978, p. 5.
206. "The Marginalization of a People," p. 64.
207. "The Gospel Is My Weapon," see note 203, this chapter.

208. On the Philippines, see above, section 3; on the emergence of such conflict in South Korea, see H.H. Sunoo, *Repressive State and Resisting Church: The Policies of the CIA in South Korea*, Korean American Cultural Association, 1976.
209. The words are by Venezuelan Bishop Mariano Parra Leon, quoted in Lernoux, *op. cit.*, p. 16.
210. *Ibid.*, pp. 17-18.
211. A Brazilian Bishop, quoted in *ibid.*, p. 19.
212. Quoted in *ibid.*
213. See chapter 1, section 9.
214. See chapter 3, section 1.
215. See, for example, the regular reports of Amnesty International, some cited above, or *Repression in Latin America*, a Report of the Russell Tribunal Session in Rome, Spokesman, Winter 1975-76. The latter is one of many studies that will never reach a U.S. audience. As in its earlier hearings on U.S. war crimes in Vietnam, the Russell inquiries lay bare the impact of the U.S. presence in their stark and brutal reality, an intolerable imposition on a free society from which its mass media thoughtfully preserve it. The Russell Tribunal on Vietnam was either ignored or vilified; the Latin American Tribunal is simply ignored. The reason for the difference is that it was impossible, under the circumstances of the 1960s, simply to ignore the Vietnam proceedings. A few years later, when it was considered appropriate by U.S. ideologists to lift the curtain on U.S. atrocities in Vietnam—that is, when powerful groups in the U.S. determined that the game was not worth the candle and that the U.S. should limit its intervention—much material of a similar sort appeared in the U.S. press, though without the systematic analysis accompanying the Russell Tribunal hearings. But that did not put an end to the denunciation of the Tribunal or of Russell personally for his association with it.

One can find occasional reference in the U.S. press to the Russell Tribunal on repression in Latin America. For example, the *Boston Globe* (1 October 1978) devoted 9 lines to a report from Rio de Janeiro that nine civilians were put on trial for having leaked information in 1969 on torture in Brazilian prisons to the Russell Tribunal, as well as to Amnesty International and the international press. The report aroused no response in a press which is in a continual uproar over the mock trials of Soviet dissidents.
216. The *New York Times*, editorializing on "Repression in Argentina" (26 May 1976), says that "what is in doubt is not General Videla's good intentions but his ability to control military men driven by obsessions..." etc. Since the abuses in question followed Videla's assumption of power, the placing of his good intentions as beyond doubt—without the slightest substantive evidence here or elsewhere of lack of control or agreement with the terror — is solid evidence of bias in favor of subfascism. Can one imagine, for example, comparable remarks in a *Times* editorial on the good intentions of the Cambodian government which is unfortunately unable to control local commanders or vengeful peasants?
217. "Argentines begin a chilly recovery in cold light of harsh economics," *Philadelphia Inquirer* (27 March 1977).
218. "Politics Are Only Part of Argentina's Difficulties," *New York Times* (20 November 1977).
219. "Rightist Terror Stirs Argentina," *New York Times* (29 August 1976).

220. Philippe Labreveux, "Argentine: La repression se poursuit sans susciter la reprobation de la communaute internationale," *Le Monde* (19 October 1977).
221. It should be noted that other powers, great and small, have found no problem in accommodating to the U.S.-sponsored terror system in Latin America. The USSR is one of Argentina's main trading partners, "unwilling to alienate this supplier of wheat without which Soviet citizens will be at the mercy of the Amercians in the case of a bad harvest;" and the Soviets are apparently quite unconcerned by torture and murder by state authorities, by economic policies that in two years halved the standard of living of the working class, or by the violent anti-communist ideology exuberantly proclaimed by the military. One of the first countries to offer its support to General Videla was democratic Venezuela, and the Third World generally has supported the Argentine regime, as have the European powers. See Jean-Pierre Clerc, "Un pays en etat de choc," *Le Monde* (6 June 1978); Labreveux, *op. cit.*; Marek Halter, "Pourquoi l'Argentine," *Le Monde* (4 February 1978).
222. Michael D. Boggs and Andrew C. McLellan, "Argentine trade unions," AFL-CIO *Free Trade Union News,* February 1978.
223. For a description of one such meeting, "virtually a meeting of the Trilateral Commission," see "The Argentine Economic Debacle," *Argentina Outreach*, March-April 1978, pp. 2-3.
224. Quoted in Christopher Knowles, "Strike wave grips Argentina," *Guardian*, New York (16 November 1977).
225. *Le Monde* (2 June 1978).
226. "Open Letter," 24 March 1977; published by the Argentine Commission for Human Rights, Washington Information Bureau, P.O. Box 2635, Washington, D.C. 20013.
227. *Amnesty International Newsletter*, April 1977, volume VII, no. 4, summarizing the report of an Amnesty International Mission of November, 1976, eight months after the coup.
228. *Matchbox* (AI) Spring, 1978, pp. 9-10.
229. "Testimony of a Prisoner," *Argentina Outreach*, July-August 1977, pp. 13-14. Ms Erb was a sociology student at the University of Buenos Aires. The junta position is that only guerrillas and left-wing suspects and extremists are ever put through their torture chambers. Juan de Onis assumes this rule to be true, despite the extensive evidence that the Argentinian police and military have killed and tortured the *children* of political enemies and despite the fact that the subfascist definition of "suspected subversive" could include his employer Arthur Sulzberger (just as it reached out to cover Jacobo Timmerman, the Jewish editor of *La Opinion*). In an article describing the Chilean secret police involvement in the assassination of Orlando Letelier, de Onis explained that the juntas exchange information and "cooperate" with one another (translation: allow one another's death squads to murder at will across state lines) "in combating left wing guerrilla groups that are also structured on regional lines." "Paraguayan Links Chilean General to Letelier Case," *New York Times* (20 July 1978). The Letelier murder nails the lie that targets of subfascist murders are confined to "left-wing guerrilla groups," but even in this specific context de Onis slides automatically into apologetics.
230. *New York Times* (30 June 1978).
231. See "Every voice can save a life...," A resource and action update on Argen-

tina, American Friends Service Committee, December 1977; William Goodfellow and James Morrell, "Small Change," 4 March 1977, mimeographed. Similar observations hold for Uruguay. Goodfellow and Morrell note that in fiscal 1976, the last year for which complete figures were available to them, the U.S. aid that has since been cut off amounted to about 7 percent of total international financing in which the United States was directly involved, since increased after the coup.

232. "Carter's Aid: A Slap on the Wrist While Money Still Flows," *Argentina Outreach,* March-April, 1977, p. 5.

233. See NACLA's *Latin America & Empire Report*, January 1977, for a fuller discussion. Also Jon Steinberg, "More than a world cup," *Seven Days*, July 1978.

234. See, among many other sources, James Petras and Morris Morley, *The United States and Chile*, Monthly Review Press, 1975; Robinson Rojas Sandford, *The Murder of Allende,* Harper and Row, 1976; John Gittings, ed., *The Lessons of Chile*, Spokesman, 1975; Amnesty International, *Chile*, AI publications, 1974.

235. *Amnesty Action*, March 1976, published by AI, U.S.A.

236. *Fellowship*, September 1977.

237. Recall the interview with Conservative leader Wilson Ferreira Aldunate, who notes that the terrorism of the Uruguayan military government began after the total destruction of the Tupamaros. (See chapter 3, pp. 90-91).

238. See A.J. Langguth, *Hidden Terrors,* Pantheon, 1978, and sources cited there. For a sympathetic Uruguayan account, see "The Tupamaros," reprinted as a booklet from *Tricontinental*, November-December 1968, January-February 1969, March-April 1970. See also James Kohl and John Litt, *Urban Guerrilla Warfare in Latin America*, MIT Press, 1974.

239. Recall the estimate by Wilson Ferreira Aldunate that the number of exiles is half a million. (See chapter 3, pp. 90-91.)

240. Juan de Onis, *New York Times* (22 November 1976).

241. See note 215. As the introduction to this volume points out, though the *Tribunal* was rather fully reported in the Italian, French and Belgian press and the Scandinavian media, the English-speaking world has ignored it, in part for reasons mentioned in note 215.

242. Cf. p. 10. Eduardo Galeano, "Un petit pays dans le 'marche commun de la mort'," *Le Monde diplomatique*, September 1977. In an accompanying article, a "Uruguayan personality" who must remain anonymous estimates on the basis of official figures that about 12% of the population is unaccounted for, presumably abroad, including a large part of the trained and educated sectors. The two articles give an account of Uruguayan fascism and its support by the U.S. (in part through international financial institutions, overcoming the "human rights" gestures) that would be difficult to find in the U.S. press.

243. Cf. Langguth, *op. cit.*, p. 253. There are similar reports of direct U.S. involvement in torture elsewhere; e.g., *ibid.*, pp. 164-65. A double agent who infiltrated the CIA from 1962 to 1970 on behalf of Cuban intelligence testified in Havana that Mitrione had personally tortured beggars to death in demonstration sessions for Uruguayan trainees. *New York Times* (5 August 1978). Cf. Langguth on Mitrione's career and the U.S. program of terrorism in Uruguay and Brazil. (See also chapter 1, note 40.)

244. A. J. Langguth, "The mind of a torturer," *The Nation*, 24 June 1978.

245. See note 236.
246. On the ways in which the Russians have regularly mimicked U.S. doctrine on regional hegemony, both in rhetoric and in practice, see Thomas M. Franck and Edward Weisband, *Word Politics,* Oxford, 1971. For still earlier interactions of this nature in the latter stages of World War II, see G. Kolko, *Politics of War*, specifically, his discussion of Italy and Rumania.
247. Cited by Laurence H. Shoup and William Minter, *Imperial Brain Trust,* Monthly Review, 1977, p. 197.
248. See chapter 3, note 34.
249. For an informative review, see Susanne Jones and David Tobis, eds., *Guatemala*, NACLA, Berkeley, 1974, and Roger Plant, *Guatemala: Unnatural Disaster,* Latin America Bureau, London, 1978. Guatemala is not the sole supplier of blood. The assassinated editor Pedro Joaquin Chamorro of Nicaragua is reported to have been murdered by agents of a company "which bought the blood of impoverished Nicaraguans and exported it to the United States." Alan Riding, *New York Times Magazine,* 30 July 1978. On the mechanism by which the poor countries of the world provide agricultural assistance to the rich, see Susan George, *How the Other Half Dies*, Allanheld, Osmun & Co., 1977; Frances Moore Lappe and Joseph Collins, *Food First,* Houghton Mifflin, 1977; Lappe and Collins, "Food First Revisited," *Ag World*, April 1978. See also several articles in *Le Monde diplomatique*, September 1978. Gonzalo Arroyo ("L'agro-business en Amerique latine") comments that the new agri-business model spreading throughout the underdeveloped world may increase production, "but it creates disequilibrium at the regional level and in types of [agricultural] production, essentially oriented towards production of primary materials for agri-industry and/or for export. Meanwhile the increase of production is null for certain other agricultural products, in particular, basic commodities for the local population," and also tends to exhaust the soil and damage the ecological system in the interests of short-term profit.
250. Plant, *op. cit.*, p. 86.
251. Plant, *op. cit.*, p. 73, citing the English sociologist Andrew Pearse.
252. *Guatemala and the Dominican Republic*, staff memorandum prepared for the use of the Subcommittee on Western Hemisphere Affairs of the Committee on Foreign Relations, U.S. Senate, 30 December 1971, U.S. Government Printing Office, Washington, 1971.
253. *Guatemala*, Amnesty International Briefing, London, 1976.
254. *Ibid.*, p. 3.
255. *Guatemala—Another Vietnam?*, Penguin, 1971, p. 293. They are quoting an embassy statement cited in a UPI dispatch by Theodore Ediger, 19 January 1968.
256. *Op. cit.*, p. 14. (See note 253.)
257. Amnesty International *Newletter*, April 1978, London.
258. Stephen Kinzer, "Guatemala beyond Bananas," *New Republic,* 5 March 1977.
259. James P. Sterba, "The quake hit a stricken land," *New York Times* (18 February 1976).
260. Jonathan Dimbleby, "Kissinger Comes to the Rescue," *New Statesman* (26 March 1976).
261. Alan Riding, "Free Use of Pesticides in Guatemala Takes a Deadly Toll," *New York Times* (9 November 1977).

262. Marlise Simons, "Guatemala Massacre of Indians," reprinted from the *Washington Post* in the *Manchester Guardian Weekly* (9 July 1978).
263. Amnesty International, *Newsletter*, September 1978.
264. "Instances of the use of United States Armed Forces Abroad, 1798-1945," pp. 82-87 (see chapter 2, note 1).
265. Alan Riding, "National Mutiny in Nicaragua," *New York Times Magazine*, 30 July 1978.
266. For an illustration, see the Reuters dispatch, "Somoza Widening His Control but Foes Vow No Letup," *New York Times* (17 February 1974).
267. Riding, *op. cit.* (See note 265.)
268. John Huey, "Human Rights and Nicaragua," *Wall Street Journal* (19 September 1978).
269. John Huey, "Business Elite Joins Struggle to Displace Nicaraguan Dictator," *Wall Street Journal* (23 February 1978).
270. Alan Riding, *New York Times* (3 March 1977).
271. Alan Riding, *New York Times* (2 March 1977).
272. See, for example, Penny Lernoux, "'Our S.O.B.s': The Somozas of Nicaragua," *The Nation*, 23 July 1977; Stephen Kinzer, "Nicaragua, a Wholly Owned Subsidiary," *New Republic*, 9 April 1977.
273. See above, section 4.4. For more extensive background supplementing Lernoux's valuable direct report, see *Nicaragua*, NACLA's *Latin America and Empire Report*, February, 1976.
274. John M. Goshko and Karen DeYoung, " 'Garbled' Rights Message," and Karen DeYoung, "Peasants Expect Little Help," side-by-side on 24 October 1977.
275. John M. Goshko, "U.S. Frees Aid to Nicaragua in a Policy Reversal," *Washington Post* (16 May 1978).
276. DeYoung, *op. cit.*
277. Alan Riding, *New York Times* (12 November 1978).
278. Smith Hempstone, "It's Logical for Israel to Continue Supplying Weapons to Nicaragua," *Washington Post* (3 December 1978).
279. See Volume II, chapter 6.
280. John Huey, "Dictator's Decline; as Nicaragua Turmoil Intensifies, Support of Somoza Evaporates," *Wall Street Journal* (12 September 1978). This report is largely concerned with the "dark mood of businessmen" whose "unity against General Somoza now is almost complete."
281. Karen DeYoung, "He Was Crying, 'Don't Kill Me, Don't Kill Me!'," *Washington Post* (20 September 1978).
282. Tad Szulc, "Rocking Nicaragua — 'The Rebels' Own Story, Anger at Carter letter and other U.S. actions motivates pro-Castro guerrillas, a spreading problem for Washington in Central America," *Washington Post* (3 September 1978). Szulc also found that the anti-Somoza campaign involved "virtually every civic organization in Nicaragua, including businessmen and the Roman Catholic Church," and that its intensity was such that "any gesture toward Somoza [from Washington] would backfire." This was the State Department assessment prior to the President's letter to Somoza.
283. UPI, "Carter phones support to Shah; troops again fire at crowd," *Boston Globe* (11 September 1978). (See also chapter 1, section 5, and notes 80, 88.)

284. Edward Cody, "The Shah of Iran Given Assurance of U.S. Support," *Washington Post* (1 November 1978).
285. See chapter 1, note 43.
286. On this matter, see *Access to Oil — The United States Relationships with Saudi Arabia and Iran*, report of the Committee on Energy and Natural Resources, Henry M. Jackson, Chairman, U.S. Senate, U.S. Government Printing Office, Washington, 1977. The report emphasizes Iran's role in blocking any "threats to the continuous flow of oil through the Gulf," which "would so endanger the Western and Japanese economies as to be grounds for general war." It notes further that "the most serious threats may emanate from internal changes in Gulf states...if Iran is called upon [sic] to intervene in the internal affairs of any Gulf state [as it already has, with U.S. blessings and in coordination with Britain and Jordan in counterinsurgency in Oman] it must be recognized in advance by the United States that *this is the role for which Iran is being primed and blame cannot be assigned for Iran's carrying out an implied assignment*" (p. 84, our emphasis). Thus "a strong and stable Iran" serves "as a deterrent against Soviet adventurism in the region" and "against radical groups in the Gulf" (p. 111). This is, of course, the real reason for the enormous build-up of the Iranian military by the United States and the reason why the United States found the Shah's regime "progressive," whatever the facts might be.
287. Alan Riding, "U.S. Strategy in Nicaragua Keeps the Time Bomb Ticking," *New York Times* (17 December 1978).
288. John M. Goshko, "Nicaragua: Case of Limits on U.S. Clout Abroad," *Washington Post* (30 September 1978). On 24 September, the U.S. Senate voted to delete from the foreign aid bill "$150,000 for military training and education [sic] in Nicaragua," already scaled down from programs totaling $579,000 in 1977 and $400,000 in 1978. *Christian Science Monitor* (25 September 1978).
289. *Le Monde* (23 September 1978); translated in the *Manchester Guardian Weekly* (1 October 1978). One wonders when the pressure of facts will lead to some skepticism in the West about this "human rights stance."
290. *Manchester Guardian Weekly* (1 October 1978).
291. *New York Times* (25 July 1978). For background on Bolivia, see Laurence Whitehead, *The United States and Bolivia*, Haslemere Group Publications, 515 Liverpool Road, London N7, 1969.
292. Alan Riding, *New York Times* (27 August 1975).
293. Alan Riding, "Fear Rules in El Salvador as Political Foes Turn Violent," *New York Times* (30 July 1978).

5 Bloodbaths in Indochina: Constructive, Nefarious and Mythical

1. Examples will appear below and in Volume II.
2. In the apologetic model, of course, the civilians were terrorized by the NLF and were thus harboring the terrorists out of fear and coercion. Most of the less

hysterical apologists knew that this coercion theory of support was highly suspect. (See sections 1.1 and 2.1, this chapter.)

3. Sidney Hook, "Lord Russell and the War Crimes 'Trial'," *New Leader* (24 October 1966); "The Knight of the Double Standard," *The Humanist*, January 1971.

4. The restriction is regrettable as the systematic character of U.S. aggression in Indochina can only be appreciated by an account that shows how the war machine was unleashed against North Vietnam, Laos and Cambodia in ever more savage efforts to maintain U.S. control at least of South Vietnam. (See Volume II, chapter 1.)

5. For our own views and background for them, see Edward S. Herman and Richard B. Du Boff, *America's Vietnam Policy, The Strategy of Deception*, Public Affairs Press, 1966; E.S. Herman, *Atrocities in Vietnam: Myths and Realities*, Pilgrim Press, 1970; Noam Chomsky, *American Power and the New Mandarins*, Pantheon, 1969; *At War with Asia*, Pantheon, 1970; *For Reasons of State*, Pantheon, 1973; and many other publications.

6. Phillipe Devillers, *Histoire du Vietnam*, Seuil, 1952, p. 337.

7. "The Problem of Democracy in Vietnam," *The World Today* (February 1960), p. 73. Later he was to write that by 1956 "it was already clear that...[Diem]...was establishing an authoritarian regime which would tolerate no political dissent" (P.J. Honey, "Viet Nam Argument," *Encounter*, November 1965), though if it was already clear in 1956, one did not learn this from his pen. The *Encounter* article was devoted to showing how much things were improving since the "popular revolt headed by the army" that overthrew Diem, that is, the U.S. backed military coup.

8. See sections 1.5 and 1.6, this chapter.

9. Jean Lacouture, *Vietnam: Between Two Truces*, Vintage, 1969, p. 29.

10. David Hotham, in Richard Lindholm, ed., *Vietnam: The First Five Years*, Michigan State, 1959, p. 359.

11. J.J. Zasloff, *Origins of the Insurgency in South Vietnam, 1954-1960: The Role of the Southern Vietminh Cadres*, Rand, March 1967, p. 11.

12. *Ibid.*, pp. 12-13.

13. See Buttinger, *Vietnam: The Unforgettable Tragedy*, Horizon, 1977, for some documentation on his advisory role and also for an account of his radical change in view, which led him to believe that "future historians may very likely regard the claims that in South Vietnam the United States was defending a free country against foreign aggression among the great political lies of this century" (p. 34) — a lie which, however, like others of its genre, is generally believed (or at least propounded) by the intelligentsia of the state that produced it. See, for example, Arthur M. Schlesinger, Jr., *A Thousand Days: John F. Kennedy in the White House*, Houghton Mifflin, 1965 (Fawcett, 1967 edition, p. 695): "1962 had not been a bad year: ...aggression checked in Vietnam." In fact, 1962 was the first year in which U.S. military forces were directly engaged in combat and combat support, bombing of villages, gunning down of peasants from helicopters, defoliation, etc. Only three years later, in April 1965, did U.S. intelligence report the presence of the first North Vietnamese battalion in the South. The "aggression" was of the sort that liberal intellectuals like to call "internal aggression"; see above, p. 99. For many more examples, see the above references of note 5. On the

internal U.S. government analysis of "North Vietnamese aggression," see Chomsky, "The Pentagon Papers as Propaganda and as History," in N. Chomsky and H. Zinn, eds., *The Pentagon Papers: Critical Essays*, published with an index to Volumes 1-4 as Volume V of the Senator Gravel edition of the *Pentagon Papers*, Beacon Press, 1971-72.

14. "Lösung für Vietnam," *Neues Forum* (August/September, 1969), p. 459. Later, Buttinger was to write that "Communist control of the whole country [North and South] was achieved without the use of force, not of course because the Vietnamese Communists reject force as a means to gain power, but for the simple reason that in the absence of any effective political resistance, the Communists needed no force to establish control over the whole of Vietnam." *Vietnam: The Unforgettable Tragedy*, p. 17. For exactly the same reason, substantial use of force was required by the United States and its clients to suppress the Viet Minh movement that had successfully withstood the French invasion. As Buttinger remarks, "It required a tidal wave of falsehood to persuade Americans into accepting the myth that not French, but Communist, aggression was responsible for the first Indochina war" (*ibid.*, p. 22), as was constantly trumpeted by Dean Acheson and a host of sycophants.

15. Jeffrey Race, *War Comes to Long An*, University of California, 1971, p. 197; to date, the best account of the origins of the insurgency under the U.S.-Diem regime. There is also important material on this subject in the massive "Vietcong Motivation and Morale Study" undertaken by the Rand Corporation. For an interesting study based on this generally ignored material, see David Hunt, "Organizing for Revolution in Vietnam," *Radical America*, vol. 8, nos. 1-2, 1974. See also Georges Chaffard, *Les deux guerres du Vietnam*, La Table Ronde, Paris, 1969. U.S. government sources, in addition to the *Pentagon Papers*, also contain much useful information: see Robert L. Sansom, *The Economics of Insurgency In the Mekong Delta*, MIT Press, 1970; Douglas Pike, *Viet Cong*, MIT Press, 1966 (here, one must be careful to distinguish the documentary evidence presented from the conclusions asserted); William A. Nighswonger, *Rural Pacification in Vietnam*, Praeger, 1967.

16. *Pentagon Papers*, Gravel edition, v. I, p. 259. See also the Government edition of the *Pentagon Papers*, U.S. Department of Defense, *United States-Vietnam Relations, 1945-67*, 12 vols., Government Printing Office, Washington, 1971; henceforth: DOD. See note 33, this chapter.

17. *Pentagon Papers*, Gravel edition, v. 1, p. 259.

18. *Ibid.*, p. 254.

19. *Ibid.*

20. *Ibid.*, p. 255.

21. *Ibid.*, p. 243.

22. Diem had publicly repudiated the Accords in January 1955 and the U.S. gave him complete support until he became a liability and was removed (indeed, eliminated) in 1963 in a U.S.-backed Generals' coup. The same record was replayed 18 years later when Washington signed a "peace agreement" in Paris in January 1973 with much fanfare (even collecting a Nobel Prize) but immediately announced with utter clarity that it had not the slightest intention of observing its terms, which it proceeded at once to subvert quite openly — all of this before the eyes of the media, which remained silent and obedient. (See Volume II, chapter 1, for some comment and references.)

23. Bernard Fall, "Vietcong — The Unseen Enemy in Vietnam," *New Society*, 22 April 1965; reprinted in Bernard Fall and Marcus G. Raskin, eds., *The Vietnam Reader*, Vintage, 1965. Fall, basically a military man, was no dove. (See chapter 3, note 44.)
24. The problem was seen to be, in part, the "tremendous sense of dependence on the U.S." of countries like the Philippines and South Korea. National Security Council Working Group Project — Courses of Action, Southeast Asia (10 November 1964), *Pentagon Papers*, Gravel edition, v. I, p. 627.
25. In the State Department's view, "a fundamental source of danger we face in the Far East derives from Communist China's rate of economic growth which will probably continue to outstrip that of free Asian countries, with the possible exception of Japan." (DOD, bk. 10, p. 1198). The Department urged that we do what we can to retard the progress of Asian Communist states. The assault on North and South Vietnam certainly contributed to that end, as did the no less violent attacks on Laos and Cambodia. We return in Volume II, chapter 1, to this theory of how to combat the dangers we face.
26. The NSC Working Group Project says that "In South Korea, there is...some discouragement at the failure to make as much progress politically and economically as North Korea (from a much more favorable initial position) has made." *Op. cit.* See note 24, this chapter. Recall that North Korea had been almost totally demolished in the Korean War, including even the bombing of dams to destroy the food supply of the population when the U.S. Air Force could find no more targets.
27. An intelligence estimate of 1959 concluded that "development will lag behind that in the North, and the GVN will continue to rely heavily upon US support...." In the North, while life is "grim and regimented...the national effort is concentrated on building for the future." (DOD, bk. 10, pp. 1191-1193). In essence, this forecast proved to be correct. See the quotes from Kellen, chapter 3, note 41, and text.
28. Revised Bundy/McNaughton Draft of November 21, 1964, *Pentagon Papers*, Gravel ed., v. III, p. 661.
29. *Ibid.*
30. Dean Acheson, *Present at the Creation*, Norton, 1969, p. 219.
31. Gabriel Kolko, "The American Goals in Vietnam," *Pentagon Papers*, Gravel ed., v. V, *Critical Essays*, p. 2.
32. On this matter, see John Dower, "The Superdomino in Postwar Asia: Japan in and out of the Pentagon Papers," in *Pentagon Papers*, Gravel ed., v. V, *Critical Essays*.
33. As should be obvious, the *Pentagon Papers*, though a useful source, must be regarded with the same caution that one would use in the case of productions, even for internal use, by scholars and bureaucrats working for other states. In fact, there is substantial misrepresentation, particularly with regard to such ideologically crucial matters as the origins of insurgency. For discussion, see Chomsky, "The Pentagon Papers as Propaganda and as History," in *Pentagon Papers*, Gravel ed., v. V, *Critical Essays*. The same is true with regard to intelligence analyses. It is necessary to study the record to see how dominated the intelligence agencies were by the framework of propaganda that they themselves were helping to construct in their disinformation campaigns. To mention one striking example, the *Pentagon Papers* analysts were able to discover only one staff paper in a record of more than two decades "which treats communist reactions

primarily in terms of the separate national interests of Hanoi, Moscow, and Peiping," rather than regarding Hanoi simply as an agent of International Communism, directed from abroad. One expects this from Dean Acheson, Dean Rusk, and the more chauvinist elements of academic scholarship, but it is surprising to find such total subordination to state dogma in the intelligence agencies as well. For discussion, see Chomsky, *For Reasons of State*, p. 51.

34. See NSC Working Group on Vietnam, Sec. 1: "Intelligence Assessment: The Situation in Vietnam," 24 November 1964, Doc. 240, *Pentagon Papers*, Gravel ed., v. III, pp. 651-56.

35. In an unpublished and untitled memorandum on pacification problems circulated within the military in 1965, a copy of which was given by Vann to Professor Alex Carey, University of New South Wales, Australia.

36. For the intellectual backup of a policy of terror and violence, see Charles Wolf, Jr., *United States Policy and the Third World*, Little, Brown, 1967. Wolf was Senior Economist for the Rand Corporation.

37. For references, and a general review of Komer's theories and policies, see Chomsky, *For Reasons of State*, pp. 84f.

38. Cited by Richard Critchfield, *The Long Charade*, Harcourt Brace and World, 1968, p. 173.

39. Douglas Kinnard, *The War Managers*, University Press of New England, 1977, pp. 75, 47.

40. Katsuichi Honda, *Vietnam — A Voice from the Villages*, published in English translation in Tokyo, though it never reached the status of a best-seller in the United States. (See note 48, this chapter; and note 53, chapter 1.)

41. Letter from a U.S. soldier in Vietnam to Senator Fulbright, reprinted in the *Congressional Record*, 16 June 1967.

42. See Rafael Littauer and Norman Uphoff, eds., *The Air War in Indochina*, revised edition, Beacon, 1971, p. 62.

43. *Ibid.*, p. 55.

44. Michael J. Uhl, Hearings Before Subcommittee of House Committee on Government Operations, *U.S. Assistance Programs in Vietnam* (July/August 1971), p. 315; henceforth, *U.S. Assistance Programs*. For a more extensive quote, see text at note 97, this chapter.

45. Quoted in Arthur M. Schlesinger, Jr., *The Bitter Heritage*, Houghton Mifflin, 1967, p. 47.

46. Indochina Resource Center, "A Statistical Fact Sheet on the Indochina War," (27 September 1972).

47. *The Air War in Indochina*, p. 63.

48. See, for example, Herman, *Atrocities in Vietnam*, Chapter 3; Seymour Hersh, *My Lai 4*, Random House, 1971; Katsuichi Honda, *Vietnam War: A Report Through Asian Eyes*, Mirai-sha, 1972; Jonathan Schell, *The Military Half: An Account of Destruction in Quang Ngai and Quang Tin*, Vintage, 1968; James Kunen, *Standard Operating Procedure*, Avon, 1971.

49. Shimkin, who was killed in Vietnam, was an International Voluntary Services (IVS) worker who had aroused the ire of the US-Saigon authorities when he "told a *New York Times* reporter about the forced use of farm labor to clear a mine field in Ba Chuc village in the Mekong Delta when American officials there refused to act even after some of the farm people were killed and several wounded" (Don Luce, "'Tell Your Friends That We're People'," in *Pentagon*

Papers, v. V, *Critical Essays*). IVS was later expelled for being "too political." Its director had protested before the Kennedy Refugee Subcommittee of the Senate on "the forced movement of the Montagnards from their mountain homes into the city slums" (Luce). Kevin Buckley was the head of the *Newsweek* Bureau in Saigon. We are indebted to Buckley for allowing us to use his original notes for the *Newsweek* article in which his account of SPEEDY EXPRESS was partially reported ("Pacification's Deadly Price," *Newsweek*, 19 June 1972). Quotes are from Buckley's notes unless identified as *Newsweek*, in which case they are from the published article.

50. See Peter Braestrup, *Big Story*, Westview, vol. II, Documents, p. 20. On this Freedom House effort to show how the media undermined our noble enterprise in Vietnam, see volume II, chapter 1.

51. On the behavior of the 9th Division and its commander, see Daniel Ellsberg, "Bombing and Other Crimes," in his *Papers on the War*, Simon & Schuster, 1972. Ellsberg writes in part on the basis of direct observation as a DOD analyst in Vietnam.

52. See the references cited in Chomsky, *For Reasons of State*, pp. xx, xxxiii.

53. Earl S. Martin, *Reaching the Other Side*, Crown, 1978, pp. 133f.

54. Gordon S. Livingston, "Letter from a Vietnam Veteran," *Saturday Review* (20 September 1969).

55. Ithiel de Sola Pool, letter, *New York Review of Books*, 13 February 1969. For news reports on the exploits of the 9th Division at the time, see Chomsky, *At War with Asia*, pp. 99f.

56. Cf. Henry Kamm, *New York Times*, 29 November 1969. This forcible evacuation complicated the task of the investigators of the My Lai massacre, he reported.

57. For references and further details, see Chomsky, *At War with Asia*, p. 104; *For Reasons of State*, p. 225; see Martin, *op. cit.*, p. 133, for an eyewitness account; also the testimony by Martin Teitel of the American Friends Service Committee, Hearing before the Subcommittee to Investigate Problems Connected with Refugees and Escapees, Committee on the Judiciary (Kennedy Subcommittee), U.S. Senate, 92nd Congress, Second Session, 8 May 1972. Teitel also describes US-GVN atrocities of April 1972 in the same area subsequent to the virtually bloodless liberation by the NLF-NVA — the victims, once again, included remnants of the My Lai massacre, whose torment was endless. (See note 199, this chapter.)

58. Guenter Lewy, *America in Vietnam*, Oxford, 1978, p. 143. Lewy could have referred not only to *Newsweek* but also to the material cited here from Buckley's original notes, which had already been published. See Chomsky, "U.S. Involvement in Vietnam," *Bridge: An Asian American Perspective*, November 1975; "From Mad Jack to Mad Henry," *Vietnam Quarterly*, Winter 1976. In the case of Operation BOLD MARINER Lewy avoids reference either to press reports or to reports by the AFSC observers at congressional hearings and elsewhere, and thus has no need to comment on purposeful destruction of dikes to deny food and the numerous recorded atrocities, again revealing his scholarly technique in this effort to show that the United States cannot justly be accused of war crimes. Cf. Lewy, *op. cit.*, pp. 139-40. We will see below (note 168, this chapter) how Lewy deals with alleged crimes of the official enemy.

59. 2000 Koreans were dispatched on 8 January 1965. The Honolulu meeting of 20 April 1965 recommended that the numbers be increased to 7,250 (just at the

time of the first notice by intelligence that there might be a North Vietnamese battalion in the South; as late as July 1965 the Pentagon was still concerned over the *possibility* that there might be such forces in or near South Vietnam). See Chomsky, *For Reasons of State*, p. 122, for references. Koreans are reported to have been involved in an attack on a Cambodian village in February 1967; see Chomsky, *At War With Asia*, p. 122.

60. Robert M. Smith, "Vietnam Killings Laid to Koreans," *New York Times* (10 January 1970).

61. Craig Whitney of the *New York Times*, who was given extensive documentation on South Korean murders by Diane and Michael Jones, summarized their findings briefly toward the end of an article focusing on the future role of the South Koreans in Vietnam. Toward the beginning of his article, Whitney states that "they [the South Koreans] have been providing a military shield [Whitney does not say for whom] in a poorly defended section of the central coast..." ("Korean Troops End Vietnam Combat Role," *New York Times* (9 November 1972).

62. A large number of South Korean murders were "random" in the sense of not being attributable to any ongoing military actions.

63. The Rand Corporation "Viet Cong Motivation and Morale Study" of 1966, which gave documentary evidence of indiscriminate South Korean murders of civilians, was classified and suppressed. See *American Report* (28 July 1972).

64. Letter in the *New York Times*, (25 January 1970).

65. "Security" is another Orwellism consistently applied to Vietnam by official spokesmen for the United Staes, and applied in analogous fashion throughout the empire. With reference to Vietnam it meant unthreatened control by the U.S. client regime in Saigon. If Saigon controlled by sheer force and violence — often the case — the people and hamlet were "secure"; if the NLF controlled without force, the hamlet and its people were "insecure". Similarly, a National Intelligence Estimate of June 1953 gloomily discussed the inability of the French "to provide security for the Vietnamese population," who warned the guerrillas of the presence of French Union forces, thus permitting them to take cover. In short, popular support for the Vietminh made it difficult for France to provide security for the population from the Vietminh. *Pentagon Papers*, Gravel ed., v. I, p. 396.

66. See "'Pacification' by Calculated Frightfulness: The Testimony of Diane and Michael Jones on the Massacres of South Vietnamese Civilians by South Korean Mercenary Troops," Pacification Monograph Number 2; edited with an Introduction by Edward S. Herman, Philadelphia, 1973.

67. The same tendencies quickly manifested themselves in the Australian "pacification" effort. See the documentation in Alex Carey, "Australian Atrocities in Vietnam," Sydney, N.S.W., 1968.

68. On the interaction of U.S.-Diem terror and NLF counter-terror, see above. Nevertheless, we will adhere to the terminology of the propaganda system here and refer to the U.S. assassination programs as "counter-terror."

69. *U.S. Assistance Programs*, p. 183.

70. We will not review the depressing record of apologetics. To cite one example, when Senator Kennedy, in Congressional Hearings, brought to the attention of William Sullivan (then Deputy Assistant Secretary of State for the Bureau of East Asian and Pacific Affairs) a Saigon government report stating that the Phoenix program was launched in order to "eradicate Communist infrastructure" and that it reported "40,994 killed by assassination," Sullivan corrected the record, noting

that it said just "killed," not "assassinated," and then added that "some could have been killed in taking part in military action." As for the Phoenix program, "the Phoenix, basically, is only a program for the interchange of information and intelligence," he asserted. Hearings before the Subcommittee on Refugees and Escapees of the Committee on the Judiciary, U.S. Senate, 92nd Congress, Second Session, 28 September 1972, pp. 21-22.

71. An earlier predecessor was the "counter-terror," or "CT" program organized by the CIA in the mid-1960s to use assassination and other forms of terror against the NLF leadership and cadres. See Wayne Cooper, "Operation Phoenix: A Vietnam Fiasco Seen From Within," *Washington Post* (8 June 1972). See also Nighswonger, *op. cit.*, pp. 136-37, on earlier U.S. efforts to develop "assassination teams" and "prosecutor-executioners."

72. *Pentagon Papers*, Gravel ed., v. II, pp. 429, 585.

73. *Ibid.*, pp. 503-504.

74. *Ibid.*, v. IV, p. 578.

75. Richard S. Winslow, a former AID employee, pointed out that Phoenix program language at one time spoke of the "elimination" of VCI. "'Elimination,' however, gave the unfortunate impression to some Congressmen and to the interested public that someone was being 'eliminated.' Now the major goal is 'neutralization' of the VCI. Of course, the same proportion of VCI are being killed....But Congress seems mollified now that suspected Vietcong are 'neutralized,' rather than 'eliminated.'" *U.S. Assistance Programs*, p. 244.

76. *U.S. Assistance Programs*, p. 207.

77. Saigon Ministry of Information, *Vietnam 1967-1971, Toward Peace and Prosperity*, 1971, p. 52.

78. *U.S. Assistance Programs*, p. 207.

79. *Ibid.*, pp. 184, 225.

80. *Ibid.*, p. 183.

81. *Ibid.*, p. 212.

82. *Ibid.*, p. 186.

83. For Robert Komer, writing in April 1967, the problem is that "we are just not getting enough payoff yet from the massive intelligence we are increasingly collecting. Police/military coordination is sadly lacking both in collection and in swift reaction." *Pentagon Papers*, Gravel ed., v. IV, p. 441.

84. *Ibid.*, v. II, p. 407, referring to the officials of Bien Hoa Province.

85. See Jon Cooper, "Operation Phoenix," Department of History, Dartmouth, 1971, mimeographed. The IVS volunteer was Don Luce.

86. *U.S. Assistance Programs*, p. 314.

87. *New York Times* (13 August 1972).

88. *Washington Post* (17 February 1970).

89. *U.S. Assistance Programs*, p. 314.

90. Dispatch News Service International, No. 376 (6 July 1972).

91. *U.S. Assistance Programs*, p. 321.

92. Tad Szulc, *New York Times* (7 April 1971). Saigon costs were also borne by the U.S., overwhelmingly.

93. Frances Starner, "I'll Do It My Way," *FEER* (6 November 1971).

94. Richard West, "Vietnam: The Year of the Rat," *New Statesman* (25 February 1972).

95. *U.S. Assistance Programs*, p. 252.
96. *Ibid.*, p. 314.
97. *Ibid.*, pp. 314-15. U.S. intelligence nets were infiltrated by right-wing Vietnamese who had their own reasons for inciting terror, according to former intelligence agents. See the report by Jeffrey Stein, an agent-handler in 1968-69, *Boston Phoenix* (10 May 1972).
98. *U.S. Assistance Programs*, p. 321.
99. *Ibid.*, p. 252.
100. UPI, *Le Monde* (5 November 1971).
101. After the Phoenix program was officially phased out, as a result of the bad publicity it received, a new program under the code name "F-6" of a similar nature was instituted, according to a number of former U.S. intelligence officers. Earl Martin came across some independent evidence in support of this not very surprising allegation. Shortly before the Saigon army fled from Quang Ngai (which, he reports, was liberated by NLF troops without a shot being fired), Martin was picked up by the Saigon army and kept briefly in the local Provincial Interrogation Center, where the main torturers had operated. He happened to notice an organizational chart on which every number began with "F-6." *Op. cit.*, p. 82.

It is interesting to see how the indiscriminate character of Phoenix murders is used by some of the current apologists for U.S. terrorism in Indochina. Guenter Lewy, for example, points out that very few of those killed under the Phoenix program were specifically targeted. He argues that "the fact that so few of those killed were on the Phoenix target list certainly undermines the charge that the Phoenix program was a program of planned assassinations" (*op. cit.*, p. 281). The logic is astounding. Actually, the facts Lewy cites merely show that this program of planned assassination degenerated into indiscriminate slaughter, as we have discussed, not a surprising fact given the background and context, which Lewy characteristically ignores in his apologetics. As in the cases noted earlier (see note 58, this chapter), Lewy selectively cites government documents, carefully omitting testimony from participants in Phoenix operations or reports by journalists and others on the scene that would permit a serious scholar to determine the character and significance of the programs he seeks to justify.
102. Nazi extermination camps, of course, occupy a place by themselves, but for systematic torture and brutalization of ordinary citizens, often using sophisticated technology, the "Free Vietnam" established by U.S. force bears comparison to European fascism.
103. For extensive documentation on this point, see *After the Signing of the Paris Agreements, Documents on South Vietnam's Political Prisoners*, Narmic-VRC (June 1973), p. 27; Communauté Vietnamienne, *Saigon: un régime en question: les prisonniers politiques*, Sudestasie, Paris, 1974; *A Cry of Alarm, New Revelations on Repression and Deportations in South Vietnam*, Saigon, 1972; Jean-Pierre Debris and André Menras, *Rescapés des bagnes de Saigon, nous accusons*, Editeurs Francais Réunis, Paris, 1973; *The Forgotten Prisoners of Nguyen Van Thieu*, Paris, May 1973; Holmes Brown and Don Luce, *Hostages of War, Saigon's Political Prisoners*, 1973, Indochina Mobile Education Project; Pham Tam, *Imprisonment and Torture in South Vietnam*, Fellowship of Reconciliation, undated; *Prisonniers Politiques au Sud Vietnam, Listes de Prisonniers, Appel des 30 Mouvements*, Saigon, February 1973.
104. Quoted in Brown and Luce, *op. cit.*, p. 14.

105. *Ibid.*, p. 15.
106. *Ibid.*, p. 32.
107. Quaker Team in Quang Ngai Province, "To Report Truthfully on the Treatment of Prisoners in 1972."
108. *After the Signing*, p. 32.
109. *U.S. Assistance Programs*, p. 314.
110. *After the Signing*, p. 27.
111. *Ibid.*, pp. 26-27.
112. *After the Signing*, p. 33.
113. *Ibid.*, pp. 33-34.
114. Michael Field, *The Prevailing Wind: Witness in Indo-China*, Methuen, 1965, p. 210.
115. "M. Thieu...appliquons la loi des cowboys," *Le Monde* (27 January 1973).
116. Nothing new in that. For example, the May 1969 meeting of the Council on Vietnamese Studies, which pretended to be a scholarly organization, was devoted to a discussion led by Harvard's Samuel Huntington on the apparently insuperable problems that would face the U.S. and its local client if compelled to enter into political competition with the NLF, admittedly "the most powerful purely political national organization." Huntington suggested various forms of deceit and chicanery that might overcome the advantages of the enemy, but apparently without convincing his more skeptical colleagues. For discussion, in the context of the plans being developed in the early 1970s by U.S. scholars for incorporating South Vietnam permanently within the U.S. system, see Chomsky, *For Reasons of State*, chapter 4.
117. *Boston Globe* (24 June 1972).
118. *San Francisco Chronicle* (4 June 1972).
119. Cited in *Saigon: un régime en question*, p. 69, from the *Washington Post* (10 November 1972), in a discussion of the intensifying terror.
120. *Le Monde* (17 May 1973).
121. Chris Jenkins, "Thieu's Campaign of Terror," *American Report* (29 January 1973); letter of the Committee Campaigning for the Improvement of the Prison System of South Vietnam (9 December 1972); *After the Signing*, pp. 35ff.
122. Sylvan Fox, "Saigon Bypasses Accord by Freeing Many Prisoners," *New York Times* (6 February 1973).
123. The press also failed to note the suspiciousness of the huge number (40,000) allegedly being released, and the illogic in the contention that the political component, numbering 10,000, had "renounced Communism." (All at once? If not, why were they held to this point?)
124. *Prison News* of the Committee Campaigning for the Improvement of the Prison System of South Vietnam (14 December 1972).
125. *Prison News* (9 December 1972); Ngo Vinh Long, "Thieu starving refugees to keep the throne," *Boston Phoenix* (12 December 1972), citing South Vietnamese newspaper reports; *Prison News* (9 December 1972); *After the Signing*, pp. 35ff.
126. *Le Monde* (3 January 1973).
127. *Ibid.*
128. *New York Times* (27 January 1973).
129. *U.S. Assistance Programs*, p. 5.

130. GAO Report (July 1972), p. 42.
131. *U.S. Assistance Programs*, p. 197.
132. *Ibid.*, p. 224.
133. *Ibid.*, p. 96.
134. *Ibid.*, pp. 177, 179. (Our emphasis.)
135. AID, Fiscal 1971 Program and Project Data Presentation to Congress; cited by Michael T. Klare, "America's Global Police," *American Report*, 15 September 1972.
136. See pp. 48-49.
137. *U.S. Assistance Programs*, pp. 186ff. One illustration of "improvement" cited by William Colby was that confessions obtained during "interrogations," which "used to be used exclusively...are not used exclusively any more." p. 197.
138. Quoted in Brown and Luce, *op. cit.*, p. 32.
139. *Ibid.*, p. 36.
140. *Ibid.*, p. 111.
141. For a discussion of the 1967 attack on Dak Son and this general issue, see Herman, *Atrocities in Vietnam*, pp. 46-54.
142. The quote is from a captured Communist document dated March 1960, cited at length in Race, *op. cit.*, pp. 116-119. The specific quote is on p. 119.
143. Douglas Pike, *Vietcong*, pp. 91-92.
144. *Ibid.*, p. 101. This conclusion is generally accepted even by scholars who bend over backwards to find evidence for Hanoi's aggression. See, e.g., King C. Chen, "Hanoi's Three Decisions and the Escalation of the Vietnam War," *Political Science Quarterly*, Summer 1975: "It was the growing military campaign of the Diem regime against the Communists with America's support that compelled Hanoi to decide to revert to war." p. 258.
145. Race, *op. cit.*, p. 184. Law 10/59 initiated a system of military courts that, within three days of a charge, were to sentence to death "whoever commits or attempts to commit...crimes with the aim of sabotage, or of infringing upon the security of the State" (Article 1), as well as "whoever belongs to an organization designed to help to prepare or to perpetrate [these] crimes" (Article 3). This law made all dissent and opposition subversive and punishable by death.
146. However absurd it may be, this picture was widely disseminated throughout the Indochina War, and still is, in essence. For example, it is seriously argued today that a tiny group of Paris-educated fanatics ("nine men at the top") held the entire country of Cambodia in their grip as they proceeded systematically to massacre and starve the population — the reason for this policy, according to the widely praised account that has reached by far the largest international audience, may be that their leader suffers from "chronic impotence." The same authorities (John Barron and Anthony Paul of the *Readers Digest*) hold that a tiny group of completely inconsequential leaders succeeded through the use of terror to organize a force capable of defeating the world's greatest military power and the government it supported. This is put forth with utter seriousness in a work lauded for its insights throughout the Western world. Meanwhile another authority regarded with much awe among the intelligentsia (Francois Ponchaud) assures us that the group of fanatics who held the terrorized country in their iron grasp were proceeding to eliminate some 5-7 million people out of a total of 8 million, including all but the young. For discussion of these ideas and the evidence that is advanced to support them, see Volume II, chapter 6. As will be seen, the characterization just given is literally accurate.

147. *Ibid.*, pp. 196-97. Emphasis added.
148. *Op. cit.*, pp. 188-89, note 25.
149. *Ibid.*, p. 104.
150. *Ibid.*, pp. 110-11.
151. *Ibid.*, pp. 94-95, 116, 184ff.
152. *Ibid.*, p. 140.
153. *Ibid.*, p. 211.
154. *Ibid.*, p. 200. After talking with the Saigon leadership in 1965, James Reston wrote: "Even Premier Ky told this reporter today that the communists were closer to the people's yearnings for social justice and an independent life than his own government." *New York Times* (1 September 1965). It was a constant refrain apart from propaganda exercises.
155. Race, *op. cit.*, p. 200.
156. These reports reached flood proportions during the DRV offensive of 1972, with the *New York Times* contributing its share in the writings of Joseph Treaster and Fox Butterfield. Their reports, heavily dependent on official handouts of Saigon and U.S. information officers, do not withstand close scrutiny. See, for example, Tom Fox, "The Binh Dinh 'Massacre'," *American Report* (15 September 1972); *Le Monde*, 28-29 May 1972 (report of interviews with refugees by an AFP special correspondent). See also notes 174, 198, 199, this chapter. (See Volume II for many additional examples.)
157. When we speak of "mythical bloodbath" we do not mean to imply that no killings took place. In fact they did, on a considerable scale. But the evidence seems to us decisive that the core of truth was distorted, misrepresented, inflated and embellished with sheer fabrication for propaganda purposes. As to the events themselves, we are not attempting to offer any definitive account, but rather to compare the evidence available with its interpretation by the government and the media.
158. This system of responsiveness extended into the military sphere, helping to explain the "astonishing" fighting capacity and "almost incredibly resilient morale" of DRV soldiers, who benefit from a system of "morale restitution... designed to lend great emotional and physical support to its members," a system which "anticipates and alleviates possible future morale troubles." Konrad Kellen, "1971 and Beyond: The View from Hanoi," Rand Corporation, June 1971, p. 9.
159. In R.N. Pfeffer, ed., *No More Vietnams?*, Harper and Row, 1968, p. 227.
160. Race, *op. cit.*, pp. 182-83, note 22.
161. Diane Johnstone, "'Communist Bloodbath' in North Vietnam is Propaganda Myth, says former Saigon Psychological Warfare Chief," *St. Louis Post-Dispatch* (24 September 1972).
162. The analysis that follows is based on D. Gareth Porter, *The Myth of the Bloodbath: North Vietnam's Land Reform Reconsidered*, International Relations of East Asia, Interim Report No. 2, Cornell, 1972. See also the abbreviated version in the *Bulletin of the Concerned Asian Scholars,* September 1973.
163. *Myth of the Bloodbath*, pp. 26-28.
164. *Ibid.*, pp. 44-45.
165. "Figure on N. Vietnam's Killing 'Just a Guess,' Author Says," *The Washington Post* (13 September 1972).

166. Late 1954 was also a period of famine in much of North Vietnam, affecting the very area in which Chi had lived, which further compromises his inferences drawn from a count of village deaths by starvation.

167. *Fire in the Lake*, Little, Brown, 1972, p. 223. FitzGerald gives no footnote reference for this estimate, but she relies heavily on Fall and her language is similar to his.

168. Author (not Congressman) Michael Harrington writes that he and other "socialist cadre...knew that Ho and his comrades had killed thousands of peasants during forced collectivization in North Vietnam during the '50s (a fact they themselves had confessed)." *Dissent* (Spring 1973). In fact, the only known "confessions" are the fabrications that had been exposed many months earlier, and neither Harrington nor other Western observers "know" what took place during the land reform. Note the claim that "Ho and his comrades had killed thousands of peasants," when in fact there is no evidence that the leadership ordered or organized mass executions of peasants.

Guenter Lewy writes that "the Communists in the North had severe problems with their own 'counterrevolutionaries'. In 1955-56 perhaps as many as 50,000 were executed in connection with the land reform law of 1953....A North Vietnamese exile puts the number of victims at one-half million" (*op. cit.*, p. 16). His two footnote references for these estimates are Chi for the latter and Fall (who appears to have relied on Chi) for the former. Lewy then adds, "Attempts by the Hanoi sympathizer D. Gareth Porter to deny the scope of this terror remain unconvincing." This exhausts Lewy's discussion, and once again reveals clearly the scholarly standards of this apologist for U.S. terror. The material just reviewed is nowhere discussed. For Lewy, an extrapolation from one execution reported in one village by a highly unreliable source to an estimate of 50,000 executions (or 500,000 victims) for all of North Vietnam is quite legitimate, and there is no need to concern oneself over Chi's demonstrated fabrications, Chau's report that the whole story was an intelligence fabrication, the results of Moise's careful study (see note 170, this chapter), or any of the abundant evidence that calls this parody into question. This reference to alleged crimes of the enemy is a natural counterpart to Lewy's efforts to deny U.S. crimes, in the manner already illustrated (see notes 58 and 101, this chapter).

169. Porter, *Myth of the Bloodbath*, p. 55. We return in Volume II to 1978 repetitions of the long-exposed propaganda fabrications, in addition to Lewy.

170. See his "Land Reform and Land Reform Errors in North Vietnam," *Pacific Affairs*, Spring 1976, and his University of Michigan Ph.D dissertation, 1978. We quote from the former.

171. The analysis below is based primarily on D. Gareth Porter, "U.S. Political Warfare in Vietnam — The 1968 'Hue Massacre'," *Indochina Chronicle*, No. 33, 24 June 1974 (reprinted in the *Congressional Record*, 19 February 1975); and Edward S. Herman and D. Gareth Porter, "The Myth of the Hue Massacre," *Ramparts*, May-June 1975. See also references cited below.

172. Stewart Harris, *London Times* (27 March 1968).

173. Marc Riboud, *Le Monde*, (13 April 1968). Riboud reports 4000 civilians killed during the reconquest of the "assassinated city" of Hue by U.S. forces.

174. Report by John Sullivan of the AFSC, 9 May 1968. He reports that none of the AFSC workers who were in Hue throughout the fighting had heard of abusive or atrocious behavior by the NLF-NVA.

175. Len Ackland, "Hue," unpublished; one of the sources used by Don Oberdorfer in his *Tet*, Doubleday and Co., 1971.
176. Richard West, *New Statesman*, (28 January 1972).
177. And despite Pike's government position and quite remarkable record as a propagandist. For some samples, see N. Chomsky, *American Power and the New Mandarins*, pp. 365-66.
178. *Fire in the Lake*, pp. 174-75. In a subsequent edition of her book, FitzGerald qualified her earlier wholesale acceptance of the myth, but the impact was slight.
179. *New York Times*, Op.-Ed. (15 June 1972). In his book, *No Exit From Vietnam*, McKay, Updated Edition, 1970, Thompson says, "Normally Communist behavior toward the mass of the population is irreproachable and the use of terror is highly selective" (p. 40); but that work, while biased, involved some effort at understanding and contained a residue of integrity, entirely absent in the *New York Times* piece.
180. Porter, "U.S. Political Warfare in Vietnam."
181. *Ibid.*
182. *Ibid.*
183. *Ibid.*
184. Quoted in Townsend Hoopes, *The Limits of Intervention*, McKay, 1969, p. 142.
185. *Vietnam Inc.*, Macmillan, 1971, p. 137.
186. Cited in Herman and Porter, *op. cit.*
187. See Harris, *op. cit.*
188. *Op. cit.*, pp. 141-42.
189. Riboud, *op. cit.*
190. See Wilfred Burchett, *Guardian* (New York), 6 December 1969.
191. Riboud, *op. cit.*
192. Interview with Mr. Tony Zangrilli (2 February 1973).
193. Alje Vennema, *The Tragedy of Hue*, unpublished; quoted by Porter, *op. cit.* Subsequently Vennema changed his views on Hue. He returned for a visit during which he collected secondary and tertiary source information, which he then used in a book in which his own personal first hand observations were shunted aside. See Alje Vennema, *The Viet Cong Massacre At Hue*, Vantage Press, 1976.
194. Oriana Fallaci, "Working Up to Killing," *Washington Monthly* (February 1972).
195. John Lengel, AP, A010 — Hue Descriptive, 10 February 1968, cited by Peter Braestrup, *Big Story*, Westview Press, volume I, pp. 268-69. After the reference to a psychological warfare program pinning the blame on the Communists, Braestrup adds a footnote that reads: "At this point, the 'Hue massacre' by the Vietcong was still unknown to newsmen." It naturally does not occur to him to ask whether this "massacre" may not relate to the psywar program so desperately needed. While Braestrup cites Porter's critique, he assumes without comment or discussion that the official line must be correct, as does his Freedom House sponsor, a typical manifestation of subservience to official dogmas. See note 168, this chapter. We return to some discussion of the Braestrup-Freedom House version of history in Volume II, chapter 1.
196. D. Gareth Porter and Len E. Ackland, "Vietnam: The Bloodbath Argument," *Christian Century* (5 November 1969).

197. *Ibid.*
198. Katsuichi Honda, *Vietnam War: A Report Through Asian Eyes*, pp. 55-69.
199. Martin Teitel, *op. cit.*, p. 17 (see note 57, this chapter); "Again, the suffering of My Lai," *New York Times* (7 June 1972). In the same Senate Hearings Teitel reports other instances of terrorism attributed to the NLF but apparently carried out by ARVN.

5 Appendix

1. Hospitalized prisoners are chained.
2. It appears, in fact, that if freedom of movement were re-established at the same time as democratic liberties, the great majority of the province would opt for the P.R.G. One of the "liberated zones" begins only three kilometers from the town of Quang Ngai (N.D.L.R.).

INDEX*

* This index covers only Names, Places, and Publications mentioned within the body of the text.

SOUTH END PRESS TITLES

Curious Courtship of Women's Liberation and Socialism	*Batya Weinbaum*
Theatre for the 98%	*Maxine Klein*
Unorthodox Marxism	*Michael Albert & Robin Hahnel*
Conversations in Maine	*James &Grace Lee Boggs, Freddy & Lyman Paine*
Strike!	*Jeremy Brecher*
Between Labor and Capital	*edited by Pat Walker*
Ba Ye Zwa	*Judy Seidman*
No Nukes!: Everyone's Guide to Nuclear Power	*Anna Gyorgy & Friends*
Science and Liberation	*edited by Rita Arditti, Pat Brennan, & Steve Cavrak*
Science, Technology and Marxism	*Stanley Aronowitz*
European Communism in the 70s	*edited by David Plotke & Carl Boggs Jr.*
Crisis in the Working Class	*John McDermott*
Social and Sexual Revolution	*Bertell Ollman*
They Should Have Served That Cup of Coffee: Radicals Remember the Sixties	*Dick Clust[illegible]*
Slice the Dreammaker's Throat	*Bill [illegible]*
Ecology and Politics	*A[illegible]*
From the Grassroots	*Mann[illegible]ole*
Women and Revolution	*edited by L[illegible]rgent*
What's Wrong With the U.S. Economy?	*Institute for Labor Education*
Indignant Heart: A Black Worker's Journal	*Charles Denby (Matthew Ward)*
The Sun Betrayed	*Ray Reece*
Trilateralism	*edited by Holly Sklar*
LOUDcracks/softHEARTS	*Jean Lozoraitis*
Creative Differences	*David Talbot & Barbara Zheutlin*

ABOUT SOUTH END PRESS

South End Press is committed to publishing books which can aid people's day-to-day struggles to control their own lives.
Our primary emphasis is on the United States—its political and economic systems, its history and its culture—and on strategies for its transformation.
We aim to reach a broad audience through a balanced offering of books of all kinds—fiction and non-fiction, theoretical and strategic, historical and cultural, for all ages and in all styles and formats.

South End Press, Box 68, Astor Station, Boston, MA 02123